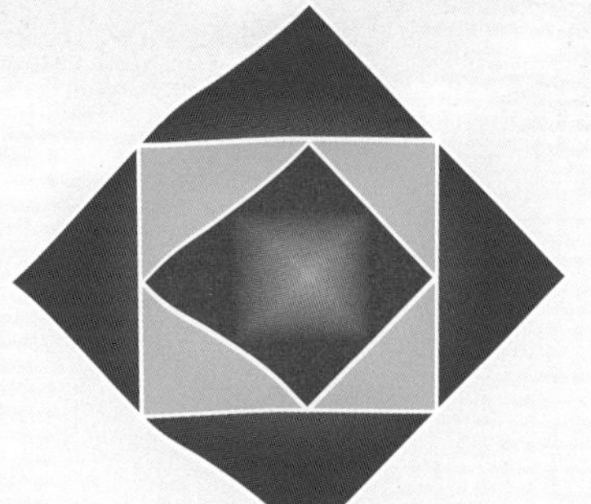

Core Physics

Series editors	Bryan Milner
	Jean Martin
	John Mills
Physics editor	Bryan Milner
***Core Science* authors**	Jenifer Burden
	Paul Butler
	Zoë Crompton
	Sam Ellis
	Peter Evans
	Jean Martin
	John Mills
	Bryan Milner
Consultants	Kate Chaytor
	Nigel Heslop
	Martyn Keeley

PUBLISHED BY THE PRESS SYNDICATE OF THE UNIVERSITY OF CAMBRIDGE
The Pitt Building, Trumpington Street, Cambridge CB2 1RP, United Kingdom

CAMBRIDGE UNIVERSITY PRESS
The Edinburgh Building, Cambridge CB2 2RU, United Kingdom
40 West 20th Street, New York, NY 10011-4211, USA
10 Stamford Road, Oakleigh, Melbourne 3166, Australia

First published 1999

Printed in Italy by G. Canale & C. S.p.A., Borgaro T.se, (Turin)

Typeset in Stone Informal 11/14 pt, 10.5/14 pt, 10/13pt

A catalogue record for this book is available from the British Library

ISBN 0 521 66637 6 paperback

Designed and produced by Gecko Ltd, Bicester, Oxon

Cover photo: Compact disc, Bald Headed Pictures/Telegraph Colour Library

Contents

How this book is organised

Core Physics is designed to cover the physics (AT4) component of the National Curriculum for Science at Key Stage 3. It also covers the physics requirement of the Common Entrance Examination at 13+.

For most pupils, Key Stage 3 comprises the first three years (Years 7, 8 and 9) of their secondary education, culminating in the Key Stage 3 SATs towards the end of Year 9.

If these pupils are to do themselves justice in the SATs tests, they really need to have made significant, recent use of all the scientific ideas that they might encounter in the SATs.

To ensure that this happens, the content of *Core Physics* is organised as follows.

BASIC CONCEPTS [for all pupils, normally in Years 7 and 8]	CONSOLIDATION [for all pupils, normally in Year 9]	+	DEVELOPMENT [for some pupils, normally in Year 9]
This section of the book: ■ covers the great majority of concepts needed for KS3 SATs up to Level 6; ■ introduces new ideas gently, one at a time, with ample opportunity for pupils to confirm their mastery of each new idea immediately after it is introduced.	This section of the book: ■ revisits all the Basic Concepts, in different contexts and at a quicker pace; ■ extends them, where necessary, so that pupils are fully prepared for KS3 SATs up to Level 6.		These additional (Core+) pages, at the end of each topic in the Consolidation section: ■ extend the Basic Concepts further and/or apply them to more difficult contexts; ■ prepare pupils for KS3 SATs up to Level 7.

Pages 8 and 9 are set out so that they show where each concept area in the Basic Concepts section is Consolidated and further Developed.

They show, for example, that:

Basic concepts about colour are covered in:	The basic concepts are consolidated and extended a little in:	The ideas are further developed and applied to other contexts in:
2.4 Colours of the rainbow	C1.4 Colour	C1.12 Mixing colours
2.5 Why do things look coloured?	C1.5 What prisms do to light	C1.13 More ways of using prisms

The links between the different sections are shown at the top of the relevant pages of the book.

It should be noted that *Core Physics* does not attempt to cover the additional content that may be required for the SATs Extension papers. The additional material needed to answer some of these questions in these papers derives from part of the Programme of Study specified by the National Curriculum for Key Stage 4. Teachers who feel that their pupils are ready for this material in Year 9 are advised to use the relevant parts of textbooks written to support Key Stage 4.

Pupils' notes

The text is liberally sprinkled with questions designed to provide pupil interaction and allow them to confirm their mastery of ideas as they are presented. The outcomes of these questions are not intended to result in a coherent set of notes for revision – this is the purpose of the summary sections (see below).

Some of these questions have a magnifier symbol printed alongside. This indicates that the answer to the question cannot be found in the text. Pupils are expected to find out the answer from elsewhere.

> A 'working notebook' for answering these text questions is recommended. This notebook might also be used for any other written work which is not intended to form a permanent record for revision purposes, such as some aspects of practical work, answers to questions from Question banks in the *Supplementary Materials*, etc.

The **key** words in each spread are highlighted in **bold**. Pupils use these words to complete the summary sections headed *What you need to remember* (WYNTR). The accumulated set of WYNTR passages comprises a record of the knowledge and understanding that pupils will need for SATs.

A separate notebook for WYNTR summaries is recommended. This will make a useful reference for revision.

Since they are to be used for revision, it is, of course, essential that pupils' completed summaries are correct. These are supplied at the back of *Core Physics* and can be used for checking.

Practical work

The content and presentation of any particular piece of practical work will depend on what the teacher considers are the main aims of that practical assignment, e.g. to make otherwise abstract ideas more concrete and meaningful or to develop and assess Sc1 skills and abilities. Consequently, practical work on a particular topic may vary considerably. So, though *Core Physics* helps to develop Sc1 skills and abilities by presenting information about investigations for pupils to interpret and evaluate, detailed instructions for pupils' practical work are not provided. It is assumed that the teacher will provide the practical work to support topics that best suits the needs of their pupils.

The text of *Core Physics* has also been presented in a way that does not depend on practical work; it is completely stand-alone.

Supplementary materials

Core Physics Supplementary Materials are available to support the pupils' text. This fully photocopiable resource assists teaching and lesson-planning by providing practical suggestions, tests, worksheets (for homework or class use) and answers to all the questions in the pupils' text. There is also a matching grid to show how *Core Physics* covers the Key Stage 3 Science National Curriculum.

These materials comprise:

- a *Commentary* for each double-page spread of the pupil's text which includes:
  - full details of the expected *Outcomes to questions* in the text, written in language that pupils themselves are expected to use;
  - *Suggestions for practical activities;*
- *Worksheets* wherever these are particularly useful;
- *Topic tests* and *Question banks.*

The Common Entrance Examination at 13+

Pupils preparing for the Common Entrance Examination at 13+ will need to have covered the material in *Core Physics* a year earlier than pupils preparing for SATs.

This can be achieved via several different approaches:

- embarking on *Core Physics* a year earlier (e.g. in the preparatory school sector);
- covering the Basic Concepts section in a single year and proceeding to the Consolidation and Development section the following year;
- visiting each topic area once only in a two-year programme, i.e. covering the Consolidation and Development section immediately after the relevant Basic Concepts section. When using this strategy, only selected aspects of the Consolidation material may be needed and the remainder omitted.

Ways through this book

The word 'CORE+' appears at the top of the Development pages as a reminder that they are needed only for the higher-tier Key Stage 3 SATs.

1.1 How to make things move

We often want to start things moving. The diagrams show some examples.

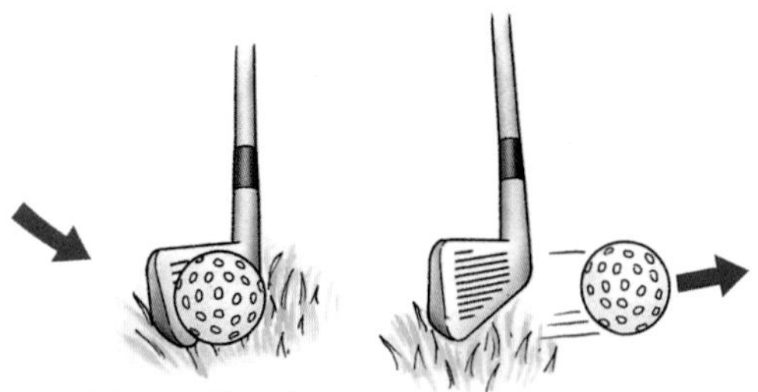

The golf club hits the ball. *The ball moves.*

1 Copy and complete the table.

	What you do to start it moving
golf ball	
drawer	
buggy	

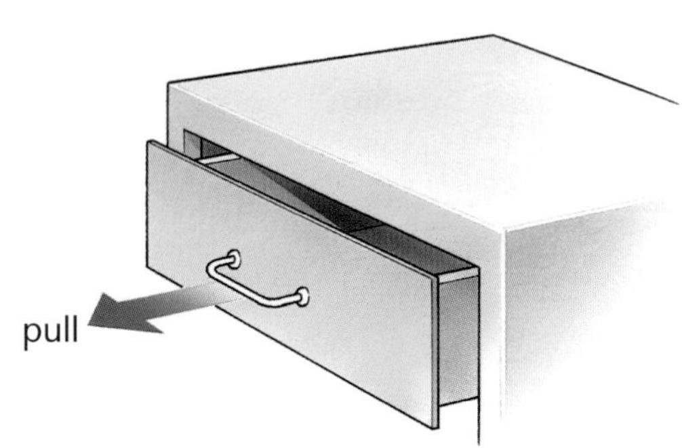

The drawer moves in the same ***direction*** *as you pull it.*

Pushing things, pulling things and hitting things are all ways of starting things moving. They move because you make a **force** act on them.

2 Look at the diagrams again. Then copy and complete the sentences.

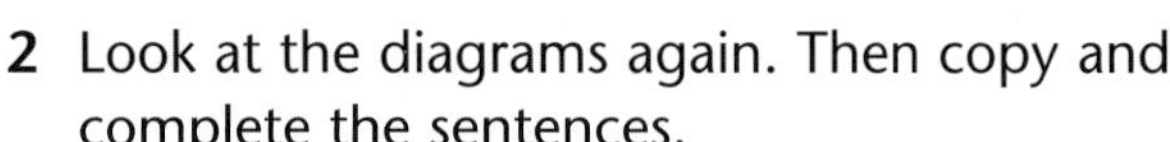

A force acting on an object makes it __________.
The object moves in the same __________ as the force.

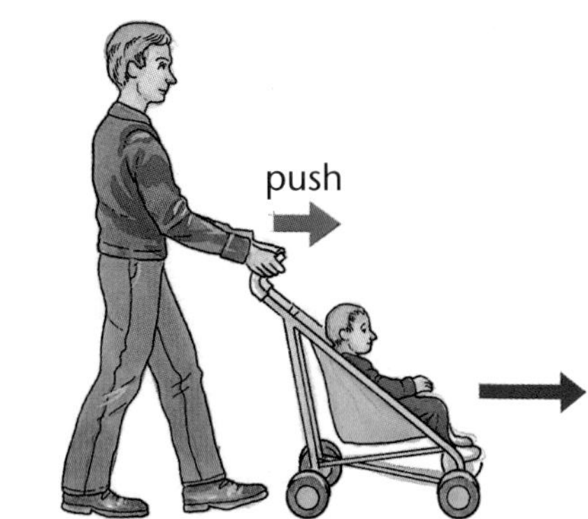

The buggy moves along.

Making things move faster

It suddenly starts raining. So the man wants to make the buggy move faster. The diagram shows how he can do this.

The buggy moves faster.

3 Copy and complete the sentences.

To make the buggy move faster, the man must push it with a bigger __________.
This force must be in the same __________ as the buggy is moving.

Making things move slower

The man with the buggy now has to go downhill. The buggy starts to move too fast, so he needs to slow it down. The diagram shows how he can do this.

A force in the ***opposite*** *direction slows the buggy down.*

4 Copy and complete the sentences.

To make something slow down you need a __________. The force must be in the __________ direction to the way the thing is moving.

Making things change direction

A football is moving <u>across</u> the goal mouth. The attacker wants the ball to go <u>into</u> the goal. The diagram shows how he can do this.

5 Copy and complete the sentences.

To change the direction that the ball is moving, the attacker must make a __________ act on it.

The attacker wants the ball to turn to the right. So he must head it with a force from the __________.

WHAT YOU NEED TO REMEMBER (Copy and complete using the **key words**)

How to make things move

To start something moving, to speed it up or to change its direction, you must make a __________ act on it. This force must be in the same __________ as you want the thing to move.

If you want to slow something down, the force must be in the __________ direction to the way it is moving.

More about moving: C2.4

1.2 Why do things slow down?

Moving things often slow down by themselves. This happens even when we <u>don't</u> want it to.

A bicycle will slow down by itself unless you keep pedalling.

1 (a) What happens to a bicycle if you stop pedalling?

(b) What must you do to keep the bicycle going at the same speed (or, in other words, to stop it from slowing down)?

Things slow down because there is a force acting on them. This force acts in the **opposite** direction to the way they are moving. We call this force a **friction** force.

movement

friction force on book

smooth table top

If you give a book a push, it will slide across a table. A table top is smooth. There is only a small friction force. The book slides a long way before it stops.

Sliding friction

When two things **slide** over each other, there is a friction force between them.

This friction force can be large or small. The diagrams show why.

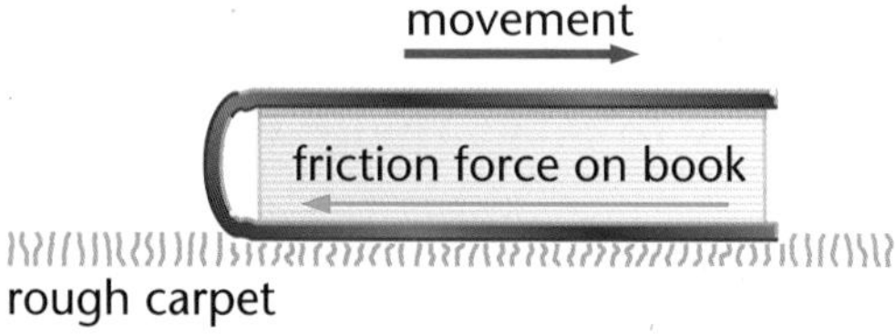

But a book won't slide very far across a carpet. A carpet isn't very smooth. There is a large friction force. The book doesn't slide very far before it stops.

2 Copy and complete the sentences.

The friction force on a moving object always acts in the opposite __________ to the way the object is moving.
So it makes the object __________ down.

There is less friction if the object is sliding over a __________ surface.

Friction with the air

In tennis, the ball is moving through the air most of the time. But this doesn't mean there isn't any friction.

There is a friction force between the ball and the air. This friction force is called air resistance or **drag**.

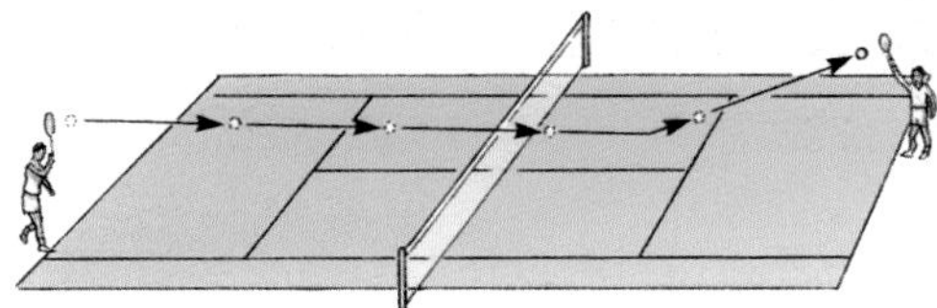

Some tennis players can serve a ball at 120 miles per hour. The ball slows down to about 90 miles per hour by the time it gets to the other player.

3 Look at the diagram. Then copy and complete the sentences.

A tennis ball __________ down as it travels through the air.
This is because of air _________ or _________.

4 A shuttlecock slows down a lot faster than a tennis ball. Explain why.

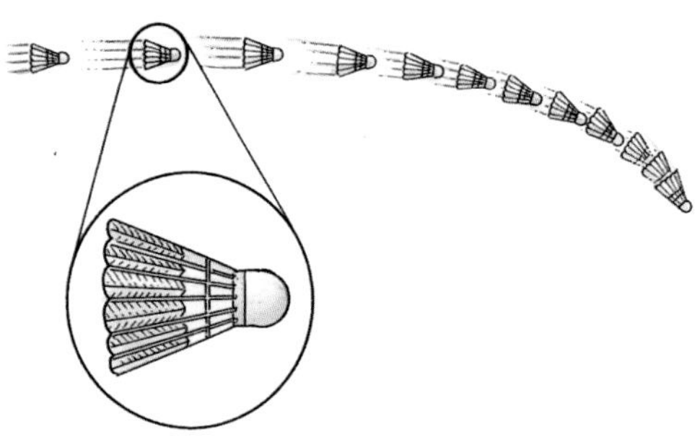

There is a lot of drag on the feathers of a badminton shuttlecock, so it slows down quickly.

Why a bicycle slows down

If you stop pedalling, a bicycle slows down. This is because of friction. The diagram shows where this friction occurs.

5 **(a)** Write down the two friction forces that slow down a bicycle.

(b) Which of these two forces slows down the bicycle more?

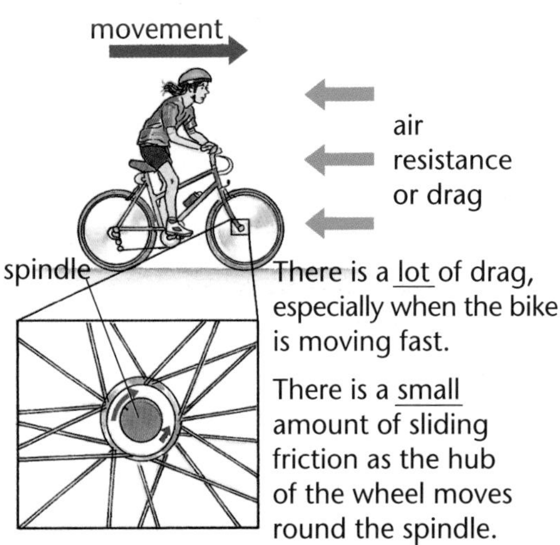
movement
air resistance or drag
spindle
There is a lot of drag, especially when the bike is moving fast.
There is a small amount of sliding friction as the hub of the wheel moves round the spindle.

WHAT YOU NEED TO REMEMBER (Copy and complete using the **key words**)

Why do things slow down?

Moving things slow down because of ____________ forces.
Friction forces act in the _____________ direction to the way an object is moving.

There is friction between things which ____________ over each other.

There is also friction when things move through the air. This is called air resistance or ________.

More about friction: C2.4

1.3 How to reduce friction

REMEMBER from pages 12–13

There is always a friction force:

- when two surfaces slide across each other;
- when things move through the air.

This friction force is always in the <u>opposite</u> direction to the movement.

When a bicycle is moving, friction forces act on it all the time. So we have to keep pedalling to keep the bicycle moving.

We want to make these friction forces as small as we can. Then we don't need to waste so much energy pedalling.

1 Write down <u>two</u> friction forces that slow down a bicycle.

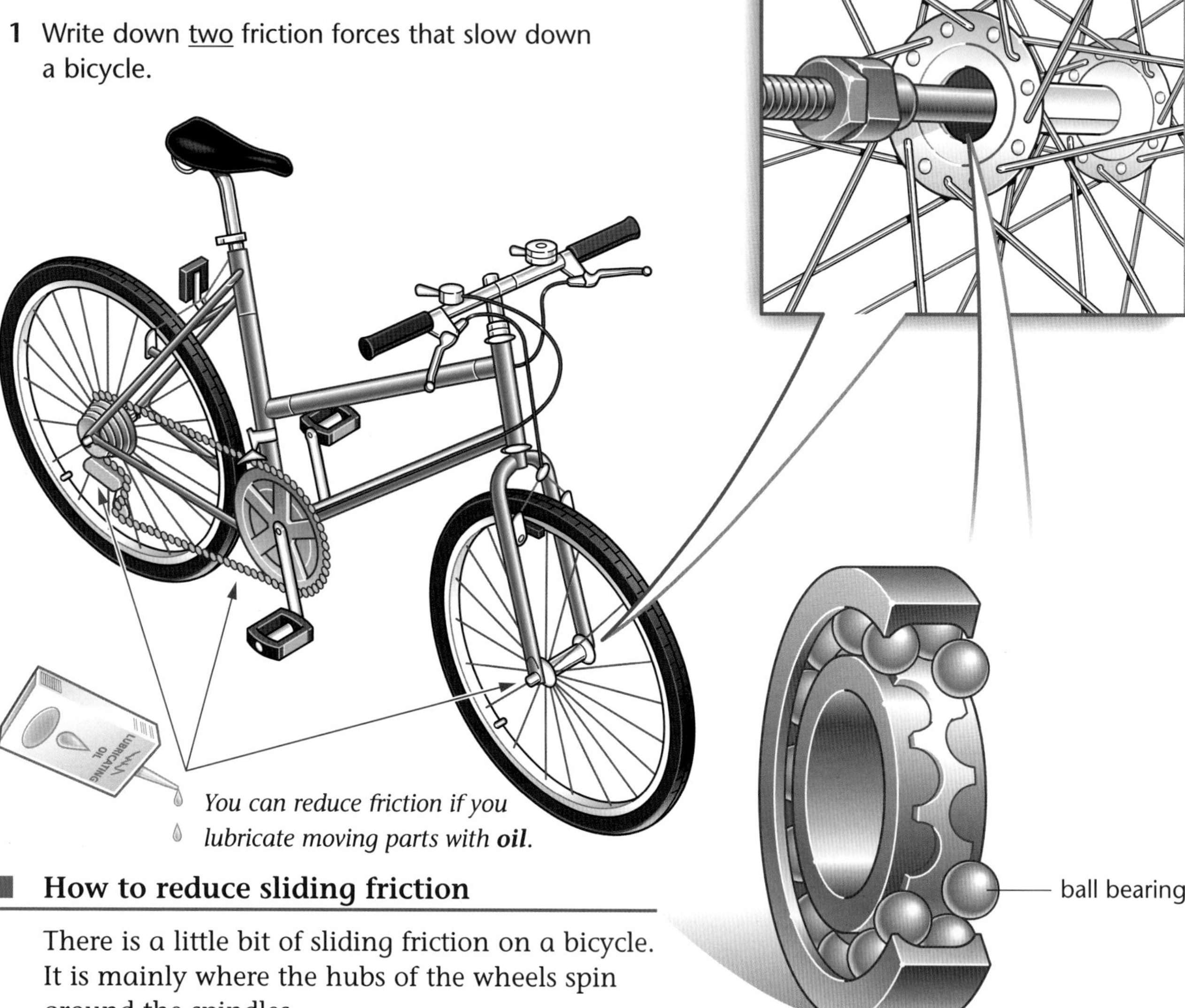

You can reduce friction if you lubricate moving parts with ***oil****.*

How to reduce sliding friction

There is a little bit of sliding friction on a bicycle. It is mainly where the hubs of the wheels spin around the spindles.

The diagrams show how we can make this friction as small as possible.

Sliding surfaces must be ***smooth****. If they are rough, or rusty, there will be a lot of friction.*
Ball ***bearings*** *reduce friction because they roll rather than slide.*

2 Write down <u>three</u> ways of reducing the friction between the hub and the spindle of a bicycle wheel.

How to reduce air resistance

When people design a car, they need to think about its air resistance or drag. They can make the air resistance smaller by changing the car's shape. The diagrams show how.

movement
air resistance
The car has to push air out of the way.

The shape of this car gives it a lot of resistance.

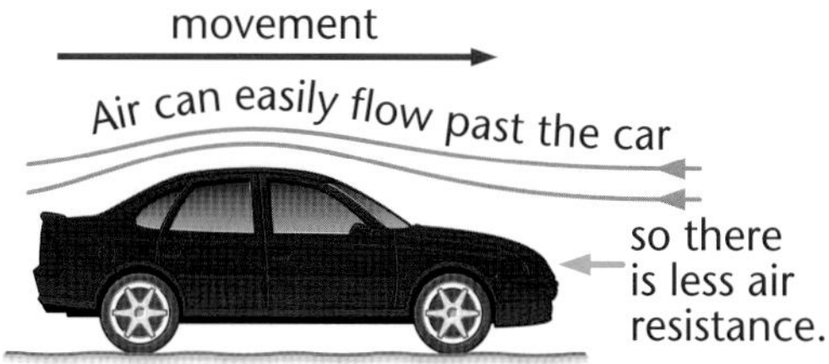

*We say this car has a **streamlined** shape.*

3 Copy and complete the sentences.

To reduce the drag on a car, we must make it a __________ shape.
The air can then __________ past it more easily.

How to save petrol

A car with a more streamlined shape uses less petrol to do the same journey at the same speed.

The diagram shows how you can do the same journey in the <u>same</u> car but using less petrol.

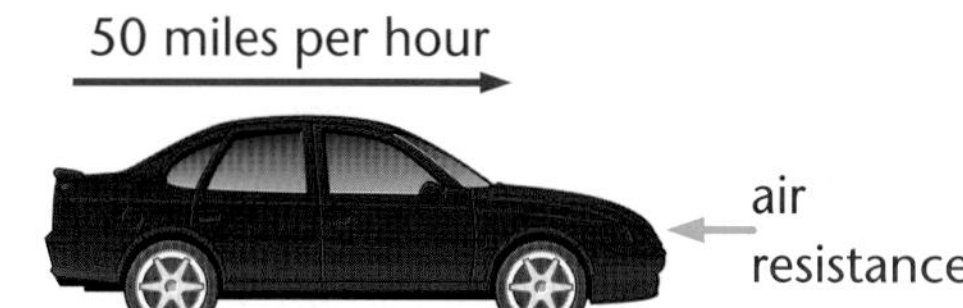

At 50 m.p.h. the car travels 50 miles on a gallon of petrol.

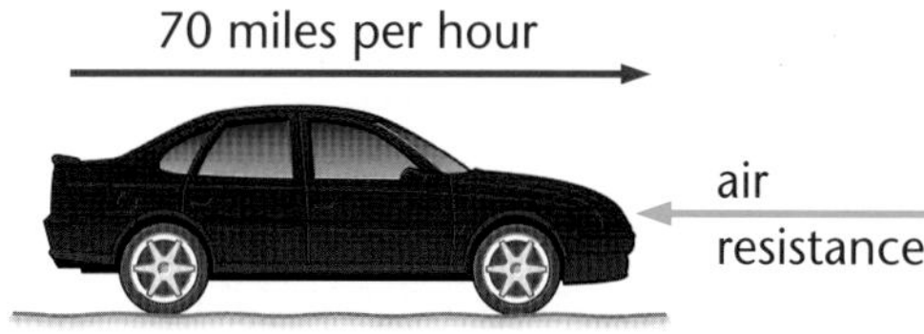

At 70 m.p.h. the car travels 30 miles on a gallon of petrol.

4 Copy and complete the table.

Speed (miles per hour)	**Petrol used (miles per gallon)**
50	
70	

5 Copy and complete the sentences.

At 70 miles per hour there is a lot more __________ __________ than there is at 50 miles per hour.

So you do [more/the same/fewer] miles on each gallon of petrol.

WHAT YOU NEED TO REMEMBER (Copy and complete using the **key words**)

How to reduce friction

You can reduce sliding friction between hubs and spindles:
- by using ______________ surfaces
- by using ball ______________
- by lubricating moving parts with ______________.

You can reduce air resistance by giving things a ______________ shape.

More about friction: C2.4

1.4 Making good use of friction

REMEMBER from pages 12–13

Friction forces slow things down. This happens whether you want it to or not.

Friction is often a nuisance. So we usually want to reduce it.

But friction can also be very helpful. Then we want to increase it.

Slowing down

To slow down a car or a bicycle, we use the **brakes**.

The diagram shows how the brakes on a bicycle work.

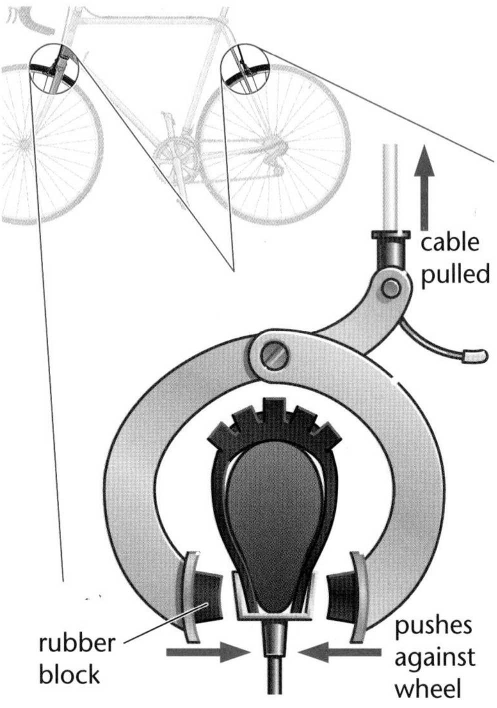

How bicycle brakes work.

1 Write down the following sentences in the right order. The first one is in the correct place.

- You squeeze the brake lever to pull the cable.
- There is a force of friction between the rubber blocks and the wheel.
- The wheel slows down.
- The rubber blocks press against the wheel.

Using drag to slow things down

Brakes use **sliding** friction to slow things down.

You can also use **air resistance** to slow things down. The diagram shows how air resistance slows down a parachutist.

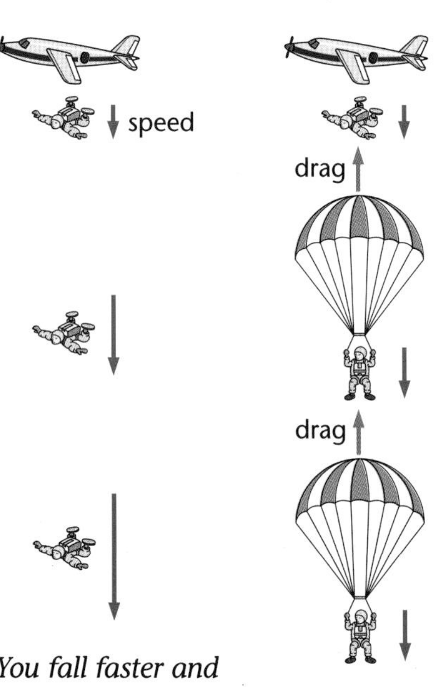

You fall faster and faster. You will be killed or injured when you hit the ground.

A parachute slows you down so you can land safely.

2 (a) Why do people use a parachute when they jump out of a plane?

(b) How does the parachute work?

Walking on ice

The friction force is sometimes big enough to stop two surfaces from sliding across each other.

You use a friction force like this when you walk. That is why it is difficult to walk on ice.

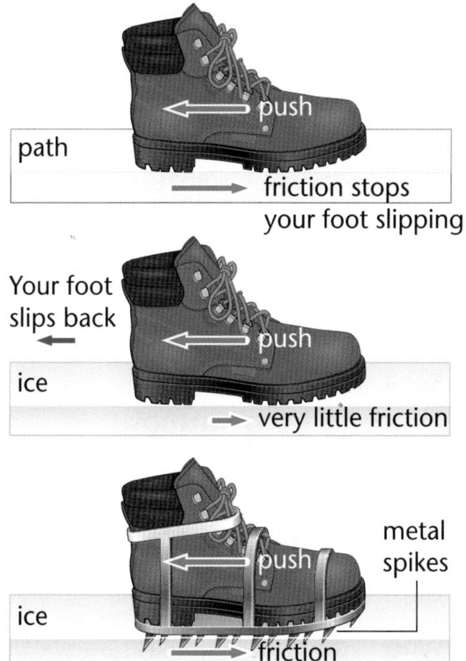

Metal spikes on crampons dig into the ice. This makes a very big friction force.

3 Look at the diagrams. What happens if you try to walk on slippery ice?

Mountaineers fasten crampons to their boots so they can walk on ice.

4 How do the crampons work?

Getting a grip

Tyres must grip the road. If they don't grip hard enough, the car or bicycle will **skid**.

5 Look at the diagram. Then copy and complete the sentences.

To make tyres grip, there must be a lot of __________ between the tyres and the road.

To make the friction forces big, we make tyres from __________ and make road surfaces __________.

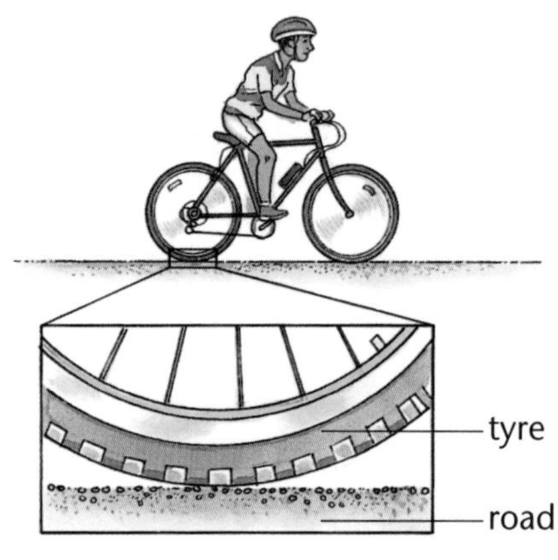

*There is a lot of **friction** between a rubber tyre and a rough road surface.*

WHAT YOU NEED TO REMEMBER (Copy and complete using the **key words**)

Making good use of friction

Between tyres and the road there must be a lot of __________.
If there isn't, the tyre might __________.

You slow down cars and bicycles by using the __________.
These use __________ friction to slow the wheels down.

A parachute uses __________ __________ to slow the parachutist down.

More about slowing down: C2.5

1.5 Balanced forces

You need a force to start something moving or to change its speed or direction.

But forces are also acting on things that are staying still and on things that are moving at a steady speed.

REMEMBER from pages 10–11

A force can:
- start something moving;
- make it move faster;
- slow it down;
- make it move in a different direction.

Holding up a suitcase

A suitcase which isn't moving still has forces acting on it. The diagram shows these forces.

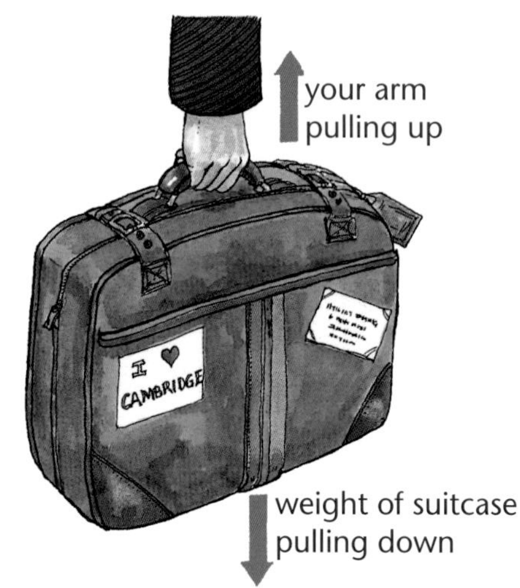
your arm pulling up
I ♥ CAMBRIDGE
weight of suitcase pulling down

The two forces balance, so the suitcase stays still.

1 Copy and complete the sentences.

When you hold a suitcase above the ground:
- the __________ of the suitcase pulls down
- your arm pulls __________.

These two forces __________, so the suitcase stays still.

If something is staying still, the forces that act on it must be **balanced**.

More things staying still

The diagrams show some more things which aren't moving.

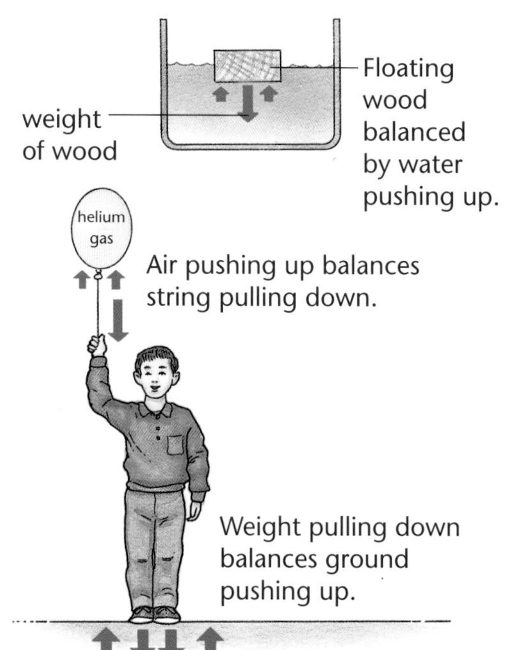
weight of wood
Floating wood balanced by water pushing up.
helium gas
Air pushing up balances string pulling down.
Weight pulling down balances ground pushing up.

2 Copy and complete the table.

	Which forces balance?	
	upwards force	**downwards force**
wood floating	water pushing	
helium balloon		
child standing		

Falling at a steady speed

The diagram shows the forces acting on a parachutist.

3 **(a)** What <u>two</u> forces are acting on the parachutist?

(b) Why does the parachutist fall at a steady speed?

When something falls at a steady speed, there are still forces acting on it. It falls at a steady speed because the forces acting on it are <u>balanced</u>.

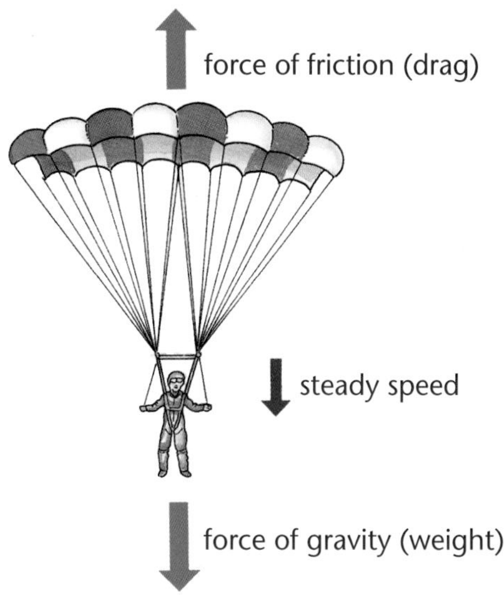

The forces balance, so the parachutist falls at a steady speed.

Cycling at a steady speed

A bicycle is moving at a steady speed.
So its speed isn't changing.

There are still forces acting on the bicycle.
But these forces are <u>balanced</u>.

4 Look at the diagram. Then copy and complete the sentences.

There are two forces that affect the speed of the bicycle:

- the force of ___________
- the ___________ force, caused by pedalling.

The bicycle goes at a steady speed because the two forces are ___________.

Balanced forces don't change the way things move. To change the way something moves, you need an **unbalanced** force.

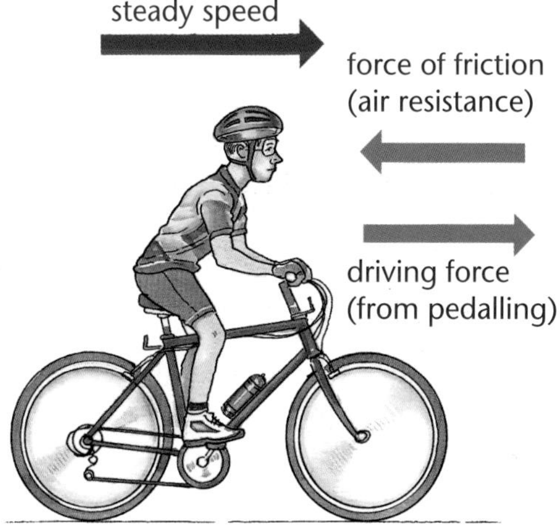

The two forces balance, so the bicycle goes at a steady speed.

WHAT YOU NEED TO REMEMBER (Copy and complete using the **key words**)

Balanced forces

A force doesn't always change the way something moves.
This is because the force may be ___________ by another force.

To change the way something moves, you need an ___________ force.

More about balanced forces: C2.5

1.6 How hard is it pressing?

Your feet sink into soft snow.

Walking on snow isn't easy.

It's a lot easier if you wear snow shoes.

1 Look at the pictures. Why do snow shoes make it easier to walk on snow?

How do snow shoes work?

You're still the same weight when you wear snow shoes. In fact, the snow shoes will make you a little bit heavier.

But you don't sink into the snow.

The diagrams at the bottom of the page show why.

2 Copy and complete the sentences.

Snow shoes work by spreading out your ________ over a much bigger __________.

When you spread your weight out over a bigger **area** of snow, you press down less on each bit of snow. We say that there is less **pressure** on the snow.

If you wear snow shoes, your feet don't sink in.

How much do snow shoes reduce the pressure?

The diagrams show the areas of an ordinary shoe and a snow shoe.

3 Copy and complete the sentences.

The area of a snow shoe is five times __________ than the area of an ordinary shoe.

So the pressure of a snow shoe on the snow is five times _____.

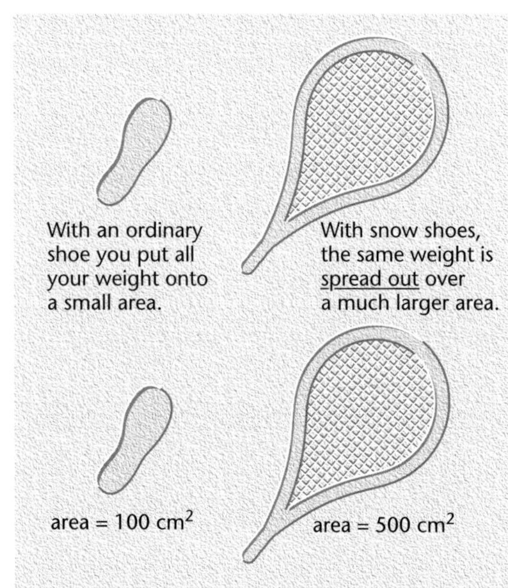

With an ordinary shoe you put all your weight onto a small area.
With snow shoes, the same weight is spread out over a much larger area.
area = 100 cm²
area = 500 cm²

Riding on soft sand

It's hard to ride a racing bike on soft sand.

It's a lot easier on a mountain bike.

The diagrams show why.

A racing bike sinks into the sand. It has thin tyres so there is a big pressure on the sand.

4 (a) Why is it hard to ride a racing bike across sand?

(b) Why doesn't the mountain bike sink into the sand so much?

5 Copy and complete the sentences.

With fatter tyres the weight is spread over a __________ area. So there is a __________ pressure on the sand.

A mountain bike has fat tyres so there is a small pressure on the sand.

Cutting cheese with a knife

It's easy to cut cheese with a sharp knife.

But it's much harder if you use the wrong side of the blade!

The diagrams show why.

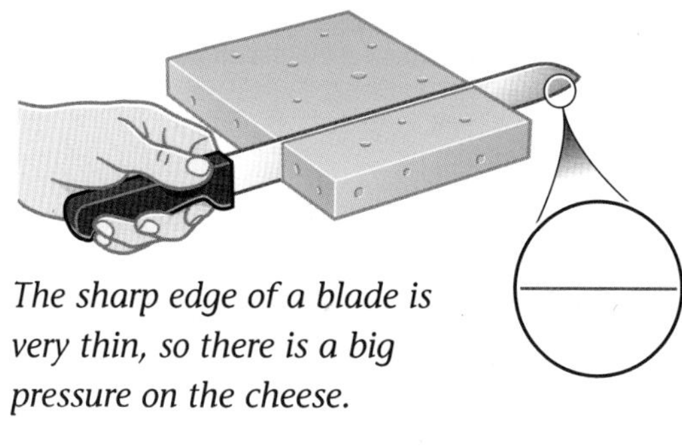

The sharp edge of a blade is very thin, so there is a big pressure on the cheese.

6 Copy and complete the sentences.

The sharp edge of a knife blade is much thinner than the __________ edge.
So the same force produces a much bigger __________ on the cheese.

7 The sharp edge of the knife is 100 times narrower than the blunt edge. How many times bigger is the pressure on the cheese, using the same force?

It's a lot harder to cut cheese with the blunt edge of a blade. This edge of the blade is 100 times thicker.

WHAT YOU NEED TO REMEMBER (Copy and complete using the **key words**)

How hard is it pressing?

If you spread out a force over a big area, it will only produce a small __________.

To get a big pressure, you must make a force act on a small __________.

More about pressure: C2.7

1.7 Using forces to make things turn

Some things are fixed to the ground, so we can't make them move along. But we can sometimes make them move round.

REMEMBER from pages 10–11

You can use a force to:
- start something moving;
- make it move faster;
- slow it down;
- make it move in a different direction.

Making a roundabout turn

The diagrams show a roundabout in a children's playground.

1 Copy and complete the sentences.

You can make the roundabout turn by __________ it.

Pushing it one way makes it turn round __________ wise.
Pushing it the other way makes it turn round __________ wise.

The roundabout turns around a point called the __________.

If you push like this the roundabout goes round the same way as the hands of a clock.
We say it turns clockwise.

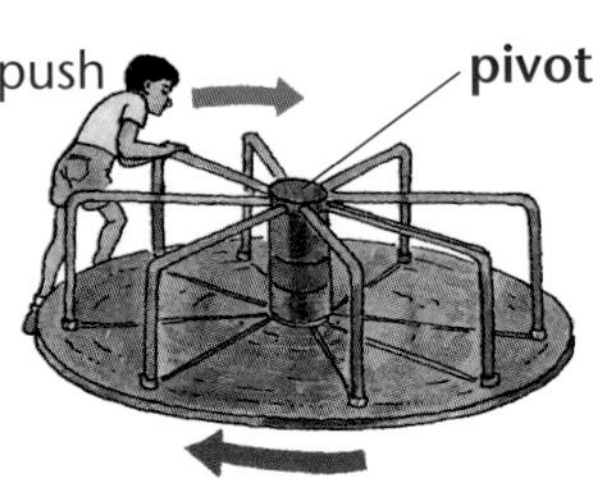

If you push the opposite way the roundabout turns **anti-clockwise.**

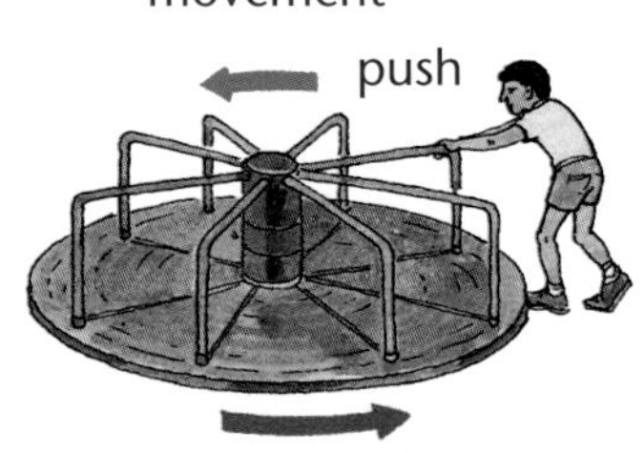

Moving a see-saw

The diagram shows what happens when a boy sits on the right-hand side of a see-saw.

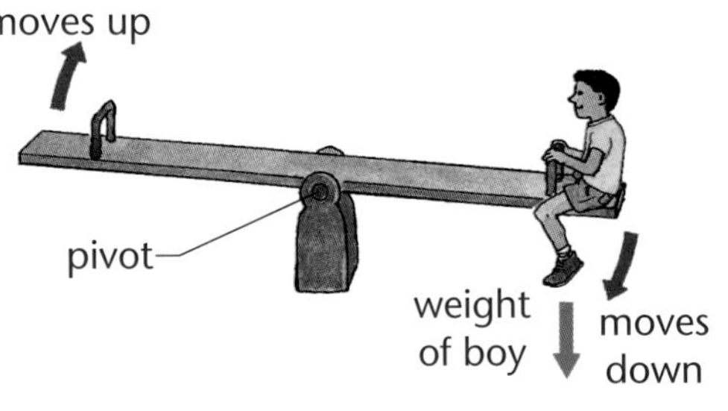

2 Copy and complete the sentence.

The see-saw turns __________ wise.
It turns around its __________ point.

3 Copy the diagram of a girl on a see-saw. Then complete it to show what happens.

Balancing a see-saw

The diagram shows how the turning forces on a see-saw can **balance**.

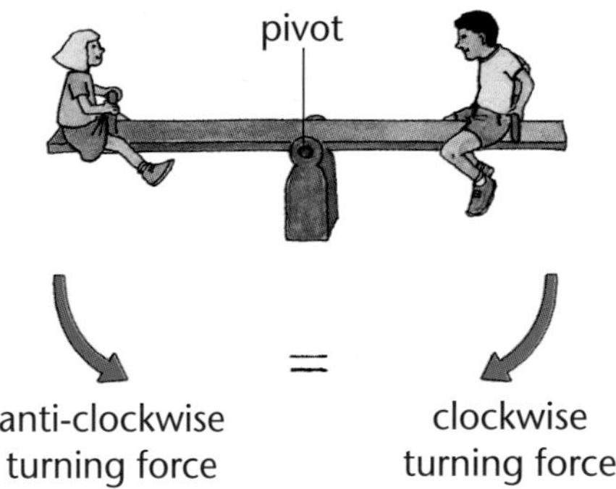

4 Copy and complete the sentences.

The clockwise turning force is the same as the ___________ turning force.
So the forces ___________.

Turning forces in everyday life

You often use a turning force to do things. For example, you can use a spanner to tighten a bolt.

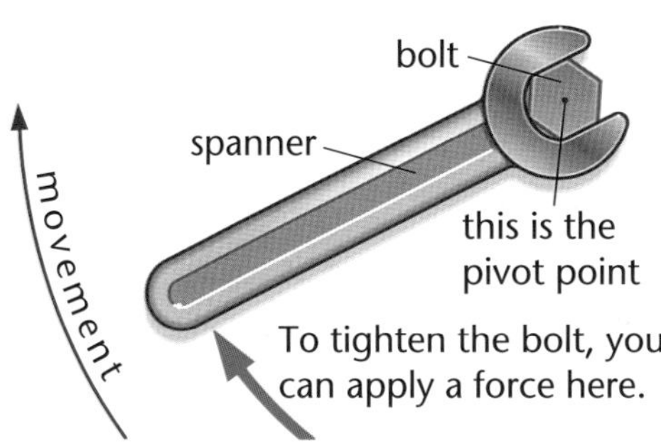

5 Which way do you turn a bolt to tighten it?

You also use a turning force to close a door.

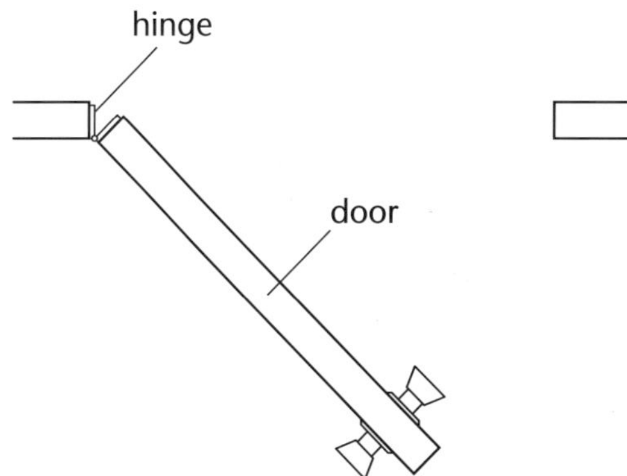

6 Make a copy of the diagram of the door. Show on the diagram:

(a) the pivot point;

(b) where you apply a force to close the door.

WHAT YOU NEED TO REMEMBER (Copy and complete using the **key words**)

Using forces to make things turn

Forces can make things turn around a ______________ point.

If a force makes something turn clockwise, the opposite force will make it turn ______________.

If a clockwise turning force is the same as an anti-clockwise turning force, the forces ______________.

More about turning: C2.8

1.8 How fast is it moving?

We sometimes want to know how fast something is moving.

Look at the top picture of a car and a lorry. They both go past a lamp-post at the same time. The lower picture shows how far the car and the lorry travel in the next second.

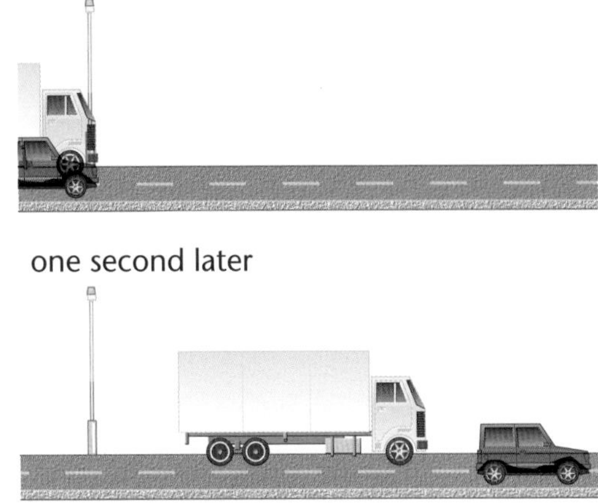

1 (a) Which is moving faster, the car or the lorry?

(b) Give a reason for your answer.

The car is moving faster than the lorry. We say that the car has a higher **speed** than the lorry.

Thinking about speed

The speed of something is how far it travels in a certain time.

For example, the lorry in the pictures travels 10 metres in one second.
So its speed is 10 metres per second.
[Note: 'per second' means 'in one second'.]

2 Look again at the pictures of the car and the lorry. What is the speed of the car?

3 Look at the pictures of the walker and the cyclists. What is the speed:

(a) of the walker?

(b) of the cyclists?

4 How far will:

(a) the walker travel in 4 hours?

(b) the cyclists travel in $2\frac{1}{2}$ hours?

The walker travels 5 kilometres in one hour.

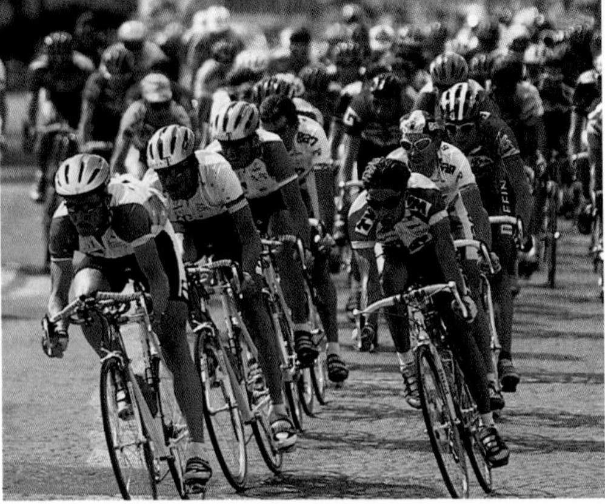

These cyclists travel 50 kilometres in one hour.

How to work out speeds

To work out the speed of something you need to know:

- how far it travels (a **distance**);
- the **time** it takes to travel this distance.

You can then work out its speed like this:

speed = distance travelled ÷ time taken

Example

A car goes 120 miles in 2 hours.

speed = distance travelled ÷ time taken
= 120 ÷ 2
= 60

So the car's speed is 60 miles per hour.

5 Work out the speeds of the things shown in the pictures on this page. (Use a calculator if you want to.)

Concorde travels 3000 miles in 2 hours.

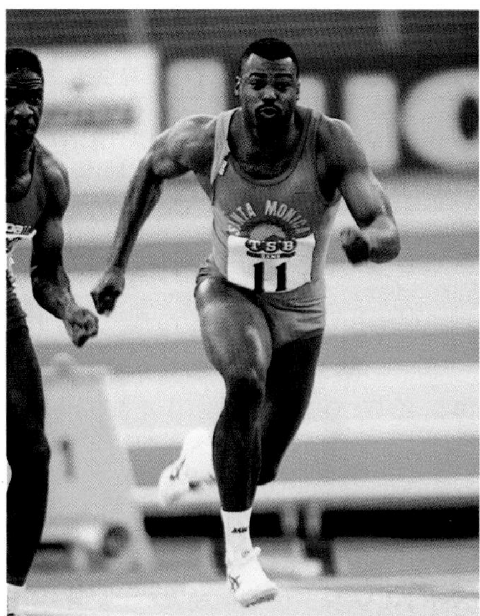

This athlete runs 100 metres in 10 seconds.

This Eurostar train travels 240 kilometres in $1\frac{1}{2}$ hours.

Average speeds

Most things don't travel at the same speed all the time. For example:

- the train stops at some stations;
- the athlete has to build up to full speed.

So the speeds you worked out were their **average** speeds.

6 The athlete runs 40 metres in the first 5 seconds of the race and 60 metres in the last 5 seconds. Work out his speed during each half of the race.

WHAT YOU NEED TO REMEMBER (Copy and complete using the **key words**)

How fast is it moving?

The distance something travels in a certain time is called its ____________.

You can work out speed like this: speed = ____________ travelled ÷ ____________ taken

Many things don't move at the same speed all the time. So the speed we work out is their ____________ speed.

More about speed: C2.6

1.9 Working out the pressure

REMEMBER from pages 20–21

You can make a force produce a smaller pressure by spreading it out over a larger area.

You can make a force produce a bigger pressure by making it act on a smaller area.

The pressure that a force produces depends on the **area** that the force acts on.

So you can get different pressures with the same force.

This idea is used with a drawing pin.

How a drawing pin uses pressure

When you use a drawing pin you get:

- a small pressure on your thumb;
- a big pressure on the notice-board.

The diagram shows how this happens.

The point of the drawing pin has a small area, so a large pressure pushes it into the board.

notice-board

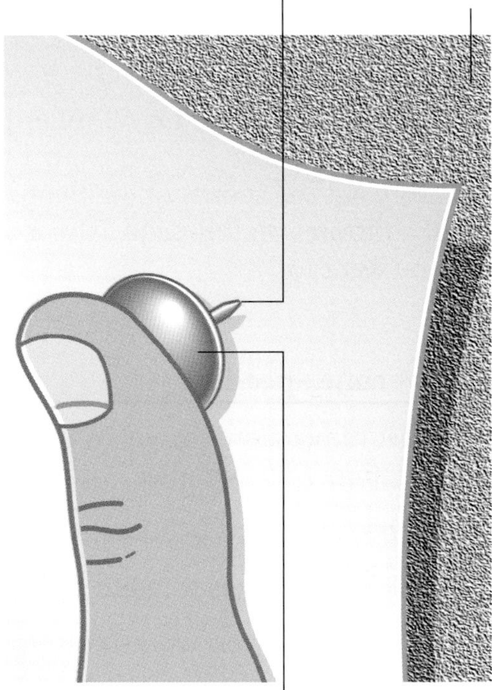

The head of the drawing pin has a large area, so the pressure is small and doesn't cut your thumb.

force on board

This is the same force, but on a much smaller area.

force of thumb

1 (a) Why do you want a small pressure on your thumb?

(b) How do you get this small pressure?

2 (a) Why is the pressure of the sharp end of a drawing pin on the notice-board very big?

(b) Why do you want this pressure to be very big?

How much bigger is the pressure on the notice-board?

The head of the drawing pin has an area a thousand times bigger than the point of the drawing pin.

The same force acts on both.

3 How many times bigger is the pressure of the drawing pin on the notice-board than on your thumb?

4 A badly made drawing pin has a blunt end.

(a) Is the area of this blunt end bigger or smaller than the area of a normal point?

(b) Will this make it easier or harder to push the drawing pin into a notice-board?

Measuring forces

We measure forces in units called **newtons** (N for short).

The diagrams give you an idea of how big a newton of force is.

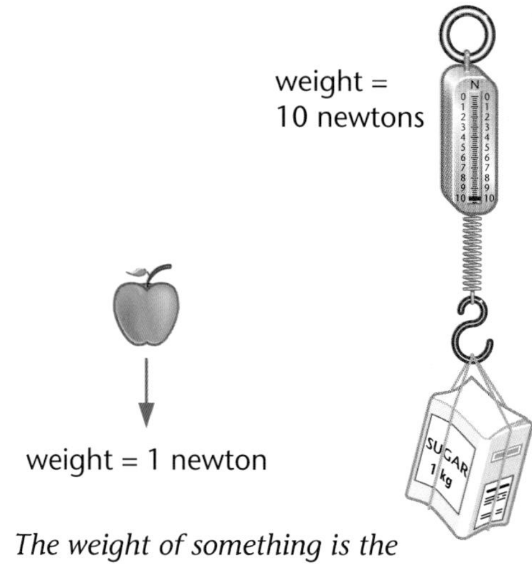

The weight of something is the force of gravity that pulls it to the Earth.

5 Copy and complete the sentences.

The weight of an apple is about ________ newton.

The force of gravity on a kilogram is about ________ N.

Working out the pressures

Pressure is the **force** on a certain area. So you can work out a pressure like this:

pressure = force ÷ area

The example shows you how to use this idea for the drawing pin.

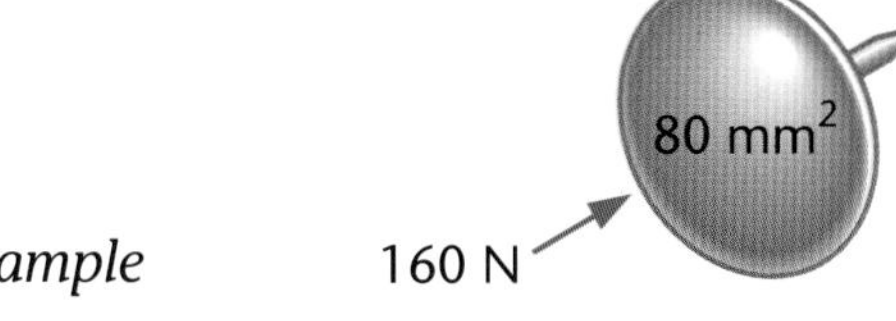

Example

On your thumb:

pressure = force ÷ area
= 160 ÷ 80
= 2 newtons per mm^2

Working out the pressure on snow

The diagrams show a girl's ordinary shoe and her snow shoe.

As the girl walks, she puts all her weight on to one foot and then on to the other foot.

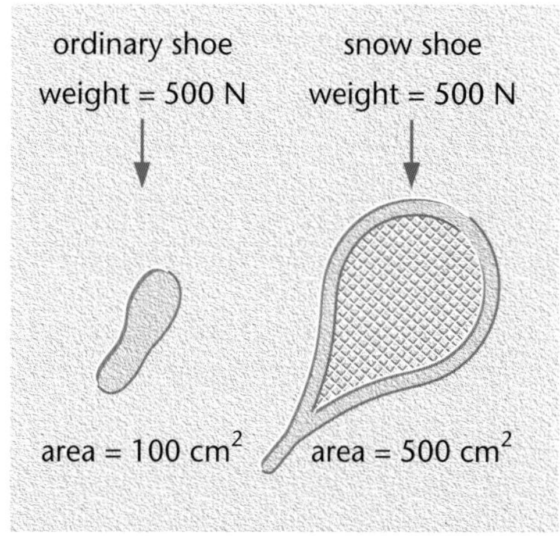

6 Work out the pressure of the girl's foot on the snow as she walks:

(a) with ordinary shoes;

(b) with snow shoes.

WHAT YOU NEED TO REMEMBER (Copy and complete using the **key words**)

Working out the pressure

The pressure of a force depends on the ____________ it acts on.

Forces are measured in ____________ (N for short).

You can work out pressure like this: pressure = ____________ ÷ area

More about pressure: C2.7

2.1 How you see things

You need **light** to see things.

When it's dark, you can't see very well.
If it's completely dark, you can't see anything at all.

*The light bulb sends out light. Other things in the room **reflect** this light. You see when light goes into your eyes.*

1 Look at the diagrams.

(a) Why can you see the light bulb?

(b) Why can you see the chair and the carpet?

(c) Why can't you see the chair or the carpet when it's dark?

2 Sometimes there is a power cut and all the electric lights go off.

Write down <u>three</u> different things you could use to give you light during a power cut.

A problem with corners

Even when it is light, you can't see round **corners**. The diagram shows why.

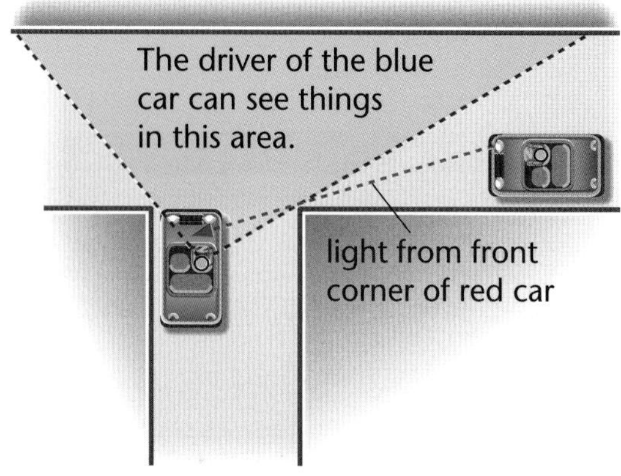
The driver of the blue car can see things in this area.
light from front corner of red car

*Light travels in **straight lines**.*

3 Copy and complete the sentences.

The driver of the blue car can't see the __________ car. This is because light from the red car travels in __________ lines.
Light doesn't travel round __________.

4 **(a)** Can the driver of the red car see any part of the blue car?

(b) Explain your answer on a copy of the diagram. (Leave out the red line so that it doesn't get in the way.)

Shadows

Light can't go through most solid things. So if you put something like a pencil in the way of a beam of light, you get a **shadow**.

The diagram shows why.

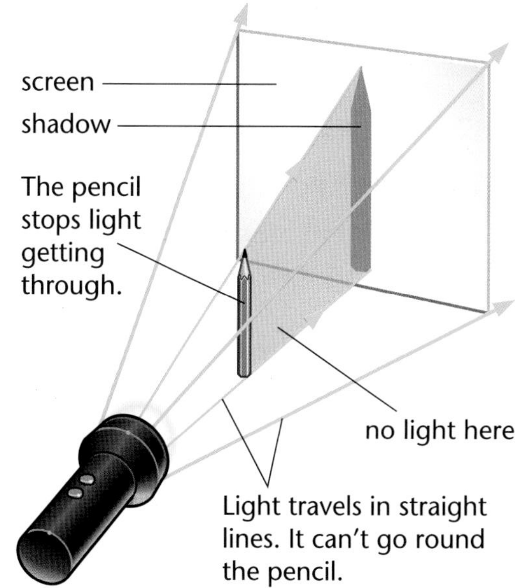

screen
shadow
The pencil stops light getting through.
no light here
Light travels in straight lines. It can't go round the pencil.

5 Copy and complete the sentences.

Light can't go through a pencil.

Light travels in straight __________.
So it can't go __________ the pencil either.

This is why the pencil makes a __________.

6 What shape is the shadow of the pencil?

Find out how you can make a shadow bigger or smaller.

Why is it light on a cloudy day?

During the day we can see because of light from the Sun.

light from Sun

Even on a cloudy day there is still plenty of light. The diagram shows why.

light from Sun
Clouds reflect some light.
But some light gets through.

7 **(a)** Why is it light on a cloudy day?

(b) Why is it not as light on a cloudy day as on a sunny day?

(c) You can't see the Sun or the sky on a cloudy day. What else don't you see on a cloudy day? (Look carefully at the picture.)

WHAT YOU NEED TO REMEMBER (Copy and complete using the **key words**)

How you see things

You can only see when there is some __________.
The things you see either give out light or __________ light into your eyes.

Light travels in __________ __________. So it can't go round __________.

When light can't pass through something, it makes a __________.

More about driving at night: C1.3

2.2 Reflecting light

Some things give out **light**. This makes them easy to see.

We can see other things because they **reflect** the light that falls on them.

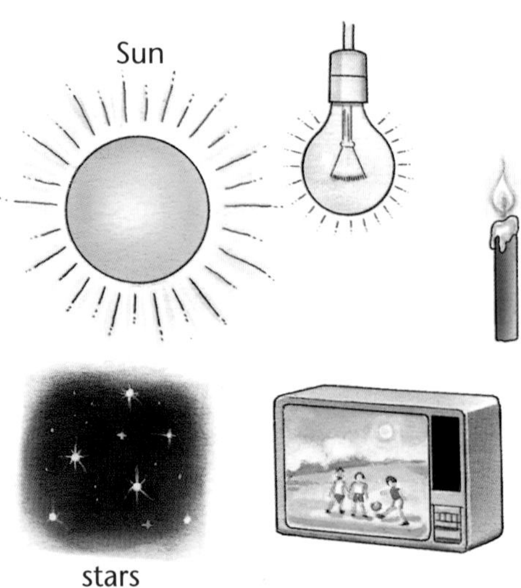

Some things give out their own light.

1 Write down the names of five things that give out light.

2 How can you see:

(a) the Moon;

(b) the pages of a book you read at night?

We can see other things because they reflect light.

How most things reflect light

A spotlight shines on a picture.

The diagram shows why you can see the picture from all parts of the room.

3 Copy and complete the sentences.

The picture reflects light in _________ directions. This is because the surface of the picture has lots and lots of tiny _________.

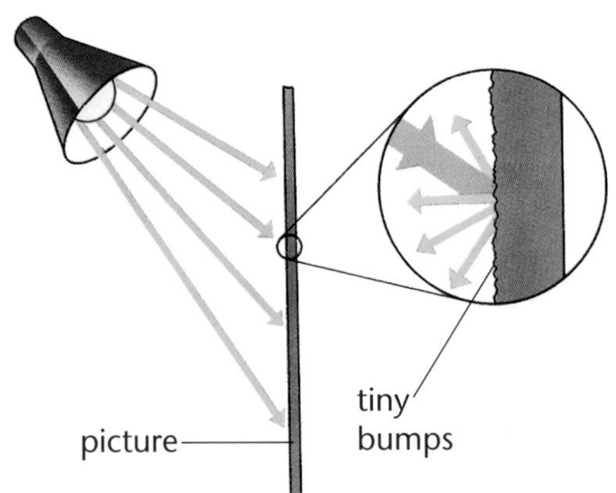

*The picture has a bumpy surface. So it reflects light in all **directions**.*

Reflection from very shiny surfaces

Shiny surfaces reflect light in a special sort of way.

4 Look at the diagrams.

(a) What can you use a very shiny surface for?

(b) Write down the names of two shiny surfaces you can see your reflection in.

Try looking at your reflection on each side of a shiny spoon.
Are there any differences?
Does it matter how far away the spoon is?

mirror (glass with silvered back)
polished metal spoon

You can see your own reflection in these.

How a mirror reflects light

Some pupils decided to find out how a mirror reflects light. The diagram shows what they did.

The pupils then moved the ray-box so the beam of light hit the mirror at a different **angle**.

The table shows their results.

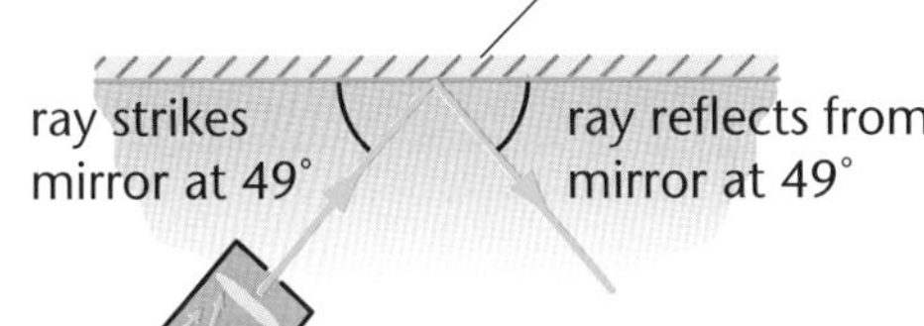
This is an easy way to show a mirror.
ray strikes mirror at 49°
ray reflects from mirror at 49°
A ray-box makes a narrow beam of light.
We call this a ray.

Angle that light strikes mirror	Angle that light reflects from mirror
20°	20°
37°	37°
49°	49°
66°	66°
81°	81°

5 Copy and complete the sentence.

A mirror reflects a ray of light at the __________ angle as it strikes the mirror.

Write your name on a piece of paper and look at it in a mirror.
What do you notice?
Now write your name on a piece of paper so that it is the right way round in a mirror.

WHAT YOU NEED TO REMEMBER (Copy and complete using the **key words**)

Reflecting light

We can see some things because they give out __________.

We can see other things because they __________ light into our eyes.

Most things reflect light in all __________.

Shiny surfaces, such as mirrors, reflect light at the same __________ as the light strikes them.

More about mirrors: C1.3

2.3 Using mirrors

Other people can see you because light is reflected from your face.

To see your own face you need to use a mirror.

The diagram shows how this works.

REMEMBER from pages 30–31

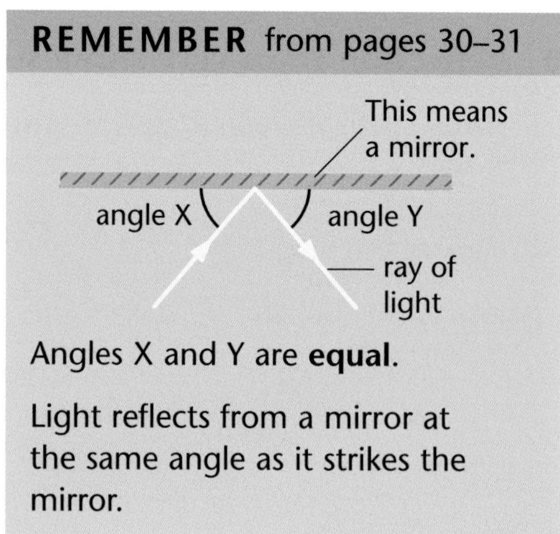

Angles X and Y are **equal**.

Light reflects from a mirror at the same angle as it strikes the mirror.

1 Copy and complete the sentence.

On the diagram angle P and angle Q are

___________.

2 Draw a diagram to show how the girl sees her own lips to put on lipstick.

We can use mirrors to do many other useful jobs.

3 Car drivers often look into their mirrors while they are driving.
Why do they do this?

Seeing round corners

You can use a mirror to help drivers to see round a dangerous corner.

The diagram shows how the driver of the blue car can see the red car through the mirror.

When she looks past the corner, the driver of the blue car can <u>just</u> see the front of the yellow car.

The driver of the blue car can also see the yellow car through the mirror.

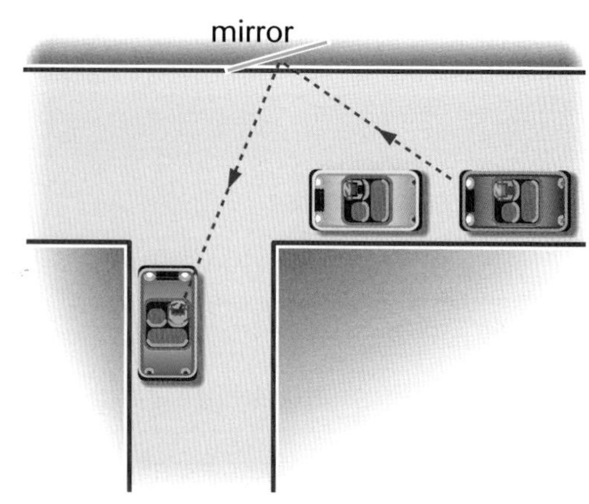

4 On a copy of the diagram, draw lines to show the <u>two</u> ways the driver of the blue car can see the yellow car. (Leave out the red lines so they don't get in the way.)

Seeing over the top of things

To see over the top of something you need to use a <u>periscope</u>.

The diagrams show some of the ways you can use a periscope.

5 Write down <u>three</u> things that a periscope can be used for.

battleship

submarine

seeing over a crowd

woodpecker

birdwatcher

How a periscope works

You can make a periscope using two mirrors.

The diagram shows how you can do this.

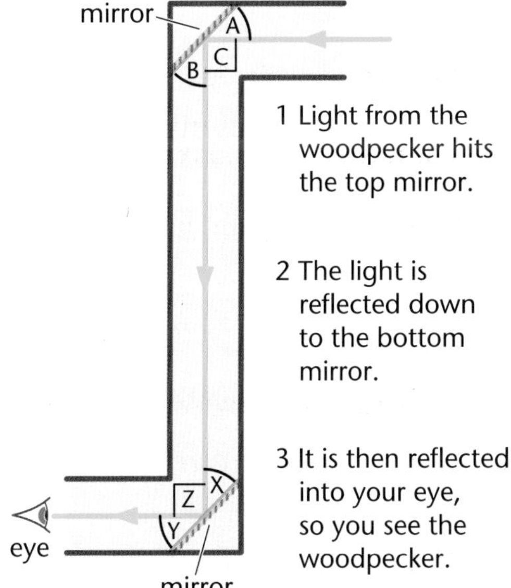

mirror
A
B
C
1 Light from the woodpecker hits the top mirror.
2 The light is reflected down to the bottom mirror.
3 It is then reflected into your eye, so you see the woodpecker.
Z
X
Y
eye
mirror

A right angle is 90°.

6 Copy and complete the table.

Angle	Number of degrees
A	45°
B	______°
C	90°
X	______°
Y	______°
Z	______°

7 Copy and complete the sentences.

At each mirror, the light changes direction by an angle of ______°.

To do this:

- it strikes the mirror at ______°
- it is reflected at ______°.

WHAT YOU NEED TO REMEMBER (Copy and complete using the **key words**)

Using mirrors

When light is reflected from a mirror, angles X and Y are ____________.

mirror

X Y

You should be able to use this idea to explain other uses of mirrors in the same sort of way as you have on these pages.

More about mirrors: C1.3

2.4 Colours of the rainbow

On pictures we often show the Sun as yellow.

But the light from the Sun is really **white**.

White light isn't just one colour. It's lots of different colours all mixed up together.

You can see all these colours in a **rainbow**.

Drops of rain can split up sunlight into all the colours of the rainbow.

1 What splits up sunlight into all the colours in a rainbow?

2 Write down a list of the colours of the rainbow in the right order. Start from the outside with red.
Use these colours in your list:
blue green orange red violet yellow

■ Making your own 'rainbow'

The diagram shows how you can use a **prism** to split up white light into all the colours of the rainbow.

We call these rainbow colours a **spectrum**.

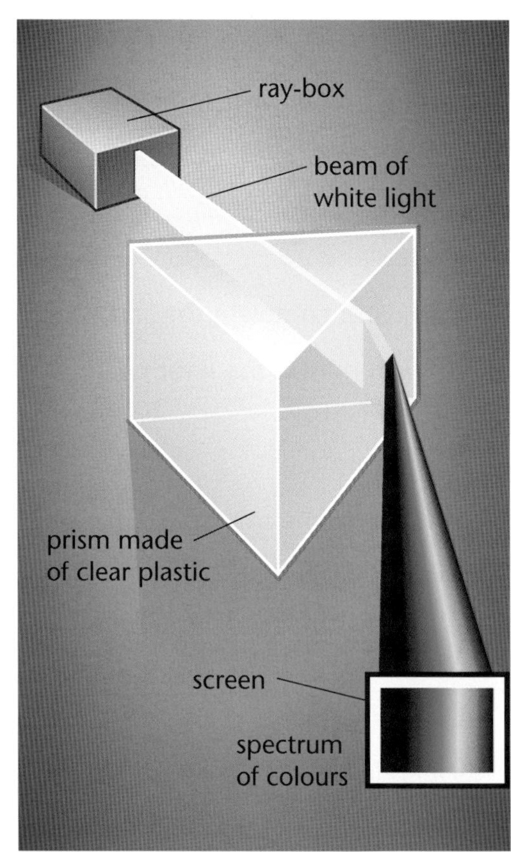

3 Copy and complete the sentences.

We can split up a narrow beam of white light using a prism made of __________ __________.

We call all the different colours of light a __________.

4 Draw a box about 5 cm wide and 2 cm high.

Colour a spectrum inside the box. (Coloured pencils are best because you can shade the colours into each other.)

Then label the colours in your spectrum.

Using coloured filters

Another way to get coloured light from white light is to use coloured **filters**.

Filters let some colours of light pass through. But they stop other colours. We say that the filters **absorb** these other colours.

The diagrams show how filters work.

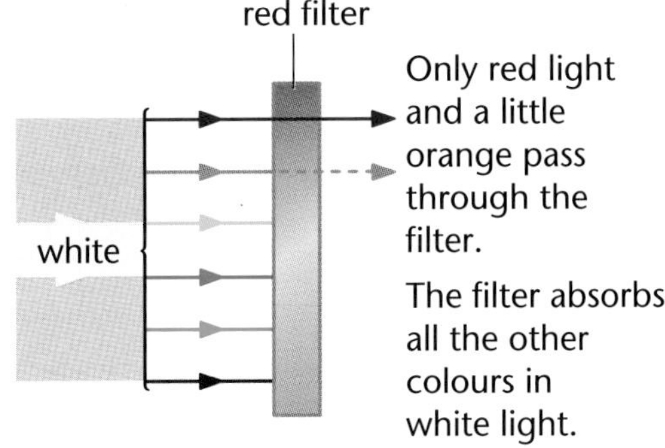
red filter
white
Only red light and a little orange pass through the filter.
The filter absorbs all the other colours in white light.

How a red filter works.

5 When you send white light through a red filter it comes out red. Explain why.

6 Copy the diagram of the yellow filter.

Then add words to the diagram to explain how it works.

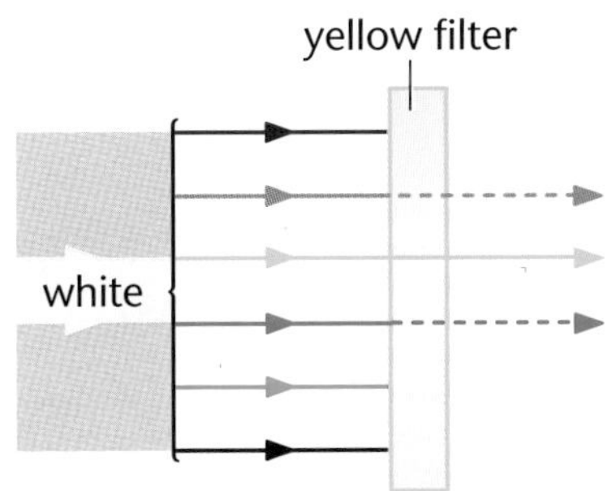
yellow filter
white

How a yellow filter works.

Using more than one filter

The diagram shows what happens when you send white light through a blue filter and then through a yellow filter.

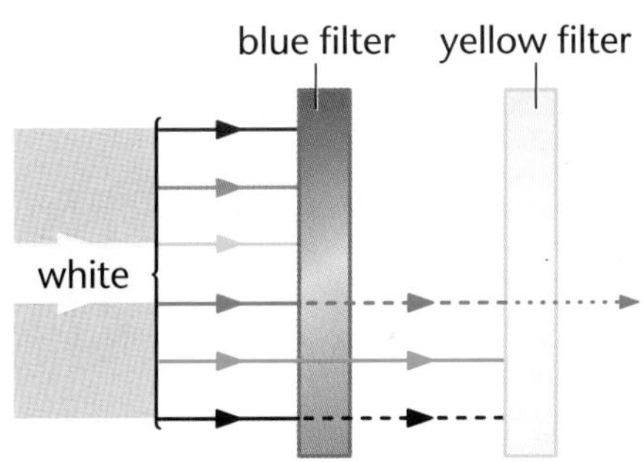
blue filter
yellow filter
white

Two filters together.

7 What light passes through both filters?

8 **(a)** What happens if you send white light through a blue filter and then through a red filter?

(b) Draw a diagram to explain your answer.

WHAT YOU NEED TO REMEMBER (Copy and complete using the **key words**)

Colours of the rainbow

Light from the Sun is ______________.

When white light is split up by drops of rain, we get a ______________.

We can split up white light into colours using a ______________ made of clear plastic.
We call the colours a ______________.

We can also make coloured light from white light by using ______________.
Filters let some colours pass through but ______________ other colours.

More about colour and prisms: C1.4, C1.5

2.5 Why do things look coloured?

REMEMBER from pages 34–35

White light is a mixture of all the colours of the rainbow.

white light

Coloured filters let some colours through. They absorb other colours. ('Absorb' means 'soak up'.)

We can see things because they reflect light.

But sunlight and the light from most lamps is white.

So we need to explain why many of the things we see are coloured.

Why a postbox looks red

A postbox looks red in white daylight.

The diagram shows why.

1 Copy and complete the sentences.

A postbox looks __________.
This is because red paint reflects mainly __________ light.
It __________ most other colours.

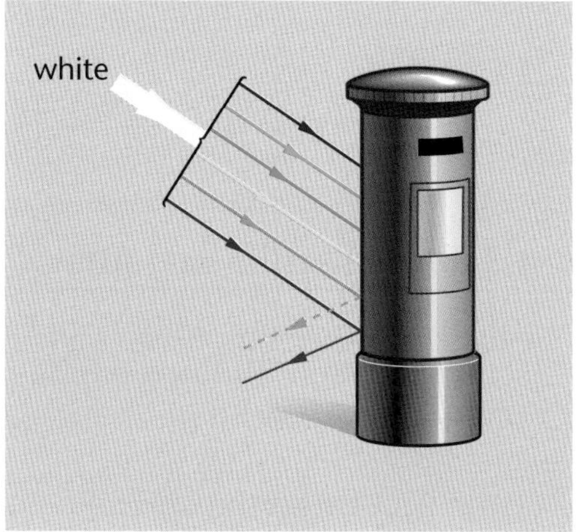

Red paint reflects red light and a little orange. It absorbs other colours.

Why grass looks green

Things look coloured because they **reflect** some colours of light and **absorb** other colours.

The diagram shows why grass looks green.

2 **(a)** What colour of light does grass mainly reflect?

(b) What other colours does grass partly reflect?

(c) What happens to the colours of light that are not reflected?

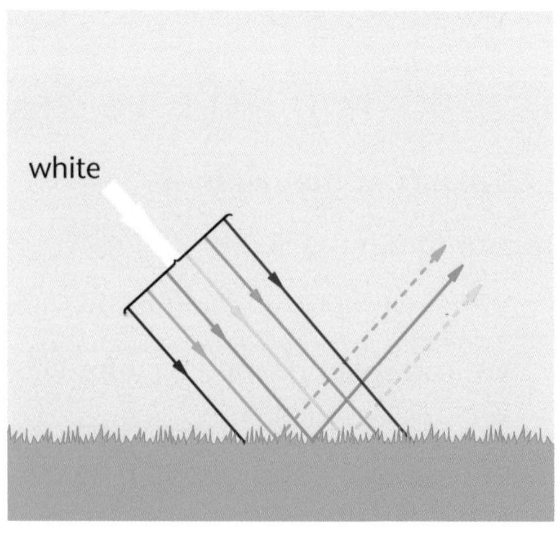

Why grass looks green.

Why isn't everything coloured?

Some things aren't coloured. They are white or black or some shade of grey.

The diagrams show why.

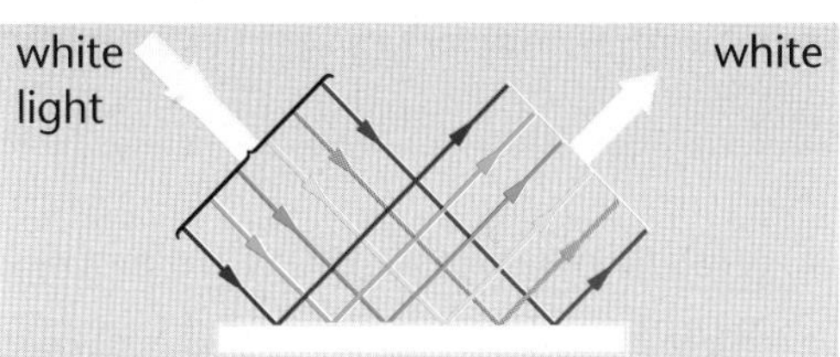

*A white surface reflects **all** colours a lot.*

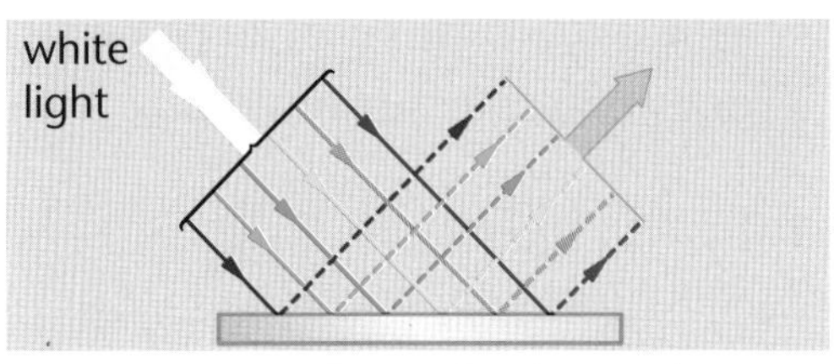

A grey surface reflects all colours a bit.

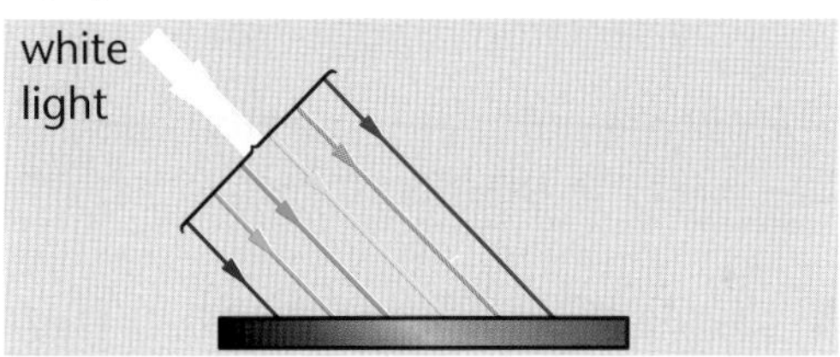

*A **black** surface hardly reflects any colour.*

3 **(a)** Copy and complete the table.

Surface	What it reflects
white	
black	
grey	

(b) Copy and complete the sentences.

White things and grey things don't look coloured. This is because the light they reflect contains all the __________ of the spectrum.

Looking at things in coloured light

Things look their normal colour when we see them in <u>white</u> light.

They look different in coloured light.

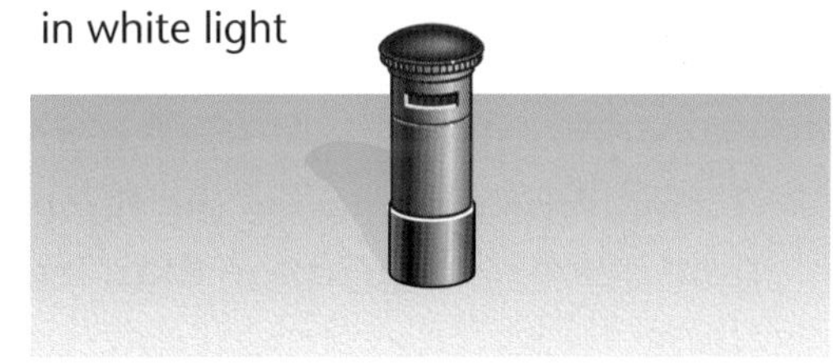

4 Look at the diagrams. Then copy and complete the table.

	How it looks in red light	How it looks in green light
postbox		
grass		

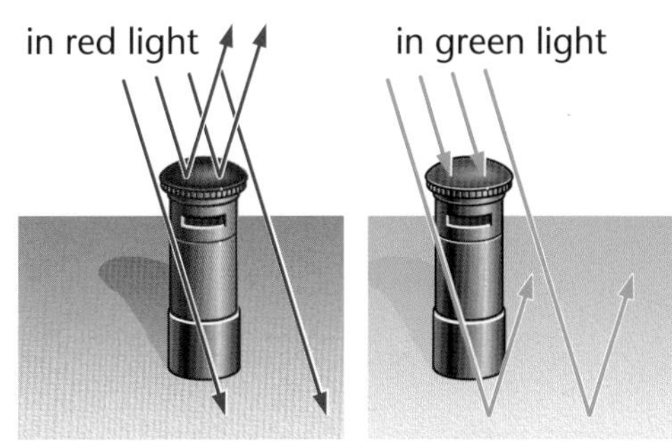

WHAT YOU NEED TO REMEMBER (Copy and complete using the **key words**)

Why do things look coloured?

Things look coloured in white light because they __________ some colours of light but __________ other colours.

White things and grey things don't look coloured because they reflect the same amount of __________ the colours of the spectrum.

Things which reflect hardly any light at all look __________.

More about colour: C1.4

2.6 Comparing light and sound

We all need to know what's going on in the world around us. We find out mainly by looking and listening.

This means that we use **light** and **sound** to find out about our surroundings.

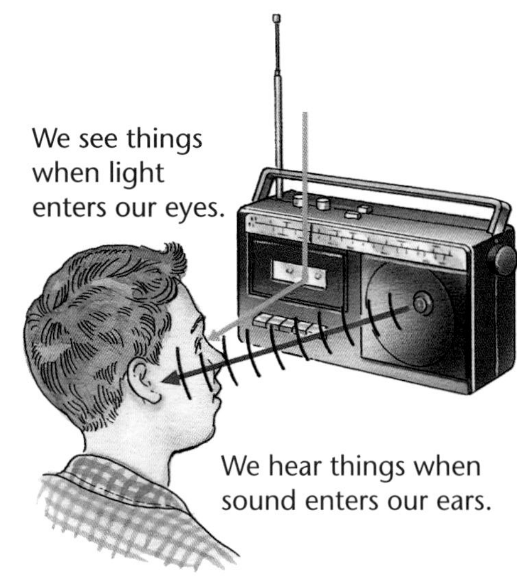

1 Look at the picture. Then copy and complete the sentences.

We use our ________ to see the ________ reflected from things around us.

We use our ________ to hear ________.

Seeing and hearing in a thunderstorm

During a thunderstorm you see flashes of lightning. These make the sound we call thunder.

Light takes hardly any time at all to travel through the air. You see the lightning a short time before you hear the thunder. The diagram shows why.

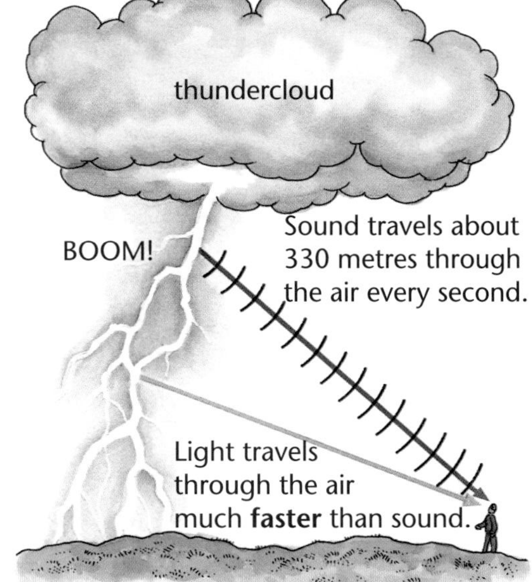

thundercloud
BOOM!
Sound travels about 330 metres through the air every second.
Light travels through the air much **faster** than sound.

2 Why do you see lightning before you hear thunder?

3 You see a flash of lightning. Three seconds later you hear thunder.

How far away was the lightning?

If you hear thunder 4 seconds after seeing lightning, the lightning is
$4 \times 330 = 1320$ metres away.

Fainter and fainter

As a thunderstorm moves further away, the sound of the thunder isn't so loud. The flashes of lightning aren't so bright either.

We say that the light and sound get **fainter**.

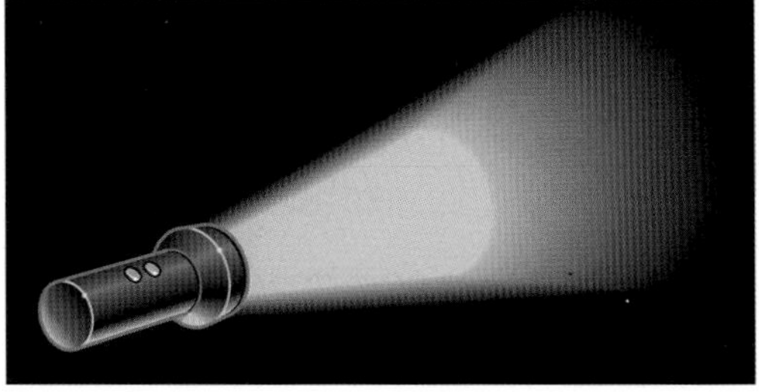
Light spreads out more as it gets further away. So it is fainter.

4 Why does light get fainter as it gets further away?

Another difference between light and sound

An accident on a satellite causes a HUGE explosion.

5 People on Earth see the explosion. But they do not hear it. Why not?

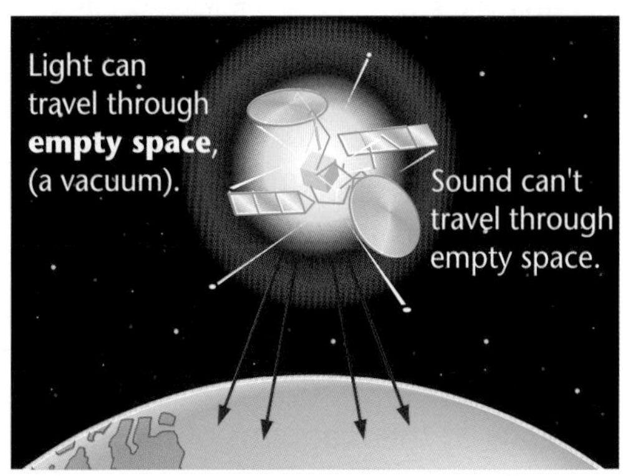

Differences between sounds

You know that light can be many different **colours**.

In the same way, sounds can have a different **pitch**.

We say that some sounds have a higher or lower pitch than others.

Small musical instruments play notes with a higher pitch than large ones.

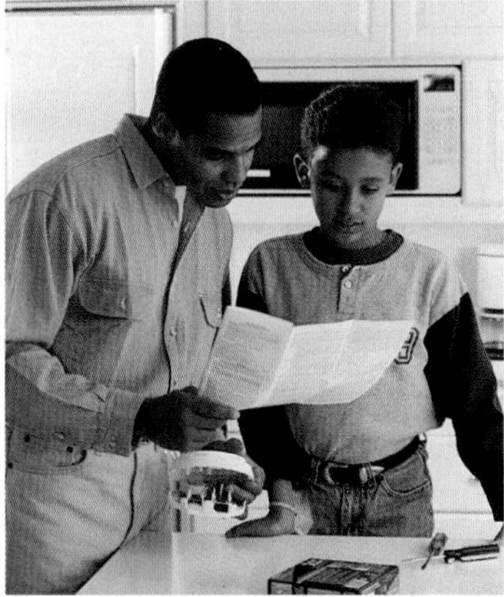

A man's voice has a lower pitch than a young boy's voice.

6 Look at the pictures. Then answer the questions below.

(a) Which plays notes of a higher pitch, a cello or a violin?

(b) During his teens, a boy's voice 'breaks'. What does this mean?

(c) Where do you find the lowest notes on a keyboard?

The pitch of notes gets higher as you move this way along the keyboard.

Each key on a keyboard plays a note with a different pitch.

WHAT YOU NEED TO REMEMBER (Copy and complete using the **key words**)

Comparing light and sound

We see when __________ enters our eyes. We hear when __________ enters our ears.

Light travels __________ than sound through the air.

The further light and sound travel, the __________ they get.

Light, but not sound, can travel through __________ __________. Light can be different __________. Sounds can have a different __________.

More about sound: C1.7

2.7 Making and hearing sounds

Things that vibrate make sounds.

There are lots and lots of different sounds. They are all made by things which **vibrate**.

We often use musical instruments to make sounds.

1 Look at the diagrams of musical instruments. Then copy and complete the table.

Instrument	What vibrates to make a sound
saxophone	the air inside it

saxophone

The air inside this vibrates when you blow.

guitar

The strings vibrate when you pluck them.

drum

The drum skins vibrate when you hit them.

Sound from radios and TVs

Many of the sounds we listen to every day come from radios, TVs and CD players.

2 Look at the diagram. What part of a radio produces sounds?

The loudspeaker in a radio produces sounds.

How sounds reach your ears

The diagram shows how the sound from a loudspeaker reaches your ears.

3 Copy and complete the following.

loudspeaker makes ____ → vibrations travel through the ____ → vibrations enter your ____

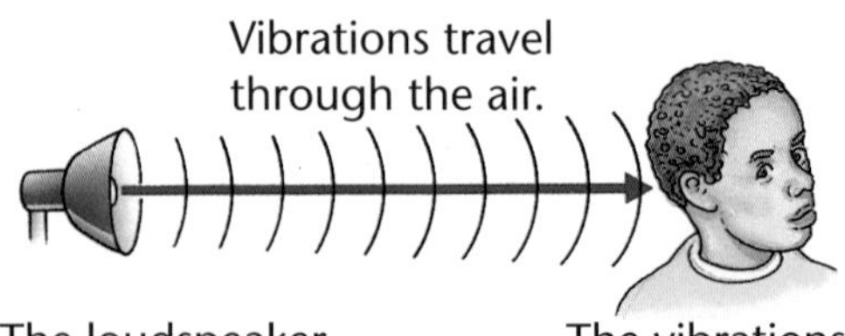
Vibrations travel through the air.
The loudspeaker makes vibrations.
The vibrations enter your ear.

What else can sound travel through?

Most of the sounds you hear travel through **air** before they reach your ears.

Sound can also travel very well through **solids** and **liquids**.

Whales can send sounds to each other for hundreds of kilometres.

4 Write down:

(a) one example of a sound travelling through a solid;

(b) one example of a sound travelling through a liquid.

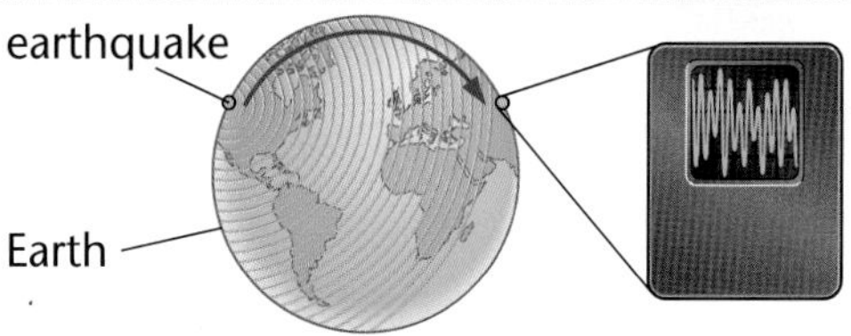

Sound vibrations from an earthquake travel through the Earth. Scientists use special instruments to 'listen' to earthquakes thousands of kilometres away.

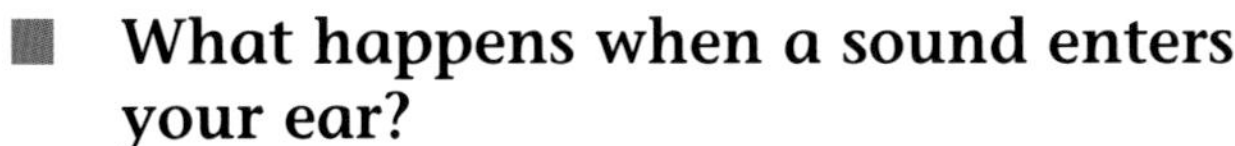

What happens when a sound enters your ear?

The diagram shows what happens when sound vibrations travel through the air into your ear.

5 Write down these sentences in the right order to explain how you hear. The first and the last are in the correct place.

- Your pinna collects sound vibrations in the air.
- Vibrations pass on to small bones inside your ear.
- The vibrations in the air strike your eardrum.
- Your eardrum vibrates.
- The vibrations in the air travel down your ear canal.
- Your inner ear sends a signal to your brain.

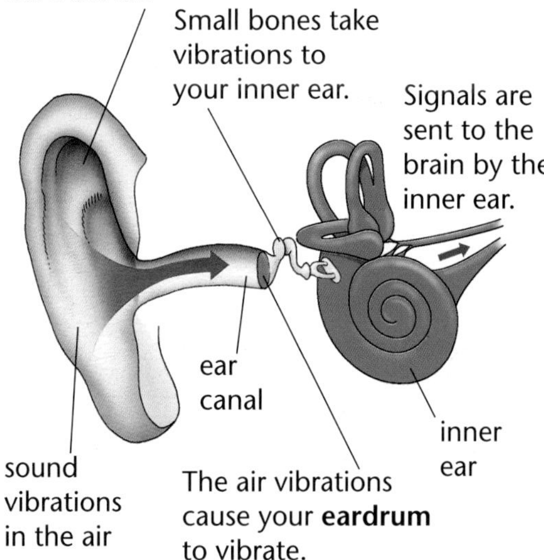

Signals are sent to the brain by the inner ear.

WHAT YOU NEED TO REMEMBER (Copy and complete using the **key words**)

Making and hearing sounds

Sounds are made when things ______________.
These vibrations then travel through the ______________ to your ears.

Sounds can also travel through ______________ and ______________.

When sounds enter your ear, they strike your ______________ and make it vibrate.

More about hearing sound: C1.7

2.8 Different sounds

There are lots of different sounds.

Some sounds are **louder** than others.

The pictures show how you can make the same sound louder.

1 Write down three ways of making a sound louder.

Why are some sounds louder than others?

All sounds are caused by **vibrations**. These vibrations are often too small to see. But you can see the strings on a guitar vibrate.

2 Look at the diagram. Then copy and complete the sentences.

When you pluck a guitar string harder, the sound is ___________.
This is because the vibrations are ___________.

Another way of saying that vibrations are large is to say that they have a big **amplitude**.

Making a louder sound.

Hit the drum harder.

Turn up the volume control.

String plucked gently:

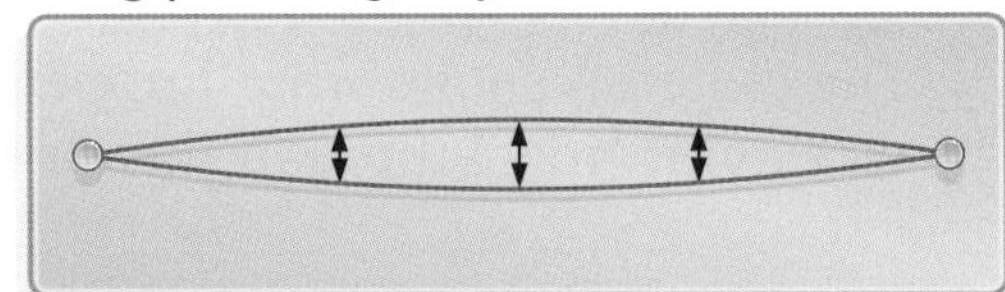

small vibrations, quiet sound.

String plucked harder:

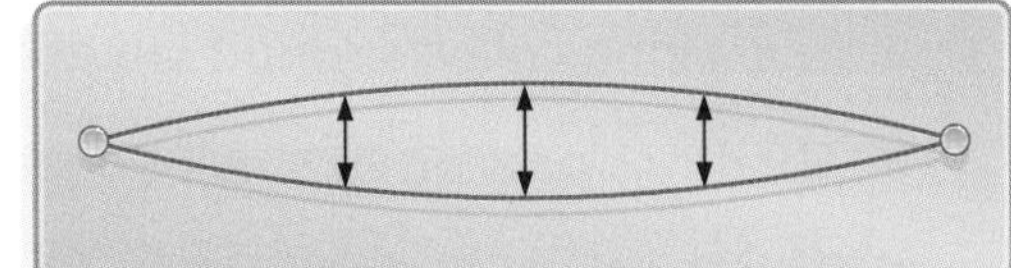

larger vibrations, louder sound.

Danger! Loud sounds

Very loud sounds can be dangerous.

3 Why are very loud sounds dangerous?

4 How can workers prevent their ears from being damaged by loud sounds?

People who work in loud noise should wear ear protectors.

Very loud sounds can damage your ears.

Another difference between sounds

Some sounds are louder than others. Sounds can also have a different **pitch**.

5 Copy and complete the sentences.

Small musical instruments make sounds with a higher __________ than larger ones.

REMEMBER from page 39

The pitch of a sound is how high or low the sound is.

Large musical instruments make sounds with a lower pitch than small ones.

Why do sounds have different pitches?

The pitch of a sound depends on **how many** vibrations there are each second.

We call this the **frequency** of the sound.

Sounds that have a high frequency also have a high pitch.

We measure frequency in **hertz** (Hz for short).

6 How does the pitch of a sound depend on its frequency?

7 Look at the diagram.

(a) What is the lowest frequency that most people can hear?

(b) What happens to the highest frequency people can hear as they get older?

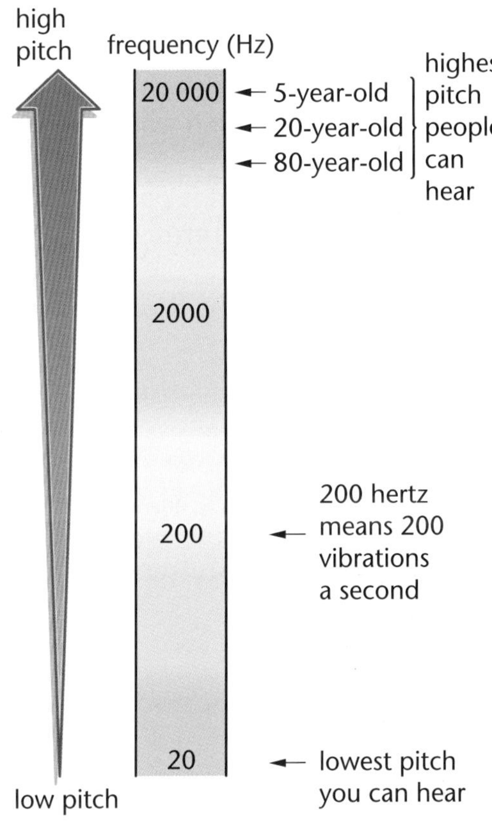

WHAT YOU NEED TO REMEMBER (Copy and complete using the **key words**)

Different sounds

Sounds can be different in two ways:
- one sound can be __________ than another;
- the sounds can have a different __________.

Loud sounds are caused by large __________. We say that these vibrations have a big __________.

The pitch of a sound depends on __________ __________ vibrations there are each second. This is called the __________ of the sound.

A frequency of 200 __________ (Hz for short) means 200 vibrations each second.

More about different sounds: C1.7, C1.8

2.9 How to bend light

REMEMBER from pages 28–29

Light travels in straight lines.
It can't go round corners.

Light usually travels in straight lines.

But you can make light bend using water.

The diagram shows you how.

1 At first, Kris can't see the coin in the metal can. Why not?

2 When Sam fills the can with water, Kris can then see the coin. Explain why.

Light bends when it passes from water into air. We say that it is **refracted**.

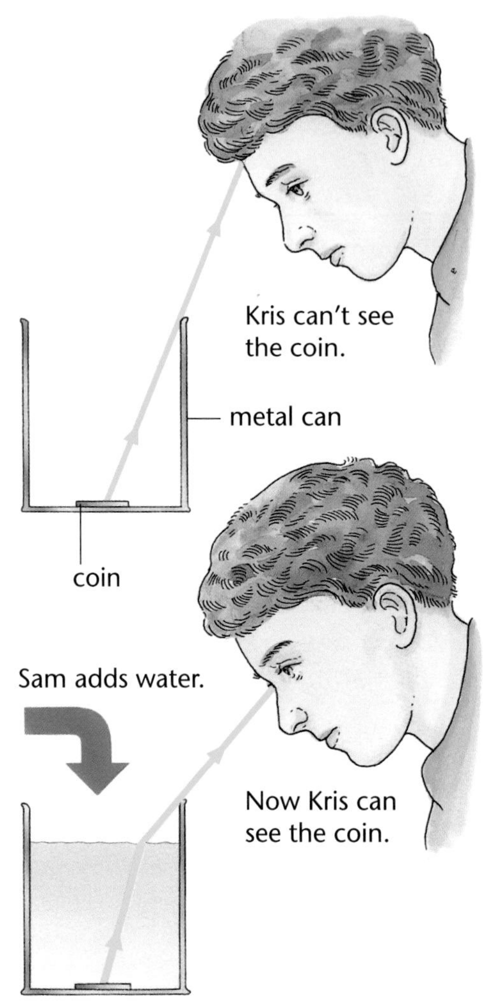
Kris can't see
the coin.
metal can
coin
Sam adds water.
Now Kris can
see the coin.

Describing refraction

We sometimes want to say which way light is refracted.

The diagram shows how you can do this.

Look carefully at the key words on the diagram.

3 Copy and complete the sentences.

Where the water ends is called a _________.

A normal is a line at _________ angles (90°) to the boundary.

When light crosses the boundary from water into air, it is refracted away from the _________.

The **normal** is a line at **right angles** to the boundary.

This ray of light is refracted **away from** the normal.

air

water

The **boundary** is where the water ends.

Refraction works both ways

Light is also refracted when it travels from air into water.

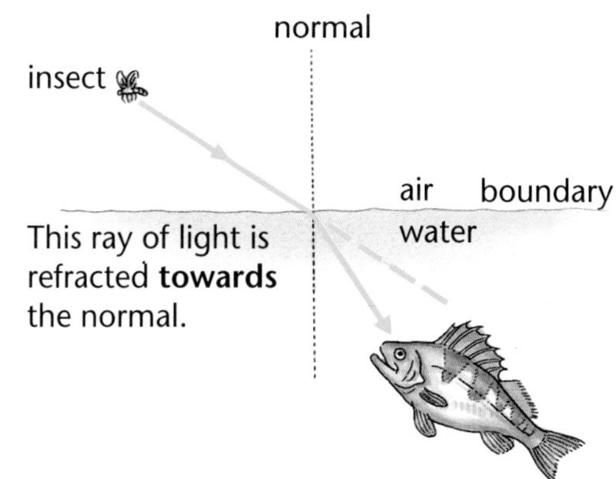

4 Look at the diagram. Describe what happens to a ray of light from the insect as it passes into the water.

More examples of refraction

The diagrams show what happens to light when it crosses the boundaries between different substances and at different angles.

Light travelling along a normal is <u>not</u> refracted.

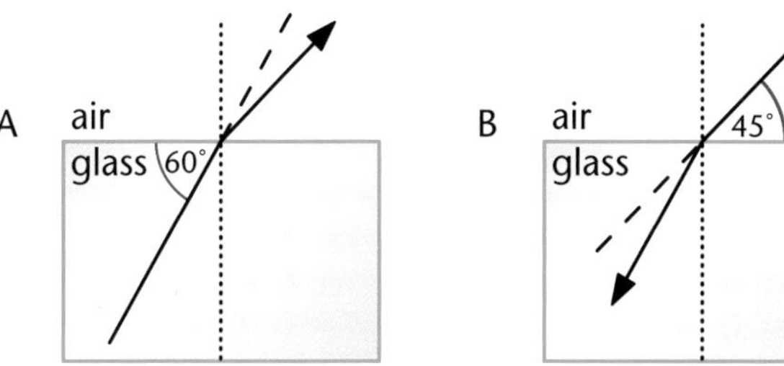

5 Copy each diagram.

Underneath each diagram describe what happens like this:

A When light passes from <u>glass</u> into <u>air</u> at <u>60°</u> to the boundary it is <u>refracted away from the normal</u>.

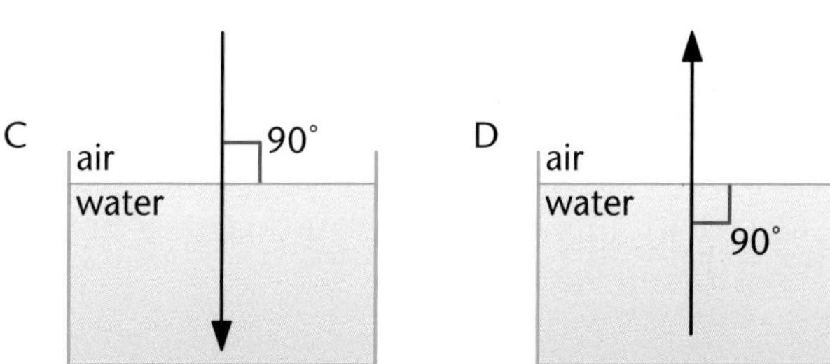

WHAT YOU NEED TO REMEMBER (Copy and complete using the **key words**)

How to bend light

Light bends when it passes across the ____________ between two different substances. We say that the light is ____________.

A line at 90° to a boundary is called a ____________.

When light passes from glass or water into air, it is refracted __________ __________ the normal.

When light passes from air into glass or water, it is refracted ____________ the normal.

When light crosses a boundary at ____________ ____________, it is not refracted.

More about bending light: C1.5, C1.6

3.1 Making electricity by rubbing

The Ancient Greeks discovered electricity thousands of years ago. The diagram shows how they discovered it.

1 **(a)** How did the Ancient Greeks make electricity?

(b) How did they <u>know</u> they had made it?

(c) How did electricity get its name?

Amber looks like orange glass. The Ancient Greeks used it to make jewellery.

When we rub amber, we say that it becomes **charged** with electricity.

The electrical charge stays on the amber. So we call it **static** electricity. ('Static' means 'not moving'.)

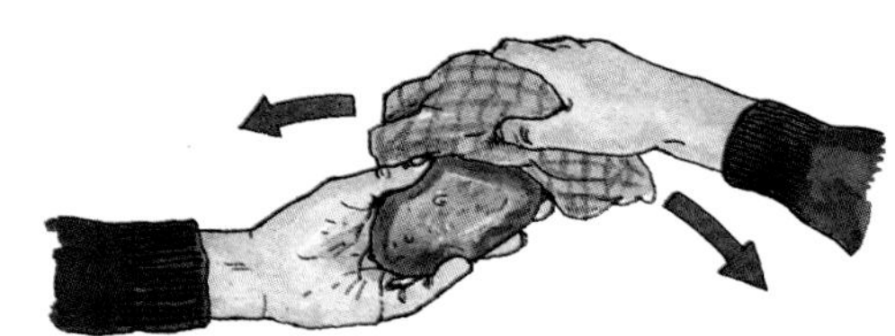

If you rub a piece of amber with a cloth, it will ***attract*** *bits of paper and dust.*

Charging a comb

We don't use amber much today. But we do make lots of things from <u>plastic</u>.

You have charged a piece of plastic with electricity lots of times. You do this when you comb your hair.

2 Look at the diagram. Then copy and complete the sentences.

When you use a comb, it rubs against your hair.
The comb becomes charged with __________.
So it will __________ small bits of paper or dust.

DID YOU KNOW?

Our word 'electricity' comes from the Greek word for amber.

When you use a comb, it rubs against your hair.

The comb will then attract bits of paper and dust.

Making a balloon stick to the ceiling

A balloon will stick to the ceiling if you charge it with electricity. The diagram shows how you can do this.

3 **(a)** How can you charge a balloon with electricity?

(b) Why does the balloon now stick to the ceiling?

Clothes are made from different materials such as wool, acrylic, cotton and polyester.

Find out which material works best for charging a balloon with electricity.

You can charge a balloon by rubbing it against your sweater.

Release the balloon near the ceiling. There is a force of attraction between the charged balloon and the ceiling. This holds the balloon up.

Making your own lightning

When you take off a sweater, it rubs against your blouse or your shirt. Sometimes you can hear crackles. If it is dark you can see tiny sparks.

4 **(a)** What causes the sparks when you take off a sweater?

(b) Why does taking off a sweater make electricity?

You can only get an electrical charge if the things you rub together are made of <u>different</u> materials.

5 A boy wears a cotton sweater on top of a cotton shirt. When he takes the sweater off, he <u>doesn't</u> produce an electrical charge. Why not?

Another way to make static electricity.

WHAT YOU NEED TO REMEMBER (Copy and complete using the **key words**)

Making electricity by rubbing

If you rub an object with a different material, it becomes ____________ with electricity.
The electrical charge stays where it is, so we call it ____________ electricity.

A charged object will ____________ other things such as bits of dust or paper.

More about static electricity: C3.4

3.2 Two sorts of charges

Two rulers are made from the same kind of white plastic.

You can charge the rulers by rubbing both of them with a cloth. The diagrams show how you can then test the electrical charges on the rulers.

1 What do the electrically charged rulers do to each other?

2 Copy and complete the sentences.

Both white rulers are made of the same kind of __________.
They are both rubbed with the same __________.
So the electrical charge on both rulers must also be the __________.

Two objects that have the <u>same</u> electrical charge repel each other.

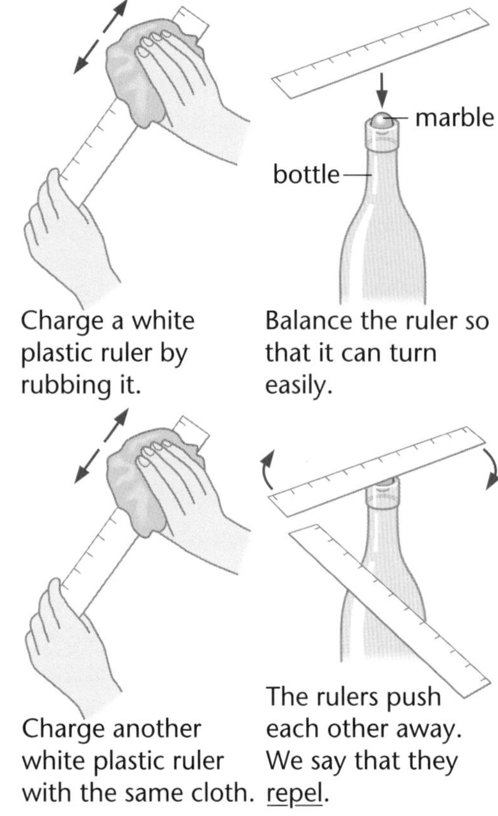

Charge a white plastic ruler by rubbing it.

Balance the ruler so that it can turn easily.

Charge another white plastic ruler with the same cloth.

The rulers push each other away. We say that they <u>repel</u>.

Testing a different plastic

A clear ruler is made from a different kind of plastic.

Some pupils charge a clear plastic ruler by rubbing it with a cloth. They then test it with a charged white plastic ruler. The diagram shows what happens.

3 Copy and complete the sentences.

The clear plastic ruler __________ the white plastic ruler.
But if two charges are the <u>same</u>, they repel each other.
So the electrical charge on the clear plastic must be __________ from the electrical charge on the white plastic.

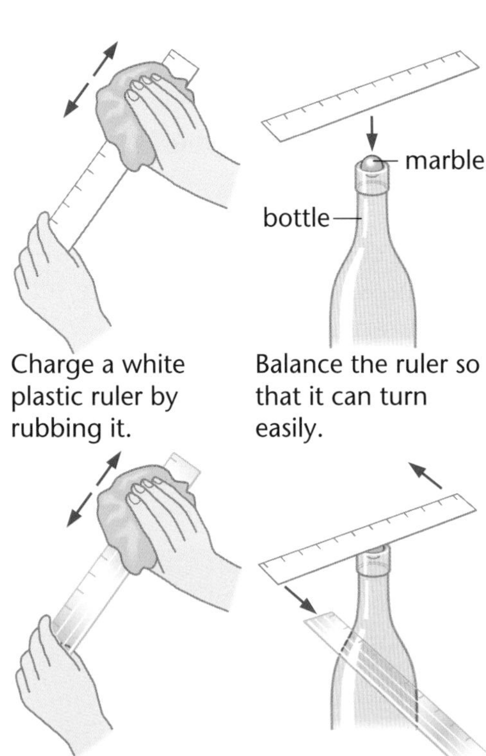

Charge a white plastic ruler by rubbing it.

Balance the ruler so that it can turn easily.

Charge a clear plastic ruler with the same cloth.

The rulers <u>attract</u> each other.

What do we call the different charges?

The charge on a clear plastic ruler is different from the charge on a white plastic ruler. This is because the rulers are made of different kinds of plastic.

A clear plastic ruler is made from acrylic plastic. When you charge something made from acrylic plastic, you give it a **positive** (+) charge.

A white plastic ruler is made from polythene. When you charge something made from polythene, you give it a **negative** (–) charge.

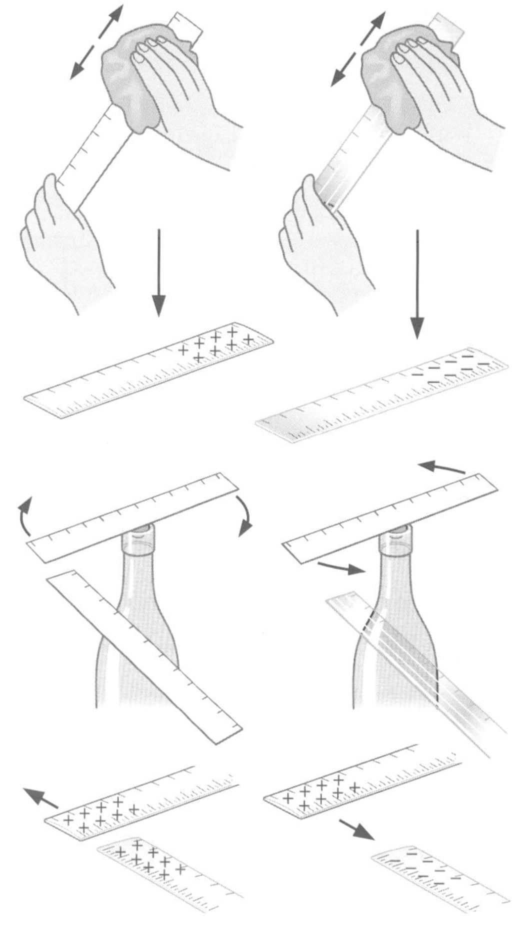

4 Copy and complete the table.

Charge on first object	Charge on second object	Do they attract or repel?
+	+	
+	–	
–	–	

Different charges **attract** each other.

Charges that are the same **repel** each other.

Another look at combing your hair

Sometimes, when you comb your hair, it won't lie flat. The diagram shows why.

Your hairs all have negative charges, so they repel each other.
The comb has a positive charge.

5 Copy and complete the sentences.

When you comb your hair you give all the hairs a ___________ charge.
So the hairs ___________ each other.

WHAT YOU NEED TO REMEMBER (Copy and complete using the **key words**)

Two sorts of charges

Electrical charges can be ___________ (+) or ___________ (–).

A positive charge and a negative charge ___________ each other. Two charges that are the same ___________ each other.

More about attracting and repelling: C2.1

3.3 Electric currents

REMEMBER from page 46

You can charge an object with electricity by rubbing it.

The charge stays where it is, so we call it static electricity.

You can make static electricity by rubbing things together. But to be really useful, electrical charges must be moving.

When charges move they make an electric current. Electric currents can do lots of useful jobs.

*You can use a **cell** to get an electric current that is safe for experiments.*

A safe electric current

We can get an electric current from the mains. You just plug in and switch on.

But mains electricity is very dangerous. For experiments, you need a safe electric current.

*Two (or more) cells joined together make a **battery**.*

1 Look at the diagrams. Then copy and complete the sentences.

To get a safe electric current we can use a __________.

If we join cells together we get a __________.

Connecting up a cell

To get an electric current from a cell, you need to connect it into a circuit. The diagram shows how to do this.

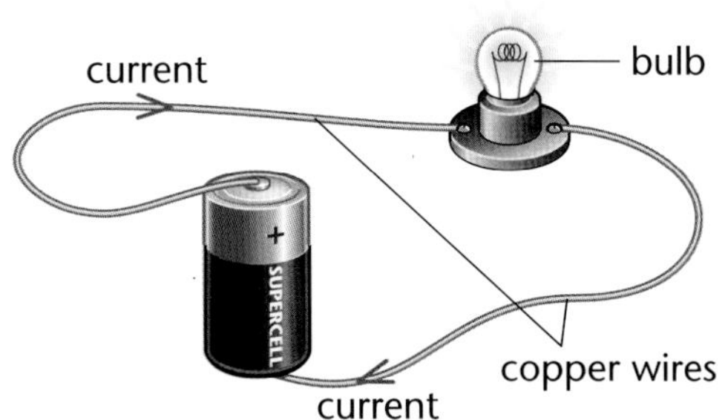

2 Copy and complete the sentence.

An electric current flows:

- from the cell,
- through a __________ wire,
- through the __________,
- through another __________ wire,
- back to the other end of the __________.

3 You can't see electricity. So how do you know that an electric current is flowing in this circuit?

Adding a switch to the circuit

If you want to turn a current on or off, you use a **switch**.

4 Look at the diagrams. Then copy and complete the sentence.

To switch off a current, you must __________ the circuit.

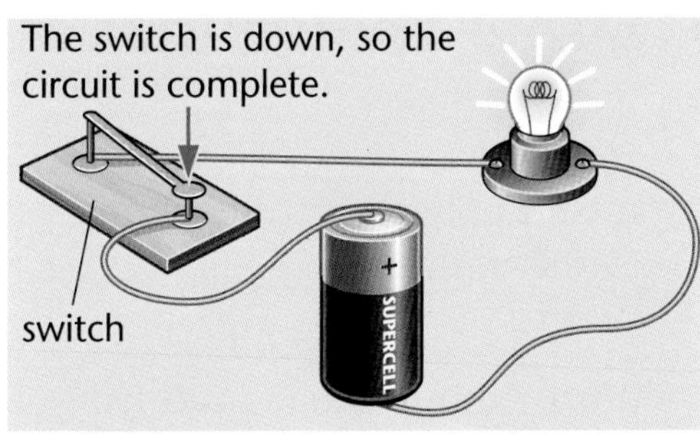

The switch is down, so the circuit is complete.
switch
+
SUPERCELL

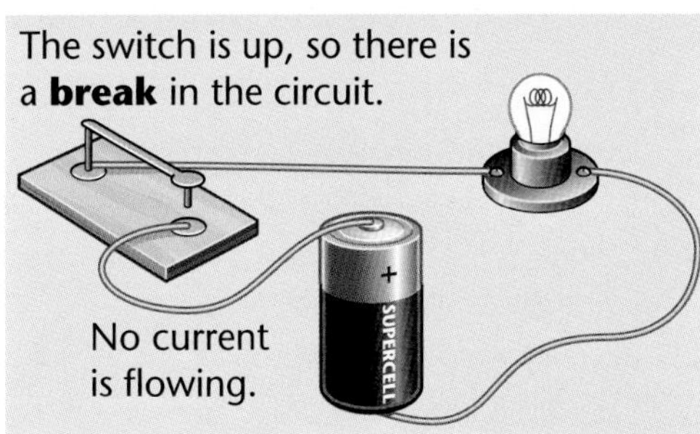

The switch is up, so there is a **break** in the circuit.
No current is flowing.
+
SUPERCELL

A current can only flow if there is a **complete** circuit.

If the circuit is broken there is no current and the bulb doesn't light.

Conductors and insulators

If you make a circuit using string, it doesn't work.

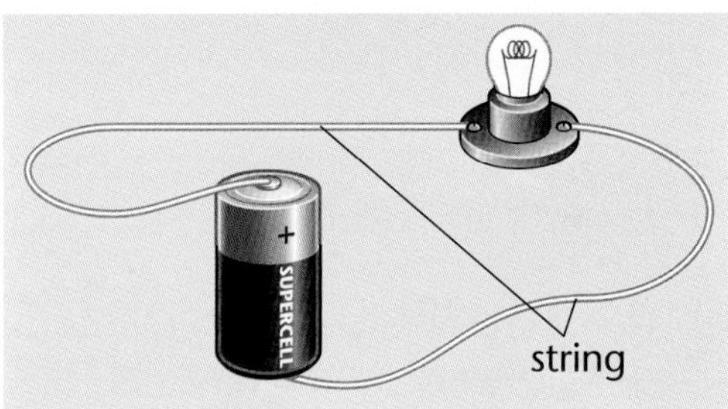

An electric current <u>won't</u> go through string. We say that string is an <u>insulator</u>.

5 How do you know that an electric current does <u>not</u> flow through the string?

6 Copy and complete the sentences.

An electric current <u>will</u> flow through copper.
So we call copper a __________.

An electric current <u>won't</u> flow through string.
So we call string an __________.

An electric current can only flow if there is a complete circuit made of **conductors**.

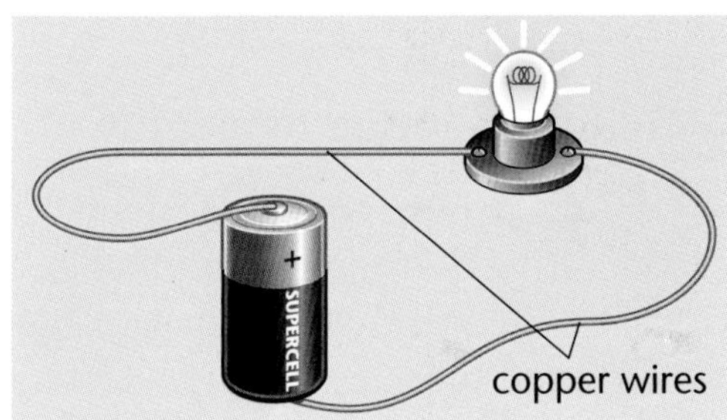

An electric current <u>will</u> go through copper. We say that copper is a <u>conductor</u>.

WHAT YOU NEED TO REMEMBER (Copy and complete using the **key words**)

Electric currents

You can get a safe electric current from a ___________.

Two or more cells joined together is called a ___________.

A current will only flow if there is a ___________ circuit of ___________.

To stop a current flowing you must make a ___________ in the circuit. You usually do this using a ___________.

More about currents: C3.4

3.4 Other things that attract and repel

It isn't only electrically charged objects that can attract things.

Some rocks that you find in the ground will attract things made from **iron** or steel. We say that these rocks are **magnetised**.

The diagrams show some of the things that magnetised rocks can do.

REMEMBER from pages 48–49

Objects that are charged with static electricity can attract or repel each other.

'Attract' means 'pull towards'. 'Repel' means 'push away from'.

Some rocks are magnetised. They attract things made of iron or steel.

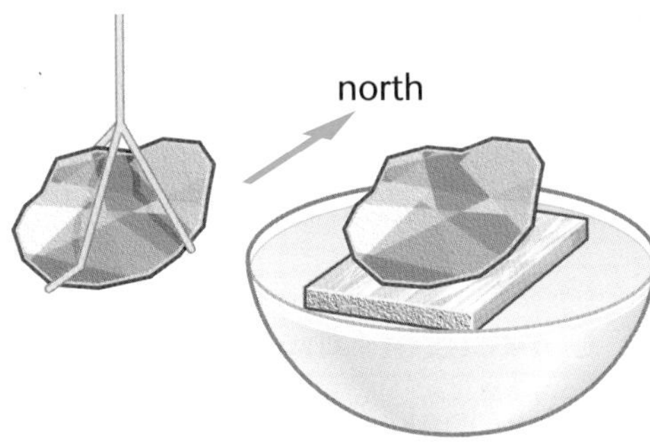

A magnetised rock always points the same way if you hang it up or float it on water.

1 What things will magnetised rocks attract?

2 Hundreds of years ago, explorers used magnetised rocks to find out the direction they were travelling. Explain how they did this.

Magnets made by people

We don't need to use magnetic rocks any more. Scientists can <u>make</u> magnets in all shapes and sizes. We use these modern magnets for many different jobs.

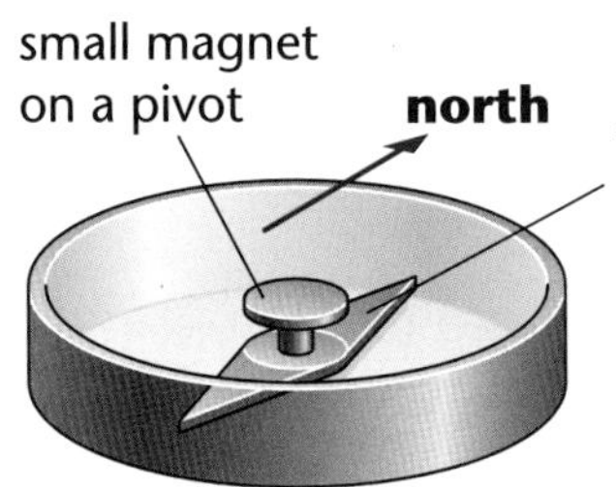

A magnetic compass tells you where north and south are.

3 Look at the diagrams. Write down <u>two</u> different uses for modern magnets.

4 (a) What do we call the end of a magnet which points north?

(b) What do you think we call the <u>other</u> end of a magnet?

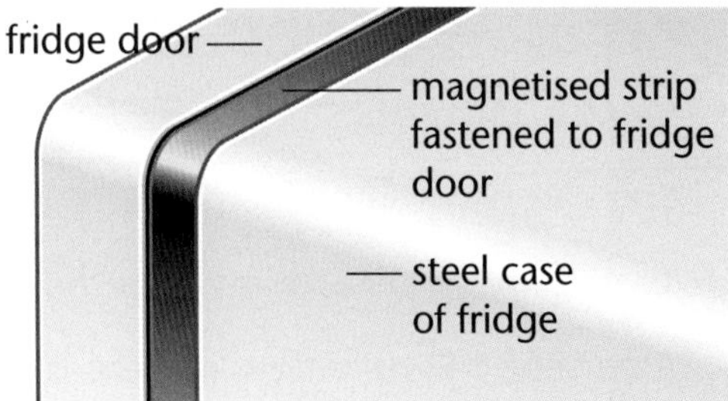

A magnetised strip keeps a fridge door closed.

What do magnets do to each other?

The diagrams show what happens when you bring the **poles** of two magnets near to each other.

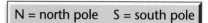

5 Copy and complete the table.

Pole of first magnet	Pole of second magnet	Do they attract or repel?
S	N	
S	S	
N	N	

Two poles that are different attract each other.

Two poles that are the same repel each other.

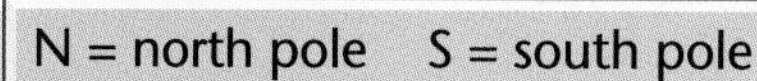

These magnets **attract** each other.

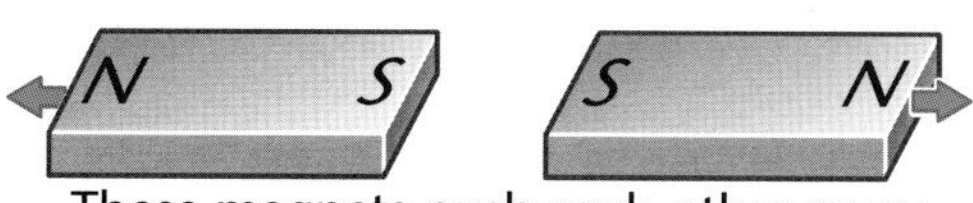

These magnets push each other away. They **repel**.

These magnets also repel.

Finding the north and south poles of a magnet

To find the north and south poles of a magnet, you can hang the magnet up or float it.

The diagrams show you another way to find out.

6 Copy and complete the sentences.

End A of the magnet is a __________ pole because it repels the __________ pole of the compass needle.

End B of the magnet is a __________ pole because it repels the __________ pole of the compass needle.

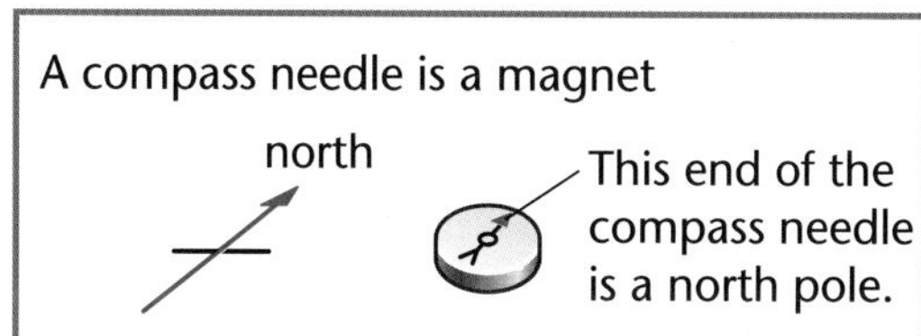

A compass needle is a magnet
north
This end of the compass needle is a north pole.

End A repels the N pole of the compass needle and attracts the S pole.

End B attracts the N pole of the compass needle and repels the S pole.

WHAT YOU NEED TO REMEMBER (Copy and complete using the **key words**)

Other things that attract and repel

Some rocks attract things made of ____________ or steel. We say that the rocks are ____________.

If a magnetised rock or a magnet is free to move, one end will point ____________ and the other end will point south. The ends of a magnet are called the ____________.

The north pole of one magnet will ____________ the south pole of another magnet. Two poles that are the same ____________ each other.

More about attracting and repelling: C2.1

3.5 Magnetic fields

Magnets attract pieces of iron or steel that are near to them. They can also attract or repel other magnets.

The area around a magnet where it pushes or pulls is called a magnetic **field**.

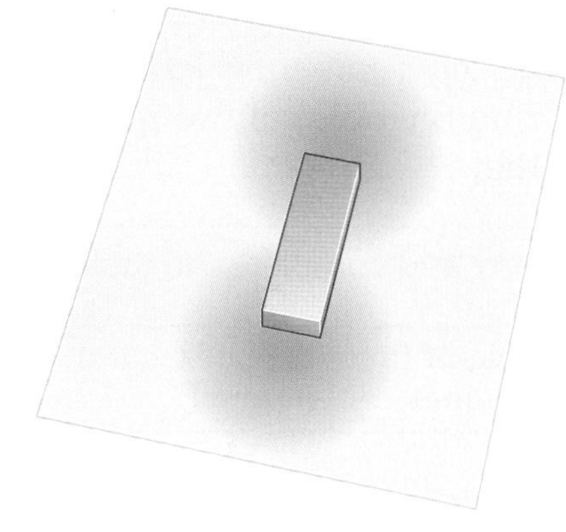

The pushing and pulling effect of a magnet gets smaller as you get further away. We say that the magnetic field gets <u>*weaker*</u>.

1 Look at the diagram. Then copy and complete the sentence.

As you go further away from a magnet, the magnetic field gets __________.

Exploring a magnetic field

You can see the shape of the magnetic field around a **bar** magnet using tiny bits of iron. We call these iron **filings**.

The diagrams show you how to do this.

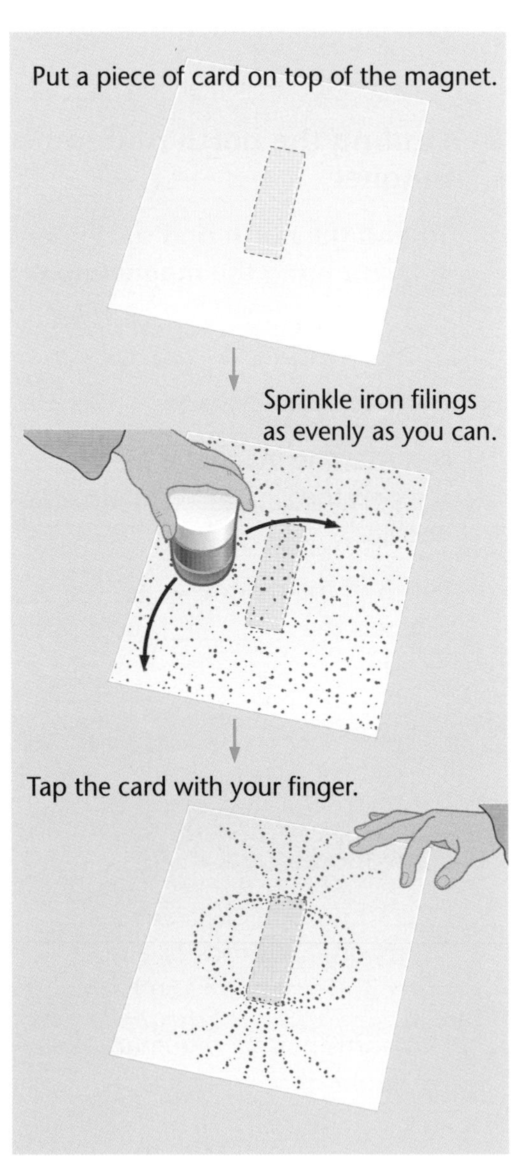

Put a piece of card on top of the magnet.
Sprinkle iron filings as evenly as you can.
Tap the card with your finger.

2 Write down the following sentences in the right order. (The first sentence is in the correct place.) Use the diagrams to help.

- Put a card on top of a bar magnet.
- Tap the card with your finger.
- Sprinkle iron filings on evenly.
- The iron filings now show you the magnetic field pattern of the magnet.

The lines that show you the shape of the magnetic field are called lines of magnetic **force**.

3 Which parts of the bar magnet do all the lines of magnetic force come out from (or go in to)?

Another way of exploring a magnetic field

You can also find the shape of a magnetic field using a small magnetic **compass**. The diagrams show you how to do this.

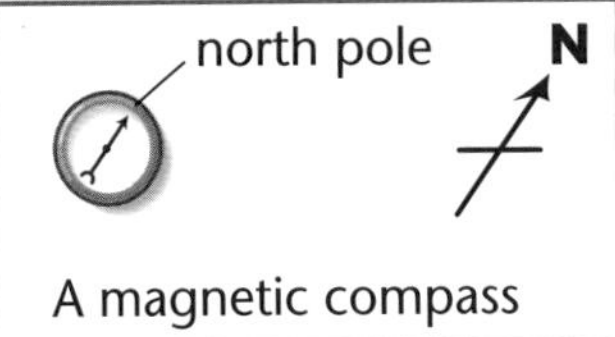

A magnetic compass

1 Put a compass anywhere in a magnetic field. Put a dot at each end of the compass needle.

2 Move the compass so that its south pole is where the north pole was before. Add a dot.

3 Keep on moving the compass in the same way. Add a dot each time.

4 Keep on until you get back to the magnet or come to the edge of the paper. Do the same thing again lots of times, starting off with the compass in a different place each time.

Join the dots to get lines of magnetic force. The arrows show which way the **north** pole of a compass points.

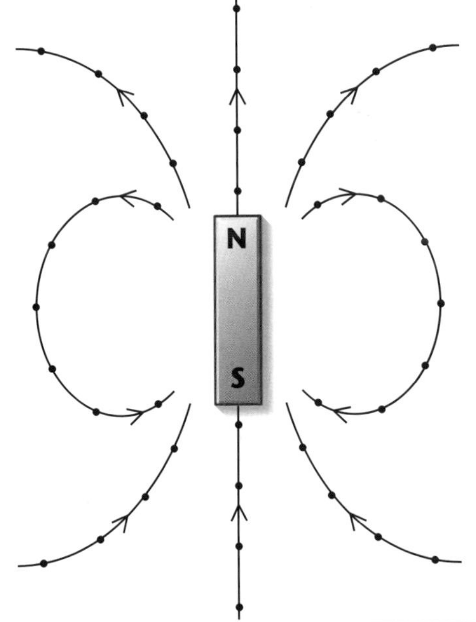

4 (a) What are the lines of the magnetic field pattern called?

(b) What do the arrows on the lines show?

WHAT YOU NEED TO REMEMBER (Copy and complete using the **key words**)

Magnetic fields

The area around a magnet is called a magnetic ______________.

You can explore a magnetic field using iron ______________ or a small magnetic ______________.

The lines on a magnetic field are called lines of magnetic ______________.

The arrows show the direction that the ______________ pole of a compass needle will point.

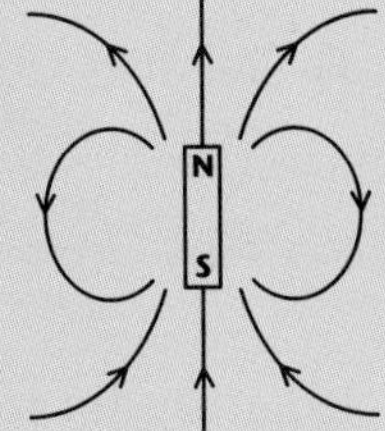

The magnetic field around a ______________ magnet.

More about magnets: C3.6

3.6 Using an electric current to make a magnet

You can get a safe electric current using a cell or a battery of cells. But cells soon run out of energy.

A low voltage power supply is often better. It will give you a safe electric current for as long as you want.

REMEMBER from pages 50–51

To get an electric current from a cell, you must have a complete circuit of conductors.

1 Look at the diagram. Then copy and complete the following.

To get a current from a low voltage power supply you must:

- switch it __________;
- connect the terminals to a __________ circuit.

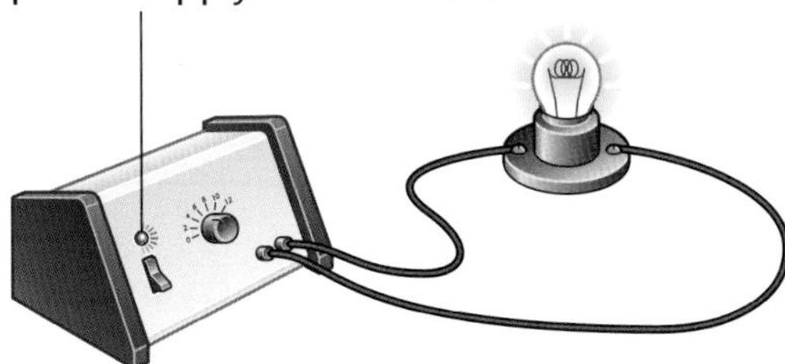

This red light tells you the power supply is switched on.

The two terminals of the power supply are connected to a complete circuit.

A bulb uses an electric current to produce light. You can also use an electric current to make a magnet.

Making a magnet

You can make a magnet by sending an electric current through a **coil** of wire.

The magnet works better if you put an iron bar down the middle of the coil. This is called an iron **core**.

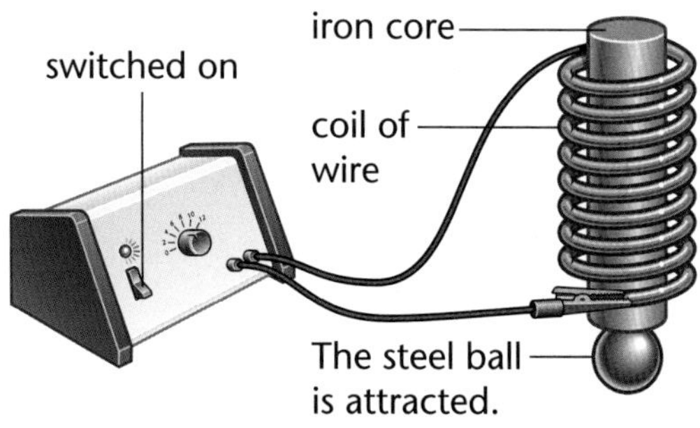

2 How can you tell that the electric current makes the coil and core into a magnet?

3 (a) What happens to the steel ball when you switch the current off?

(b) Why does this happen?

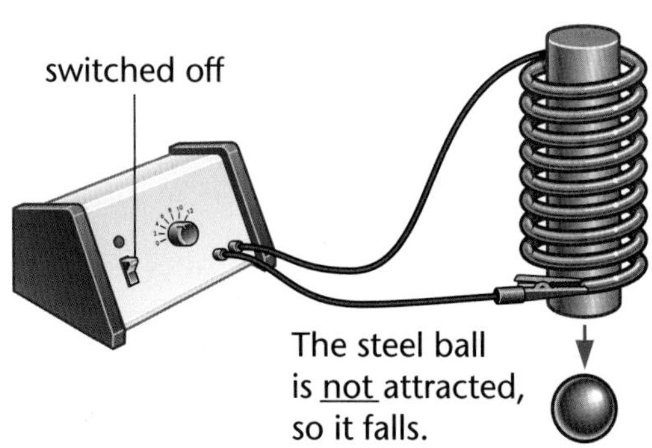

switched off
The steel ball is not attracted, so it falls.

This magnet needs an electric current to make it work, so we call it an **electromagnet**.

Find out what difference it makes to an electromagnet if you have more turns on the coil.

Picking up paper clips

Suppose you drop a packet full of paper clips on to a fluffy rug. An easy way to pick up the paper clips is to use a magnet.

4 Look at the diagrams.

(a) You can pick up the paper clips with a permanent magnet. What's the problem with this?

(b) How would an electromagnet solve this problem?

A bar magnet stays magnetised all the time. We call it a permanent magnet.

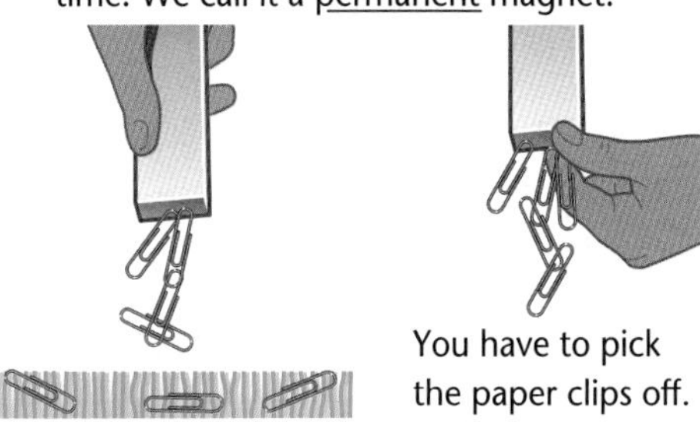

You have to pick
the paper clips off.

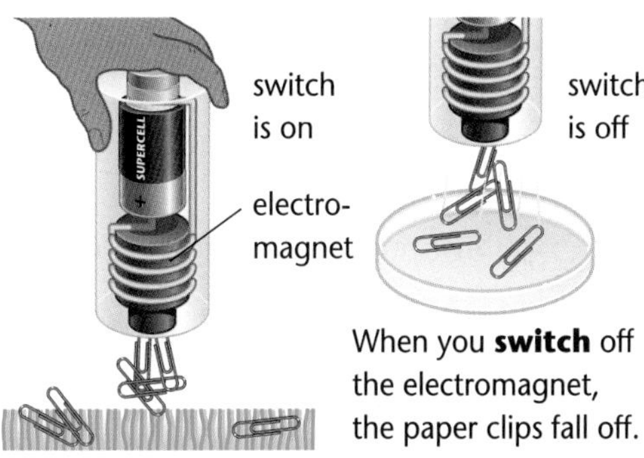

When you **switch** off the electromagnet, the paper clips fall off.

The magnetic field around an electromagnet

You can find the shape of a magnetic field around an electromagnet with a small magnetic compass. Lines of magnetic force show you the shape of a magnetic field.

5 Copy and complete the sentences.

End X of the electromagnet is a magnetic __________ pole.
End Y of the electromagnet is a magnetic __________ pole.

The lines of magnetic __________ around the magnet show you the shape of its magnetic __________.

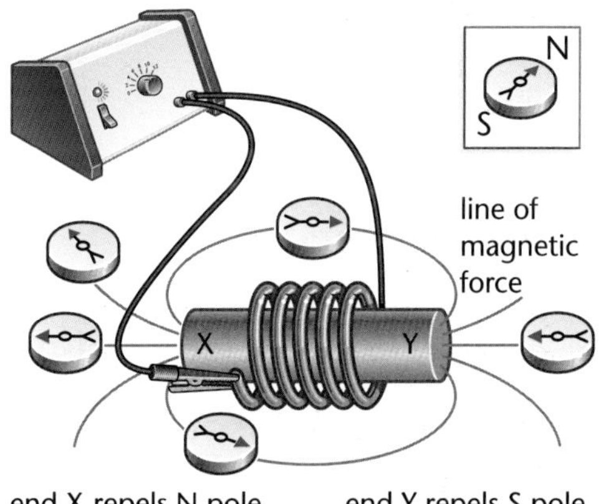

The magnetic field of an electromagnet is the same shape as the field of a ***bar*** *magnet.*

WHAT YOU NEED TO REMEMBER (Copy and complete using the **key words**)

Using an electric current to make a magnet

You can make a magnet by passing an electric current through a ____________ of wire. This is called an ____________.

The magnet works better with an iron ____________ inside the coil.

The magnetic field of the electromagnet is the same shape as for a ____________ magnet.

An electromagnet is very useful because you can ____________ it off.

More about electromagnets: C3.6

3.7 Building up circuits

You can make a simple circuit by connecting a bulb to a cell.

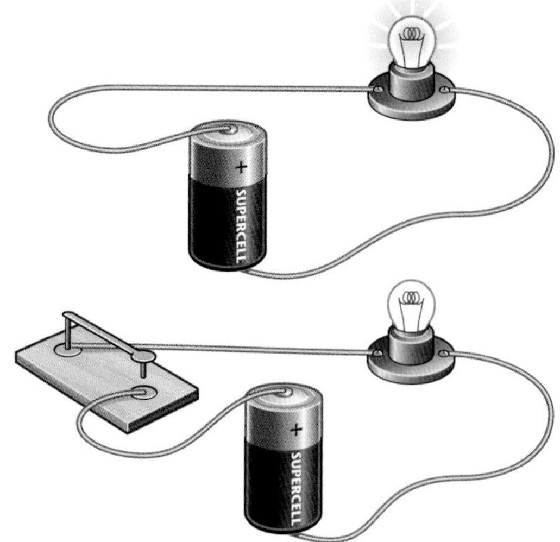

Adding a switch to the circuit

The circuit is more useful if you add a switch. The diagram shows how you can do this.

You can break the circuit with a switch. No current then flows.

1 How does a switch turn a current off?

2 Copy and complete the sentences.

When the switch is on, an electric current flows through the switch and then through the __________.

We say that the switch and the bulb are connected in __________.

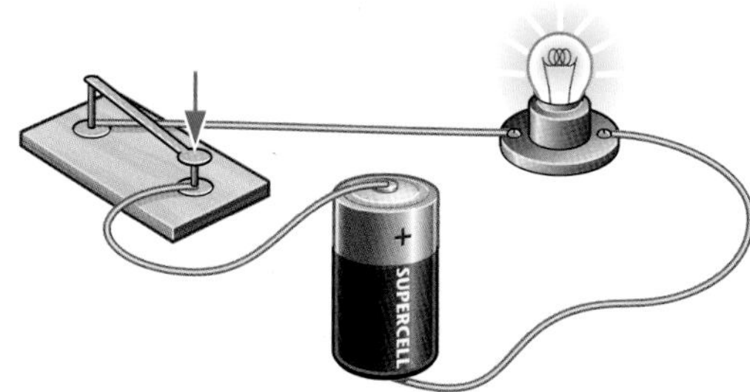

*When the circuit is complete, a current flows through the switch and then through the bulb. So we say that the switch and the bulb are connected in **series**.*

Adding another bulb to the circuit

You can add another bulb to the circuit in two different ways. The diagrams show you how.

3 Copy and complete the table.

	How the bulbs are connected	How bright the bulbs are
circuit A	in _______	
circuit B	in _______	

Parallel lines run alongside each other.

In a television series, each programme follows on from the previous one.

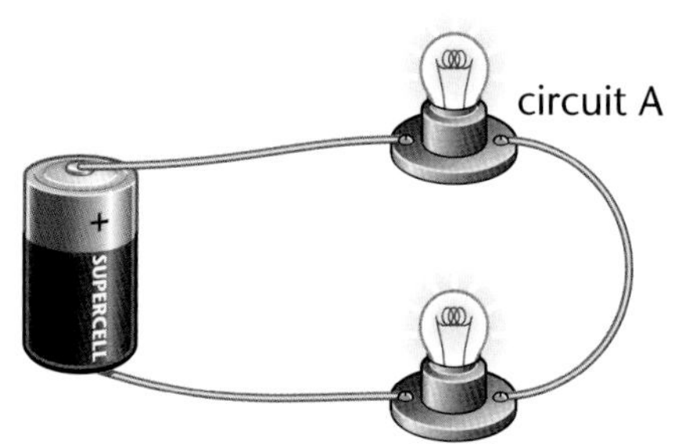

A current flows through one bulb and then through the other.

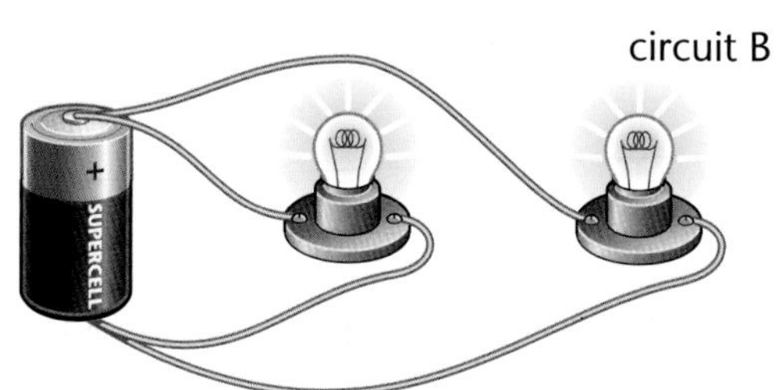

*Each bulb is connected separately to the cell. We say they are connected in **parallel**.*

An easy way to draw circuits

It's useful to have a quick and easy way to draw electrical circuits. You can do this using special **symbols** for bulbs, cells and switches. The diagram shows you how.

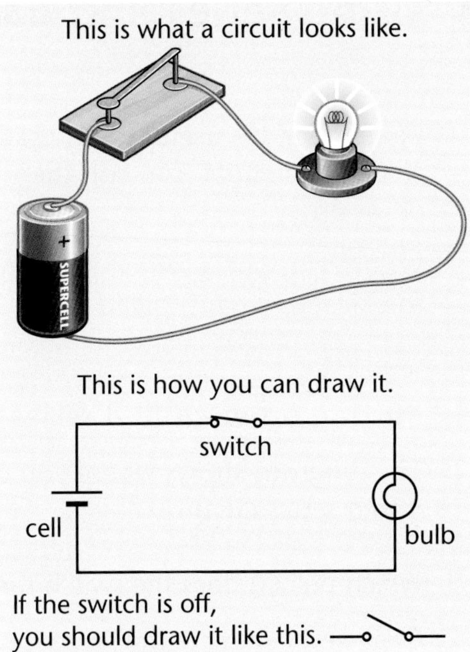

This is what a circuit looks like.
SUPERCELL
This is how you can draw it.
switch
cell
bulb
If the switch is off,
you should draw it like this.

4 Copy and complete the table.

	Symbol
cell	
bulb	
switch (on)	
switch (off)	

When we draw circuits using symbols, we call them **circuit diagrams**.

Find out the symbols for three more things we use in electric circuits.

Looking at circuit diagrams

The diagrams show three different circuits, X, Y and Z.

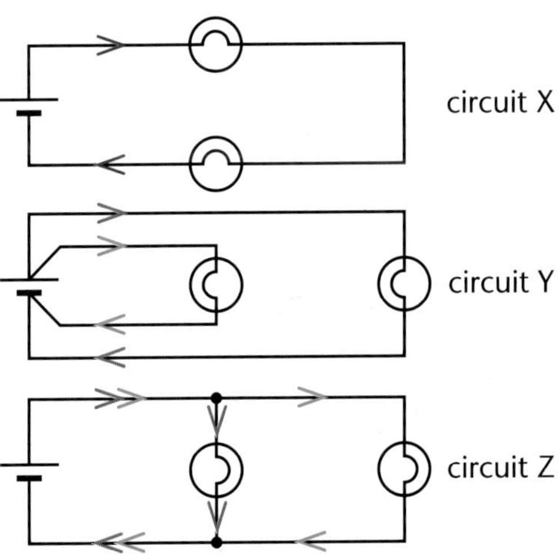

5 Copy each circuit diagram. Then copy and complete this sentence underneath each diagram (three times altogether).

The bulbs in this circuit are connected in __________ with each other.

WHAT YOU NEED TO REMEMBER (Copy and complete using the **key words**)

Building up circuits

If a current flows through one bulb and then through another, we say that the bulbs are connected in __________.

If two bulbs are connected separately to a cell or a power supply, we say that they are connected in __________.

We can draw circuits using special __________ for cells, bulbs, and switches. Circuits drawn with these symbols are called __________ __________.

You should know the symbols for bulbs, cells and switches.

More about circuits: C3.5

3.8 Using series and parallel circuits

Remember, it's useful to have switches in electrical circuits. You can then turn the current on or off.

Where you put a switch in a circuit depends on the kind of circuit it is in.

REMEMBER from pages 58–59

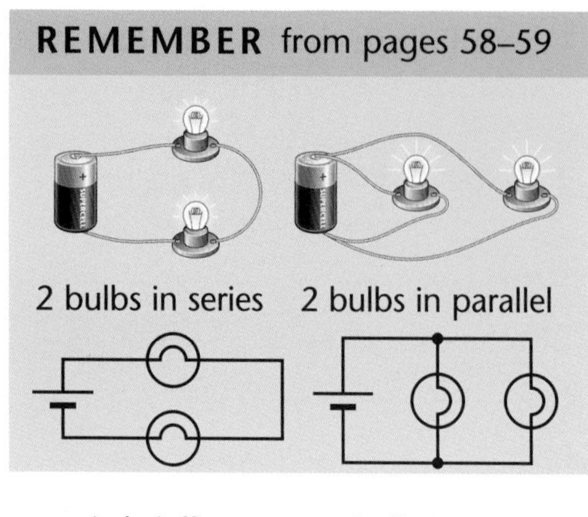

Putting a switch in a series circuit

The diagram shows where you can put a switch into a series circuit.

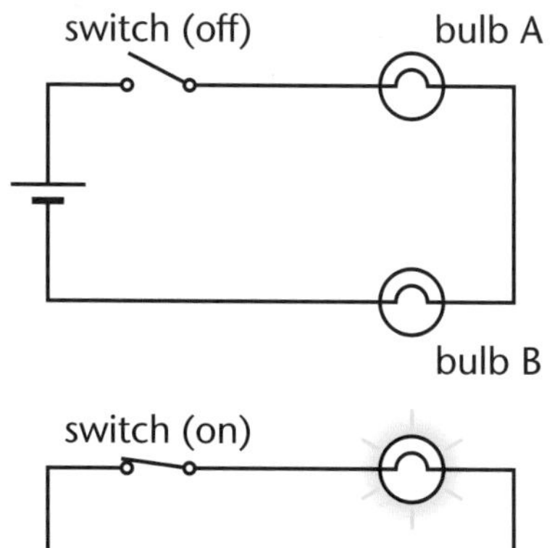

1 Which bulb(s) does the switch turn on and off?

2 Copy and complete the sentence.

The switch is put in __________ with the two bulbs in the circuit.

You could also put the switch at position P or position Q in the circuit. It will still be in **series** with both bulbs.

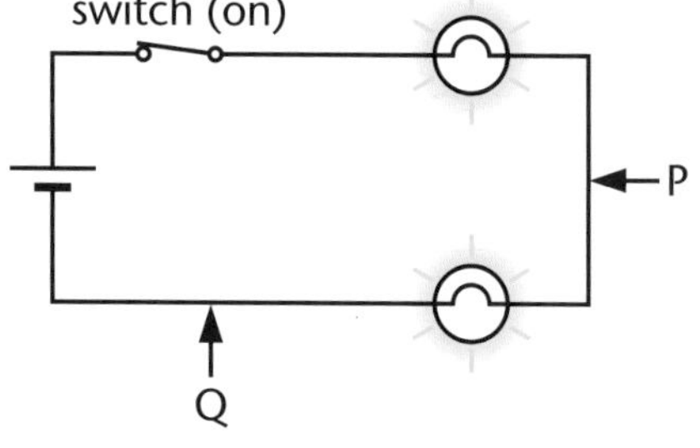

3 Draw a circuit diagram with the switch (on) at position P.

If two bulbs are connected in series, the same switch turns **both** of them on or off.

What if one bulb breaks in a series circuit?

The diagram shows a circuit with two bulbs connected in series. Neither of the bulbs lights up.

The filament of a bulb gives out light when a current flows through it.

This bulb has a broken filament ...

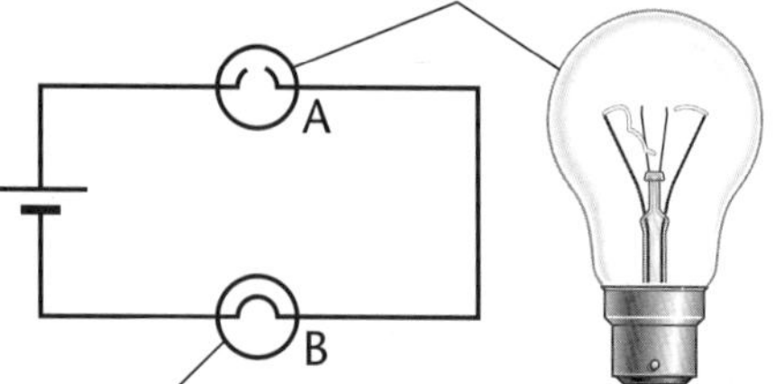

... so this bulb **doesn't light** either.

4 (a) Why doesn't bulb A light up?

(b) Why doesn't bulb B light up?

The bulb with a broken filament is just like a **switch** which is off.

Putting a switch in a parallel circuit

In a parallel circuit, you need to decide whether you want the switch to switch off both bulbs or just one bulb. Then you can choose the right place to put the switch.

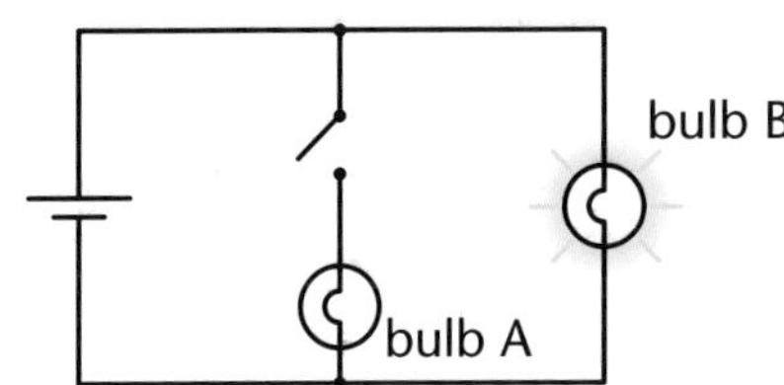

5 Look at circuit X. Which bulb does the switch turn on and off?

6 Draw a circuit diagram which has a switch for turning bulb B on and off, but <u>not</u> bulb A.

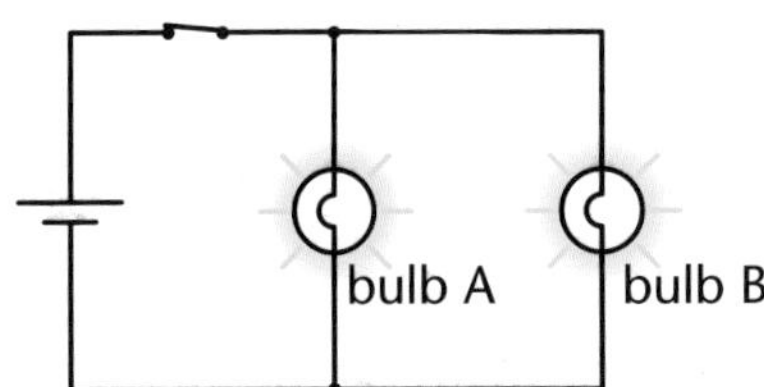

Circuit Y shows where a pupil puts a switch.

7 The pupil breaks the circuit with this switch. What happens to each bulb?

What if one bulb breaks in a parallel circuit?

The diagram shows what happens if the filament of one of the bulbs breaks.

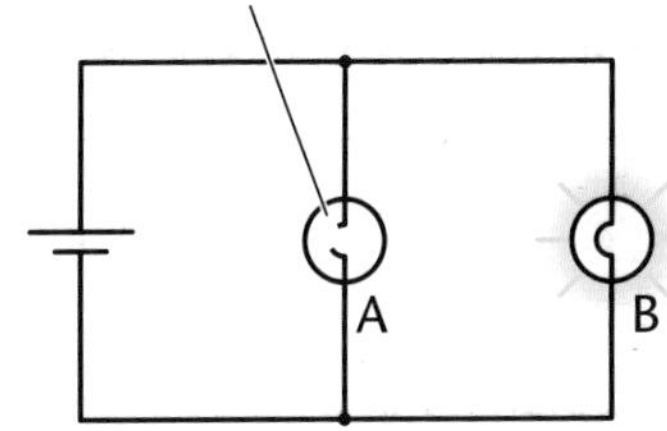

8 **(a)** Why doesn't bulb A light up?

(b) Why does bulb B stay lit?

WHAT YOU NEED TO REMEMBER (Copy and complete using the **key words**)

Using series and parallel circuits

You must put a switch in ____________ with the bulb that you want to switch on or off.

If two bulbs are in series, the switch will turn off the current to ____________ of them.

A bulb with a broken filament is just like a ____________ which is off.

In a series circuit, if one bulb breaks, the other bulb ____________ ____________.

In a parallel circuit, if one bulb breaks, the other bulb ____________ ____________.

More about circuits: C3.5

3.9 Using electromagnets

You can **switch** electromagnets on and off. This makes them useful for many jobs. For example, you can use an electromagnet to make a relay or a buzzer.

REMEMBER from pages 56–57

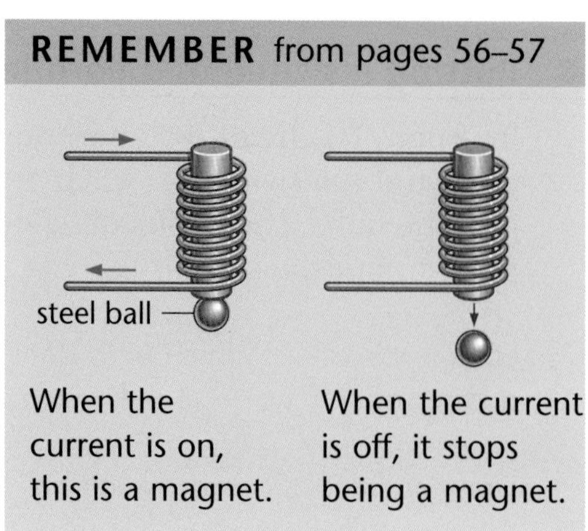

When the current is on, this is a magnet.

When the current is off, it stops being a magnet.

A relay

A relay is a special kind of switch. It uses a small current to switch on a much larger current.

Diagram (a) shows a simple relay. The current to the relay is switched off.

1 Copy and complete the sentences.

The springy __________ strip is not touching the contact.
So there is a __________ in the circuit that goes to the powerful lamp.
This means that the lamp is switched __________.

Diagram (b) shows what happens when you switch on the current to the relay.

2 Write down the following sentences in the right order. (The first sentence is in the correct place.) Use the diagram to help.

- You press the switch.
- The electromagnet becomes magnetised.
- The springy steel strip touches the contact.
- A large current flows through the lamp.
- A small current flows through the coil.
- The electromagnet pulls the steel strip down.

When you stop pressing the switch, the springy steel strip moves away from the contact. This switches the powerful lamp off.

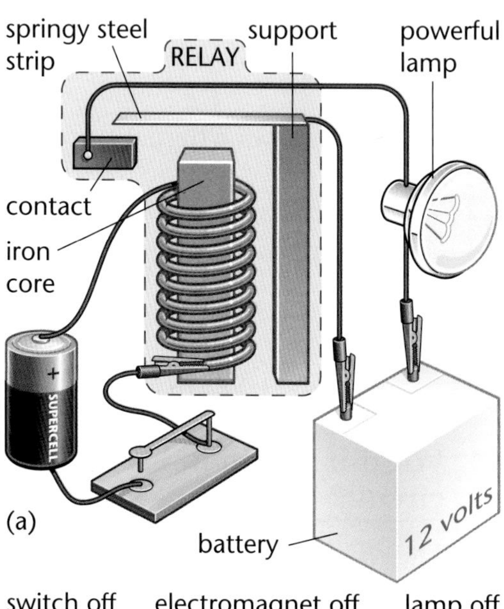

(a)

switch off electromagnet off lamp off

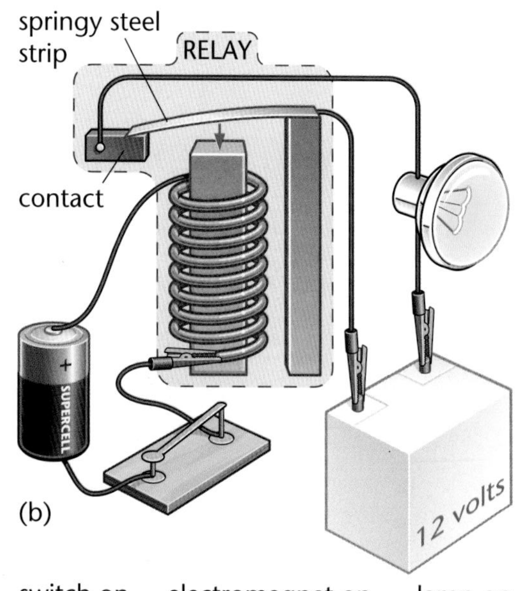

(b)

switch on electromagnet on lamp on

A buzzer

The diagram shows how you can make a buzzer.

When you press the switch, the springy steel strip vibrates. This makes a buzzing sound.

3 What is used for the core of the electromagnet in the buzzer?

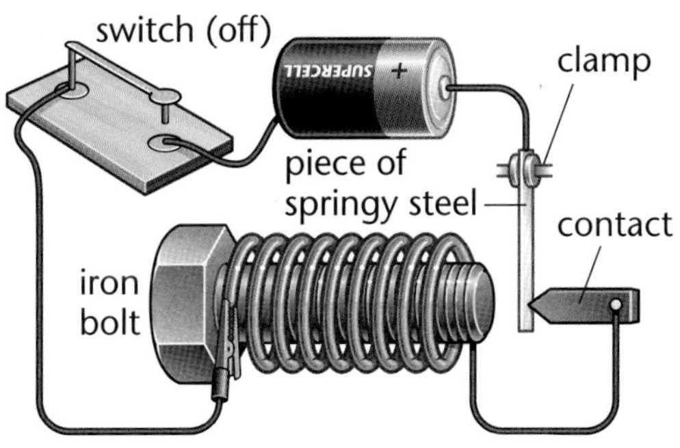

How to make a buzzer.

The diagrams show how the buzzer works.

4 Copy and complete the flow chart.

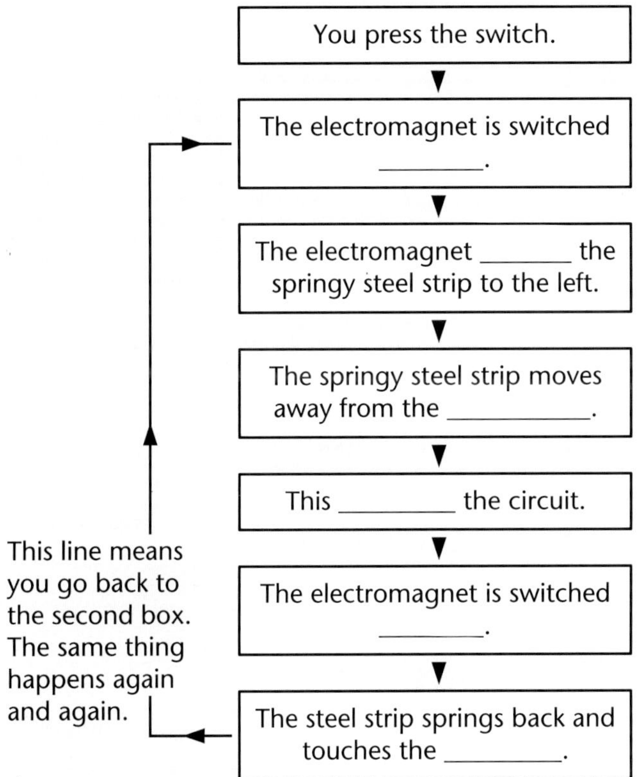

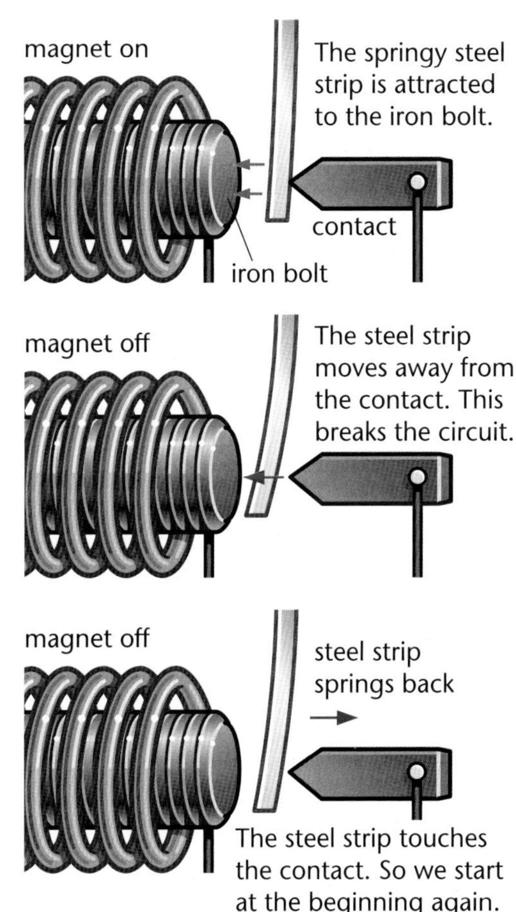

How the buzzer works.

WHAT YOU NEED TO REMEMBER (Copy and complete using the **key words**)

Using electromagnets

Electromagnets are very useful because you can easily ____________ them on and off.

You may be given a diagram of something which uses an electromagnet.
You must be able to explain how it works, like you did with the relay and buzzer.
Electromagnets can do lots of different jobs, but they all work in the same way.

More about electromagnets: C3.7

4.1 Switch on for energy

We need energy for many different things.

1 Look at the pictures. Then write down <u>four</u> things that we need energy for.

Getting the energy we need

We often get the energy we need from **electricity**.

Suppose you need some hot water to make a cup of coffee. All you have to do is put water into a kettle, plug it in and switch it on.

2 Look at the pictures again. Then copy and complete the table.

What we need energy for	What we can switch on to get it
to make something hot	■ kettle ■ ________
to make something move	■ ________ ■ ________
to produce sound	■ ________ ■ ________
to produce light	■ ________ ■ ________

Talking about energy

To make a light bulb work, we must supply it with electricity. We say that we <u>transfer</u> energy to the light bulb by electricity.

The bulb gives out light to its surroundings. We say that the bulb **transfers** energy to its surroundings by light.

drill
food mixer
We need energy to make things **move**.
light bulb
TV set
We need energy to produce light.
kettle
microwave oven
We need energy to make things hot.
cassette player
PA system
We need energy to produce sound.

We can get all these kinds of energy from electricity.

Describing energy transfers

You transfer energy to an electric kettle by electricity.

The electric kettle then transfers energy to the water inside it. This makes the water hotter. So we say that the electric kettle transfers energy to the water as **thermal** energy.

Here is a simple way to write down the energy transfers to and from the kettle:

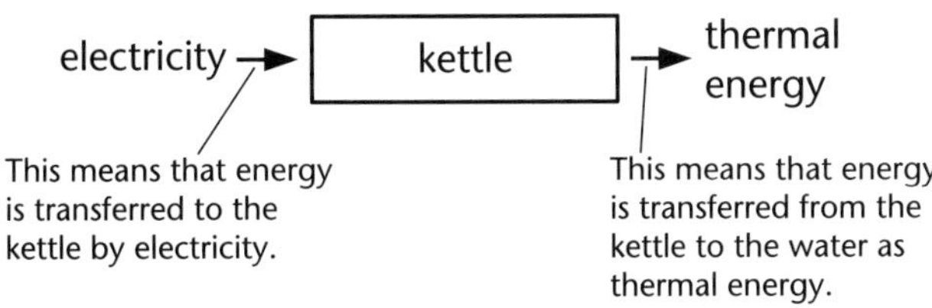

This means that energy is transferred to the kettle by electricity.

This means that energy is transferred from the kettle to the water as thermal energy.

3 Look at the pictures. Then copy and complete the following.

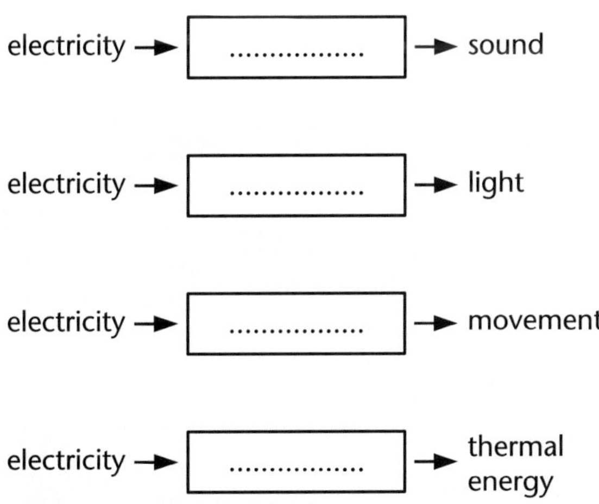

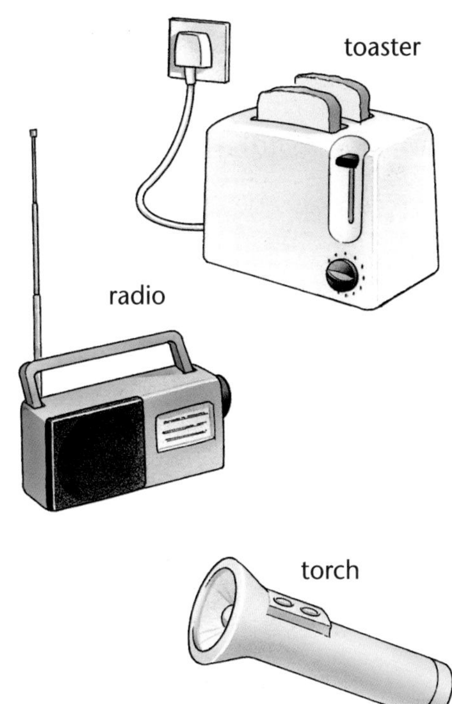

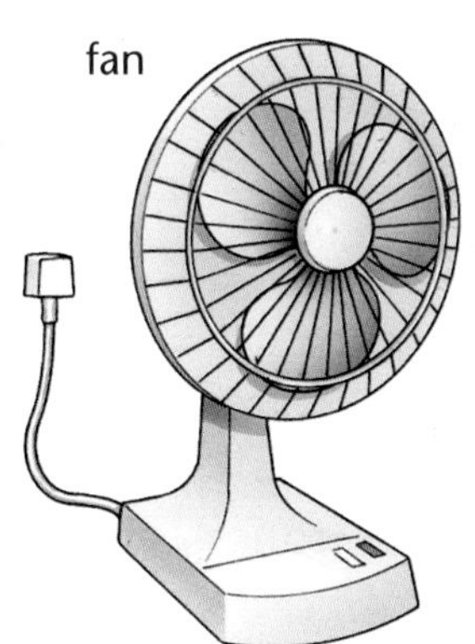

We transfer energy to all these things by electricity. They then transfer energy to their surroundings.

WHAT YOU NEED TO REMEMBER (Copy and complete using the **key words**)

Switch on for energy

We need energy for light, for sound, to make things hot and to make things ____________.

We transfer energy to a light bulb by ____________. The bulb then ____________ energy to its surroundings by light.

When something becomes hotter, it has more ____________ energy.

More about using electricity: C3.3

4.2 Energy from fuels

We often get the energy we need from electricity.

We can also get energy by burning things. The things we burn to get energy are called **fuels**.

1 Look at the pictures. Then write down the names of five fuels.

People used to burn coal to heat their homes.

Today, most people prefer gas.

Car engines burn petrol or diesel fuel.

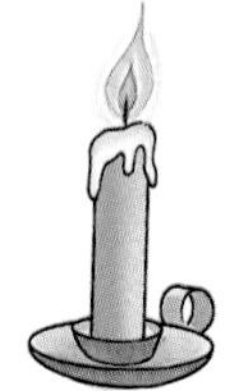
During a power cut you can burn a wax candle.

Many people burn gas for cooking.

In some parts of the world, most people burn wood for cooking.

What happens when fuels burn?

We burn fuels to transfer energy from them.

2 Look at the pictures. Then write down three reasons why we want to transfer energy from fuels.

Burning fuels always makes the things around them hotter. So we say that burning fuels transfers **thermal** energy to the surroundings.

3 Copy and complete the following.

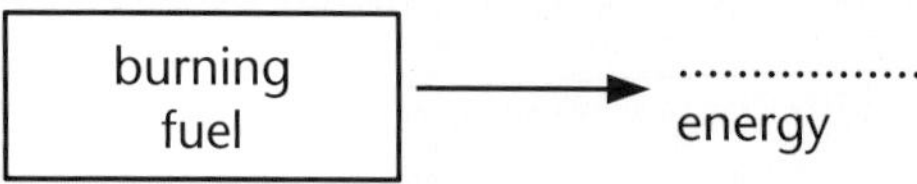

We burn fuels to make things hotter.

We burn fuels to produce light.

We burn fuels to make things move.

Why fuels can transfer energy

When we burn a fuel, it transfers energy to its surroundings. So the fuel must <u>store</u> energy to start off with.

4 Look at the diagrams. Then copy and complete the sentences.

Fuels store energy in the chemical __________ that they are made of.
So we say that they store __________ energy.

*Fuels, like everything else, are made of chemical substances. The chemical substances in fuels store energy. So we say that fuels store **chemical** energy.*

stored chemical energy → burning fuel → thermal energy

What else do fuels need to burn?

Fuels by themselves won't burn. The diagrams show what else they need so that they can burn.

5 **(a)** What else do fuels need so they can burn?

(b) Where do they usually get this from?

You also need to <u>start</u> fuels burning by using a match or a spark.

In a petrol engine, petrol and air are mixed together in exactly the right amounts before the mixture is set alight.
What is the part of the engine called where they are mixed?
How is the mixture set alight?

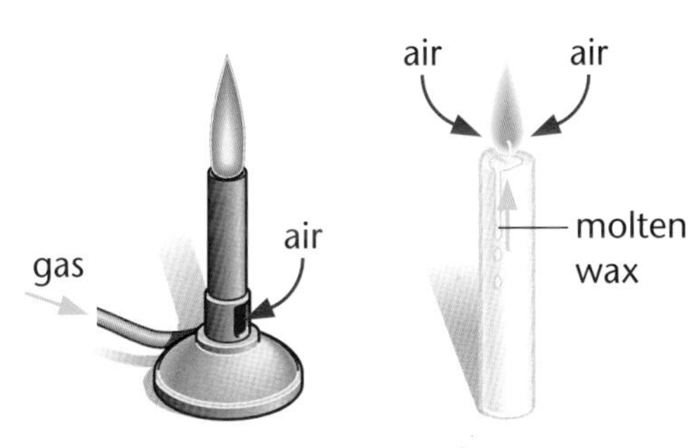

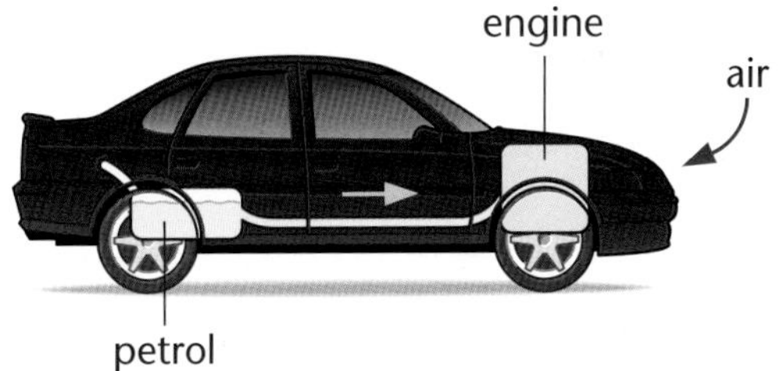

*Fuels won't burn without **oxygen** from the air.*

WHAT YOU NEED TO REMEMBER (Copy and complete using the **key words**)

Energy from fuels

We sometimes get the energy we need by burning __________.
The energy stored in fuels is called __________ energy.

When we burn fuels, energy is transferred to the surroundings as __________ energy.

For fuels to burn, __________ is also needed.

4.3 Using fuels to make electricity

Electricity is very handy when we want to transfer energy.

But we don't find electricity just lying around ready for us to use. We have to <u>make</u> electricity. We say that electricity has to be **generated**. This happens at a power station.

To generate electricity, we need to have some energy to start off with. We say that we need an energy <u>source</u>.

Most electricity is generated using the energy from **fuels**.

Power stations burn mainly these fuels.

1 Write down the names of the <u>three</u> main fuels that are burned in power stations.

What happens at a power station

The diagram shows how electricity is generated using the energy from coal.

Coal stores **chemical** energy.

The coal is burned.

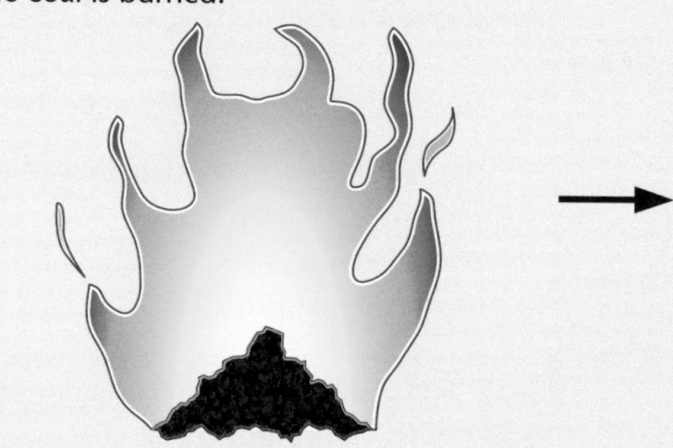

This transfers the stored energy as **thermal** energy.

2 Copy and complete the sentences.

The energy stored in coal is called ________ energy. Burning coal makes things hotter. So we say that ________ energy is transferred to the surroundings.

3 Copy and complete the energy flow diagram for a power station.

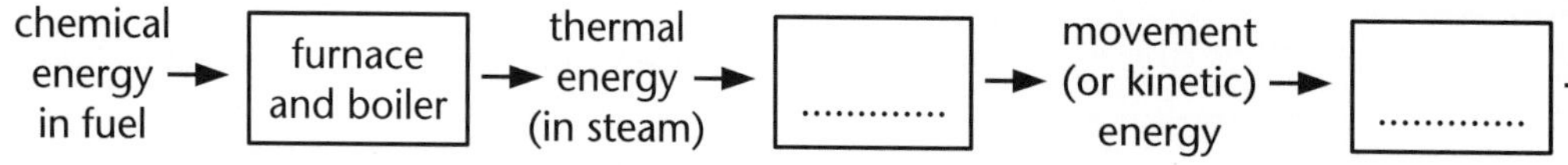

REMEMBER from pages 64–65

We can take electricity to where we want it through wires.
Then we can transfer the energy to the surroundings the way we want to:

- by light;
- as thermal energy;
- by sound;
- as movement.

Nuclear power stations

Nuclear power stations use a fuel called uranium.

The box tells you about the differences between nuclear power stations and power stations that burn coal, gas or oil.

4 Write down one difference between nuclear fuel and fuels like coal, gas and oil.

5 (a) Why are nuclear reactors dangerous?

(b) How are workers in a nuclear power station protected from this danger?

Using nuclear fuel

You don't burn uranium. You put it into a nuclear reactor. It then splits up into other substances and transfers a lot of thermal energy to its surroundings. This energy is transferred to water to make steam.

Nuclear reactors give out very dangerous radiation. So thick walls are built round them to protect workers in a nuclear power station.

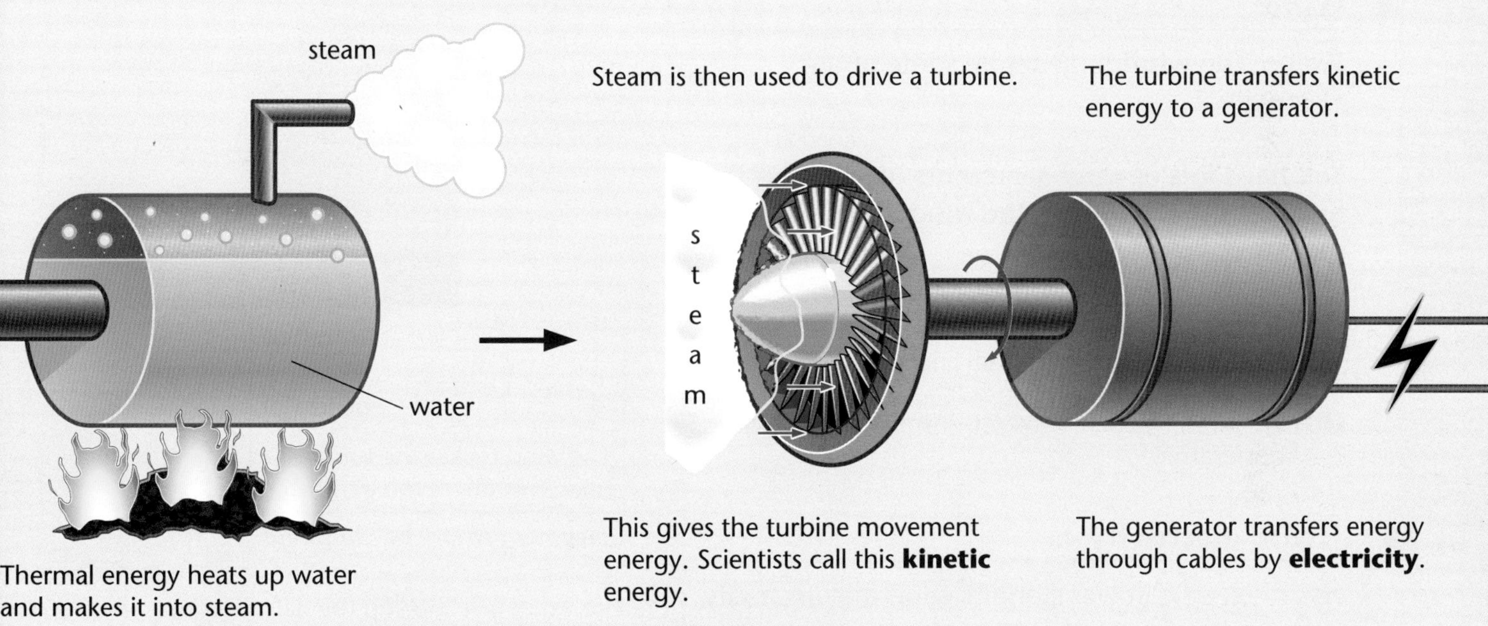

steam
water
Steam is then used to drive a turbine.
The turbine transfers kinetic energy to a generator.
steam

Thermal energy heats up water and makes it into steam.

This gives the turbine movement energy. Scientists call this **kinetic** energy.

The generator transfers energy through cables by **electricity**.

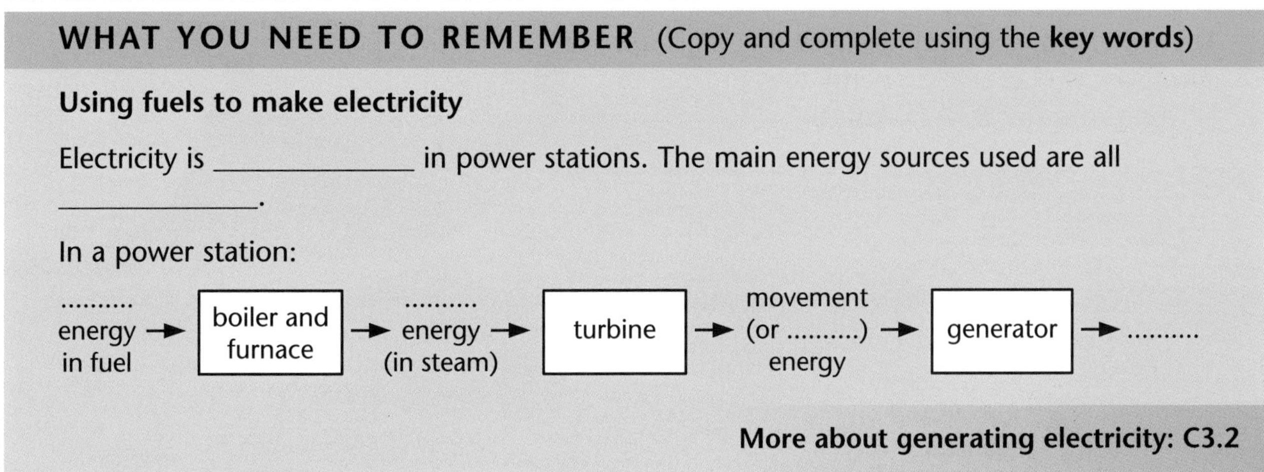

WHAT YOU NEED TO REMEMBER (Copy and complete using the **key words**)

Using fuels to make electricity

Electricity is ______________ in power stations. The main energy sources used are all ______________.

In a power station:

More about generating electricity: C3.2

4.4 Some other ways of generating electricity

To generate electricity we must first have energy of some other kind. We say that we need an energy **source**.

We often use fuels as our energy source.

One problem with fuels is that they produce harmful substances when they burn. We say they cause pollution.

The pictures on this page and the next show some cleaner energy sources we can use to generate electricity. But these energy sources still cause problems.

Power stations which burn fuels pollute the air with harmful gases.

Wind

We use the **wind** to generate some of our electricity.

You need lots of wind generators, usually on the tops of hills. Even then, the wind doesn't blow all the time.

1 **(a)** Write down one advantage of using wind generators rather than ordinary power stations.

(b) Write down two disadvantages of using wind generators.

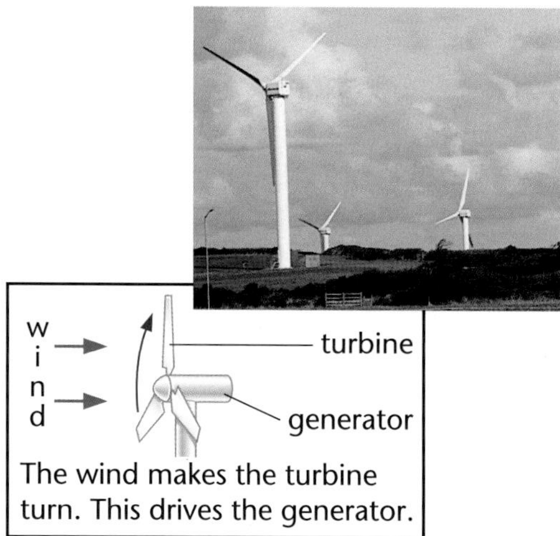

wind
turbine
generator
The wind makes the turbine turn. This drives the generator.

Generating electricity from wind.

Hydro-electricity

Hydro-electric power stations generate electricity using **water trapped behind dams**.

The water stores energy because it is high up. We can transfer this stored energy to a turbine by letting the water flow downhill.

2 What do we call the energy stored by things which are high up?

3 Copy and complete the energy transfer diagram for a hydro-electric power station.

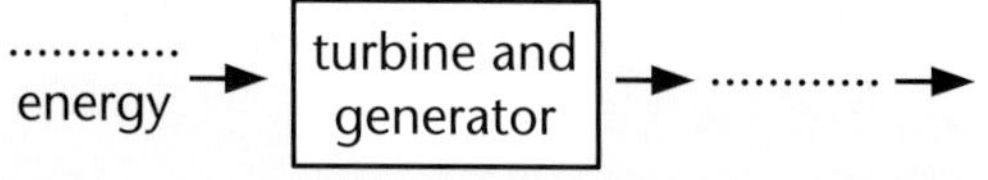

The water level behind the dam is high, so the water stores energy. We call this potential energy.

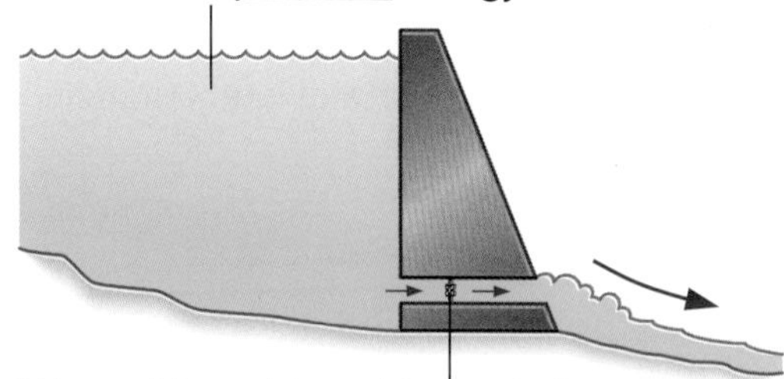

Water drives this turbine as it flows past, and the turbine drives a generator. The generator transfers energy through cables by electricity.

Producing hydro-electricity.

Waves

Energy from the **waves** could generate a lot of electricity.

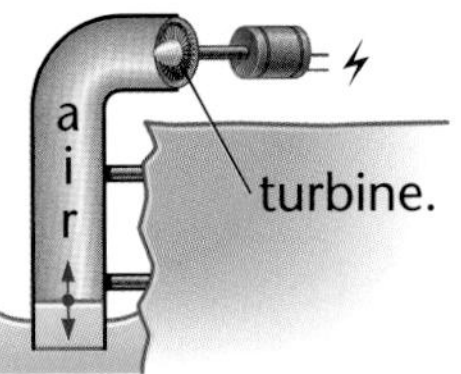

Water moves up and down inside the tube. This drives air through the turbine.

Small machines fastened to cliffs work all right. Nobody has built really big machines out at sea yet.

4 The wave machines we have at the moment don't make very much electricity. Why not?

Tides

At the coast, the level of the sea gets higher twice every day. We say that there is a <u>high tide</u> twice a day.

The diagrams show how we can use the **tides** to generate electricity.

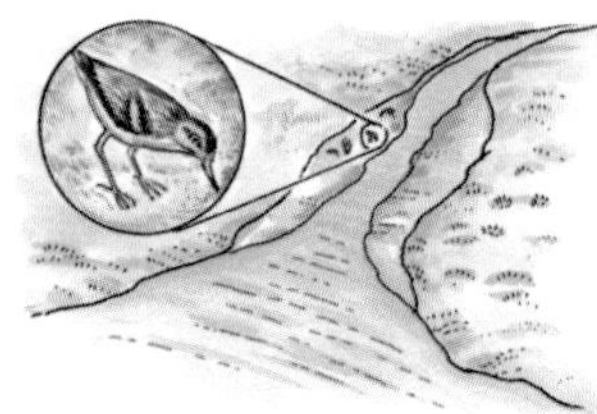

When the tide goes out there is plenty of food in the mud for wading birds.

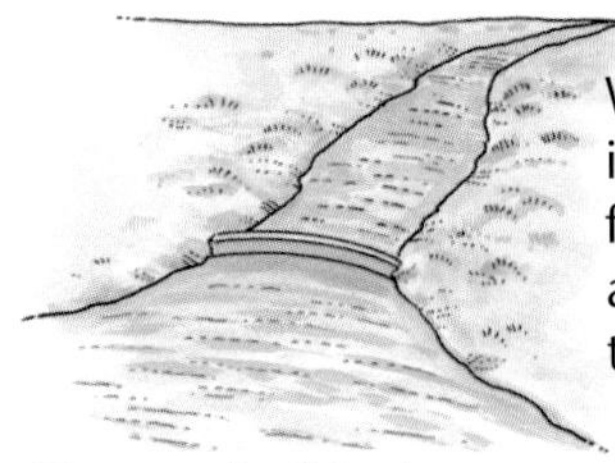

When the barrage is built the mud flats in the estuary are flooded all the time.

You can build a barrage across an estuary. This traps water when the tide comes in. When the tide goes out, the water is higher behind the barrage. So you can generate electricity just like you can with a dam. Lots of wading birds find food in the mud in estuaries. Their feeding ground will be flooded by building a barrage.

5 Copy and complete the sentences.

Water is trapped behind a __________ at high tide.

When the tide goes out, the water behind the barrage is __________ than the sea outside. So the water stores __________ energy.

You can transfer this stored energy to a __________ as kinetic energy. This then drives a generator.

6 Bird-lovers do <u>not</u> like tidal barrages. Why not?

Energy from hot rocks

Deep down in the ground the rocks are hot. You can use the hot rocks to change water into steam. Then you can use the steam to generate electricity.

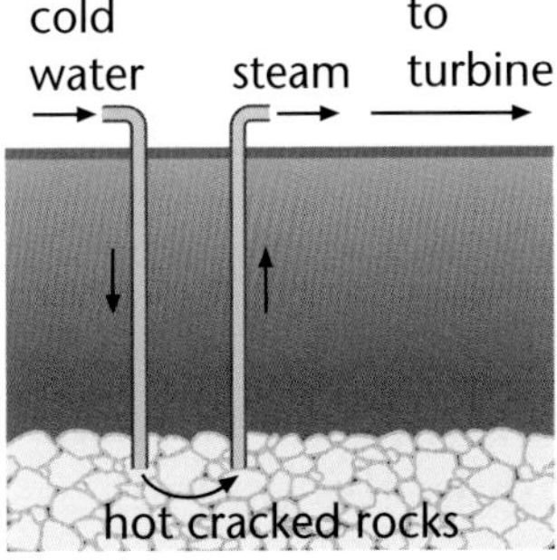

The energy in hot rocks is called **geo-thermal** energy. 'Geo' means 'Earth'.

7 Why is the energy stored in hot rocks called <u>geo-thermal</u> energy?

WHAT YOU NEED TO REMEMBER (Copy and complete using the **key words**)

Some other ways of generating electricity

To generate electricity we need an energy __________.

Some of the energy sources we can use, besides fuels, are: *[name <u>five</u> other sources].*

More about generating electricity: C3.2

4.5 Thank you, Sun!

Lots of energy reaches us from the **Sun** every day. The diagrams show how we can transfer this energy.

1 Copy and complete the following.

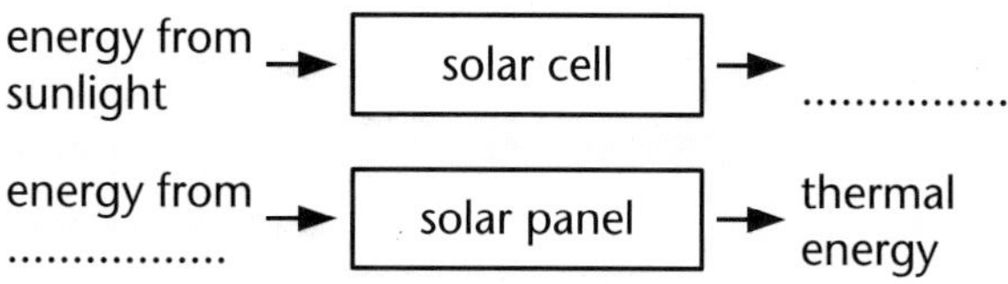

The Sun is very important to us. Most of our other energy sources wouldn't be there without the Sun.

Wood

Trees need energy from the Sun to grow.
This energy is stored in the wood the trees are made of.

Without the Sun there would be no wood.

2 Copy and complete the sentence.

Wood stores __________ energy.

All plants store energy as they grow. We say that they store energy in their biomass.

Fuels from the ground

Coal, gas and oil were all formed millions of years ago under the ground.

The diagrams show how coal was formed.

3 (a) What was coal made from?

(b) What other fuels were made in the same sort of way?

(c) Coal, gas and oil are called fossil fuels. Why is this?

Energy is transferred to solar cells and solar panels by sunlight.

solar energy

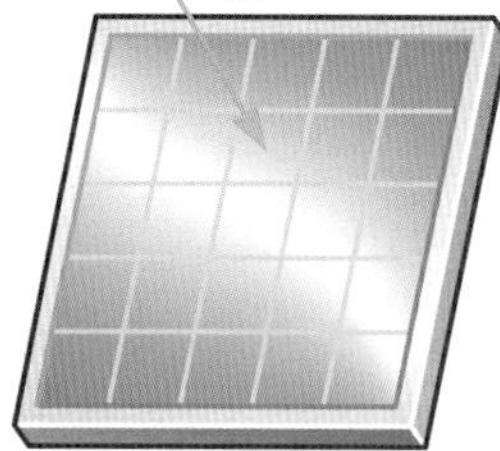

array of solar cells

Energy is transferred from solar cells by electricity. The cells are very expensive to make for the amount of electricity they produce.

solar energy

solar panel

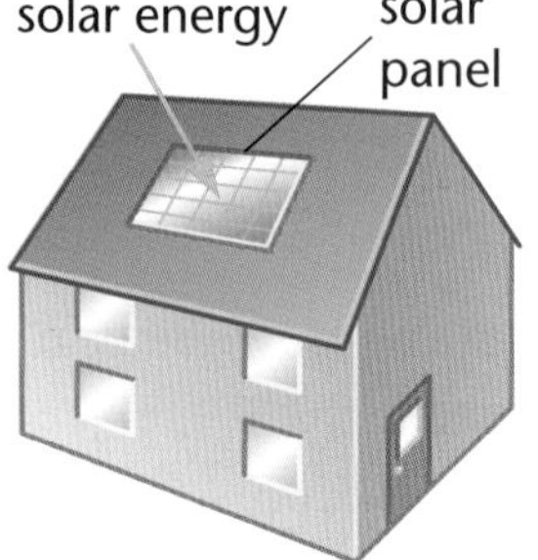

Energy is transferred from solar panels as thermal energy. This heats water to use in the house.

Energy is transferred to trees by sunlight. Trees store this energy as they grow. So trees are stores of chemical energy. You can burn the wood as a fuel.

How coal was formed.

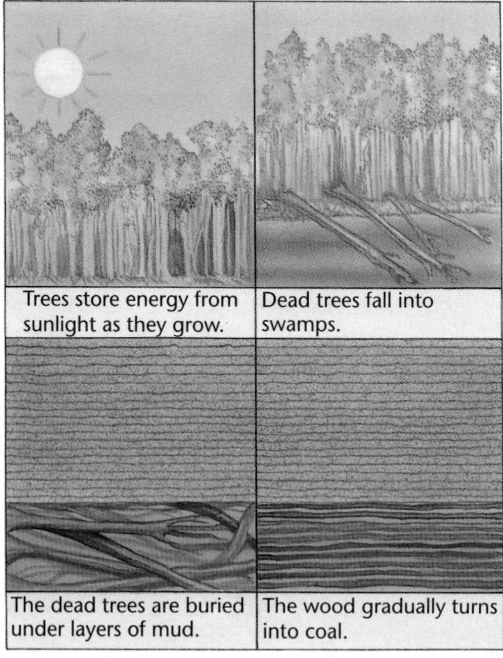

Trees store energy from sunlight as they grow.

Dead trees fall into swamps.

The dead trees are buried under layers of mud.

The wood gradually turns into coal.

Oil and gas are formed in the same way from plants and animals that lived in the sea. Because these fuels are made from the remains of dead plants and animals, they are called fossil fuels.

Wind, waves and rain

The Sun heats up some places on Earth more than others. This is what causes winds.

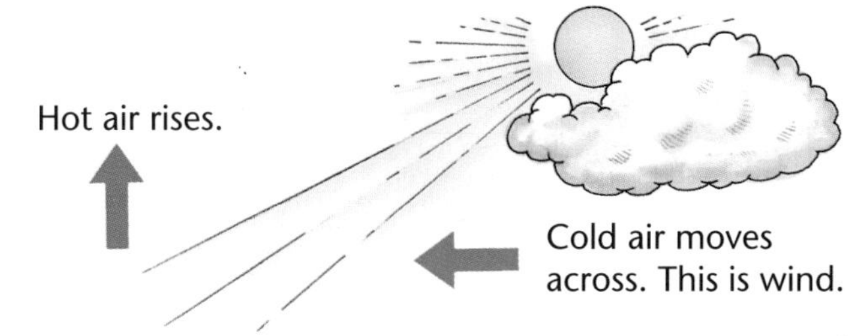

Hot air rises.
Cold air moves across. This is wind.

Without the Sun there would also be no waves and no rain. The diagram on the right shows why.

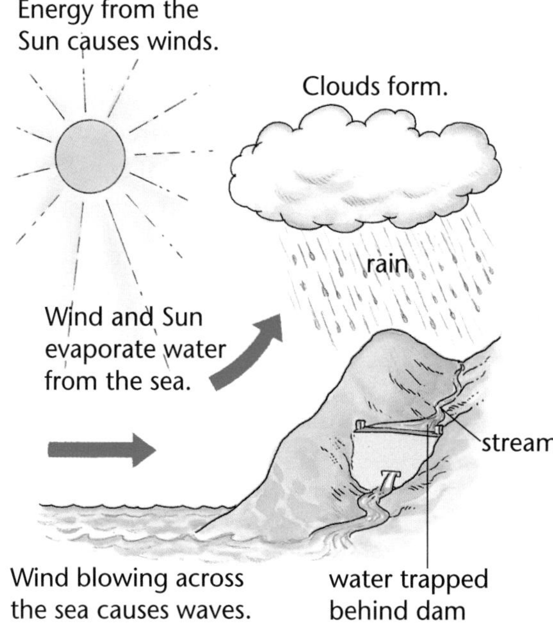

Energy from the Sun causes winds.
Clouds form.
rain
Wind and Sun evaporate water from the sea.
stream
Wind blowing across the sea causes waves.
water trapped behind dam

4 Explain how energy from the Sun:

(a) produces wind;

(b) produces waves;

(c) keeps on filling up the water behind dams.

No Sun needed

The diagrams show a few energy sources that <u>don't</u> need the Sun.

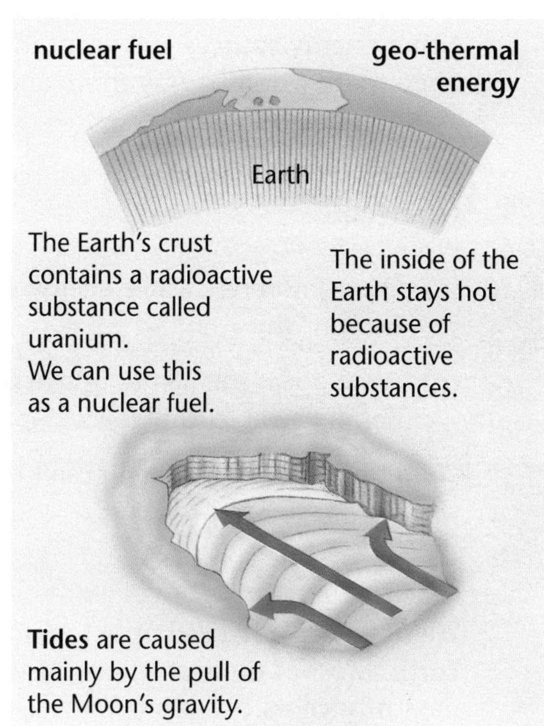

nuclear fuel
geo-thermal energy
Earth
The Earth's crust contains a radioactive substance called uranium. We can use this as a nuclear fuel.
The inside of the Earth stays hot because of radioactive substances.
Tides are caused mainly by the pull of the Moon's gravity.

5 (a) Which <u>two</u> energy sources depend on radioactive materials?

(b) Which energy source depends mainly on the Moon?

WHAT YOU NEED TO REMEMBER (Copy and complete using the **key words**)

Thank you, Sun!

Most of our energy sources depend on energy from the ___________.

Energy sources which <u>don't</u> depend on the Sun are: *[name <u>three</u>]*

More about energy sources: C3.1

4.6 Will our energy sources last for ever?

Some of our energy sources will last for billions of years. They won't run out because the energy is being **replaced** all the time.

We say that these energy sources are **renewable**.

The Sun will keep on shining for about 5 billion more years.

So solar energy is a renewable energy source.

1 Solar energy is a renewable energy source. Explain why.

Oil takes millions of years to form. We get most of our oil and gas by drilling through the rocks under the North Sea.

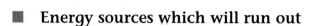

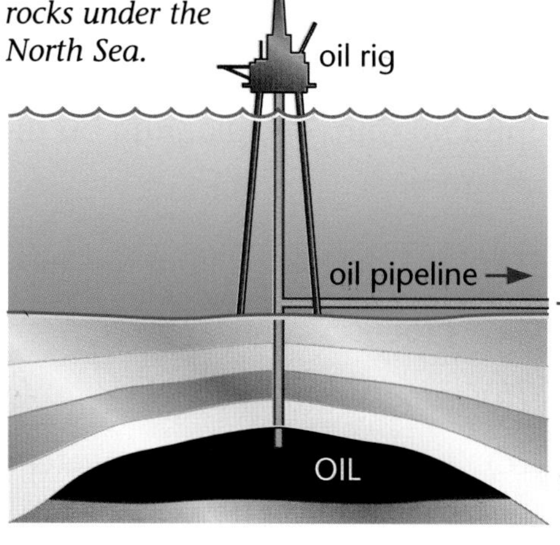

Energy sources which will run out

Other energy sources will eventually get used up. Then there won't be any more energy from those energy sources.

So we say that these energy sources are **non-renewable**.

2 (a) Oil is a non-renewable energy source. Explain why.

(b) Write down the names of two other non-renewable fossil fuels.

(Turn back to page 72 if you can't remember.)

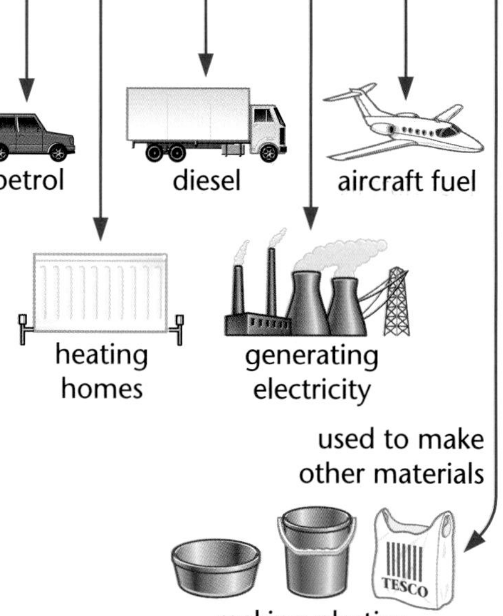

We have already used up a lot of the oil on Earth. Most of the rest will be used up during the next fifty years.

3 Most of the oil is burned as fuel. Write down five things that we use fuels from oil for.

4 What else is oil used for besides fuel?

Renewable or non-renewable?

Solar energy is a renewable energy source.

Oil is a non-renewable energy source.

The pictures show most of our other energy sources.

5 For each picture:

(a) write down the name of the energy source;

(b) say whether it is renewable or non-renewable;

(c) give a reason for your answer.

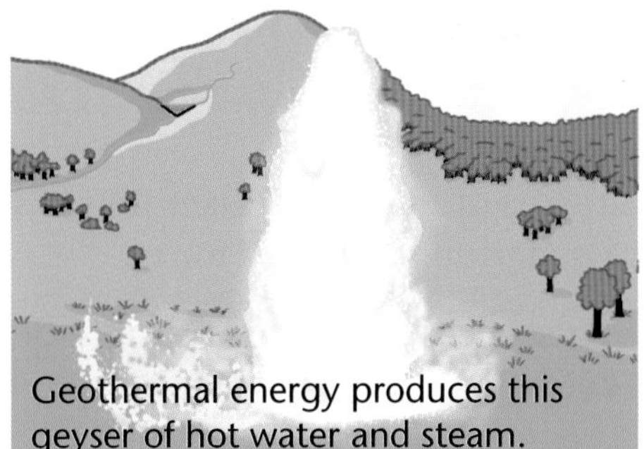

Geothermal energy produces this geyser of hot water and steam.

There is enough radioactive material left to keep the Earth hot inside for at least a billion years.

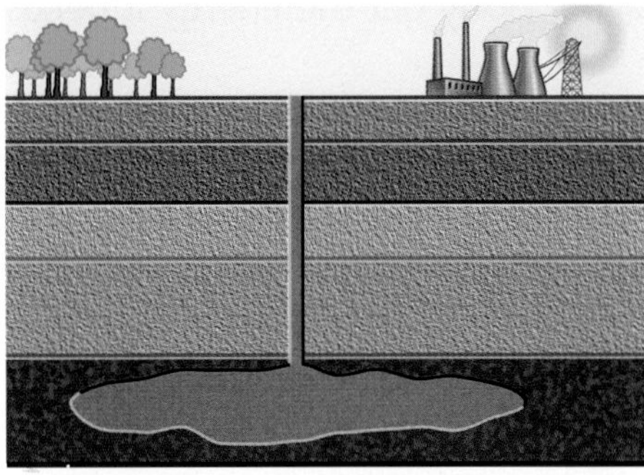

Coal was formed from trees which died millions of years ago.

Winds are caused because the Sun heats up the Earth more in some places than in others.

Tides are caused mainly by the Moon as the Earth spins round each day.

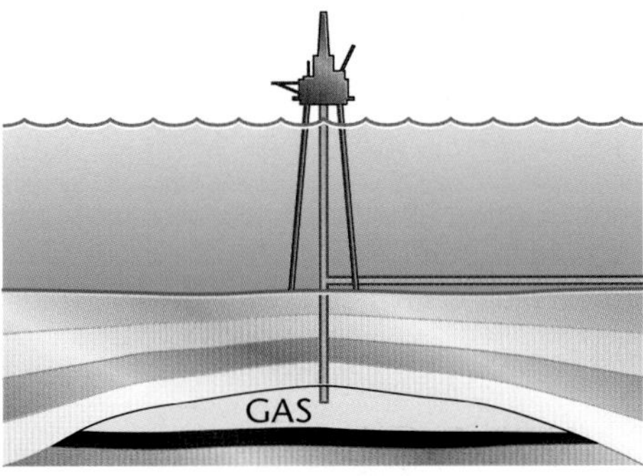

Gas was formed from the dead bodies of things which lived in the sea millions of years ago.

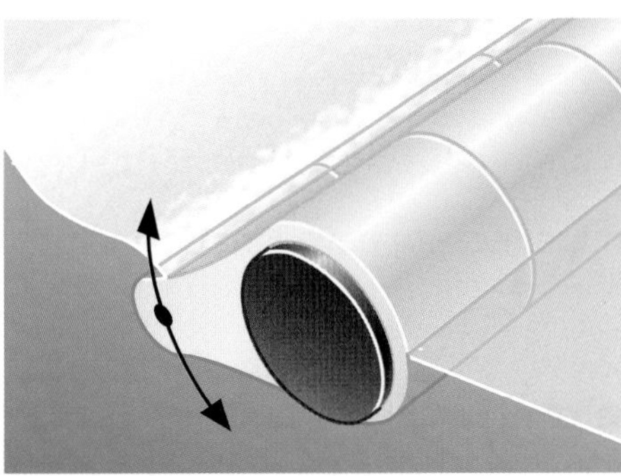

Waves are caused when the wind blows across the sea.

Waves can transfer energy to rocking 'ducks'.

WHAT YOU NEED TO REMEMBER (Copy and complete using the **key words**)

Will our energy sources last for ever?

Some energy sources will last for ever because the energy is constantly being ____________. We say that these energy sources are ____________.

Some energy sources will eventually run out. We say they are ____________ energy sources. *You should know whether or not each energy source on these pages is renewable.*

More about energy sources: C3.1

4.7 Energy for your body

We need sources of energy to keep power stations working to generate electricity for us.

Our bodies also need a constant supply of energy to keep them alive and well.

1 How does your body get the energy it needs?

2 (a) What two types of food supply most of your energy?

(b) Write down three examples of each of these types of food.

3 Copy and complete the sentence.

The food we eat stores __________ energy.

These foods give you most energy.

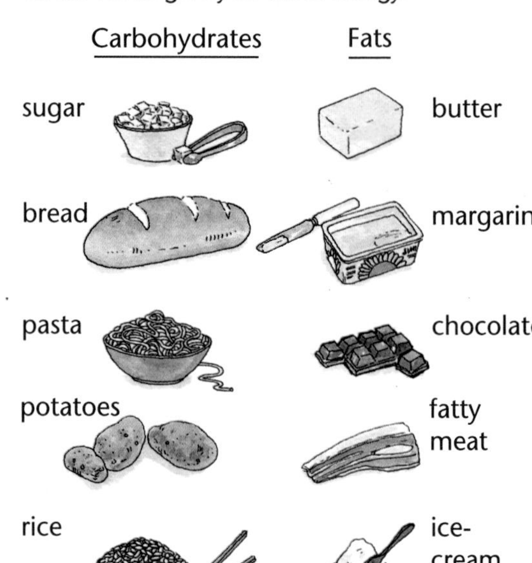

***Foods** like these store **chemical** energy.*

What does your body need energy for?

Your body is made of lots of tiny cells. All these cells need energy to work properly.

The photos show two other reasons why your body needs energy.

REMEMBER from pages 65 and 69

Things which are hot have a lot of **thermal** energy.

Things which are moving have **kinetic** energy.

4 Look at the photographs.
Then copy and complete the following energy transfer diagrams.

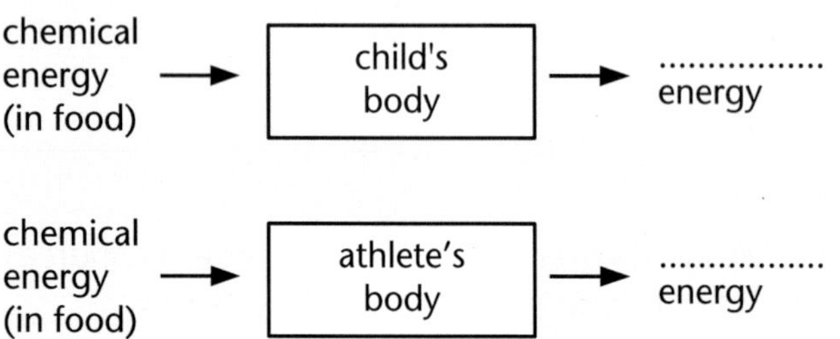

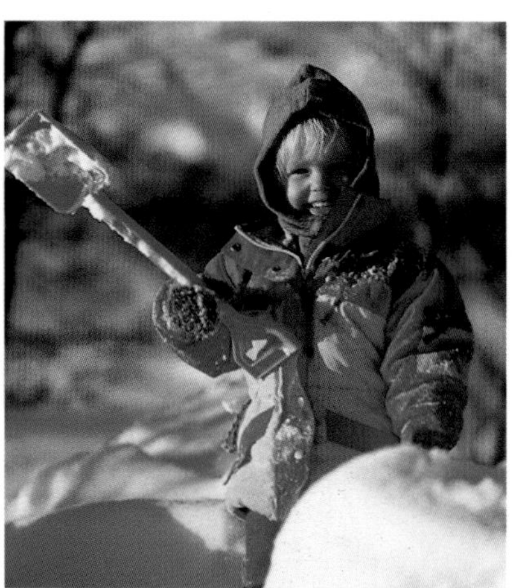

The girl needs energy to keep warm.

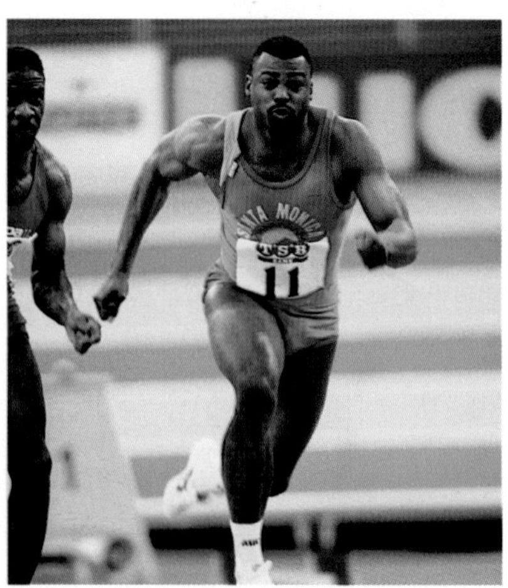

The athlete needs energy to move.

Energy for lifting things

Things which are high up store energy. So to lift things up you have to transfer energy to them.

You transfer more energy walking uphill than walking the same distance on the flat.

REMEMBER from page 70

The higher something is, the more **potential** energy it has.

5 What do we call the energy something has because it is high up?

Who transfers most energy?

Three girls are all the same weight. The drawings show what each girl does one afternoon.

Daisy lies on the sofa reading a book.

Rose walks along a flat beach.

Rani walks up a steep hill.

6 **(a)** Which girl transfers most energy? Which girl transfers least energy?

(b) Give reasons for your answers.

7 Copy and complete the following.

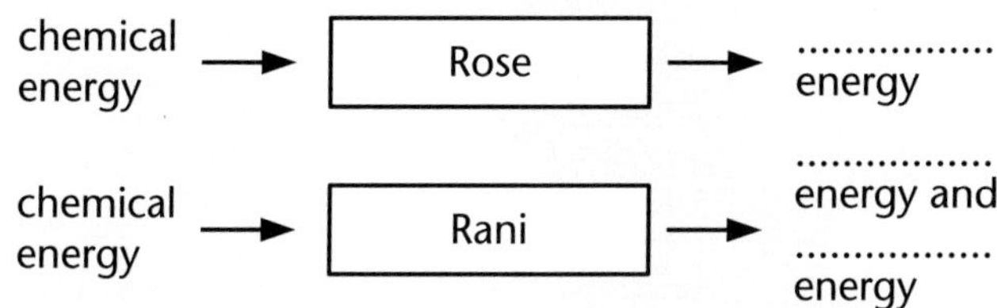

A falling book

Daisy falls asleep. Her book falls to the floor.

8 Copy and complete the following.

________ energy $\xrightarrow[\text{book falls}]{\text{as the}}$ ________ energy

WHAT YOU NEED TO REMEMBER (Copy and complete using the **key words**)

Energy for your body

Your body gets the energy it needs from ____________.

Food stores ____________ energy. Your body transfers the energy from food mainly as ____________ energy and ____________ energy.

When you lift something up, you give it more ____________ energy.

4.8 Ways of storing energy

Fuels and food store energy.

Many other things store energy too. The energy can be stored in several different ways.

Storing energy in chemicals

All the things in the diagram store **chemical** energy.

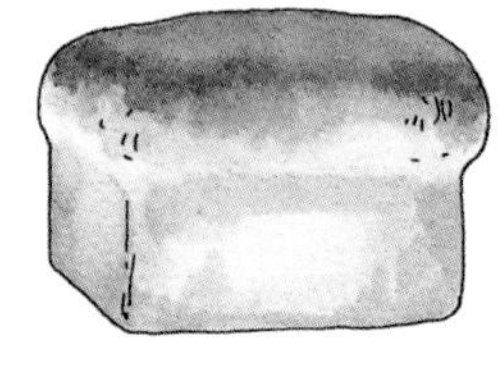

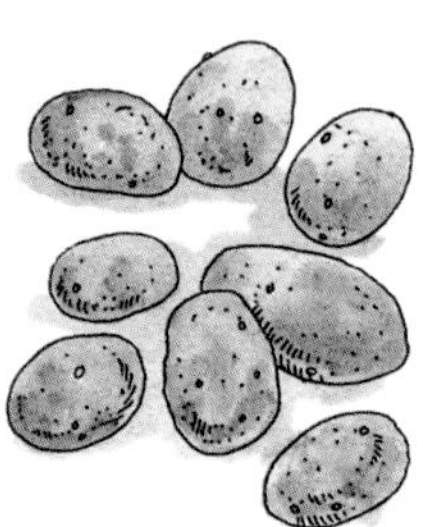

1 Copy and complete the table.

Chemical energy

What stores it	Is it a food or a fuel?	What you do to transfer the stored energy
potatoes	food	eat them
firewood		
petrol		
bread		

Storing energy by lifting things up

We can store energy in things by lifting them up. This stored energy is called <u>potential</u> energy.

Because we lift things up against the force of gravity, the energy they store is **gravitational** potential energy.

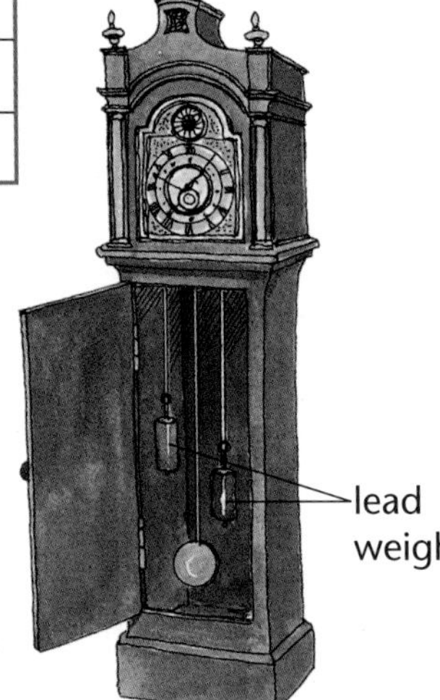

When you wind up the clock, you lift up the weights. Energy stored by the weights is transferred to the clock as the weights slowly fall <u>down</u>.

2 Look at the diagrams. Then write down <u>two</u> things that work by transferring gravitational potential energy.

3 Copy and complete the sentence.

You can transfer gravitational potential energy by letting the things that store it move __________.

Water is at a higher level behind the dam. In a hydro-electric power station, the energy stored by the water is transferred to generate electricity. This happens when the water flows <u>down</u>.

Another kind of potential energy

We can store energy in some things by changing their shape. We can do this by stretching them, bending them or squeezing them.

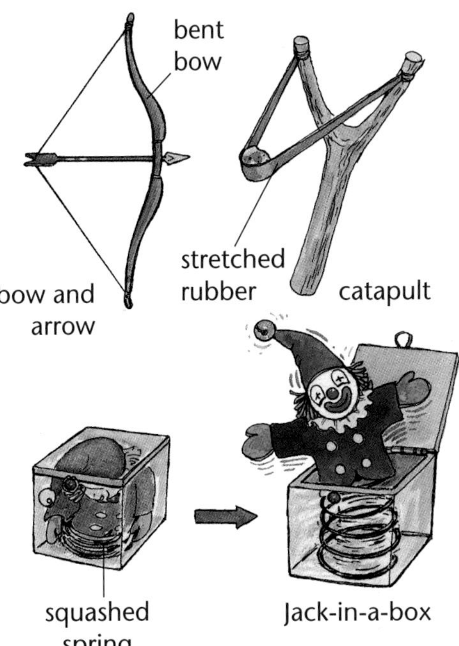

4 Look at the diagrams. Then copy and complete the table.

What changes its shape	How do we change its shape?
bow	
catapult rubber	
spring	

The stored energy is called **elastic** potential energy.

5 Copy and complete the sentence.

A bent bow, stretched rubber and a squashed spring all store __________ potential energy.

A problem with electrical energy

Electricity is great for **transferring** energy. But you can't **store** electricity.

You have to store energy in some other way. Then you can transfer the stored energy to give you electricity when you need it.

This is what happens with batteries.

6 Copy and complete the sentences.

A battery stores __________ energy. It transfers energy by __________ when you connect it into a circuit.

Charging up batteries.

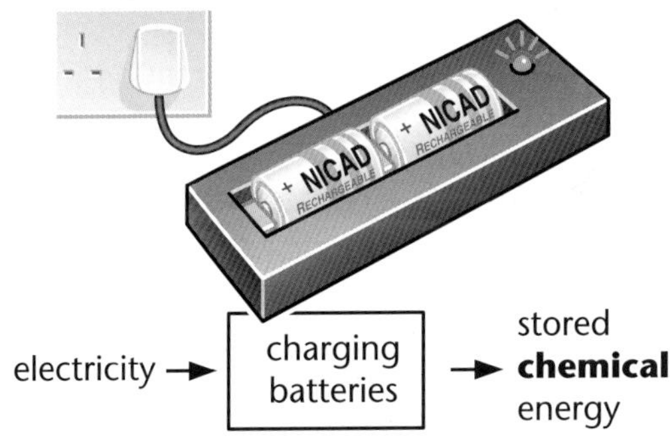

electricity → charging batteries → stored **chemical** energy

Using the batteries in a circuit.

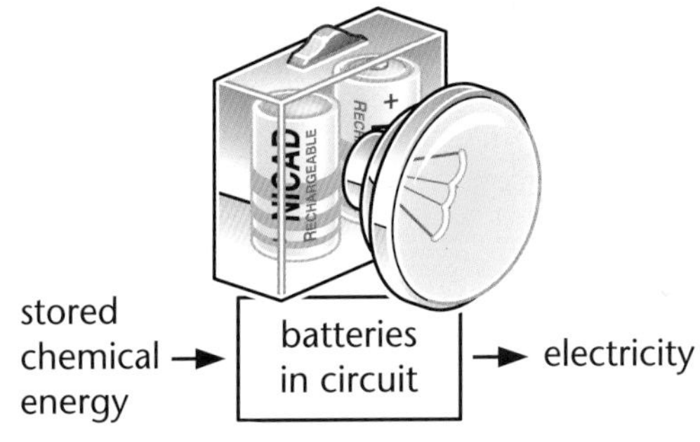

stored chemical energy → batteries in circuit → electricity

WHAT YOU NEED TO REMEMBER (Copy and complete using the **key words**)

Ways of storing energy

You can store energy as _____ energy, _____ potential energy or _____ potential energy.

Electricity is great for _____ energy, but you can't _____ electricity.

Batteries store energy as _____ energy.

More about storing energy: CORE+ C3.16

4.9 You don't only get what you want

When it gets dark, we just switch on a light bulb. The light bulb transfers energy to its surroundings as light.
But not all the electrical energy that we transfer to the bulb is transferred from the bulb as light.

1 Look at the diagram. Then copy and complete the sentences.

Energy is transferred from a light bulb only partly by ________.
Energy is transferred from a light bulb mostly as ________ energy.

This light bulb transfers energy to its surroundings :
- *partly by light;*
- *mostly as thermal energy.*

All the energy goes somewhere

Whenever you transfer energy:

- only part of the energy is transferred in the way you want;
- but **all** the energy is transferred in some way.

The diagram shows what happens to all the energy transferred to a light bulb.

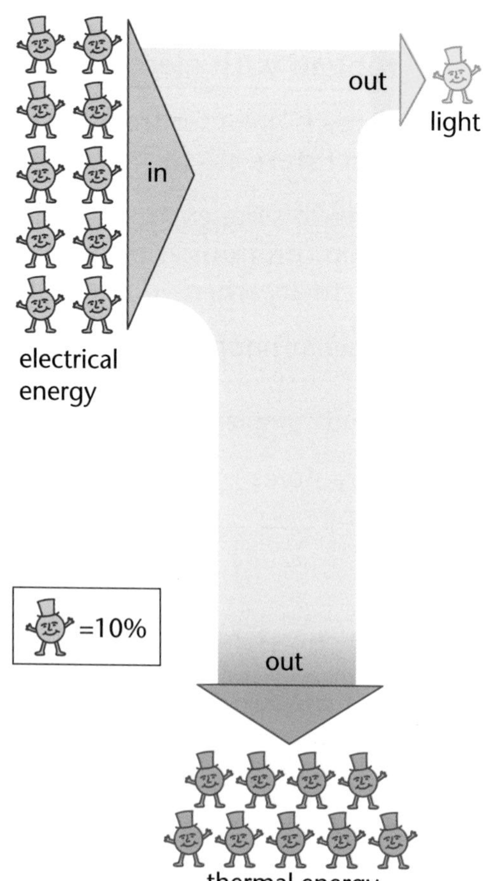

2 Copy and complete the following.

Energy transferred TO the light bulb	Energy transferred FROM the light bulb
electricity	light + thermal energy
100%	____% + ____%
	total: 100%

So:

energy IN = energy OUT

3 30% of the energy that you supply to a yellow sodium street lamp is transferred as light.

Draw an energy transfer diagram for this lamp.

Energy transfers in a car engine

The diagram shows what happens to the energy transferred from petrol in a car engine.

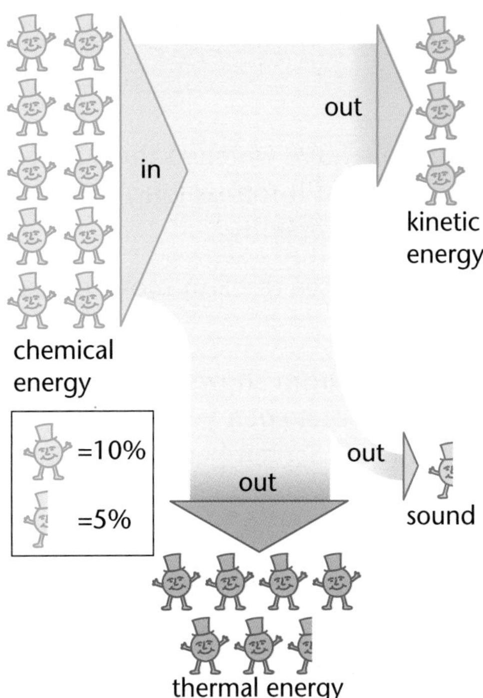

4 Copy and complete the following.

Energy IN to engine	**Energy OUT from engine**
from fuel	kinetic energy + thermal energy + sound
100%	____% + ____% + ____%
	total: 100%

So:

energy IN = energy OUT

Whenever we transfer energy, some is always transferred in ways we don't really want. This energy isn't lost, but it is **wasted** as far as we are concerned.

What a waste!

In fact, all the energy we transfer is wasted in the end. The diagram shows why.

5 What eventually happens to all the energy that a light bulb transfers to its surroundings?

Energy that is transferred to the surroundings gets very **spread out**. This means that it isn't easy to transfer it again.

Energy is transferred from a light bulb by light and as thermal energy. This energy is transferred to the things in the room. It makes everything in the room a tiny bit warmer.

WHAT YOU NEED TO REMEMBER (Copy and complete using the **key words**)

You don't only get what you want

When energy is transferred, it is __________ transferred in some way.
But some is transferred in ways we don't really want, so it is __________.

In the end, all transferred energy is wasted because it gets very __________ __________.

More about energy transfers: C3.3, C3.8

5.1 The Sun and the stars

WARNING!

You should never look directly at the Sun (not even if you're wearing sunglasses). You can badly damage your eyes.

People have watched the Sun for thousands of years. But it took a long time to work out what is really happening.

You can see the Sun move across the sky each day.

The diagram shows what you see on around March 21st each year. You see exactly the same thing on September 23rd each year too.

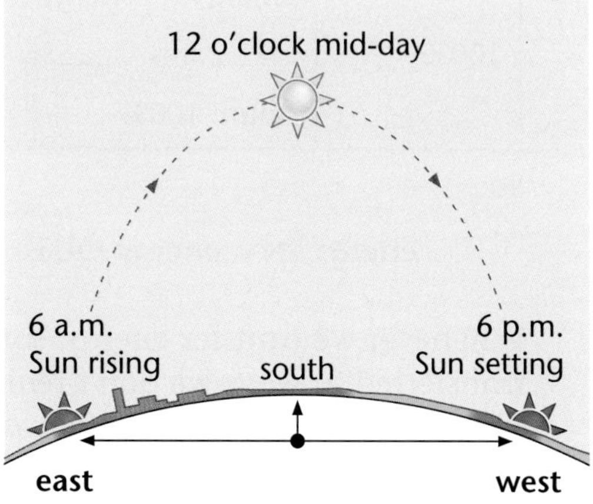

1 **(a)** Where does the Sun rise on these days?

(b) Where does the Sun set?

(c) When is the Sun at its highest point in the sky?

2 How many hours are there between sunrise and sunset on March 21st and September 23rd?

Watching the stars

People have also watched the stars for thousands of years.

A person in the UK looks towards the north on a clear night. The diagram shows the pattern of stars she can see in the sky. This pattern of stars is called the Plough.

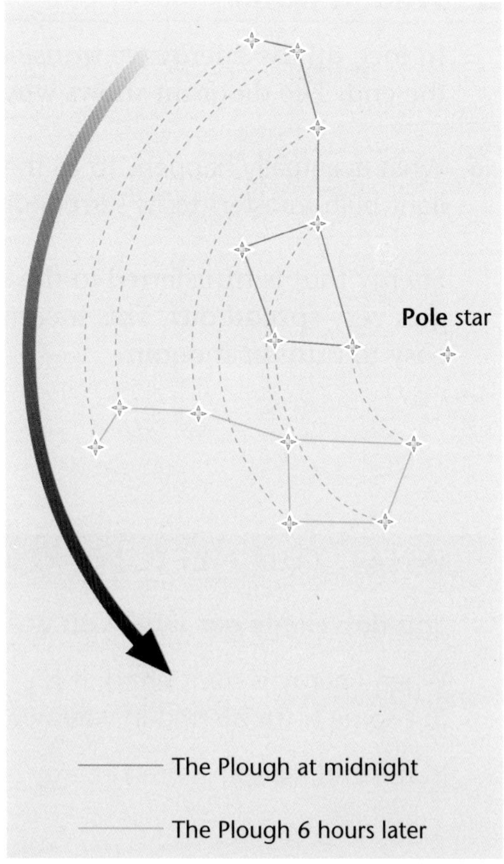

3 **(a)** How do most of the stars seem to move?

(b) Which star doesn't seem to move?

On a clear night:
- find the Plough;
- use this to find the Pole Star.

The Pole star shows you which direction is north.
You can use this to check a magnetic compass.

Explaining what we can see

The Sun and the stars both seem to move across the sky. The diagrams show two ways of explaining this.

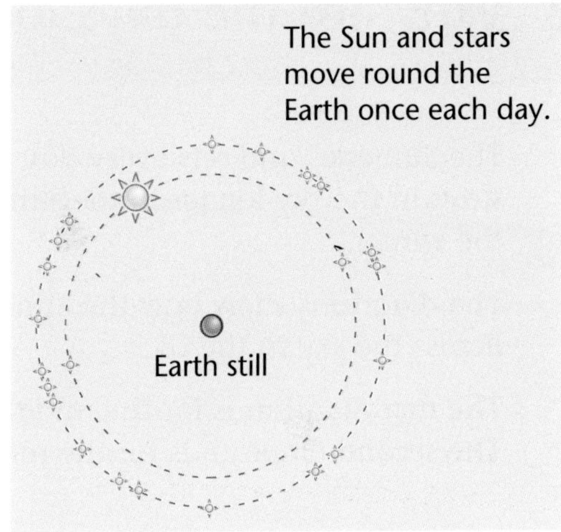

What people used to think happens.

4 Copy and complete the sentences.

Either: The Sun and the stars move around the __________ once every __________.

Or: The _________ and the stars stand still and the _________ spins round once every _________.

Which is the right explanation?

It doesn't seem like the Earth is spinning round all the time. So people used to think that the Sun and the stars move round the Earth.

Then some scientists started to say that the Earth is spinning. Most people found this very hard to believe.

5 Why did people find it hard to believe the Earth is spinning?

Today, most people do believe that the Earth **spins** round once a day. It doesn't seem like we're spinning because everything around us is also spinning at exactly the same speed.

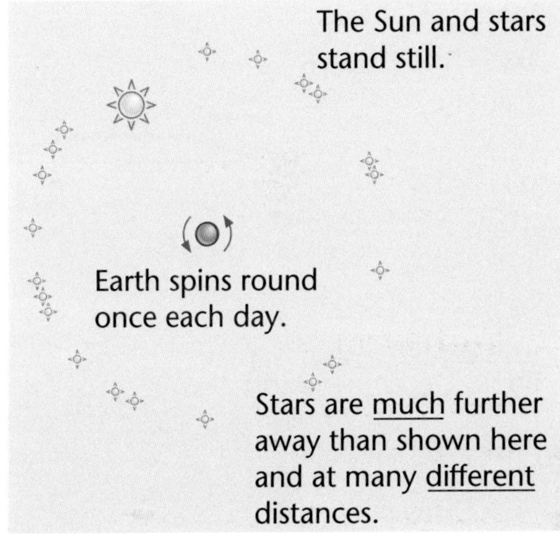

The Sun and stars stand still.
Earth spins round once each day.
Stars are much further away than shown here and at many different distances.

What we now think happens.

WHAT YOU NEED TO REMEMBER (Copy and complete using the **key words**)

The Sun and the stars

Every day the Sun seems to move across the sky from ____________ to ____________.

Every night the stars seem to go around the ____________ star.

This is because the Earth ____________ round once each day.

More about the solar system: C1.2

5.2 Why are the days longer in summer?

The Sun rises and sets every day. The Sun also stays in the sky longer in the summer than in the winter.

The diagrams show how the Sun seems to move across the sky in the UK.

The first diagram is for the middle of winter. The second diagram is for the middle of summer.

WARNING!

You should never look directly at the Sun. You can badly damage your eyes.

REMEMBER from page 82

On around March 21st and September 23rd

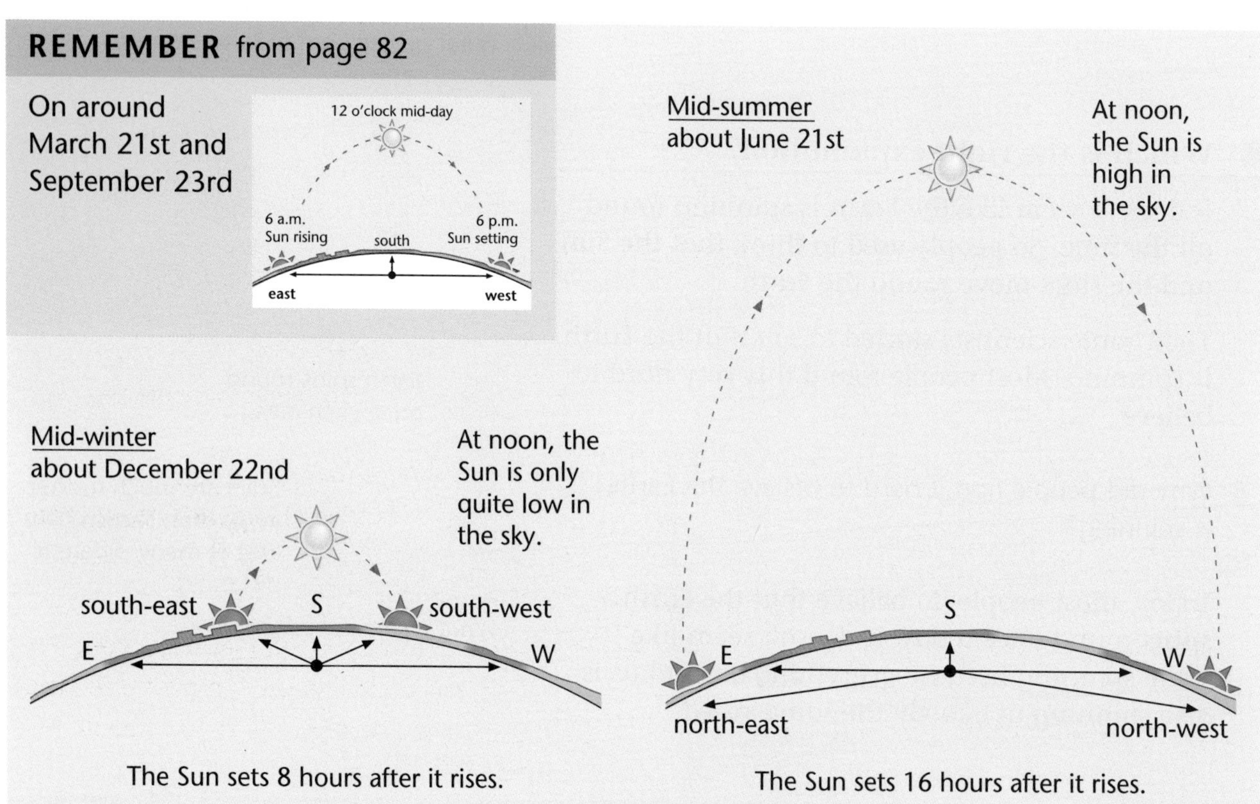

The Sun sets 8 hours after it rises.

The Sun sets 16 hours after it rises.

1 Copy and complete the table.

Date	How high is the Sun at noon?	How many hours between sunrise and sunset?	What direction is sunrise?	What direction is sunset?
March 21st				
June 21st				
September 23rd				
December 22nd				

Explaining what we can see

The diagrams show why the days are **longer** in the summer than in the **winter**.

REMEMBER from page 83

The Earth spins round once each day.

The Earth goes round the Sun once a **year**.

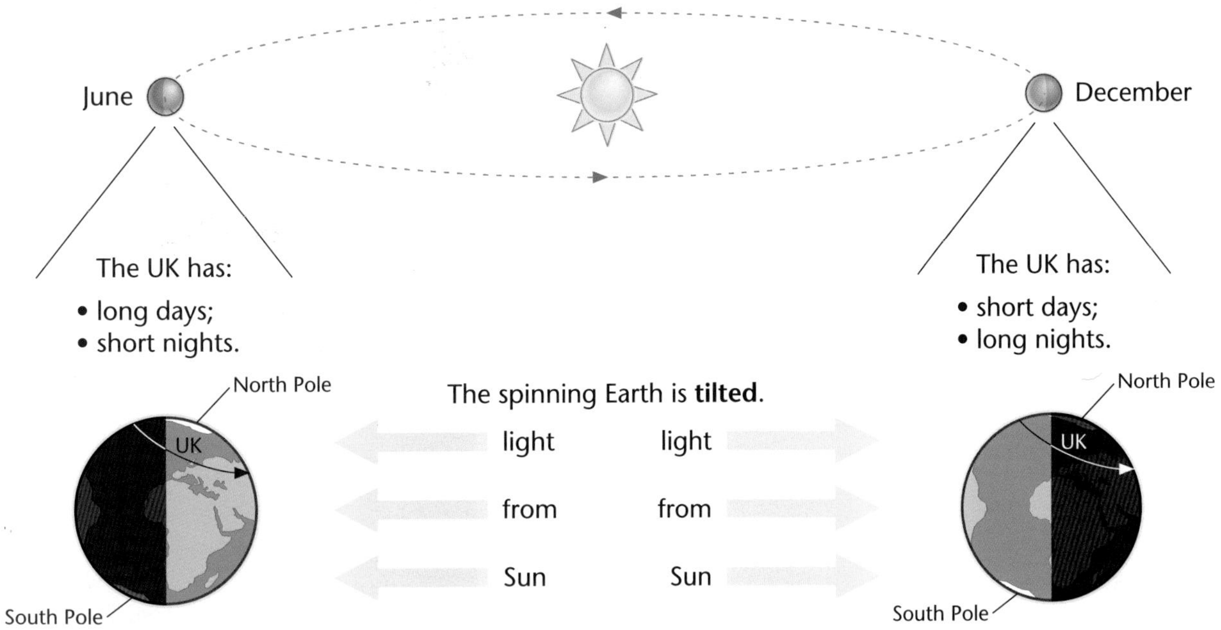

June

December

The UK has:

- long days;
- short nights.

The UK has:

- short days;
- long nights.

The spinning Earth is **tilted**.

North Pole

UK

South Pole

light from Sun

It is summer in the UK.

North Pole

UK

South Pole

light from Sun

It is winter in the UK.

2 Copy and complete the sentences.

The Earth moves round the __________.
It does this once every __________.

The Earth also spins round once every __________.

But the Earth doesn't spin straight up.
The Earth is __________.

In June the north of the Earth is tilted __________ the Sun. The UK spends more time in the __________ than in the __________.
So it is summer in the UK.

In December the north of the Earth is tilted __________ the Sun. The UK spends more time in the __________ than in the __________.
So it is winter in the UK.

WHAT YOU NEED TO REMEMBER (Copy and complete using the **key words**)

Why are the days longer in summer?

The Earth moves around the Sun once each __________.

When it is summer in the UK, the north of the Earth is __________ towards the Sun.
This means that the days are __________ than the nights.

When the north of the Earth is tilted away from the Sun, it is __________ in the UK.
This means that the nights are __________ than the days.

5.3 Stars and planets

When you look at the sky at night, stars and planets look just the same as each other. They all look like tiny pin-pricks of light.

But if you look very carefully, you can spot the difference.

1 Look at the diagrams. How can you tell the difference between a planet and a star?

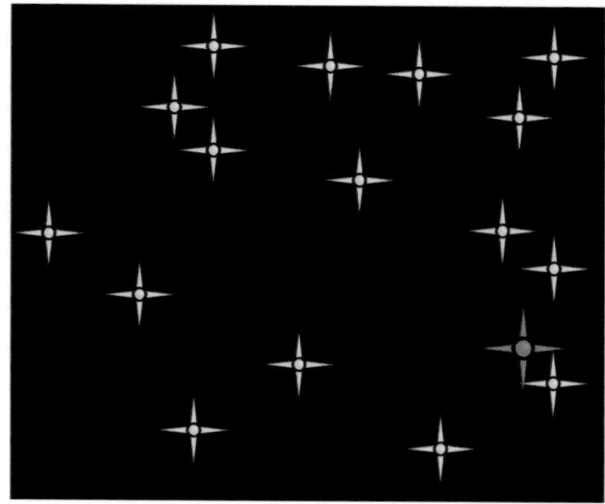

Part of the night sky.

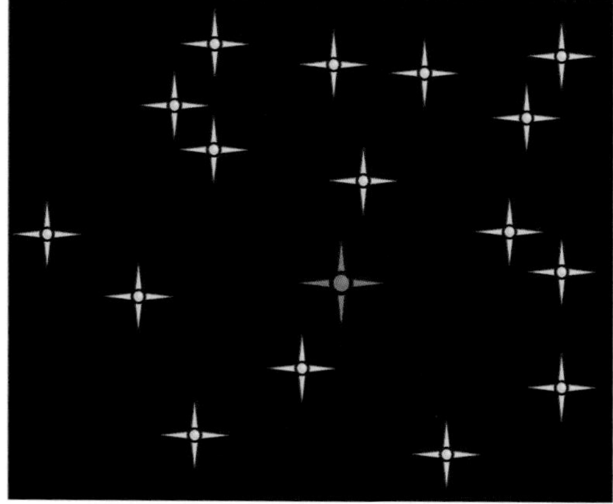

The same part of the night sky a few weeks later. All the stars are in the same places. But the planet has moved.

The word 'planet' means 'wanderer'. Stars stay in fixed places, but planets seem to wander about among the stars.

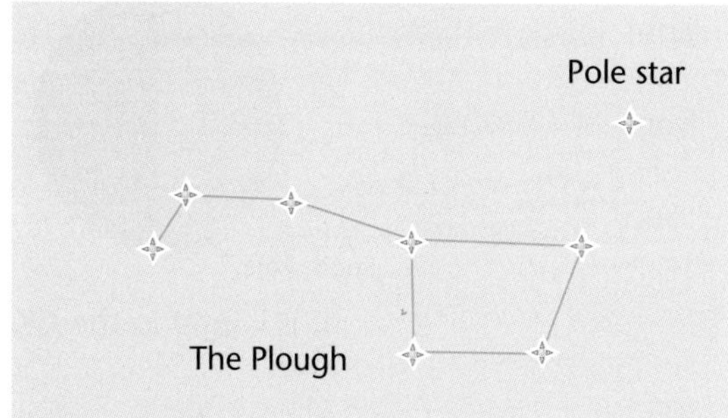

Stars stay in the same patterns. We call these constellations.

Looking through a telescope

If you look at stars and planets through a telescope, you can see another difference. The pictures show what this difference is.

2 (a) What difference can you see?

(b) How can you explain this difference?

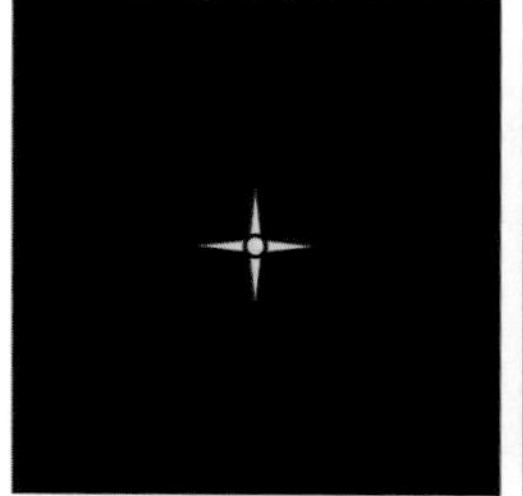

If you look at stars through a telescope, they still look exactly the same size. This is because they are so far away.

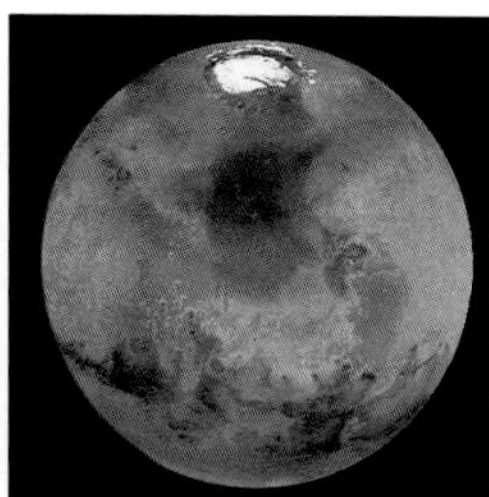

If you look at Mars through a telescope, it looks a lot bigger. This tells us that Mars isn't too far away from the Earth.

Find out:
- which planets you can see in the night sky at the present time;
- where in the sky you can see them.

Stars

Stars are a very long way away. We can see them because they send out huge amounts of **light** energy, just like the **Sun**.

In fact, the Sun is a star. It is our nearest star.

Look at the diagram.

3 Which is the brightest star in the sky (not counting the Sun)?

4 How does Sirius compare with the Sun:

(a) for size?

(b) for the amount of light it sends out?

5 Why doesn't Sirius look as bright as the Sun?

Planets

Planets go round the Sun just like the Earth does. So the Earth is also a **planet**.

Planets are different from stars because they don't give out their own light.

6 Explain how we can see planets.

7 Why do planets seem to wander about among the stars?

REMEMBER from pages 30 and 82

The Sun gives out huge amounts of light energy all the time.

Sirius is the brightest star in the sky. It is much bigger than the Sun and it sends out much more light. But it is a lot further away from Earth.

This diagram is not to scale.

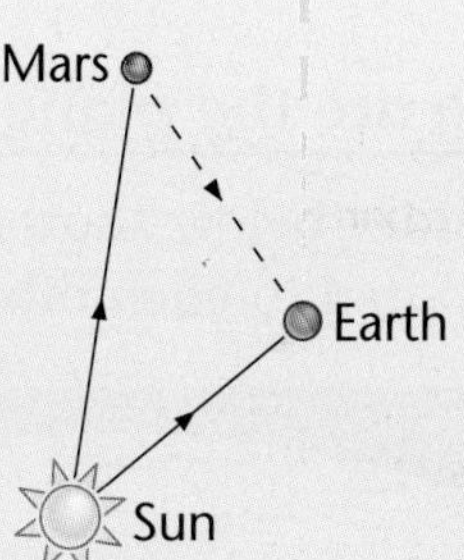

We see planets because they **reflect** light from the Sun. Planets, like the Earth, go round the Sun. So they seem to move among the stars.

WHAT YOU NEED TO REMEMBER (Copy and complete using the **key words**)

Stars and planets

All the stars except the ____________ are a very long way away. Like the Sun, they give out their own ____________.

The planets all go round the ____________. They ____________ light from the Sun.

The Earth is a ____________.

More about stars: C1.2

5.4 The solar system

The planets look like stars, but they aren't stars. They don't give out their own light.

They also go round the Sun just like the Earth does. We say that they **orbit** the Sun.

We call the Sun and all its planets the **solar system**.

1 (a) Copy the table.

Planet	**Average distance from Sun (millions of kilometres)**
Mercury	58
Venus	108
Earth	150

(b) Then add the names of the other planets in order. Start with the planet nearest to the Sun.

(c) Next add the distance of each planet from the Sun.

How big are the planets?

The diagram below shows how big the planets are compared to each other and to the Sun.

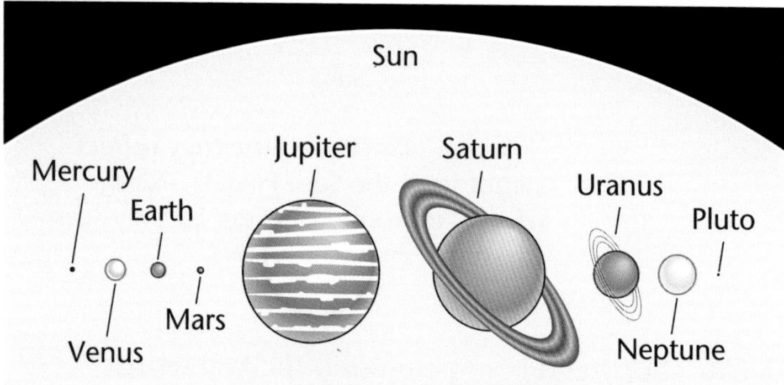

2 Write down the planets in order of size. Start with the biggest planet.

Pluto has a very egg-shaped orbit. Usually it is a lot further away from the Sun than Neptune, but sometimes it is nearer.

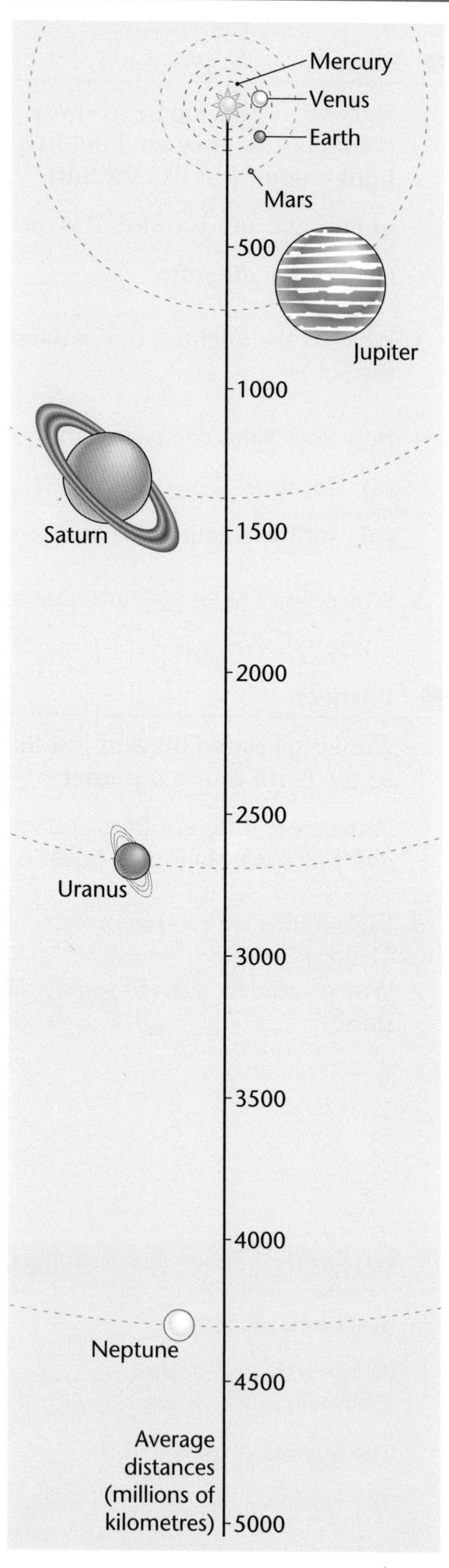

Why do some planets look brighter than others?

You can sometimes see Mercury, Venus, Mars, Jupiter and Saturn without using a telescope. We say you can see them with your naked eye.

The main reason you can see these planets with your naked eye is because they are not too far away. To see the other planets you need to use a telescope.

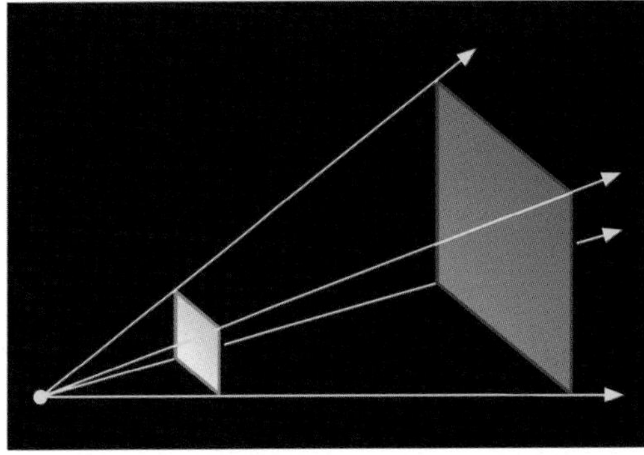

The further light travels, the more spread out it is. So it gets fainter and fainter.

3 You can't see Uranus, Neptune or Pluto with your naked eye. Why not?

4 Why is it difficult to see Pluto even with a telescope?

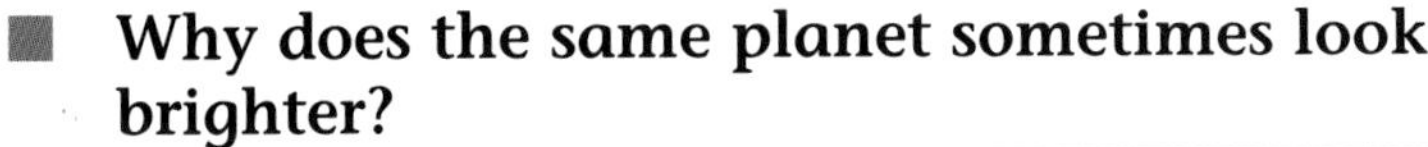

Why does the same planet sometimes look brighter?

Mars looks much **brighter** at some times than it does at other times. The diagrams show where Mars is when it looks bright and when it looks dim.

5 Where is Mars, in relation to Earth, when it looks bright?

6 Why does Mars look bright in this position?

My	Very	Easy	Method	Just	Speeds	Up	Naming	Planets
e	e	a	a	u	a	r	e	l
r	n	r	r	p	t	a	p	u
c	u	t	s	i	u	n	t	t
u	s	h		t	r	u	u	o
r				e	n	s	n	
y				r			e	

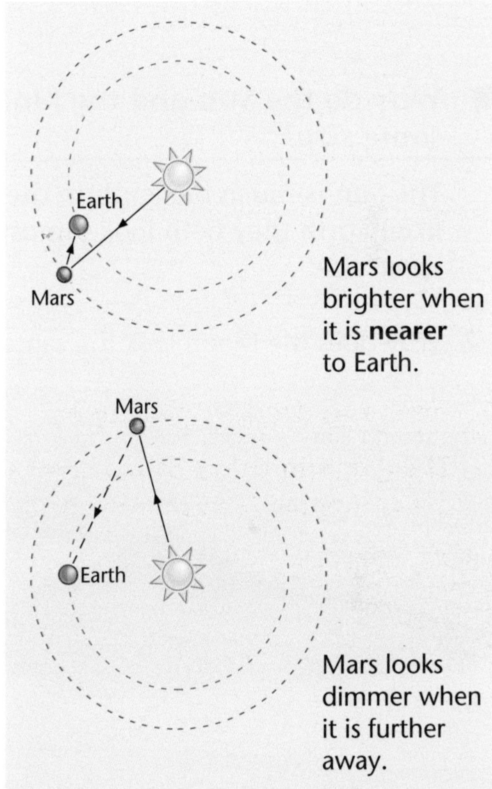

Mars looks brighter when it is **nearer** to Earth.

Mars looks dimmer when it is further away.

WHAT YOU NEED TO REMEMBER (Copy and complete using the **key words**)

The solar system

All the planets, including Earth, go round the Sun. We say they ____________ the Sun.

The Sun and all the planets make up the ____________ ____________.

We can see some planets more easily than others. This is mainly because they come ____________ to Earth. The nearer to Earth a planet is, the ____________ it looks.

More about orbits: C2.3

5.5 Moons

The Earth moves in an orbit round the Sun.

The Moon moves in an orbit round the Earth.

The diagram shows the distances between the Sun, the Earth and the Moon.

1 (a) How far is the Earth from the Sun?

(b) How far is the Moon from the Earth?

(c) How many times further away from Earth is the Sun than the Moon?

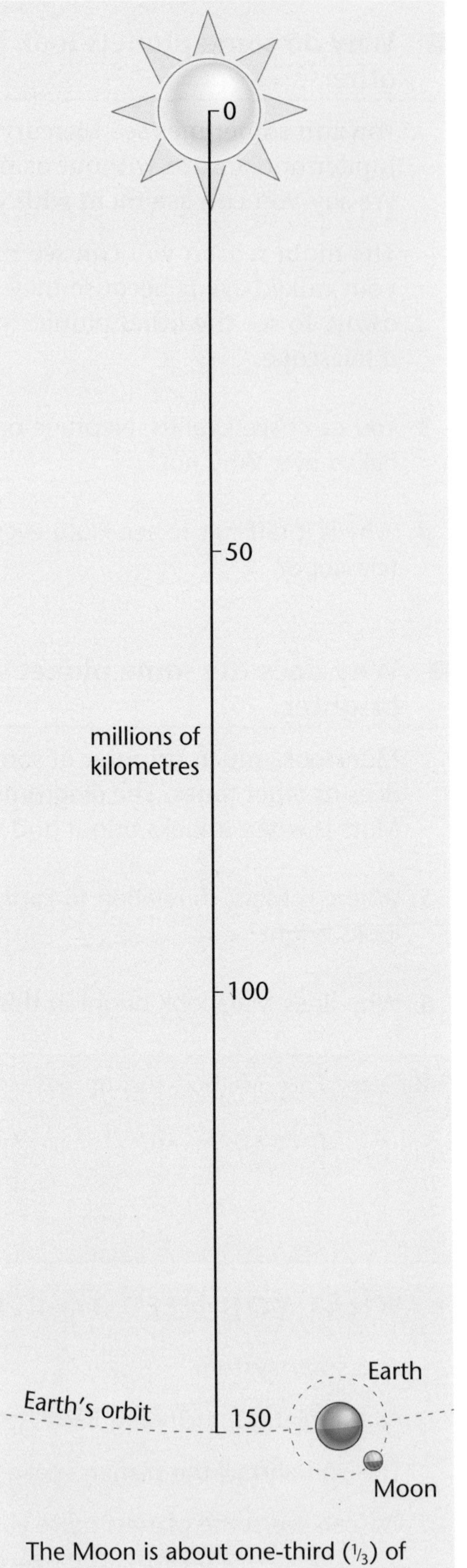

The Moon is about one-third ($^1/_3$) of a million kilometres from the Earth.

Why do the Sun and the Moon look the same size?

The Sun is much bigger than the Moon. But from Earth they both look almost exactly the same size.

2 Why does the Moon look the same size as the Sun?

the Moon in exactly the same direction at a different time

The Sun and the Moon look the same size.

Other 'moons'

It isn't just the Earth that has a Moon. Most of the other **planets** have 'moons' too. The proper name for each of these 'moons' is a **satellite**.

Satellites of another planet were first discovered by Galileo about 400 years ago.

3 (a) Around which planet did Galileo discover satellites?

(b) How many satellites did Galileo discover orbiting this planet?

(c) How many satellites do we now think Jupiter has?

4 Sometimes you can only see <u>three</u> of Jupiter's four biggest satellites. Why do you think this is?

The telescope was invented in 1609. Galileo used a telescope to look at Jupiter.

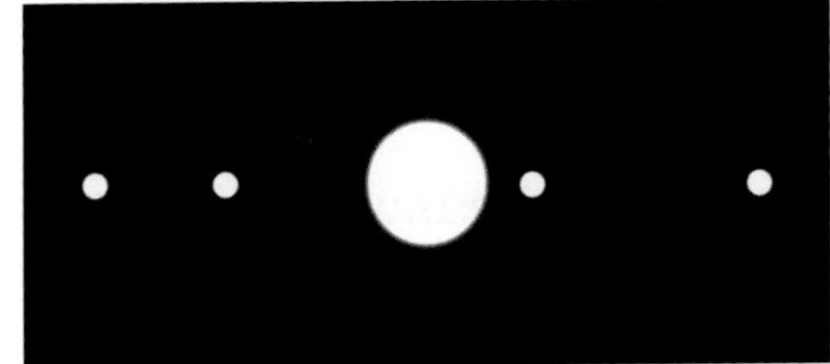

one night in 1610

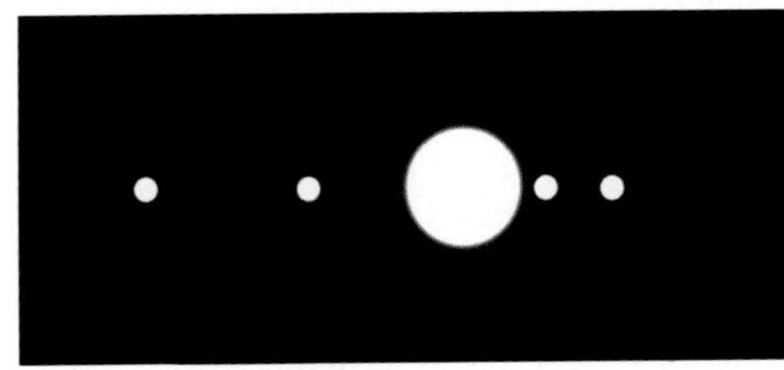

a few days later

12 more satellites of Jupiter were discovered later using more powerful telescopes.

Eclipses of the Moon

Sometimes the full Moon quickly goes dark. We call this an <u>eclipse</u> of the Moon. The diagrams show how this happens.

5 (a) Why can we normally see the Moon?

(b) Why is there sometimes an eclipse of the Moon?

Find out what happens to cause an eclipse of the Sun.

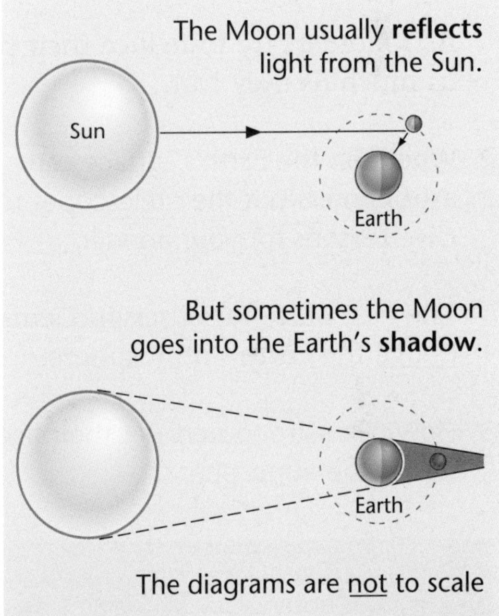
The Moon usually **reflects** light from the Sun.
Sun
Earth
But sometimes the Moon goes into the Earth's **shadow**.
Earth
The diagrams are <u>not</u> to scale

WHAT YOU NEED TO REMEMBER (Copy and complete using the **key words**)

Moons

The Moon is the Earth's ____________.

Most of the other ____________ also have satellites.

We can see the Moon because it ____________ light from the Sun.

An eclipse of the Moon happens when the Moon moves into the Earth's ____________.

More about moons: C1.1

5.6 Artificial satellites

The **Moon** is the Earth's satellite.

Satellites orbit most of the other planets in the solar system. These are called natural satellites.

We can also put **artificial** satellites into orbit around the Earth.

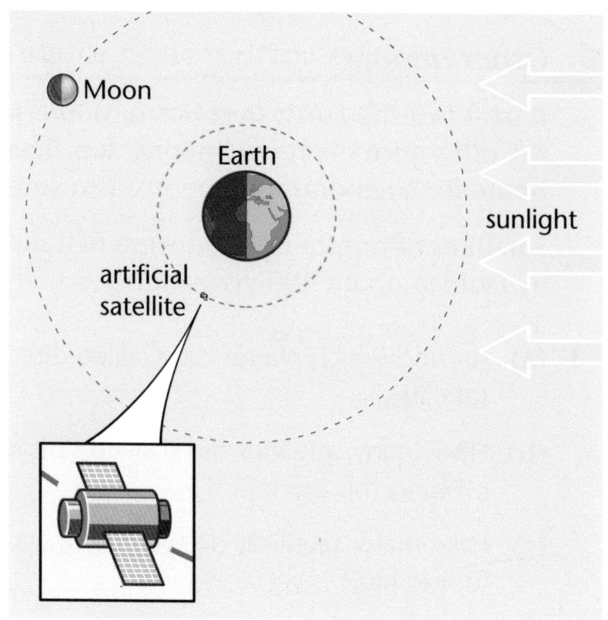

Using satellites to observe the stars

Astronomers often have problems trying to observe stars from Earth. The pictures show you why.

1 Why do astronomers have these problems?

Astronomers try to reduce their problems as much as they can.

2 Where on the Earth's surface can astronomers put their telescopes to do this? Give reasons for your answer.

The best place for observing stars is from above the Earth's atmosphere.

3 How can astronomers get their telescopes above the atmosphere?

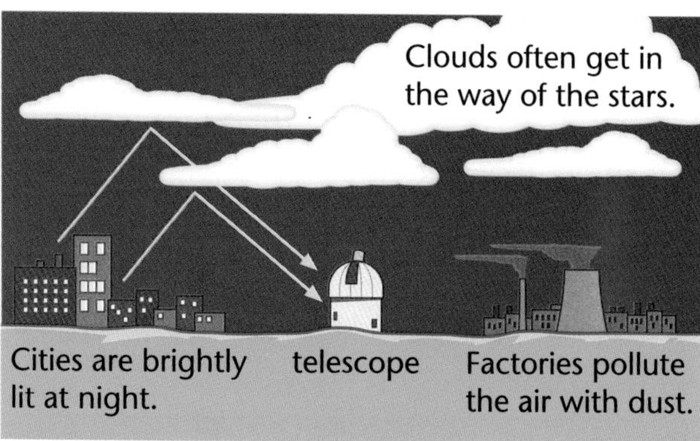

Clouds often get in the way of the stars.
Cities are brightly lit at night.
telescope
Factories pollute the air with dust.

Astronomers have problems trying to see the stars.

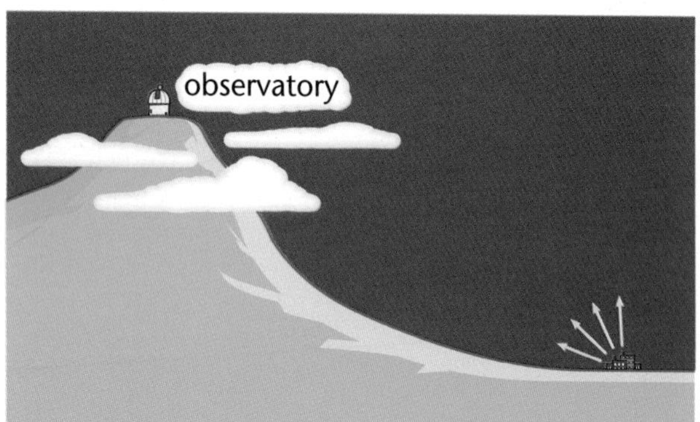

So they often put their telescopes on the tops of remote mountains.

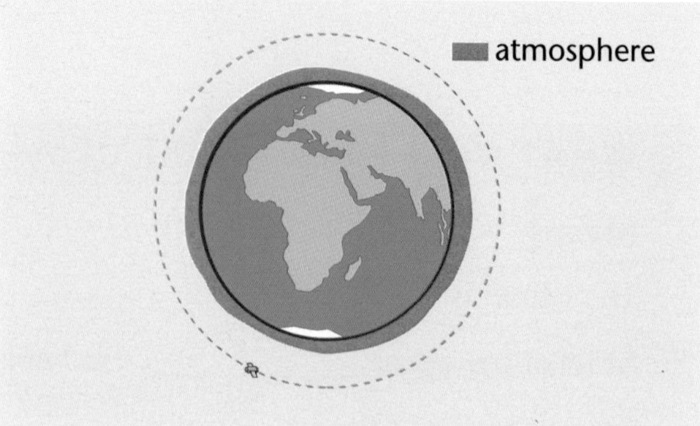

The best place to put a telescope is on a satellite.

Observing the Earth from a satellite

Satellites are useful for **observing** things on Earth as well as things in space. The pictures show some of the things on Earth we can observe from satellites.

4 Write down two of the things on Earth we can observe from satellites.

Satellite image of weather.

Satellite image of fields shows what crops are growing.

The orbit of an observation satellite

The diagram shows the kind of orbit that is often used for an observation satellite. This type of orbit is called a **polar** orbit.

5 Why is this type of orbit called a polar orbit?

As the satellite goes round its orbit, the Earth spins round underneath.

6 Look at the diagram. Then copy and complete the sentences.

The satellite takes ________ to make one orbit of the Earth. So it makes ________ orbits in a day.

The Earth spins round ________ ° each day.
So during one orbit of the satellite the Earth spins round ________ °.

During each 24-hour period, the satellite can observe everywhere on Earth.

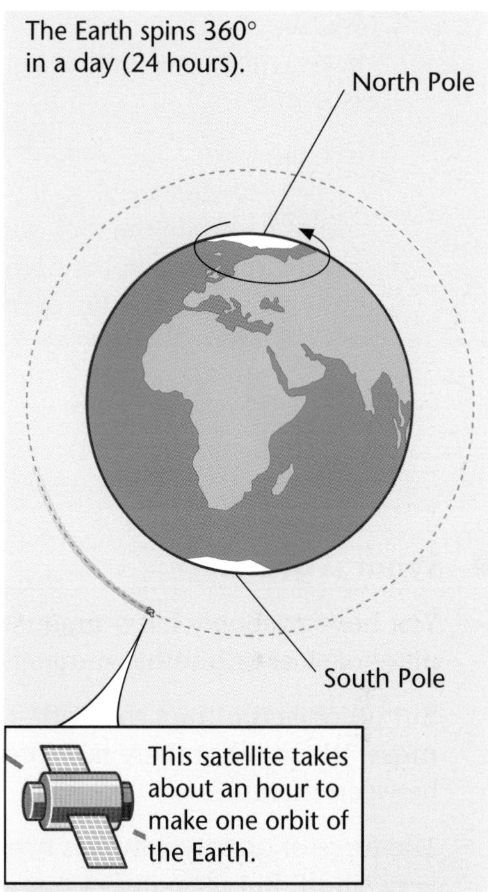
The Earth spins 360° in a day (24 hours).
North Pole
South Pole
This satellite takes about an hour to make one orbit of the Earth.

WHAT YOU NEED TO REMEMBER (Copy and complete using the **key words**)

Artificial satellites

The natural satellite of the Earth is called the ____________.

We can also put ____________ satellites into orbit around the Earth. These can be used by ____________ for observing stars.

Artificial satellites can also be used for ____________ things on Earth.
Observation satellites are usually put into a ____________ orbit.

More about orbits: C2.3

5.7 What holds the solar system together?

The planets move in their orbits round the Sun, and satellites move in their orbits round planets.

All of this can happens because of the force of **gravity**.

The idea that gravity holds the solar system together was first thought about by Isaac Newton.
He also made many other important discoveries.

Find out:

- when Newton lived;
- what gave him the idea about gravity keeping planets in their orbits;
- one other scientific discovery Newton made.

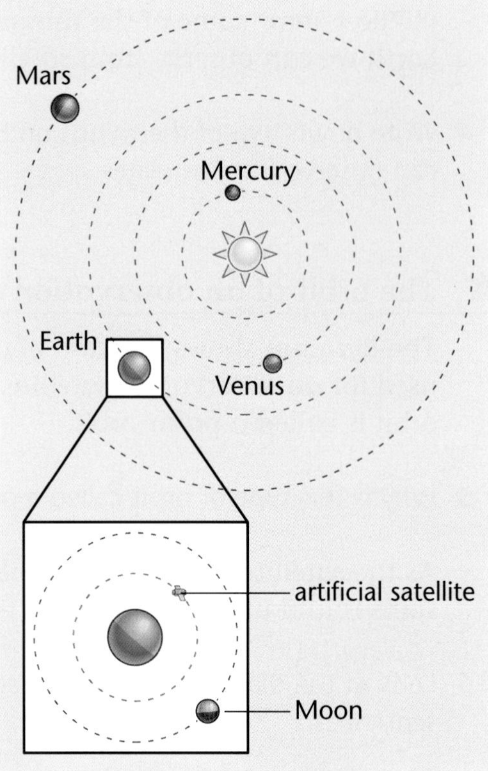

What is gravity?

You have probably felt a <u>magnet</u> attracting a piece of steel or another magnet.

But <u>all</u> objects attract each other because of their **mass**. We say that there is a force of gravity between them.

The force of gravity between two small objects is very small. But if an object has a very large mass, it can produce large forces of gravity.

1 **(a)** Why is there only a very small force of gravity between two apples?

(b) Why is there a very much larger force of gravity between an apple and the Earth?

The force of gravity between two apples is <u>very</u> small. This is because they don't have much mass.

mass = 100g

The force of gravity between an apple and the Earth is quite large. This is because the Earth has a <u>very</u> large mass.

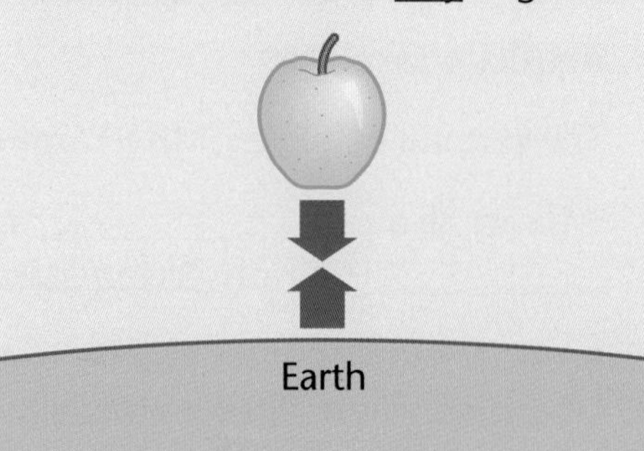

mass = billions of tonnes

Why do planets and satellites stay in their orbits?

Planets and satellites stay in their orbits because of two things:

- because they are **moving**;
- because of the force of gravity.

2 What would happen to planets and satellites if the force of gravity suddenly disappeared?

3 What would happen to planets and satellites if they suddenly stopped moving?

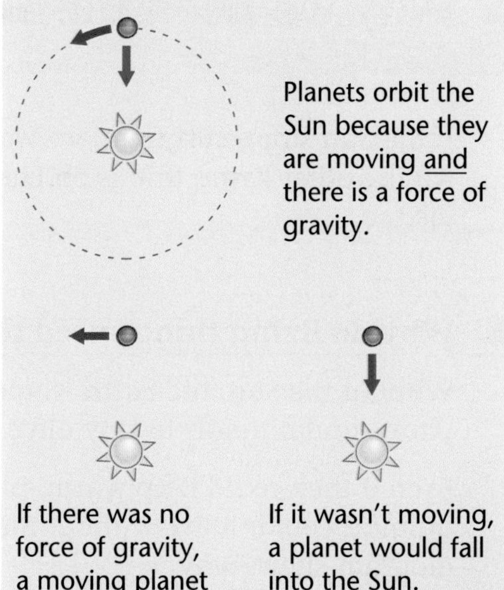

If there was no force of gravity, a moving planet would speed off into space.
If it wasn't moving, a planet would fall into the Sun.

Gravity acts both ways

The Earth attracts the Sun with exactly the **same** size of force as the Sun attracts the Earth.

But the Earth goes round the Sun because the Sun has a much bigger mass than the Earth.

4 Copy and complete the sentences.

A satellite attracts the Earth with the __________ force as the Earth attracts the __________.
But the satellite __________ the Earth because the Earth has a much bigger __________.

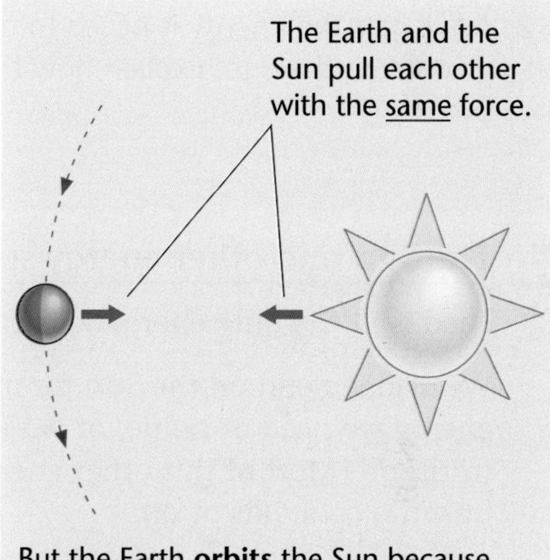

The Earth and the Sun pull each other with the same force.

But the Earth **orbits** the Sun because the Earth has a much smaller mass.

WHAT YOU NEED TO REMEMBER (Copy and complete using the **key words**)

What holds the solar system together?

Planets and satellites stay in their orbits because of the force of ______________, and because they are ______________.

The force of gravity between two objects is the ______________ on both objects.
But a planet has a lot less ______________ than the Sun, so the planet orbits the Sun.

A satellite has a lot less mass than a planet, so the satellite ______________ the planet.

More about gravity: C2.2

5.8 Why we need the Sun

If the Sun stopped shining we would all soon die. All the other living things on Earth would die too.

Why do living things need the Sun?

Without the Sun, the Earth would be too cold for plants and animals to stay alive.

Even if they could keep warm, plants and animals couldn't live without the Sun. The diagram shows why.

1 Write down why plants need energy from the Sun.

2 A fox gets the energy it needs to move and to grow from the Sun. Explain how this happens.

light from the Sun

Plants need **energy** from the Sun to make food. They use this food to grow.

Animals eat plants or other animals. They need the energy stored in this food to move and to grow.

The Sun and other energy sources

Food isn't the only energy we get from the Sun.

We also depend on the Sun for most of the other energy we need at home, at work and for transport. Most of this other energy comes from burning coal, gas or oil.

3 How does the energy stored in coal, gas and oil depend on the Sun?

We can also get energy from the wind, from the waves and from rainwater trapped behind dams.

4 Explain how these other energy sources also depend on the Sun.

Fossil fuels

Coal, gas and oil are fossil fuels. They were formed from the bodies of plants and animals which lived millions of years ago.

Energy from the Sun causes all our weather.

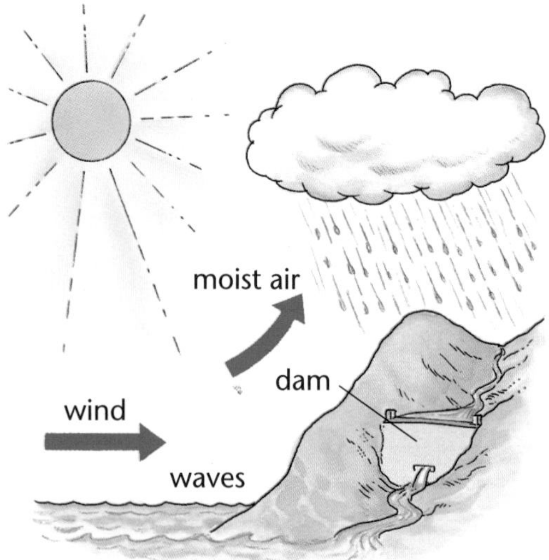

You can read about these energy sources on pages 70–71.

How long has the Sun been shining?

Scientists think that the Sun formed about 5 **billion** years ago. Later, the Earth formed and then life on Earth began.

A billion years is a thousand million years.

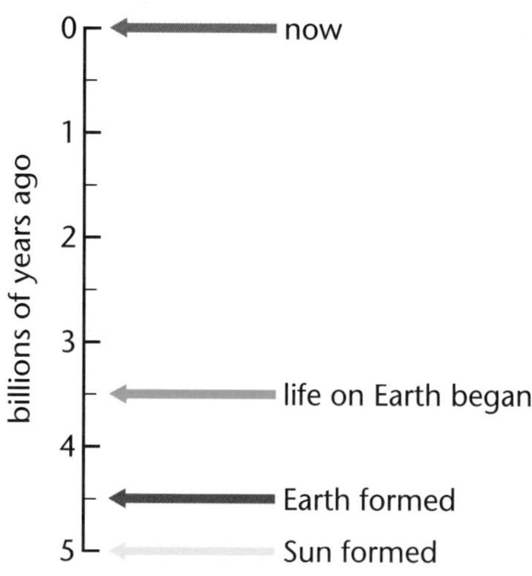

5 Look at the time chart.

(a) About how long ago was the Earth formed?

(b) When did life on Earth begin?

How can the Sun keep on shining for so long?

The Sun sends out HUGE amounts of energy all the time. Only a very small part of this energy reaches Earth.

The Sun isn't just burning like a fire. Otherwise it would have burnt out long ago. The Sun is more like a hydrogen bomb. This releases about a billion times more energy from each gram of hydrogen than just burning it.

Scientists think that the Sun has already used up about **half** of its nuclear fuel.

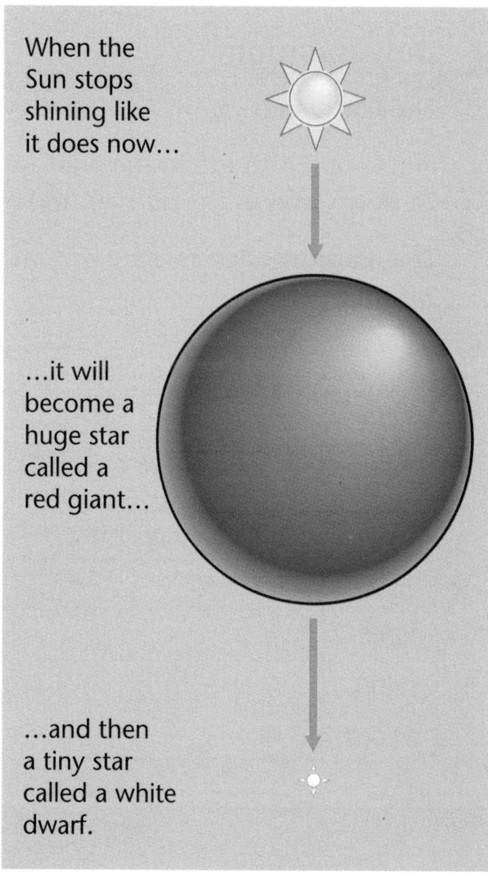

When the Sun stops shining like it does now...
...it will become a huge star called a red giant...
...and then a tiny star called a white dwarf.

6 How many years more will the Sun keep on shining like it is now?

7 Copy and complete the sentences.

When the Sun stops shining like it is now:

- it will first change into a ________ ________;
- later it will become a ________ ________.

WHAT YOU NEED TO REMEMBER (Copy and complete using the **key words**)

Why we need the Sun

All life on Earth depends on ____________ from the Sun.

The Sun has been shining for about 5 ____________ years. During that time it has used up about ____________ of its nuclear fuel.

Follows on from: 5.5

C1.1 The Sun and the Earth's satellites

When it is daytime on one half of the Earth, it is night on the other half. The diagram shows why.

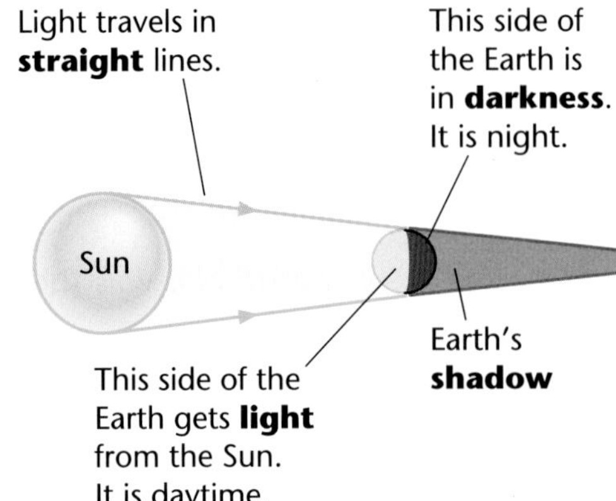
Light travels in **straight** lines.
This side of the Earth is in **darkness**. It is night.
Sun
Earth's **shadow**
This side of the Earth gets **light** from the Sun. It is daytime.

1 Copy and complete the sentences.

Light travels in __________ lines.
So the side of the Earth that faces away from the Sun is in __________.

Day and night

The Earth spins on its axis once every 24 hours.

Places on Earth are in the light for part of each 24 hours and in the dark for the rest.

The diagram shows where Britain is during a 24-hour period.

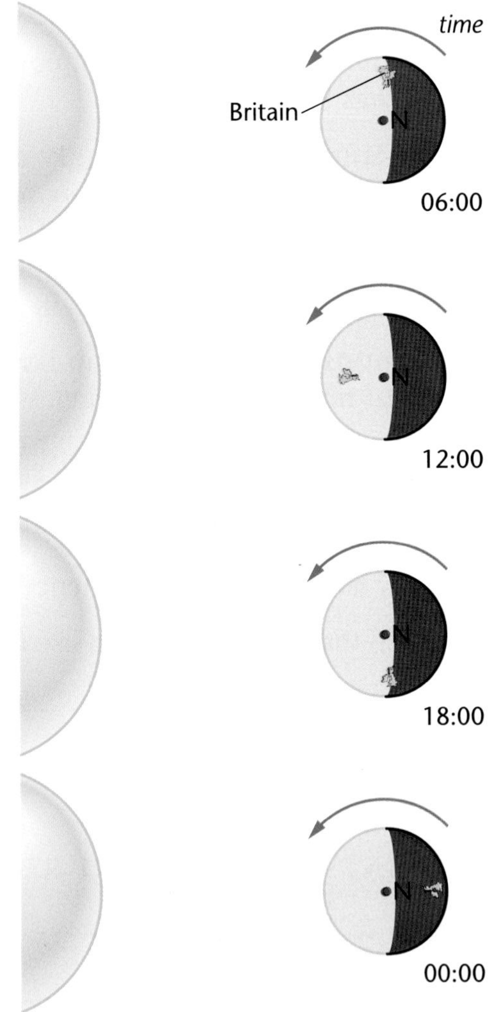
time
Britain
N
06:00
12:00
18:00
00:00

Looking down on the Earth for 24 hours in mid-March.

2 Copy and complete the table using the following words.

coming light   going dark   mid-day   midnight

Time	What's happening in Britain
06:00	
12:00	
18:00	
00:00	

On around March 21st and September 23rd there are 12 hours between sunrise and sunset everywhere on the Earth.
Find out:

- what we call these two days;
- on which date there are the most hours of daylight in the UK;
- on which date there are the fewest hours of daylight in the UK.

Moonlight

The Sun is very hot. So it gives out **light** as well as heat.

The Moon doesn't send out its own light. But we can still see it. The diagram shows why.

3 Why can we see the Moon?

The Moon goes round the Earth. We say that the Moon **orbits** the Earth. We also say that the Moon is a **satellite** of the Earth.

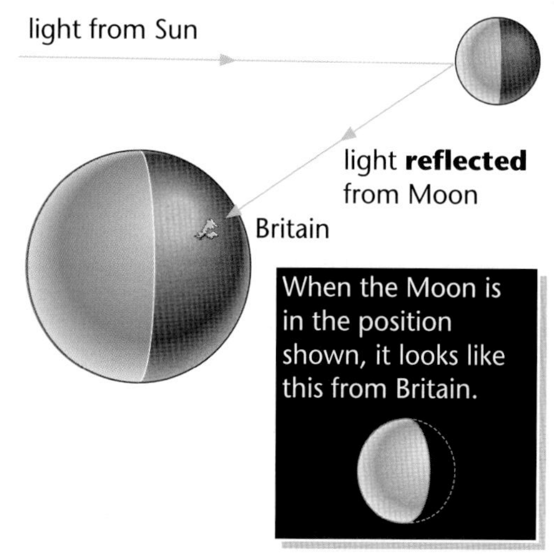

Watching other satellites

Humans have put lots of small satellites into orbit around the Earth. We can sometimes see these satellites in the night sky. They look like stars but you can see them moving.

4 Satellites don't give out their own light. So how can we see them?

The diagram shows a satellite in different positions as it orbits the Earth.

5 (a) Why can't you see the satellite from Earth when it is in position A?

(b) You can see the satellite from Earth when it is in position B. Explain why.

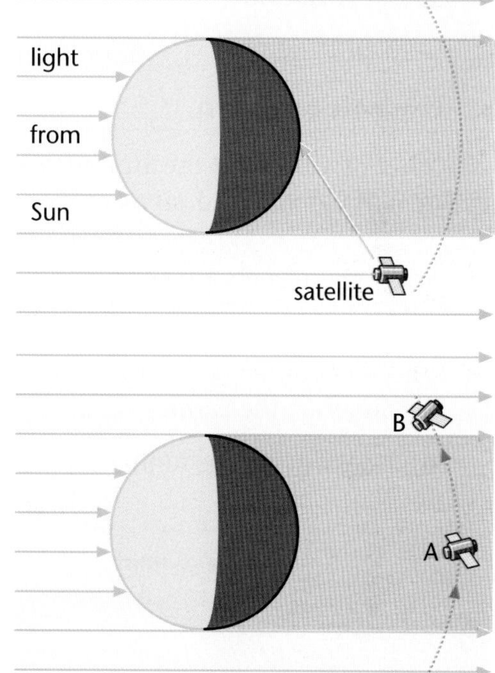

WHAT YOU NEED TO REMEMBER (Copy and complete using the **key words**)

The Sun and the Earth's satellites

The Sun gives out its own ____________.

Light travels in ____________ lines.

The side of the Earth that faces away from the Sun is in ____________.
This is because it is in the Earth's ____________.

The Moon ____________ the Earth. We say that it is a ____________ of the Earth.

We can see the Moon and other satellites because light from the Sun is ____________ from them.

More about shadows: CORE+ C1.9

Follows on from: 5.1, 5.3

C1.2 The solar system and the stars

The Sun is about 400 times further away from Earth than the Moon is.

The Sun's diameter is about 400 times bigger than the Moon's diameter.

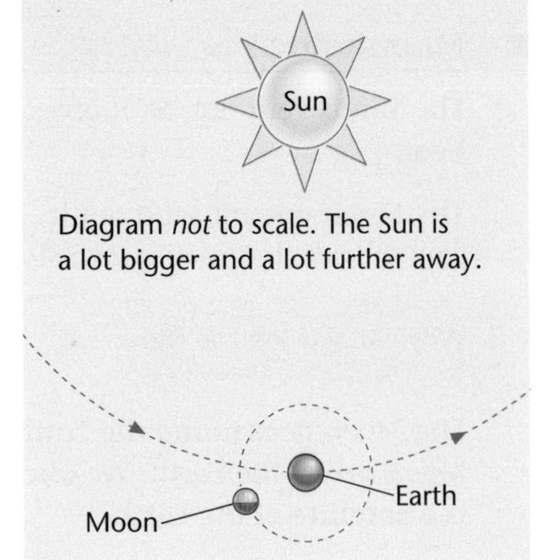

Diagram *not* to scale. The Sun is a lot bigger and a lot further away.

1 Copy and complete the sentence.

The Moon is much nearer to __________ than the Sun is.

2 The Sun and the Moon both look the same size from Earth. Explain why.

The solar system

Other planets orbit the Sun just like the Earth does. We call the Sun and all its planets the <u>solar system</u>.

Planet	Average distance from Sun (millions of kilometres)
Mercury	58
Venus	108
Earth	150
Mars	225
Jupiter	780
Saturn	1430
Uranus	2870
Neptune	4500
Pluto	5900

3 Which two planets are nearer to the Sun than the Earth is?

4 **(a)** Which planet is the next furthest away from the Sun than the Earth?

(b) How many times further away is it than the Earth?

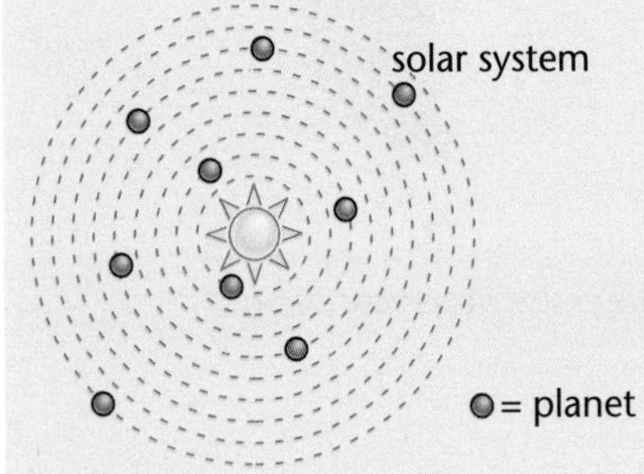

Diagram *not* to scale. The stars are a lot further away.

Stars

The **Sun** is a star.

All the other stars are <u>much</u> further away from Earth than the Sun is.

5 Many stars give out a lot more light than the Sun. But they look a lot fainter. Explain why.

Stars give out their own light. The Sun is our nearest star. The next nearest star is about a quarter of a million times further away from the Earth than the Sun is.

How we see planets

We can sometimes see other planets from Earth. The diagram shows how.

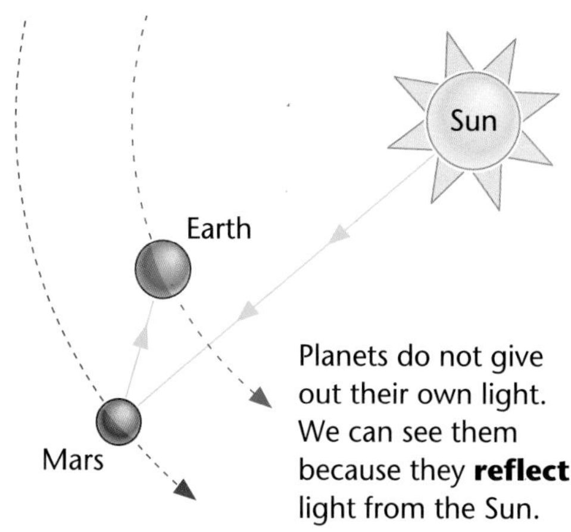

Sun
Earth
Mars
Planets do not give out their own light. We can see them because they **reflect** light from the Sun.

6 Why can we sometimes see other planets?

Planets and stars both look like small points of light in the night sky.

Stars stay in fixed patterns called **constellations**. But planets seem to move slowly through the constellations of stars.

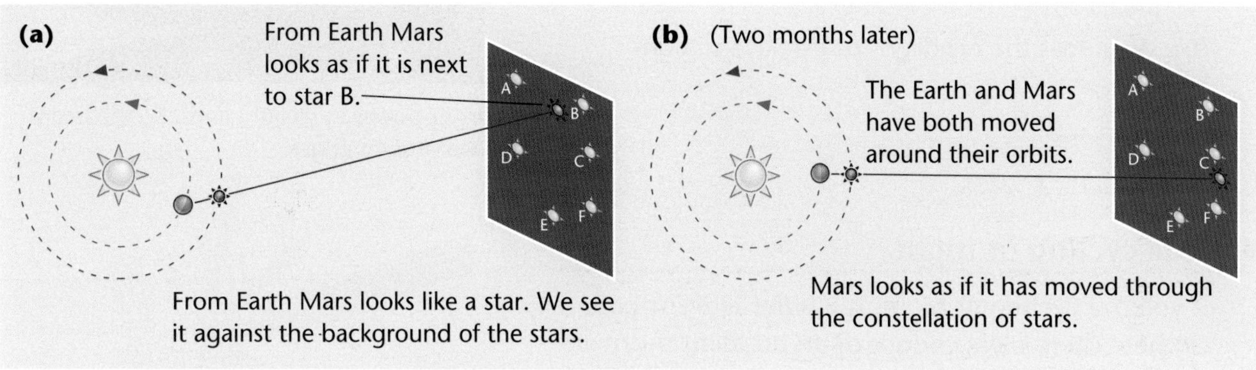

(a)
From Earth Mars looks as if it is next to star B.
A
B
C
D
E
F
From Earth Mars looks like a star. We see it against the background of the stars.
(b) (Two months later)
The Earth and Mars have both moved around their orbits.
Mars looks as if it has moved through the constellation of stars.

7 Copy and complete the sentences.

Planets seem to __________ through the constellations of stars.

In diagram (a), Mars looks as if it is next to star __________.

Two months later, Mars looks as if it is next to star __________.

8 During each night the constellations of stars seem to move across the sky. Why is this?

The Earth **spins** round in one direction.

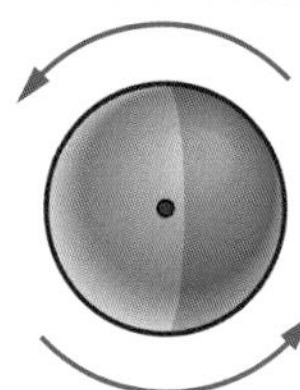

The stars and planets seem to move in the opposite direction.

WHAT YOU NEED TO REMEMBER (Copy and complete using the **key words**)

The solar system and the stars

You can see stars because they give out their own light, just like the __________.

You can see planets because they __________ the Sun's light.

Planets seem to move through the __________ of stars.

The constellations seem to move across the sky because the Earth __________.

More about movements in space: CORE+ C1.10

Follows on from: 2.1, 2.2, 2.3

C1.3 Driving at night

REMEMBER from page 30

We can see some things because they give out their own light.

We can see other things because they reflect light that comes from something else.

At night there is no light from the Sun.

In towns, street lights come on at night. But cars still need lights so that other people can see them.

Outside of towns, cars need headlights so that drivers can see where they are going.

1 Look at the diagram.

(a) Explain how the driver sees the bend sign.

(b) Why does the headlight beam have straight edges?

Light travels in straight lines. So the beam has straight edges.

Safe cycling at night

If you are cycling at night, it is safer to wear pale clothes. There's less chance of an accident if drivers can see you easily.

2 Why can drivers see pale clothes more easily?

3 What happens to most of the light that falls on dark clothes?

White things and pale things **reflect** most of the light that falls on them.

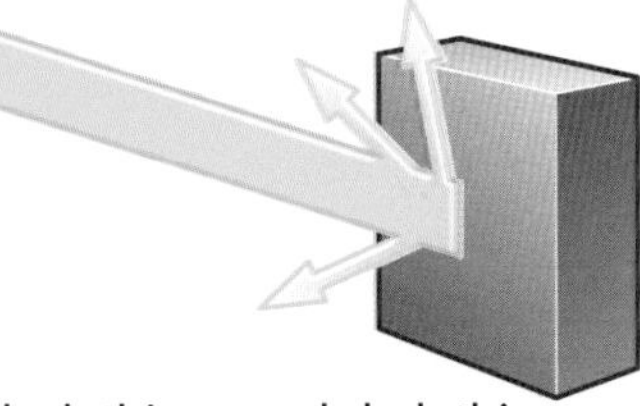

Black things and dark things reflect very little of the light that falls on them. They absorb most of the light.

The photograph shows some other ways to make cycling at night safer.

4 Write down three other things cyclists can do to make sure they are easy to see at night.

Cars and bicycles have rear lights so that people behind them can see them more easily in the dark.

Some cyclists also use rear lights that flash on and off all the time.

5 Why are these lamps better than ones that stay lit all the time?

Cyclists need to be easy to see at night.

Car mirrors

Car drivers need to see the traffic behind them as well as the traffic in front of them. They do this using mirrors.

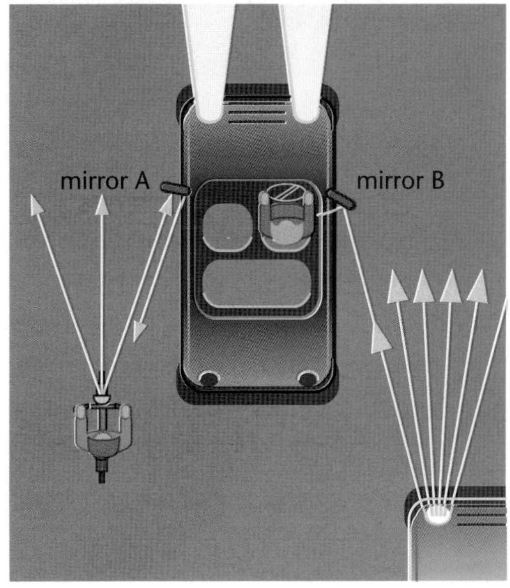

6 Look at the diagram.

(a) Which mirror does the driver of the red car use to see the car that is overtaking her?

(b) When the driver of the red car looks at mirror A she can't see the cyclist that she is overtaking. Explain why.

(c) What should the driver do to mirror A as soon as she gets the chance?

What's special about mirrors?

A mirror and a piece of white paper both reflect most of the light that falls on them. But you can't see things in a piece of white paper.

A mirror and a piece of white paper reflect light in different ways. The diagrams show how.

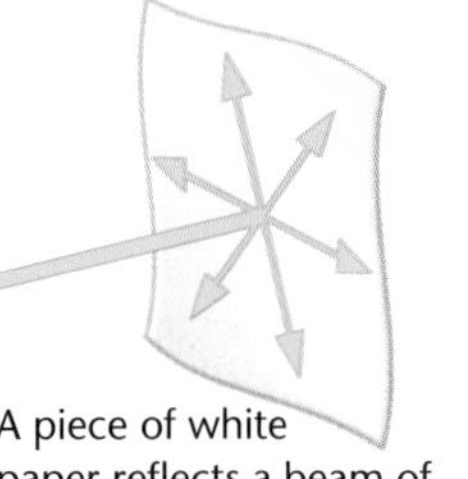

A piece of white paper reflects a beam of white light in *all* directions. We say that it **scatters** the light.

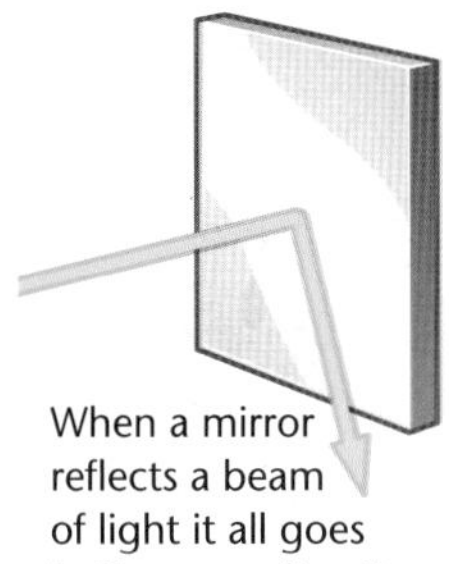

When a mirror reflects a beam of light it all goes in the *same* direction.

7 Copy and complete the sentences.

A piece of white paper reflects a beam of light in all __________.

A mirror reflects a beam of light in just __________ direction. The beam is reflected at the same __________ as it strikes the mirror.

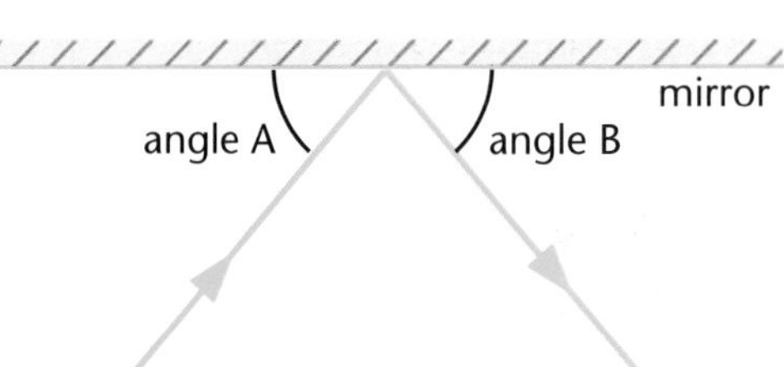

The mirror reflects a beam at the same angle as it strikes the mirror.
So angle A and angle B are **equal**.

WHAT YOU NEED TO REMEMBER (Copy and complete using the **key words**)

Driving at night

White or pale surfaces ____________ light better than black or dark surfaces.

A piece of white paper reflects light in all directions; it ____________ the light.

The diagram shows how a mirror reflects a beam of light.

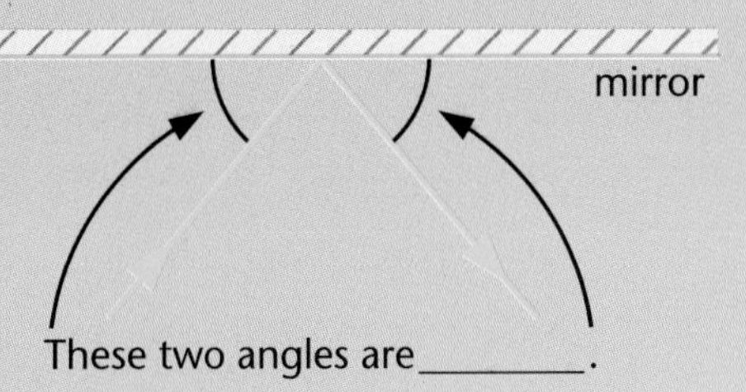

More about mirrors: CORE+ C1.11

Follows on from: 2.4, 2.5

C1.4 Colour

Daylight comes from the Sun. It doesn't look coloured, so we say that it is white light.

Although light from the Sun looks white, it is in fact a **mixture** of many different colours. The diagram shows how we know this.

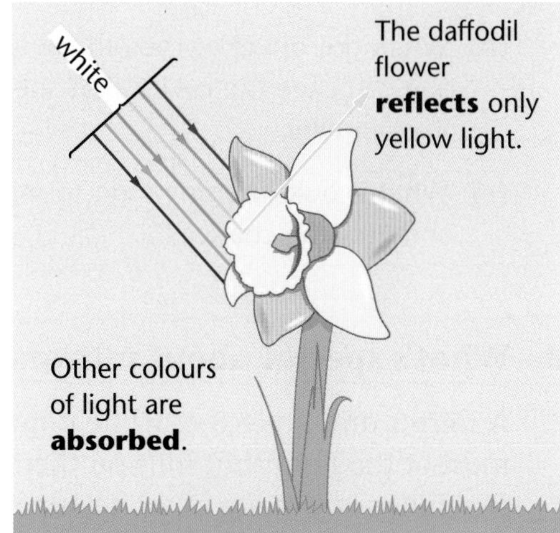

We call these bands of colour a **spectrum**.

1 Copy and complete the sentences.

We can use a prism to __________ white light into colours. The band of colours that we get is called a __________.

Why daffodils look yellow

In daylight, daffodil flowers look yellow. The diagram shows why.

2 Why do daffodil flowers look yellow?

3 Why do the stems and leaves of daffodils look green?

How to make daffodils look black

If you look at a daffodil flower through a blue filter, it looks black. The diagram shows why.

A daffodil through a blue filter.

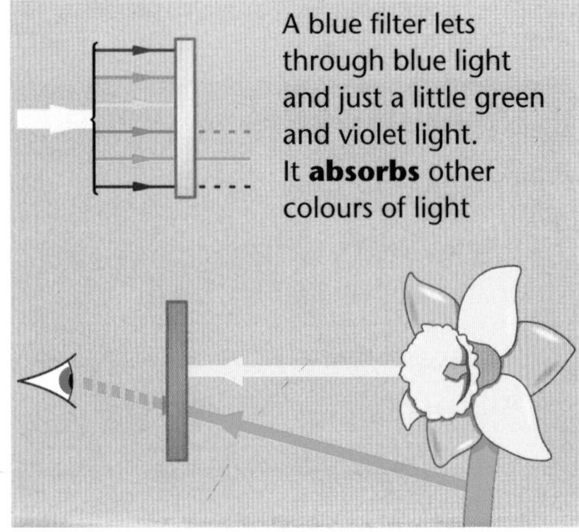

A blue filter lets through blue light and just a little green and violet light.
It **absorbs** other colours of light

4 Copy and complete the sentences.

The blue filter lets through mainly __________ light. But the daffodil flower doesn't __________ any blue light. So it looks __________.

5 The daffodil stem looks dark but not black. Explain why.

Try looking at different colours (for example clothes, cars, lipsticks) under different types of street lights.

Safety: Don't wander about at night unless an adult that you know goes with you.

Daylight and artificial light

Some street lights definitely look yellow.

Light bulbs and fluorescent tubes seem to give out white light. But the mixture of colours isn't quite the same as it is in daylight.

The bar graphs show the differences.

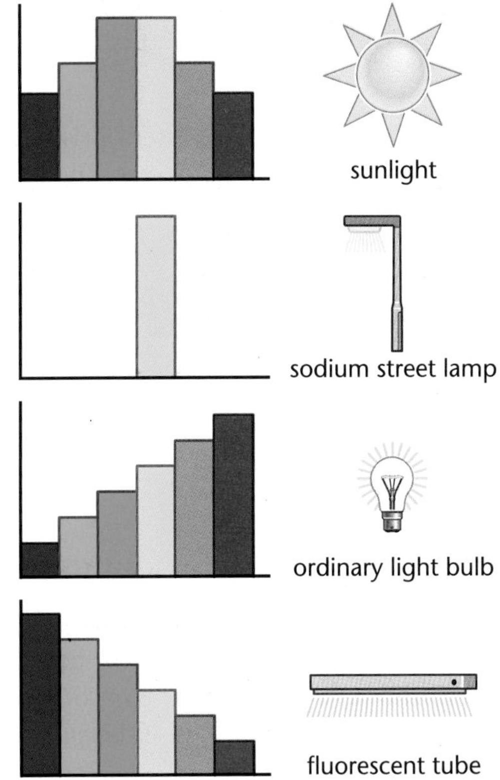

6 Copy and complete the table.

Type of light	Mixture of colours
sunlight	more or less the same amount of all ________ slightly more in the ________ of the spectrum
sodium street light	only ________ light
ordinary light bulb	more of the colours at the ________ end of the spectrum
fluorescent tube	more of the colours at the ________ end of the spectrum

Looking at colours in artificial light

Things often look a different colour in artificial light than they do in daylight.

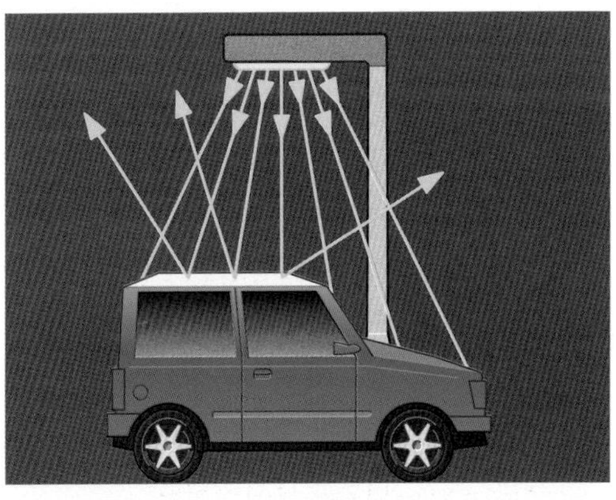

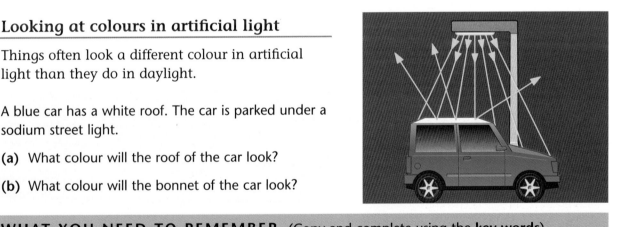

7 A blue car has a white roof. The car is parked under a sodium street light.

(a) What colour will the roof of the car look?

(b) What colour will the bonnet of the car look?

WHAT YOU NEED TO REMEMBER (Copy and complete using the **key words**)

Colour

White light is a ______________ of many different colours.

We can split white light into a ______________ using a glass or plastic prism.
We say that the prism ______________ the white light.

An object looks coloured because it ______________ only some of the colours in white light.
The other colours from the white light are ______________.

A coloured filter only lets some colours pass through; it______________ other colours.

More about mixing colours: CORE+ C1.12

Follows on from: 2.4, 2.9

C1.5 What prisms do to light

You can use a transparent prism to split white light into a spectrum of colours. The diagram shows what happens.

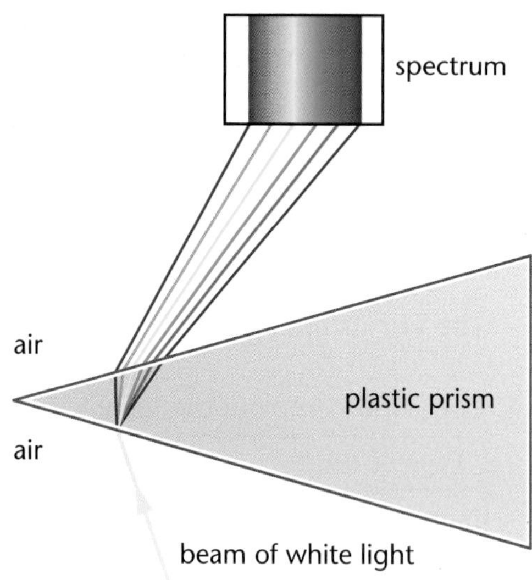
spectrum
air
plastic prism
air
beam of white light

1 Copy and complete the sentences.

The beam of light passes from the air into the __________ that the prism is made from. Then it travels through the __________. Finally, it passes out of the plastic and back into the __________.

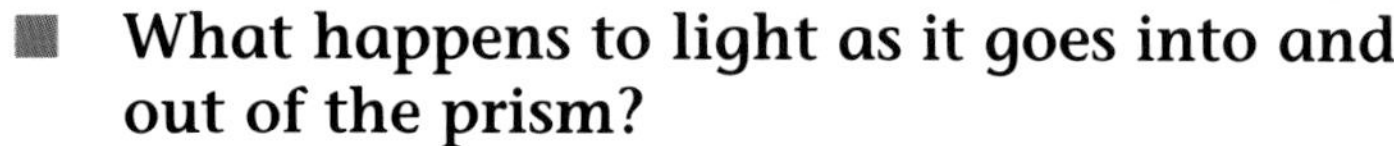

What happens to light as it goes into and out of the prism?

Some pupils shine a narrow beam of blue light through a prism. The beam of blue light bends as it passes into and out of the prism. We say that it is **refracted**.

The diagram shows what happens.

A line at right angles to the edge of a prism is called a **normal**.

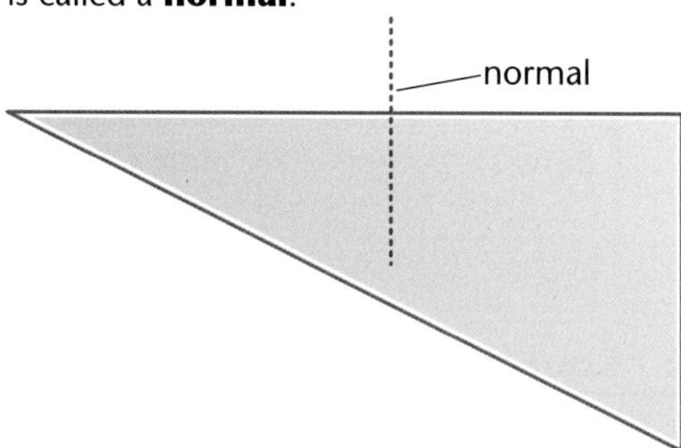
normal

We can use normals to say which way light is refracted (bent).

2 Copy and complete the sentences.

When the beam of light goes into and out of the prism, it is __________.

When it goes into the prism, the light is refracted towards the __________.

When it comes out of the prism, the light is refracted __________ from the normal.

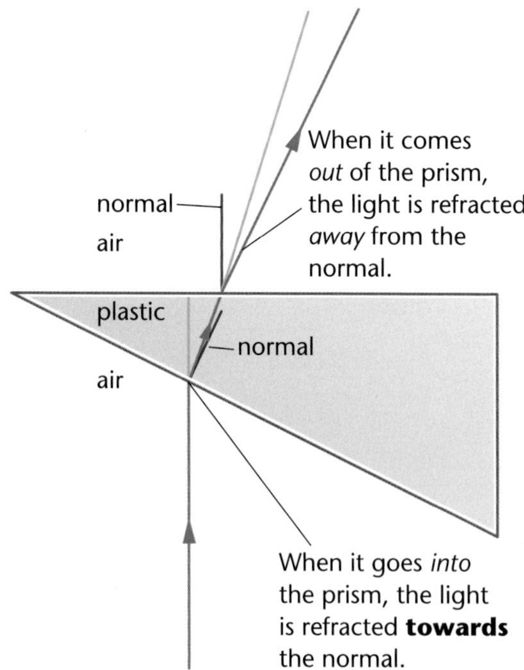
When it comes *out* of the prism, the light is refracted *away* from the normal.
normal
air
plastic
normal
air
When it goes *into* the prism, the light is refracted **towards** the normal.

The prism splits a beam of white light up into colours. This is because the prism refracts some colours more than others.

The colours in white light separate because of refraction as the light goes into the prism. They separate even more because of refraction as the light comes out of the prism.

Which colour does a prism refract most?

The diagram shows what happens to beams of red light and violet light as they pass through a prism.

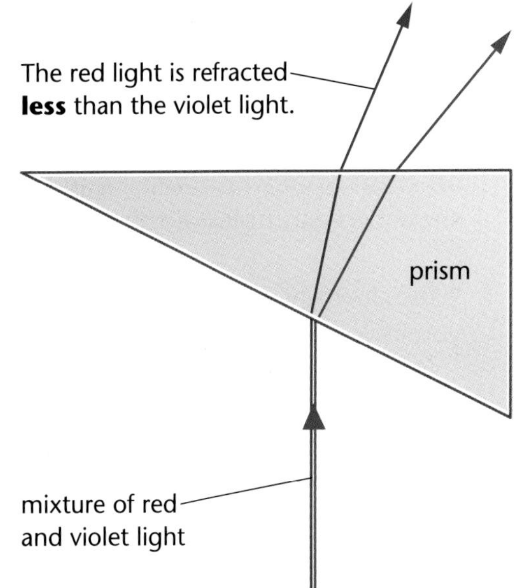

3 Copy and complete the sentences.

Violet light and red light are both __________ when they go into and out of a prism. But violet light is refracted __________ than red light.

Violet light is refracted more than any other colour of light. Red light is refracted less than other colours.

How the prism makes a complete spectrum

The different colours in white light are all refracted different amounts. So when a beam of white light goes through a prism a spectrum is formed.

4 Copy and complete the following. Put the colours of the spectrum in the right order.

refracted least — red

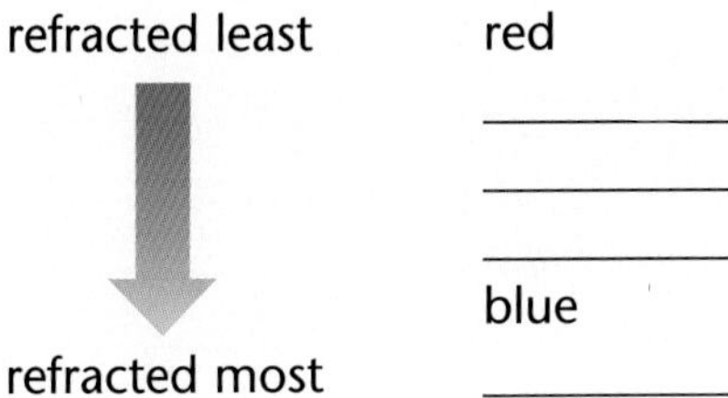

____

____

____

blue
(indigo is sometimes added between blue and violet)

refracted most — __________

There are lots of colours in a spectrum. We usually group them into six or seven broad bands.

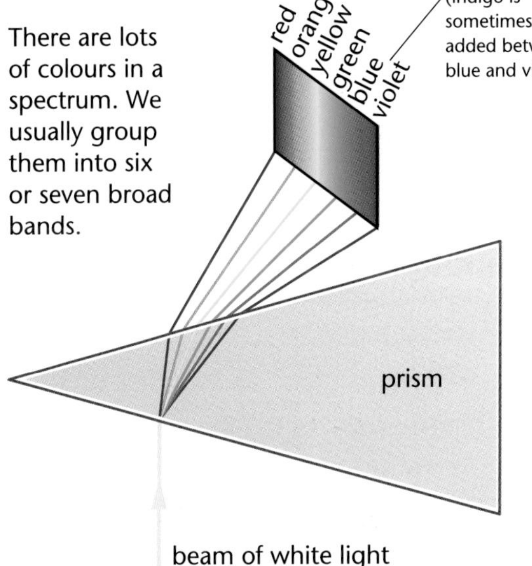

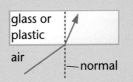

WHAT YOU NEED TO REMEMBER (Copy and complete using the **key words**)

What prisms do to light

When light passes from one substance into another, it is __________.

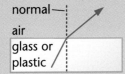

normal
air
glass or plastic

This beam of light is refracted away from the _______.

glass or plastic
air
normal

This beam of light is refracted ______ the normal.

Light at the red end of the spectrum is refracted __________ than light at the violet end of the spectrum.

More about using prisms: CORE+ C1.13

C1.6 'Bent' rulers and 'shallow' water

When you look into water, things can look different from what they really are. The diagrams show two examples of this.

1 Write down two ways that you can be tricked when you look into water.

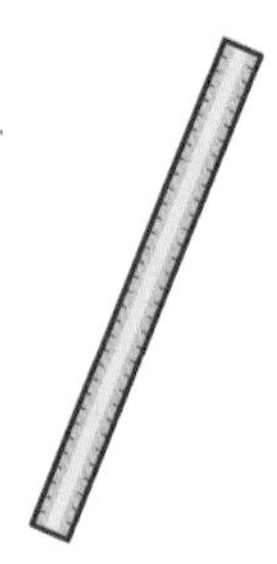

This ruler is straight

But if you dip it into water it looks **bent**.

The water in this pool looks shallow enough for the swimmer to stand up in.

But it isn't really. The swimmer looks smaller too when he is under the water.

Why does the water trick you?

Light bends when it comes out of water into **air**. We say that it is **refracted**. This makes things look different.

2 Copy and complete the sentences.

A narrow beam of light is often called a __________. When a ray of light passes from water into air, it is refracted away from the __________.

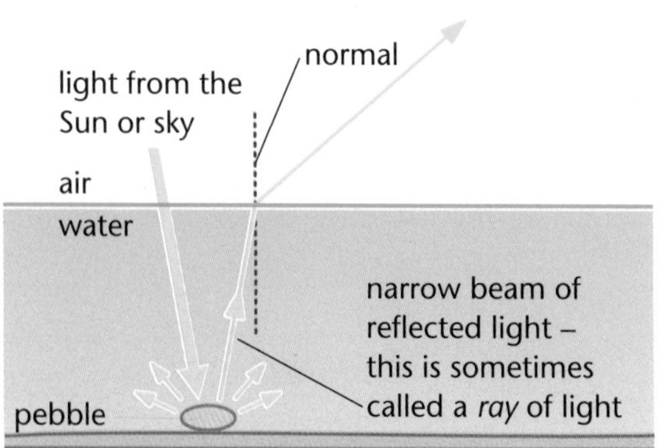

We see this pebble because it reflects light that falls on it.

Why water looks shallower than it is

Water looks **shallower** than it really is because light is refracted as it comes out of the water. The diagram shows what happens.

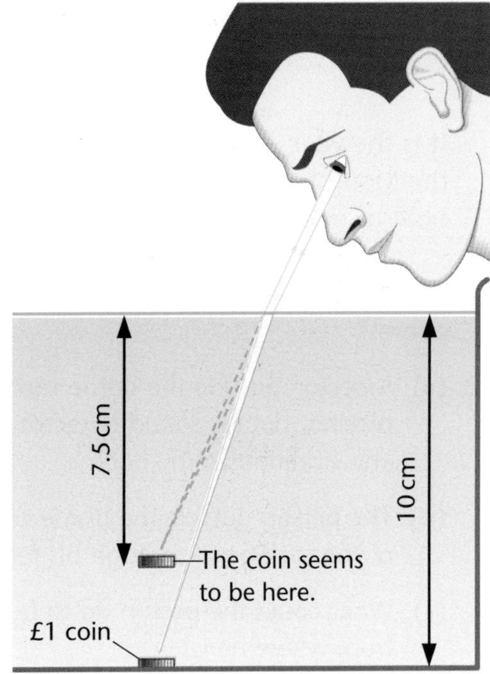

3 Copy and complete the sentences.

Light is refracted as it passes from water into __________. So water which is 10 centimetres deep only looks __________ centimetres deep.

Why a ruler looks bent

Water always looks only three-quarters as deep as it really is. So part of a ruler which is 2 cm below the surface looks as if it is only 1.5 cm below. The same sort of thing happens to all the other parts of the ruler.

The diagram shows where four different parts of the ruler seem to be.

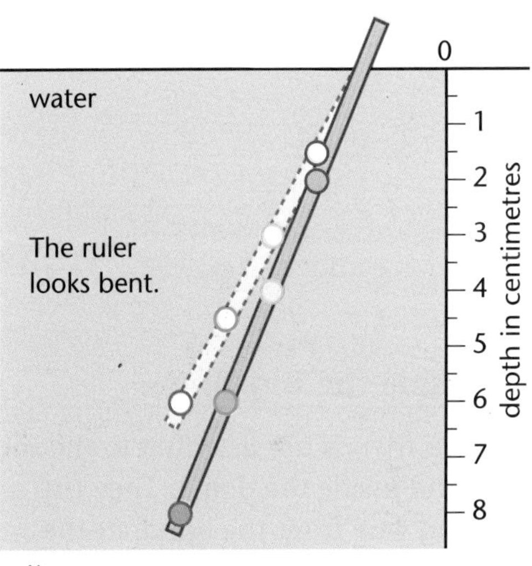

4 Copy and complete the table.

How far under water parts of the ruler really are	How far under water parts of the ruler seem to be
2 cm	1.5 cm
4 cm	
6 cm	
8 cm	

These points are joined on the diagram. They show you why the ruler looks bent.

WHAT YOU NEED TO REMEMBER (Copy and complete using the **key words**)

'Bent' rulers and 'shallow' water

Water always looks __________ than it really is.
A ruler that dips below water looks __________.
These things happen because light is __________ away from the normal when it passes from water into __________.

More about refraction: CORE+ C1.14

C1.7 A rock band on the Moon

It is the year 2120. Humans have been living on the Moon for 100 years. To celebrate, they decide to hold a rock concert in the Big Dome.

1 Why do people on the Moon have to live inside domes?

2 (a) A person outside the dome can see the band playing, but his sound detector doesn't pick up any vibrations. Why not?

(b) The person outside the dome could feel the beat of the rock band through his feet. Explain why.

(c) What could the person do to hear the rock band from where he is?

REMEMBER from pages 38–41

All sounds are made by **vibrations**.

Vibrations can travel through solids, liquids and gases. But they can't travel through empty **space** (a **vacuum**).

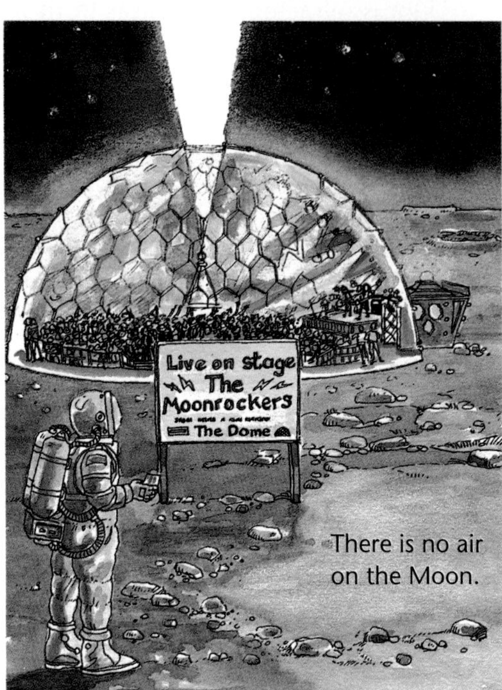

There is no air on the Moon.

Inside the Big Dome

Two friends are listening to the rock band inside the dome. They are a long way from the band, at the opposite side of the dome.

They see the drummer hit the cymbals. A fraction of a second later they hear the sound. Then they hear faint echoes of the sound.

3 (a) Why is there a delay between seeing the drummer hit the cymbal and hearing the sound?

(b) Why do they hear faint echoes?

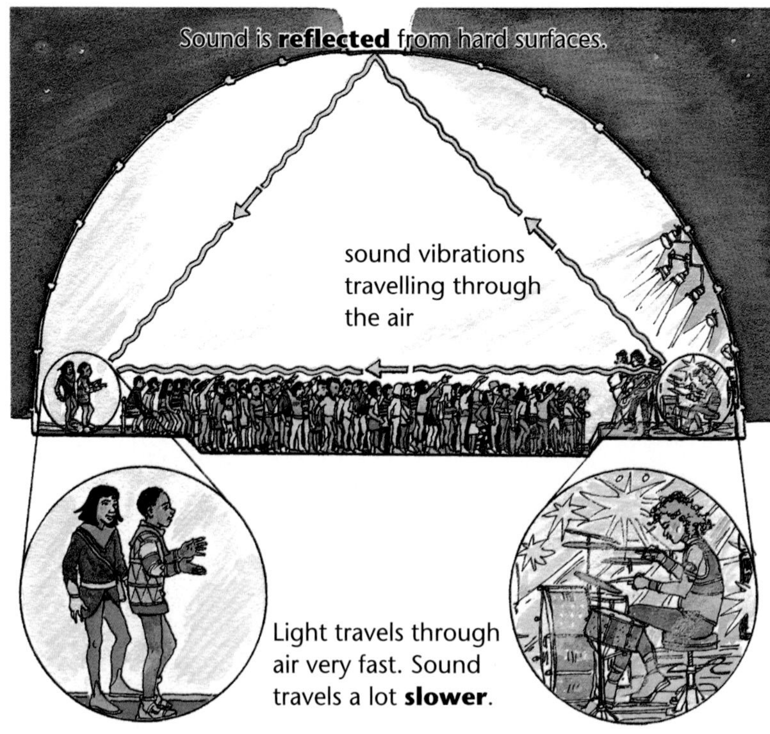

Light travels through air very fast. Sound travels a lot **slower**.

Making the sound louder

Rock music is often played very loud. We say that the sounds are amplified.

You can look at sound vibrations using an oscilloscope. You can then see the difference between a loud sound and a quieter one.

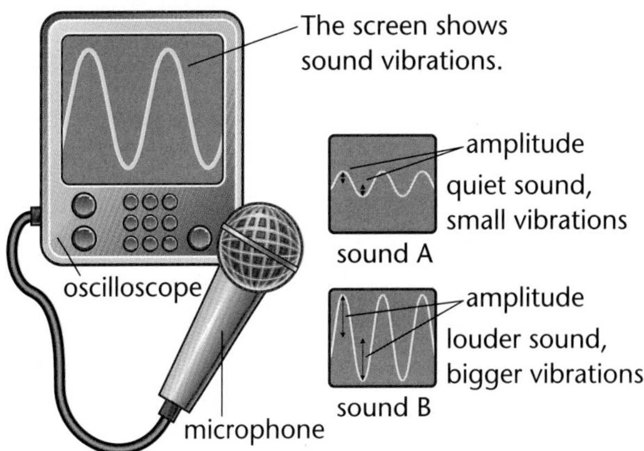

We say that the vibrations in sound B have a bigger ***amplitude****.*

4 What do you need to be able to look at sound vibrations?

5 Copy and complete the sentences.

Sound B is __________ than sound A. This is because the vibrations have a bigger __________.

6 Rock musicians quite often have damaged hearing. Explain, as fully as you can, how this can happen.

REMEMBER from page 41

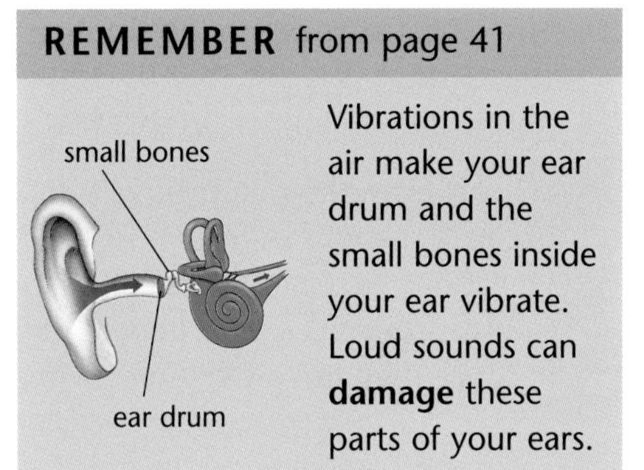

Vibrations in the air make your ear drum and the small bones inside your ear vibrate. Loud sounds can **damage** these parts of your ears.

Back on Earth

During the concert, the dome is on the dark side of the Moon. Back on Earth, people can't possibly hear the band, but they can see the laser lights from the dome.

7 Copy and complete the sentence.

People on Earth can see the laser lights on the Moon because light can travel through a __________.

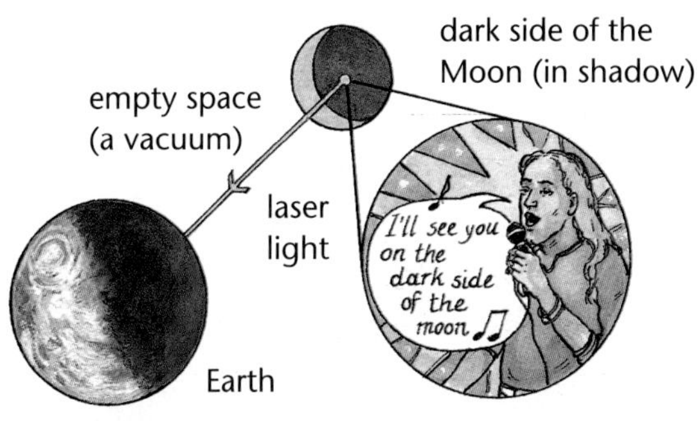

WHAT YOU NEED TO REMEMBER (Copy and complete using the **key words**)

A rock band on the Moon

All sounds are caused by ____________.
These can travel through solids, liquids or gases but not through empty ____________.
Another word for empty space is a ____________.

Sound travels a lot ____________ than light does.

Sound can be ____________, especially from hard surfaces.

Loud sounds are made by vibrations which have a large ____________.
Loud sounds can ____________ your ears.

More about the speed of sound: CORE+ C1.15

Follows on from: 2.8

C1.8 Two different stringed instruments

The photographs show an electric guitar and a cello.

1 (a) Which parts of the guitar and the cello vibrate to make sounds?

(b) What must you do to make these parts vibrate?

High notes and low notes

The guitar strings produce higher notes than the cello strings. We say that the notes played by the guitar have a higher **pitch**.

Sounds from the guitar have a higher pitch because the vibrations are faster. The number of vibrations each second is called the **frequency**. So sounds from the guitar have a higher pitch because they have a higher frequency.

2 Copy and complete the sentence.

Vibrations that have a high frequency produce sounds which have a __________ pitch.

The box shows what the frequency of a vibrating string depends on.

To get vibrations with a higher frequency:

- you can make a string tighter;
- you can make a string shorter;
- you can use a thinner string.

3 The cello plays notes with a lower pitch than the guitar.

(a) What <u>two</u> differences between the strings that you can <u>see</u> would explain this?

(b) What else affects the pitch of the note that a string plays?

REMEMBER from page 40

All sounds are made by vibrations.

When playing a guitar, you pluck the strings to make them vibrate.

When playing a cello (you say this 'chello'), you use a bow to make the strings vibrate.

Tuning a guitar

Each string on a guitar has to be tuned so that it plays exactly the right note.

4 How do you tune the strings?

5 One of the strings of a guitar is out of tune. The pitch is too low. What should you do to make it in tune?

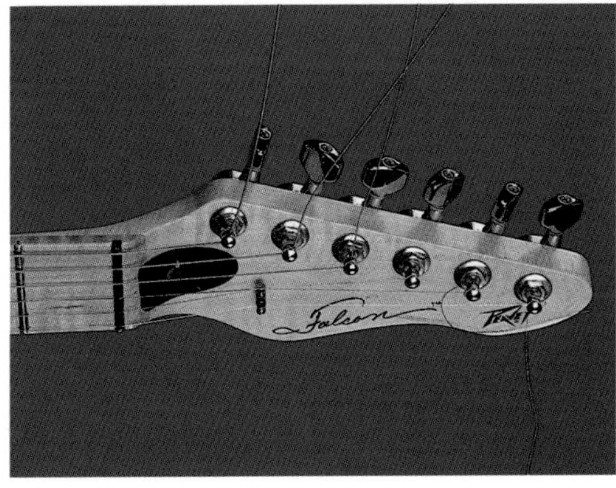

You turn the keys to make the strings tighter or slacker.

Playing a guitar

You can play many different notes on the same string of a guitar.

6 **(a)** What must you do to get different notes?

(b) Explain why this works.

What notes can we hear?

The frequencies of sound that people can hear depend on their age. The information in the box tells you what happens.

An elderly guitarist can hear the highest pitched notes he plays on his guitar. But he can't hear the very high pitched note a grasshopper makes.

7 Why can't the guitarist hear the grasshopper?

REMEMBER from page 43

Most children can hear sounds with frequencies between 20 and 20 000 hertz (20–20 000 Hz).

As you get older, the highest frequency you can hear gradually falls to about 10 000 Hz, or even lower.

WHAT YOU NEED TO REMEMBER (Copy and complete using the **key words**)

Two different stringed instruments

If a string vibrates faster, we say that it has a higher ____________.

Vibrations with a high frequency produce sounds with a high ____________.

You also need to know what is in the 'Remember' boxes.

More about frequency: CORE+ C1.16

CORE +
Follows on from: C1.1

C1.9 Another look at shadows

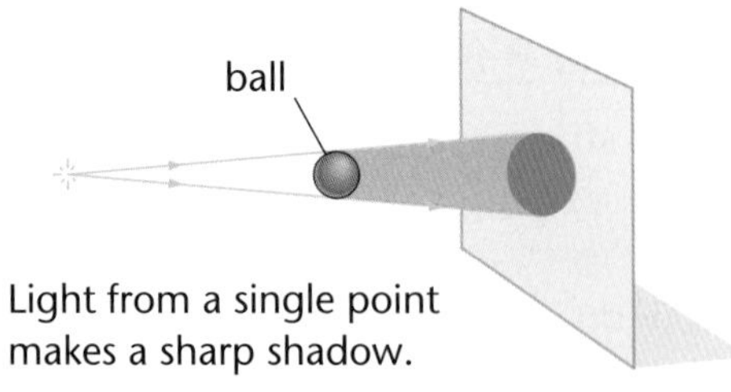

Light from a single point makes a sharp shadow.

We get shadows because light travels in straight lines. Light can't get round things that are in the way.

Looking at the edges of shadows

Shadows cast by light from a light bulb are blurred at the edges. The diagram shows why.

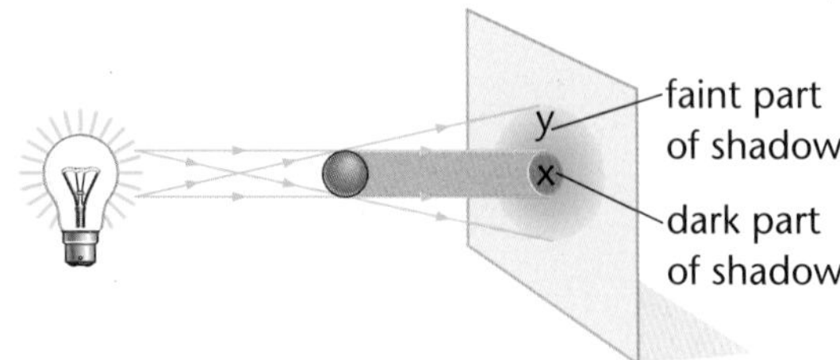

Light from a bulb doesn't all come from one point.

The shadow now has a blurred edge.

1 Copy and complete the sentences.

Light from a bulb doesn't all come from a single __________.

In the centre of the shadow, no light from the bulb gets past the object so there is a __________ shadow.

At the edges of the shadow, light from part of the bulb gets past the object so there is only a __________ shadow.

What you see if you're in the faint part of the shadow

The diagram shows what you see if your eye is at position Y in the faint part of the shadow.

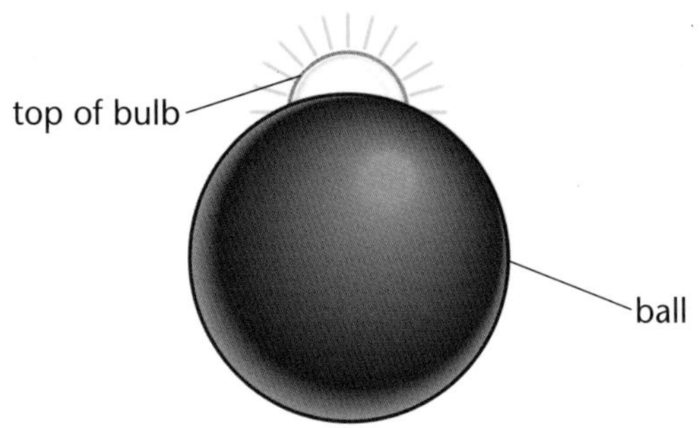

What you can see from Y.

2 Copy and complete the sentence.

From the faint part of the shadow you see just the __________ of the bulb.

3 Draw what you would see from position X in the shadow.

The diagram shows what happens during an eclipse of the Sun.

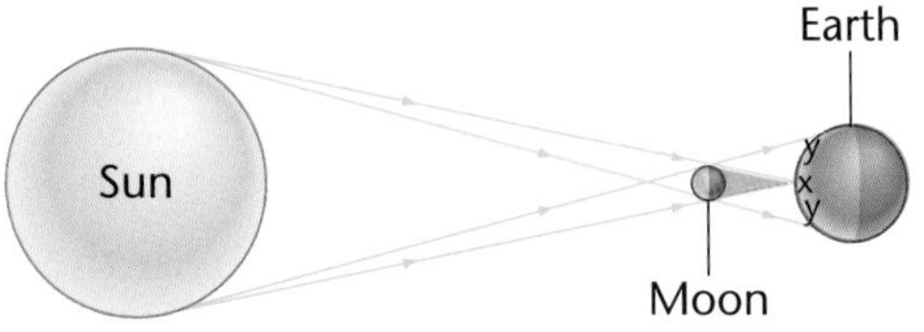

An eclipse of the Sun happens when the Earth is in the Moon's shadow.

x = total eclipse   y = partial eclipse

4 Copy and complete the table.

At a place on Earth in the dark part of the shadow ...	... there is a __________ eclipse.
At a place on Earth in the faint part of the shadow ...	... there is a __________ eclipse.

WARNING!

It is very dangerous to look directly at the Sun, even during an eclipse.

WHAT YOU NEED TO REMEMBER

Another look at shadows

You will need to use Core ideas in different ways like you have on this page.

C1.10 Some astronomical speeds

REMEMBER from page 25

speed = distance ÷ time

so distance = speed × time

Even when you are standing still, you are moving very fast. This is because the Earth is moving in two ways.

The spinning Earth

You are moving all the time because the Earth is spinning all the time. How fast you move depends on where you are on the Earth.

1 How fast, in kilometres per hour, does a person move because of the Earth's spin:

(a) at the equator? **(b)** in London?

(c) at the north pole?

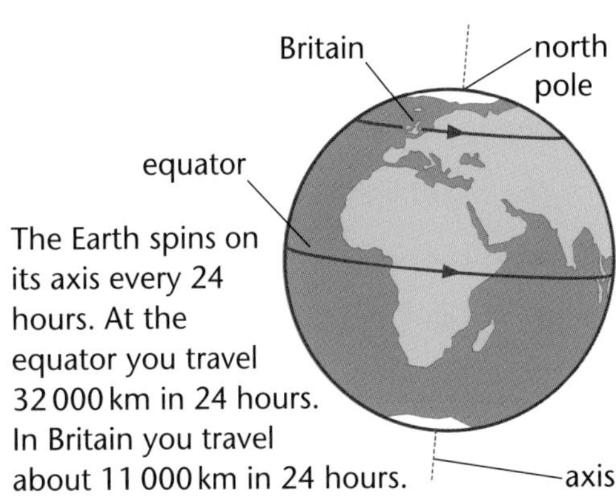

The Earth spins on its axis every 24 hours. At the equator you travel 32 000 km in 24 hours. In Britain you travel about 11 000 km in 24 hours.

The orbiting Earth

The Earth takes a year to orbit the Sun. But it travels a long way in this time. So it still moves quite fast.

2 How fast does the Earth move round its orbit, in kilometres per hour?

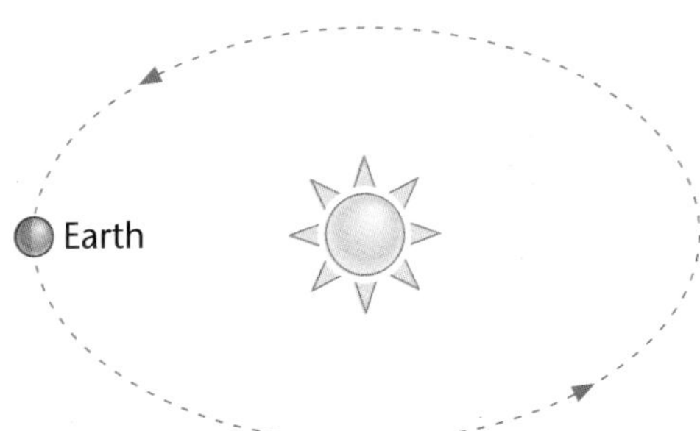

The Earth travels about 1 billion kilometres around its orbit in a year (365¼ days).

How fast does light travel?

The Earth travels a billion kilometres in a year. Light travels a billion kilometres in about an hour. This is 300 000 kilometres every second.

A <u>light-year</u> is the distance that light travels in a year. This is a very long way.

Stars are a very long way away. So we can measure the distances to stars in light-years.

3 About how far away is the next nearest star from the Earth:

(a) in light-years? **(b)** in kilometres?

solar system

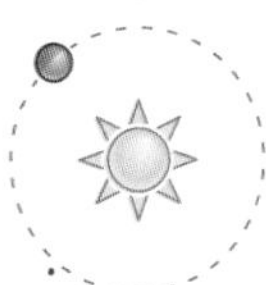

nearest star

It takes more than 4 years for light to travel from the next nearest star to the Earth. We say that this is more than 4 *light-years* away. Diagram *not* to scale.

WHAT YOU NEED TO REMEMBER

Some astronomical speeds

You will need to use Core ideas in different ways like you have on this page.

CORE +
Follows on from: C1.3

C1.11 Using two mirrors together

REMEMBER from page 31

Light is reflected from a mirror at the same angle as it strikes the mirror.

You can put two mirrors together at right angles to each other. A ray of light is then reflected from one mirror on to the other mirror.

The first diagram shows what happens to a ray of light that strikes one of the mirrors at 45°.

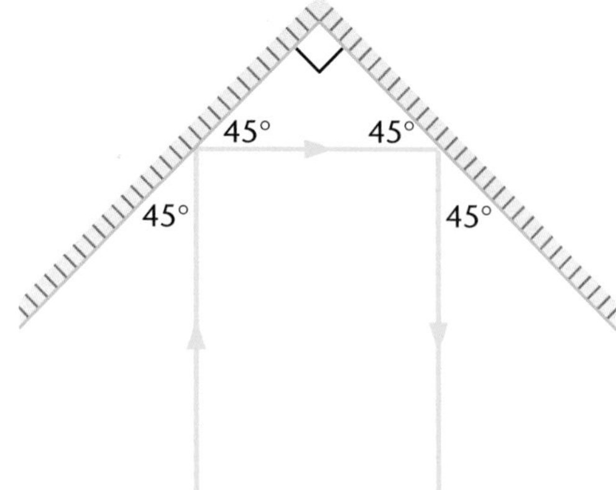

This ray of light ends up travelling in the opposite direction.

1 Copy and complete the following.

The ray of light:

- strikes one mirror at 45°;
- is reflected from this mirror at __________°;
- then strikes the other mirror at __________°;
- is reflected from this mirror at __________°;
- ends up travelling in the __________ direction to the direction it started off.

The second diagram shows what happens to a ray of light that strikes one of the mirrors at 20°.

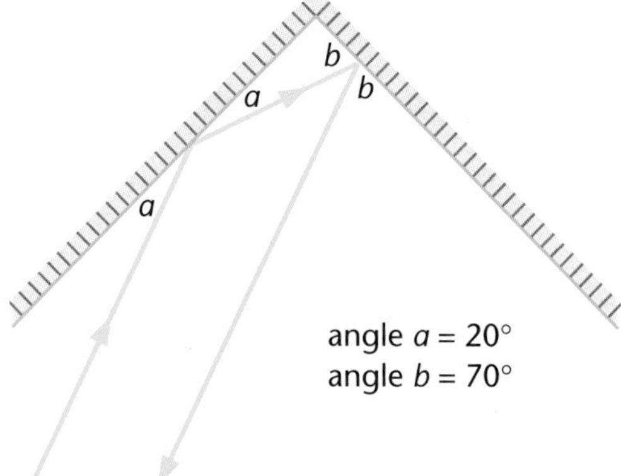

All rays of light end up travelling back to where they came from.

2 What direction does this ray of light travel in after it has been reflected from both mirrors?

It doesn't matter what direction a ray of light is coming from. After it has been reflected from both mirrors, it ends up travelling back to where it came from.

3 Draw a diagram showing how a ray of light that strikes one of the mirrors at 30° is reflected.

4 Describe an example of when we want light to be reflected back the way it came.

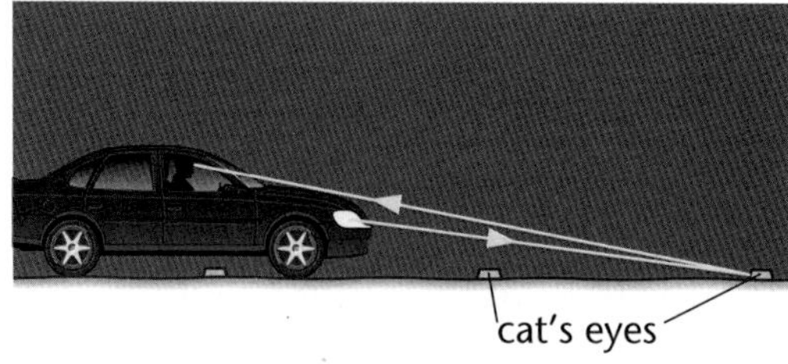

The lanes on a road are marked with cat's eyes. These have reflectors at right angles inside them. So they reflect light back to where it came from.

WHAT YOU NEED TO REMEMBER

Using two mirrors together

You will need to use Core ideas in different ways like you have on this page.

CORE +
Follows on from: C1.4

C1.12 Mixing colours

You can split white light into different colours using a prism. You can then mix all the colours back together again using a second prism. The diagram shows what happens.

This was first done by Isaac Newton to prove that prisms don't make white light coloured.

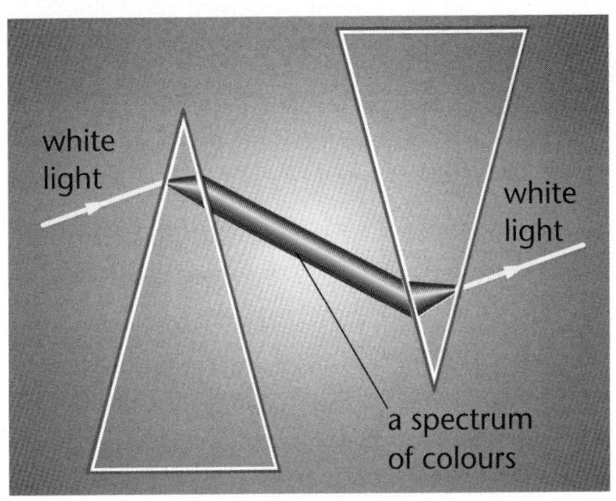

1 Copy and complete the sentence.

If you mix together all the colours from a spectrum, you get __________ light back again.

Each part of this colour wheel reflects its own colour of light.

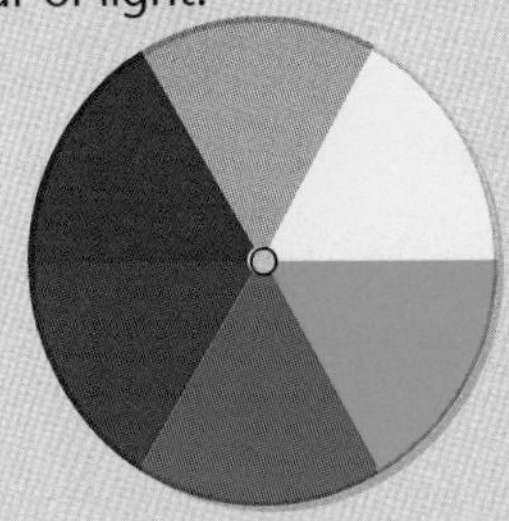

Another way to make white light

The diagram shows a colour wheel. If you spin it quickly, the colours seem to disappear and the wheel looks white. The diagrams show why this happens.

As the wheel spins, every colour is reflected in turn. Your eyes see all the colours added together. So the wheel looks white.

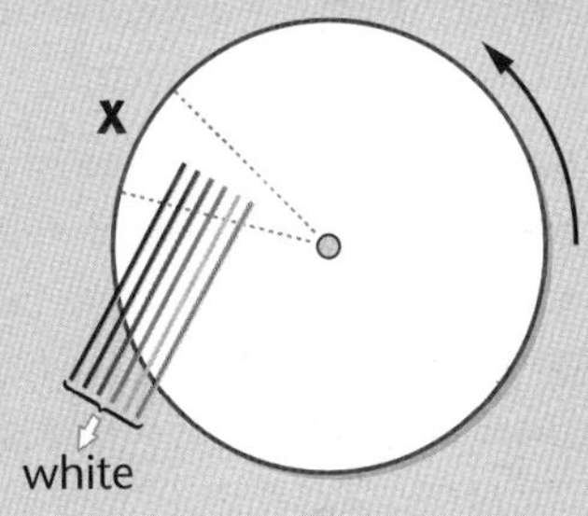

2 Copy and complete the sentences.

The red sector of the colour wheel looks red because it reflects __________ light. The same applies to all of the other coloured sectors of the wheel.

As the wheel rotates, the part of the disc at X reflects first red light, then __________ light, then __________ light, and so on. Altogether it reflects colours from __________ part of the spectrum. So it looks __________.

Mixing paints

The diagram shows what happens when you mix together red and green paint.

This mixture absorbs most of the colours. So it looks very dark (usually brownish).

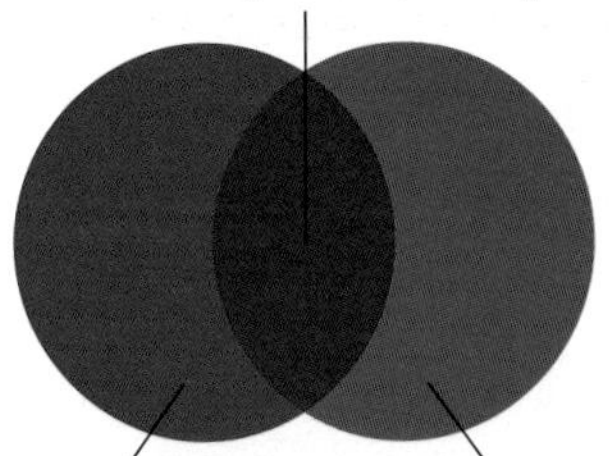

This paint absorbs most of the colours in white light except red.

This paint absorbs most of the colours in white light except green.

3 (a) What colour do you get?

(b) Why do you get this colour?

(c) Why does a mixture of blue paint and yellow paint give a green colour that isn't very bright?

WHAT YOU NEED TO REMEMBER

Mixing colours

You will need to use Core ideas in different ways like you have on this page.

CORE +
Follows on from: C1.5

C1.13 More ways of using prisms

Prisms don't always split white light into a spectrum of different colours. The diagrams show some other things that can happen.

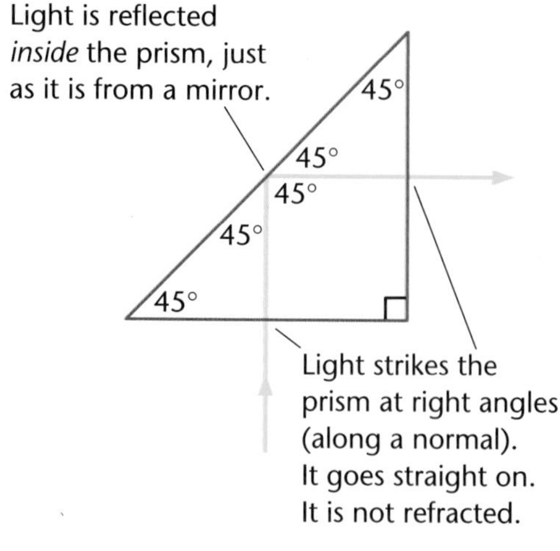
Light is reflected
inside the prism, just
as it is from a mirror.
45°
45°
45°
45°
45°
Light strikes the
prism at right angles
(along a normal).
It goes straight on.
It is not refracted.

1 Make a large copy of the second diagram. Then label it in the same sort of way as the first diagram.

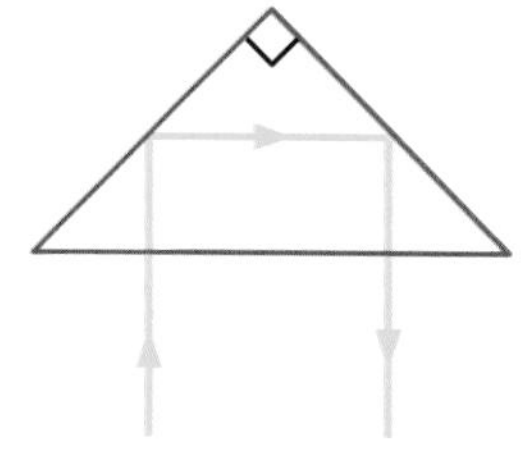

You can use the prism like this to send light back in the opposite direction.

Using prisms in a periscope

You can use prisms instead of mirrors to make a periscope.

2 Draw a diagram of a periscope with prisms instead of mirrors.

You can use a periscope to see over the top of things.

Using prisms in a telescope

To make a telescope, you need to have the right kind of lenses and you need to have them the right distance apart.

The diagrams show two different telescopes made from the same two lenses. These particular lenses need to be 20 cm apart.

3 Copy and complete the sentences.

Binoculars are two __________ side by side.
Prisms are often used so that these telescopes are much __________.

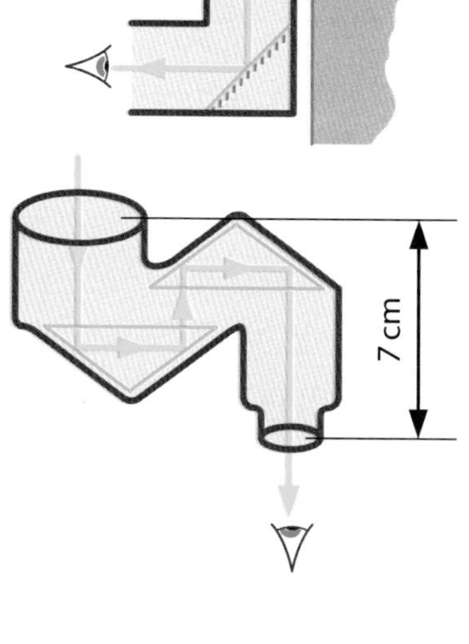
7 cm

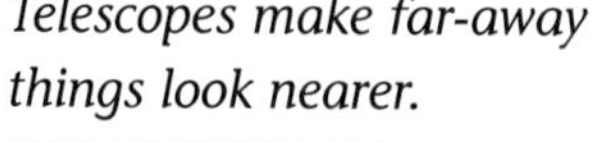

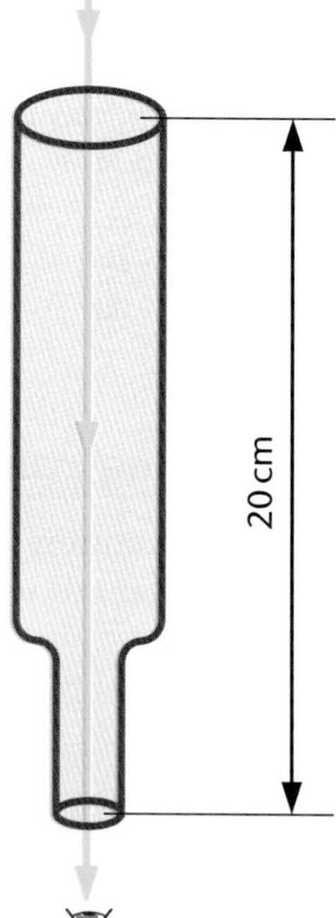
20 cm

Telescopes make far-away things look nearer.

Prisms are often used in binoculars. These are two telescopes side by side.

WHAT YOU NEED TO REMEMBER

More ways of using prisms

You will need to use Core ideas in different ways like you have on this page.

CORE +
Follows on from: C1.6

C1.14 Why glass and plastic look thinner than they are

A piece of glass always looks thinner than it really is. The diagram shows why.

(Don't worry about the very large eye. It just helps to make the diagram clearer.)

REMEMBER from page 108

Water always looks shallower than it really is. This is because light is refracted as it passes from water into air.

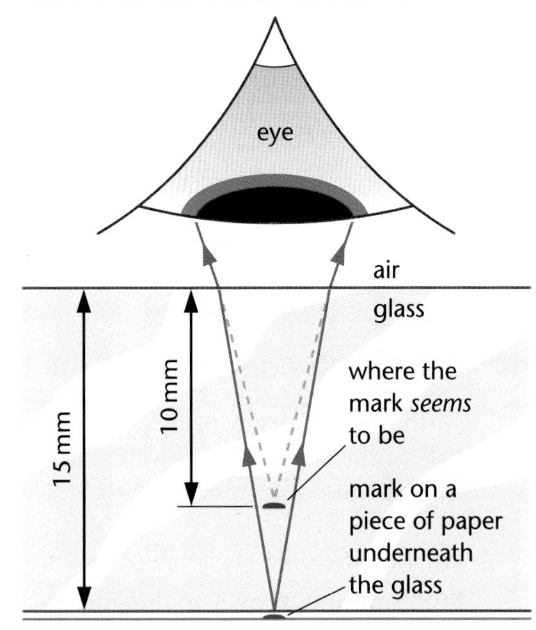

1 Copy and complete the sentences.

The glass is really __________ millimetres (mm) thick but it only looks __________ mm thick. This happens because light is __________ as it passes from __________ into __________.

2 What fraction of its real thickness does the glass seem to be?

The water in a swimming pool only looks three-quarters as deep as it really is.

Measuring how thick plastic looks

The diagram shows a way of measuring how thick a piece of plastic seems to be.

3 Copy and complete the sentences.

You have to move the microscope up __________ mm to bring the mark back into focus. So the mark seems to be ________ mm higher up than it really is.

The plastic is really ________ mm thick, but it only looks ________ mm thick.

4 What fraction of its real thickness does the plastic seem to be?

5 The more a substance refracts light, the less thick or deep it seems to be. Which substance – glass, water or plastic – refracts light (a) most, (b) least?

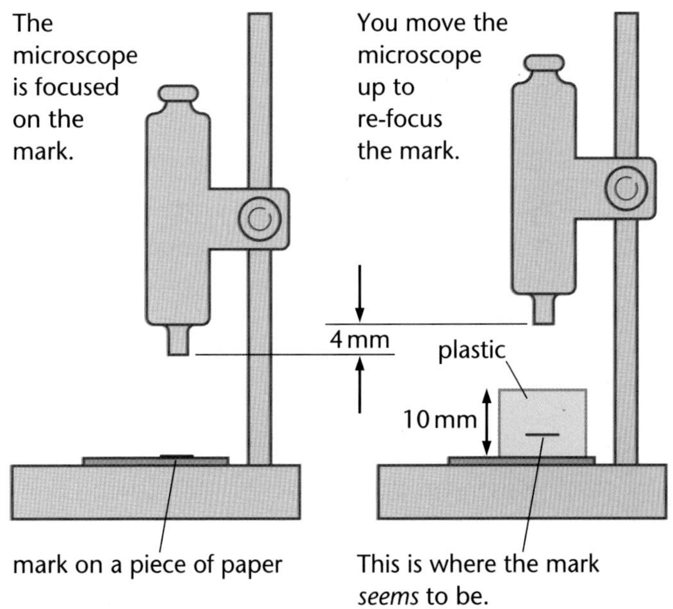

WHAT YOU NEED TO REMEMBER

Why glass and plastic look thinner than they are

You will need to use Core ideas in different ways like you have on this page.

C1.15 The speed of sound

REMEMBER from page 25

speed = distance ÷ time

Sound travels quite fast through the air.

But light travels through air very fast indeed. It takes light hardly any time at all to travel a few kilometres.

This gives us a way of measuring the speed of sound. The diagram shows what we can do.

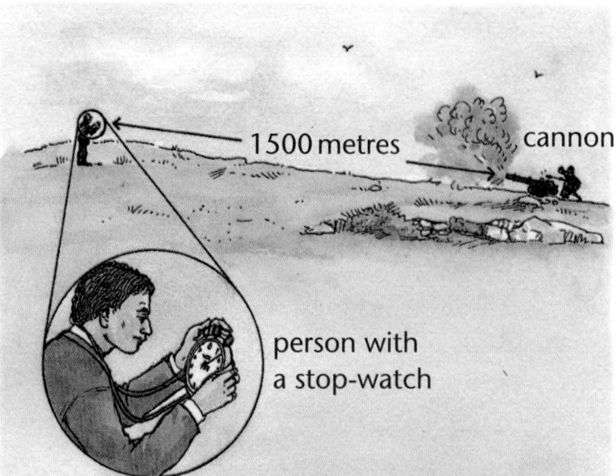

The person with the watch starts it when they see the smoke. They stop the watch when they hear the sound. The watch shows 5 seconds.

1 Copy and complete the following.

The sound travels ________ metres in ________ seconds.

So its speed is ________ ÷ ________
= ________ metres per second

Back to the dark side of the Moon

At the rock concert in the Big Dome, people at the far side of the dome hear the cymbal $\frac{1}{3}$ of a second after they see the drummer hit it.

2 Work out how far away the people are from the drummer. (Show your working.)

Note: The speed of sound through air is not always the same. It depends, for example, on the pressure of the air.

High speed jets

The speed of an aircraft is often compared to the speed of sound. A speed of Mach 2 means twice the speed of sound.

Blackbird can reach speeds of around Mach 3.

3 What is the speed of Blackbird:

(a) in metres per second?

(b) in kilometres per hour?

WHAT YOU NEED TO REMEMBER

The speed of sound

You will need to use Core ideas in different ways like you have on this page.

C1.16 More about frequency

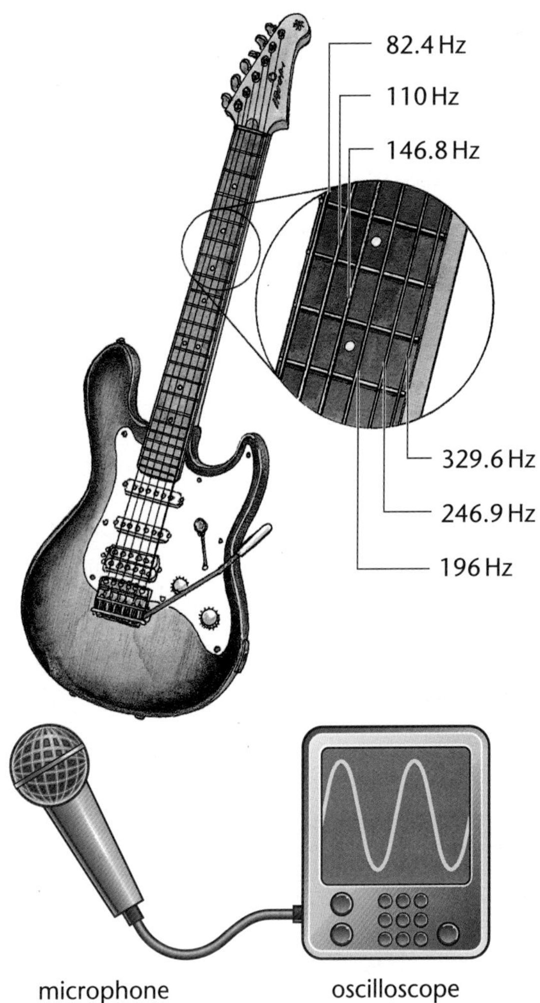

We measure frequencies in units called hertz (Hz, for short). A string that makes 110 complete to-and-fro vibrations per second has a frequency of 110 Hz.

The diagram shows the frequencies that the different strings of a guitar are usually tuned to.

1 Copy and complete the table.

String	Frequency (Hz)
1st (thinnest)	329.6
2nd	
3rd	
4th	
5th	
6th (thickest)	

Measuring frequency

The diagram shows how you can measure the frequency of any sound using a microphone and an oscilloscope.

microphone oscilloscope

= one complete vibration

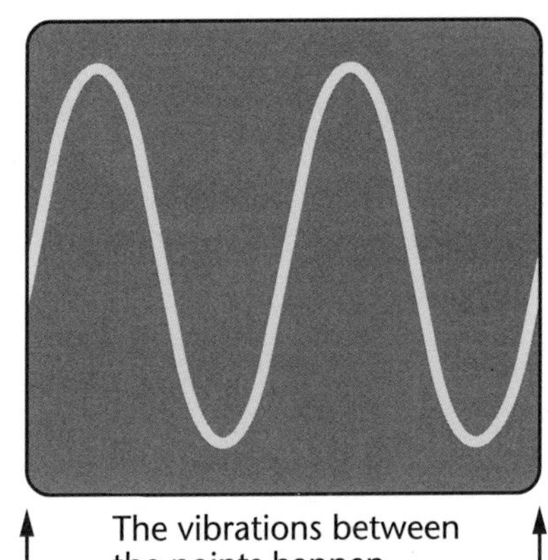

The vibrations between the points happen in 1/100 of a second.

2 (a) How many complete vibrations are shown on the oscilloscope screen?

(b) How much time did it take for this number of vibrations to be made?

(c) How many vibrations would there be in a whole second?

(d) What is the frequency of the sound?

3 (a) The same note one octave higher has double the frequency (400 Hz). Draw what this would look like on the oscilloscope screen.

(b) Which two of the guitar strings play the same note <u>two</u> octaves apart? Explain your answer.

WHAT YOU NEED TO REMEMBER

More about frequency

You will need to use Core ideas in different ways like you have on this page.

C2.1 Things that can attract or repel

Magnets

Two magnets can attract each other or they can repel each other. It depends which way round the magnets are. The diagrams show what happens with two bar magnets.

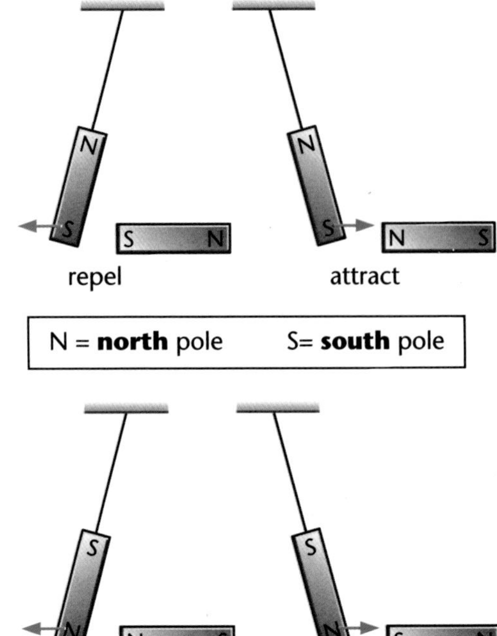

1 What are the ends of the bar magnets called?

2 Copy and complete the sentences.

Two north poles __________ each other.
Two south poles __________ each other.
A north pole and a south pole __________ each other.

We say that:

- like poles **repel**;
- unlike poles **attract**.

Why the poles of a magnet are called north and south

The diagram shows what happens if a magnet is free to turn.

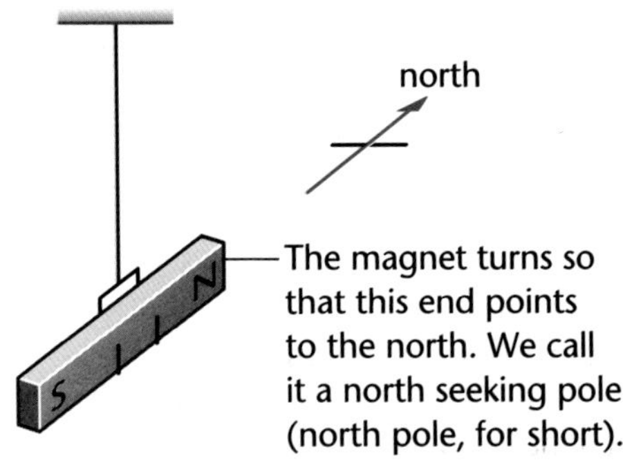

north
N
S
The magnet turns so that this end points to the north. We call it a north seeking pole (north pole, for short).

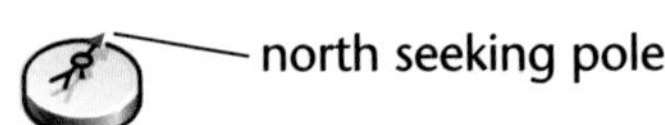

north seeking pole

A magnetic compass is a small magnet balanced on a short point so that it can turn.

3 Copy and complete the sentences.

The end of a magnet which points north is called the north seeking __________.

The other end of a magnet points south. So we call it the south __________ pole.

We can use a magnetic __________ to tell us where north and south are.

We often leave out the word 'seeking'.
We call the poles of a magnet the north pole and the south pole.

A magnetic compass does <u>not</u> point <u>exactly</u> to the north.
Find out how far a magnetic compass is wrong at the present time in the UK.
(Hint: This information is given on Ordnance Survey maps.)

Electric charges

Two objects that have electric charges either attract each other or repel each other. It depends on what kinds of charge the objects have.

The diagrams show which charges attract and which charges repel.

REMEMBER from pages 46–49

You can give an object an electric charge by rubbing it with a different material.

Electric charges can be **positive** (+) or **negative** (–).

4 There are two types of electrical charge. What are they called?

5 Copy and complete the sentences.

Two positive charges __________ each other.
Two negative charges __________ each other.
A positive charge and a negative charge __________ each other.

We say that:

- **like** charges repel;
- **unlike** charges attract.

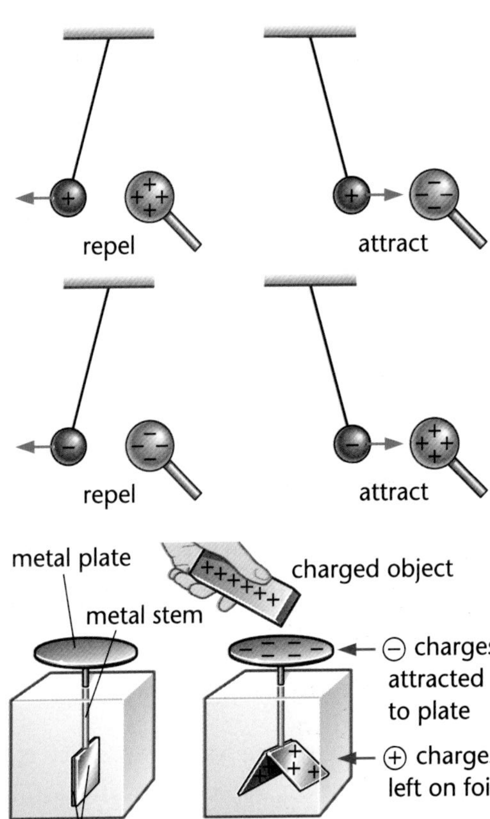

A simple charge detector

We can use the idea that like charges repel to make a charge detector. This is called an electroscope.

6 **(a)** What can you see happen when a charged object is brought near to an electroscope?

(b) Why does this happen?

WHAT YOU NEED TO REMEMBER (Copy and complete using the **key words**)

Things that can attract or repel

A magnet has a __________ pole and a __________ pole.
Like poles __________.
Unlike poles __________.

Electric charges can be __________ (+) or __________ (–).
__________ charges repel.
__________ charges attract.

You also need to know what is in the 'Remember' box.

More about magnets: CORE+ C2.9

Follows on from: 5.7

C2.2 Gravity – a force that attracts

Two magnets or two objects with electric charges may attract each other or they may repel each other. But a force called **gravity** can only attract. It never repels.

There is a force of gravity between <u>any</u> two objects. The objects don't have to be magnets, or have electric charges. The force of gravity between objects happens just because they are made of stuff and have a <u>mass</u>.

The diagrams show another way that the force of gravity is different from the forces between magnets or between objects that have electric charges.

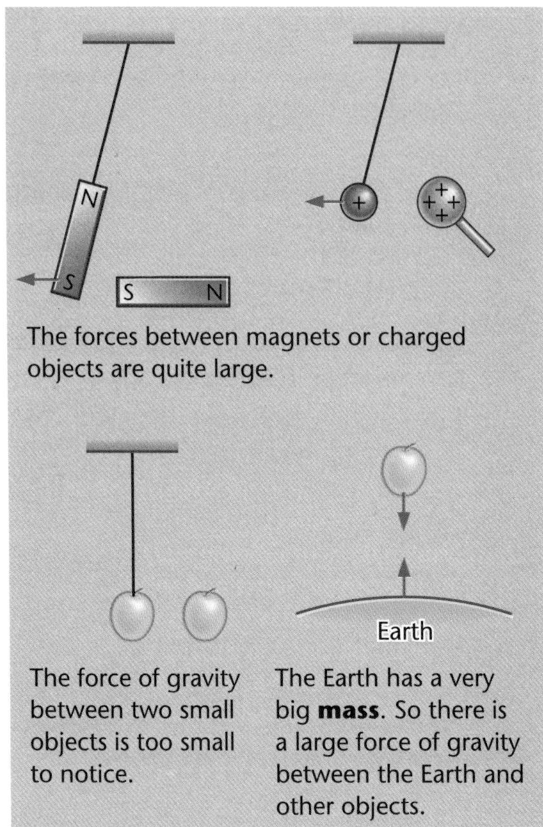

The forces between magnets or charged objects are quite large.

The force of gravity between two small objects is too small to notice.

The Earth has a very big **mass**. So there is a large force of gravity between the Earth and other objects.

1 Write down <u>two</u> differences between the force of gravity and the forces between magnets or between objects with electric charges.

Gravity and weight

Gravity is what gives you weight.

The **weight** of an object on Earth is the force of the Earth's gravity that acts on it.

The force of the Moon's gravity is smaller. So the weight of an object is smaller on the Moon than it is on Earth.

Mass is how much stuff there is.
We measure mass in kilograms (kg).

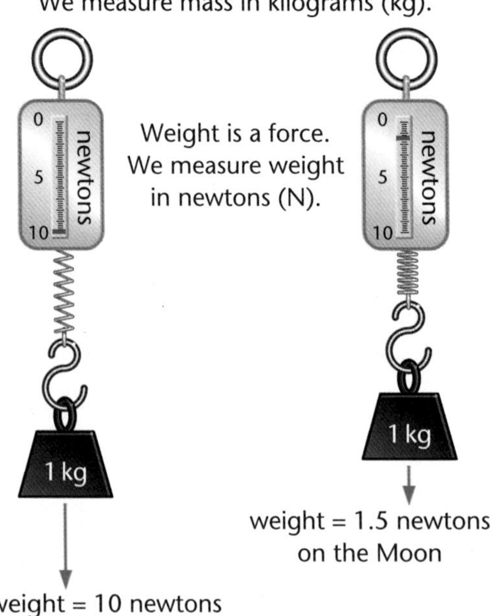

2 Look at the diagram. Then copy and complete the table.

What a 1 kilogram mass weighs	
on Earth	
on the Moon	

3 An astronaut has a mass of 80 kg. What is the astronaut's weight:

(a) on Earth? **(b)** on the Moon?

Who were the first two men to walk on the Moon?
When did they do this?

Gravity and the solar system

The Sun is made of a lot more stuff than any of the planets. It has a much bigger mass.

The force of gravity between the Sun and the planets holds the solar system together.

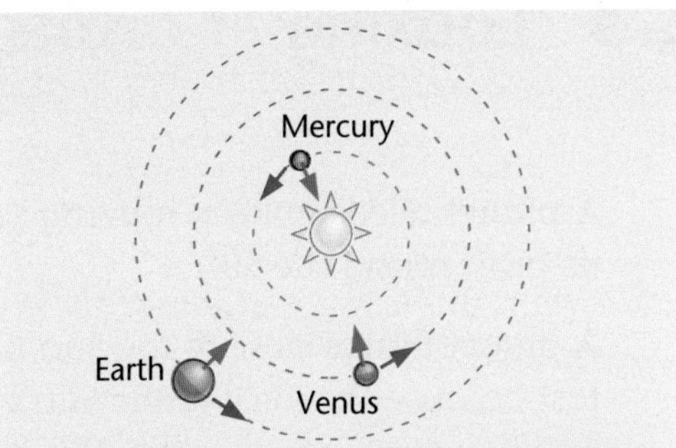

The planets move quickly. So the Sun's gravity doesn't make them fall into the Sun. But the Sun's gravity does stop them moving off into space. So the planets move in orbits round the Sun.

4 **(a)** Why doesn't the Sun's gravity make all the planets fall into the Sun?

(b) Why don't the planets move off into space?

Gravity and satellites

The Moon is a <u>satellite</u> of the Earth. This means that it moves in an **orbit** around the Earth.

Humans have put lots of artificial satellites into orbit around the Earth. The diagram shows the forces of gravity acting on an artificial satellite.

The Moon, the Earth and the Sun

The Moon is a lot nearer to the Earth than it is to the Sun. So the Earth's gravity keeps it in orbit around the Earth.

The Earth and the Moon orbit the Sun <u>together</u>.

5 Why does the Moon move in an orbit round the Earth? Why doesn't it just orbit the Sun like the Earth does?

6 Artificial satellites stay in orbit. Why don't they shoot off into space or fall to Earth?

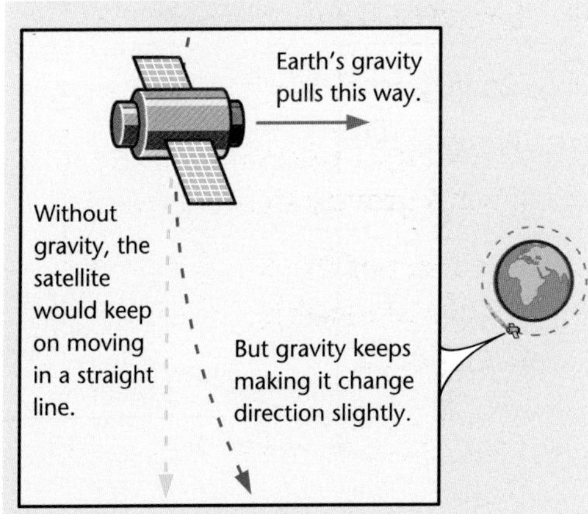

Earth's gravity pulls this way.
Without gravity, the satellite would keep on moving in a straight line.
But gravity keeps making it change direction slightly.

Satellites move in a circle round the Earth because the force of the Earth's gravity keeps changing the **direction** in which they are moving.

7 As the Earth orbits the Sun once, the Moon orbits the Earth 13 times. Use this information to draw a diagram of the Moon's journey around the Sun.

WHAT YOU NEED TO REMEMBER (Copy and complete using the **key words**)

Gravity – a force that attracts

Any two objects attract each other with a force called ____________.
This force is very weak unless one (or both) of the objects has a large ____________.

The force of gravity that acts on an object is what we call its ____________.

Gravity keeps a planet or a satellite moving around its ____________.
The force of gravity keeps changing the ____________ in which planets and satellites move.

More about gravity and distance: CORE+ C2.10

Follows on from: 5.4, 5.6

C2.3 Looking at orbits

A planet needs to keep moving so that it stays in its orbit round the Sun.

A planet that is close to the Sun has to move very fast because the force of the Sun's gravity is very big.

A planet that is further away from the Sun can move more slowly because the force of the Sun's gravity is smaller.

The graph shows how the time it takes for a planet to go once round its **orbit** depends on its distance from the Sun.

REMEMBER from pages 94–95

Planets and satellites stay in their orbits because of the combined effects of their speed and the force of gravity.

Planet	Distance	Orbit time
Mercury	0.4	0.25
Venus	0.7	0.6
Earth	1.0	1.0
Mars	1.5	1.9

The planets in this table are too small to show on the graph clearly.

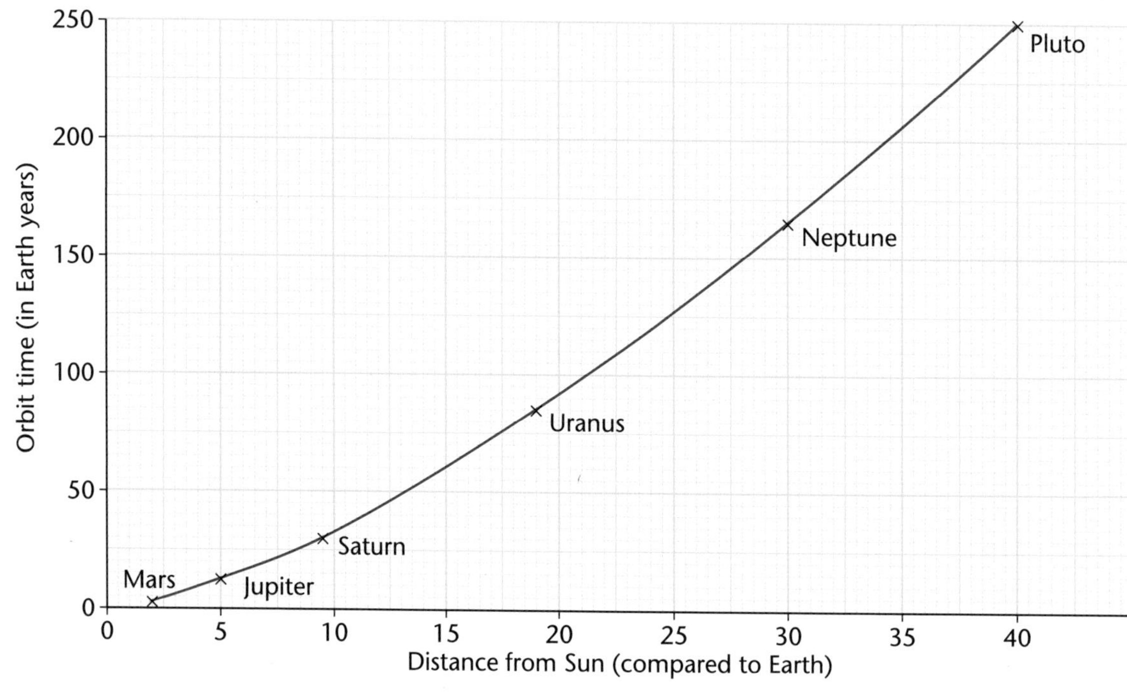

1 Copy and complete the sentence.

A planet that is further from the Sun takes a ___________ time to orbit the Sun.

2 Copy and complete the table. Put the planets in order of their distance from the Sun, starting with the nearest.

Planet	Distance from Sun (compared to Earth)	Orbit time (Earth years)
Mercury	0.4	0.25

3 **(a)** Earth is sometimes called Planet 3. Explain why.

(b) Which planet is Planet 7?

(c) What could you call Mars?

Satellites and the Earth's atmosphere

Artificial satellites need to be well above the Earth's atmosphere. The diagrams show why.

4 Write down three reasons why satellites need to be in orbit above the Earth's atmosphere.

Many different artificial satellites now orbit the Earth. Find out the names of some of these satellites and what they are used for.

The Earth's atmosphere gradually fades away. All the weather is in the first 20 kilometres above the Earth's surface.

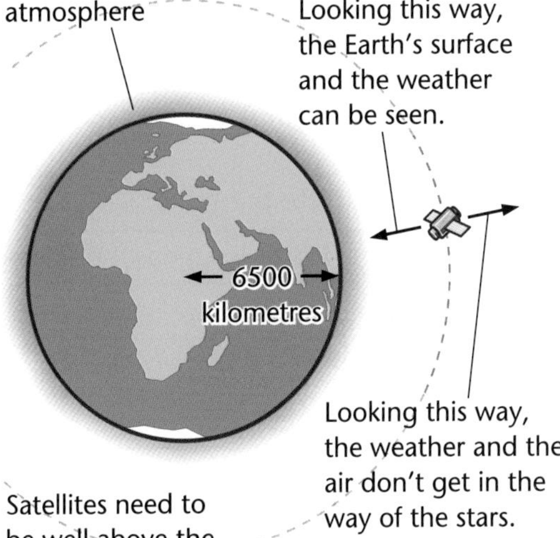

atmosphere
Looking this way, the Earth's surface and the weather can be seen.
6500 kilometres
Looking this way, the weather and the air don't get in the way of the stars.

Satellites need to be well above the atmosphere or they will be slowed by **friction** and fall to Earth.

Satellites that watch the Earth

We use satellites to watch the weather on Earth and to watch what's happening on the Earth's surface. These satellites are put into quite **low** orbits so that they can see as much detail as possible.

The graph shows how the orbit time of a satellite depends on its height.

5 How long does it take a satellite 15 000 kilometres above the Earth to make an orbit?

6 How high above the Earth must a satellite be:

(a) to have an orbit time of 6 hours?

(b) to have an orbit time of 24 hours?

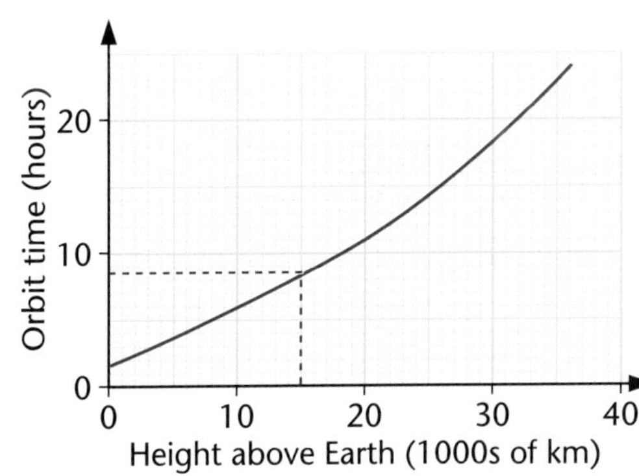

The Earth spins round once every 24 hours. So a satellite in orbit 36 000 kilometres above the equator looks like it isn't moving at all.

WHAT YOU NEED TO REMEMBER (Copy and complete using the **key words**)

Looking at orbits

The further away from the Sun a planet is, the longer is its ____________ time.

Artificial satellites need to be above the atmosphere so they aren't slowed down by ____________ with the air.

Satellites that are used to watch the Earth are put into quite ____________ orbits.

You also need to know the order of the planets in the solar system (page 89).

More about orbits: CORE+ C2.11

C2.4 Getting things moving

REMEMBER from pages 12–13

When you start something moving, or when you try to start it moving, a **friction** force acts in the opposite direction.

We sometimes use forces to start things moving.

The diagrams show what happens when some children try to push a box along the floor.

The children push the box. It doesn't move.

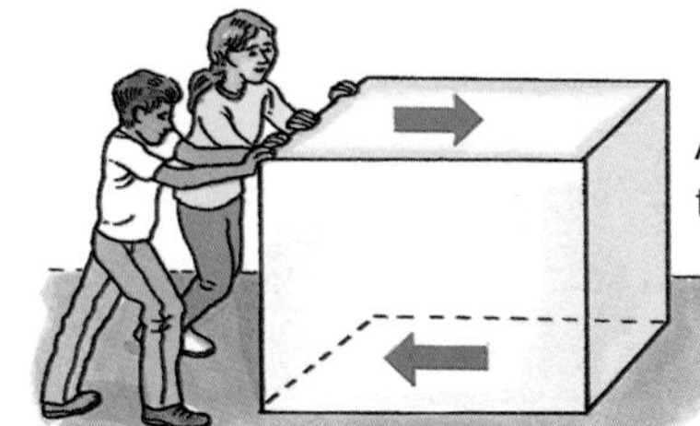

A friction force balances the pushing force.

The children push harder. The box still doesn't move.

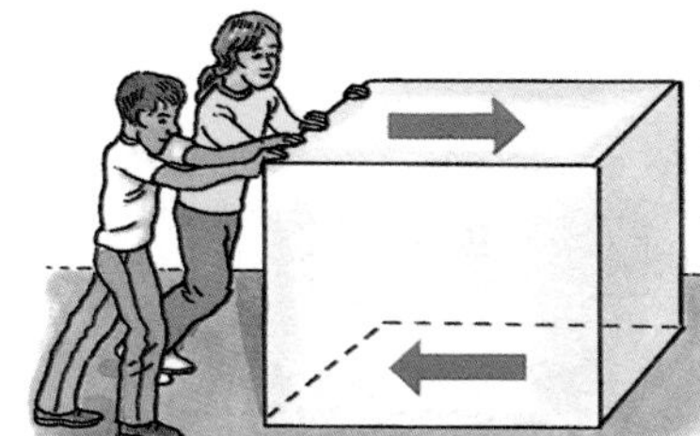

The friction force gets bigger. It still balances the pushing force.

The children push harder still. Now the box moves.

The friction force can't get any bigger. The pushing force is now bigger than the friction force. There is an unbalanced force. So the box moves.

1 Copy and complete the table.

Size of force	What happens	Reason
small		
medium		
large		

To start something moving you need an **unbalanced** force.

Trying a different surface

The children push the box off the carpet and on to a polished wooden floor. The diagram shows what now happens.

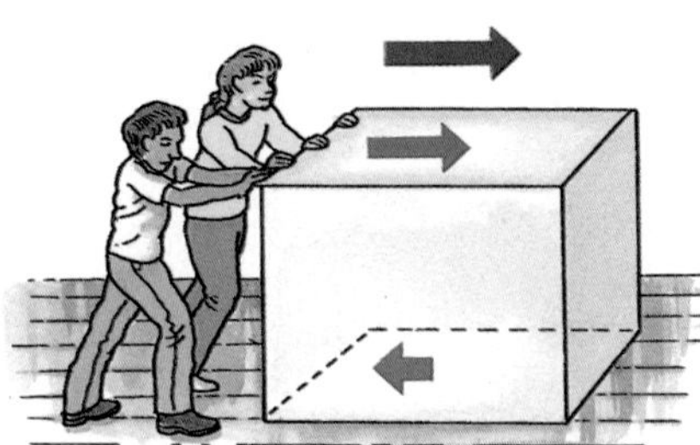

The friction force is smaller than it is on the carpet.

On a polished wooden floor, the box moves with a much smaller pushing force. If the children move the box faster, the friction force stays the same.

2 Copy and complete the sentences.

The children can push the box along the polished floor with a ___________ force. This is because there is less ___________.

3 What happens to the friction force if the children move the box faster?

It is even easier to push the box if you use rollers.

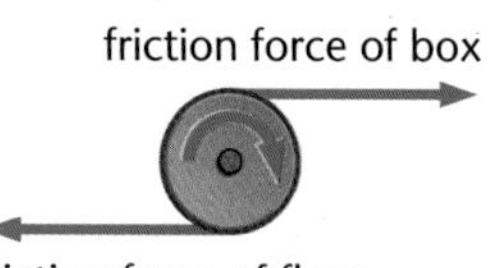

4 What effect do friction forces have on a roller?

Friction with air

When an object moves through the air, there is a friction force between the moving object and the air. This friction force can also be called **air resistance** or drag.

5 Look at the diagrams. Then write down two differences between air resistance and the friction force between two solids which can slide over each other.

Friction with liquids

When an object moves through a liquid, there is a friction force between the object and the liquid. This friction force is like air resistance but it is a lot bigger.

The diagrams show the force needed to pull two different blocks of wood through water.

It takes a force of 3 N to pull this block of wood through the water.

It takes a force of only 1 N to pull this block of wood through the water at the same speed.

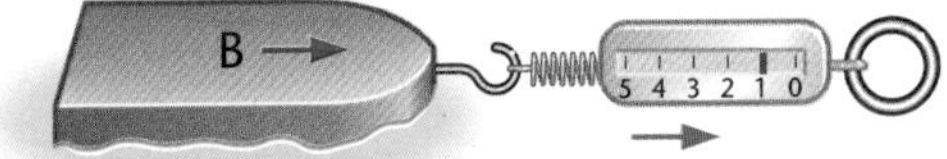

Block B has a more **streamlined** shape.

6 **(a)** Which block needs the smaller force to pull it through the water?

(b) Why does this block need a smaller force?

7 A fish is a good shape for moving through water. Explain why.

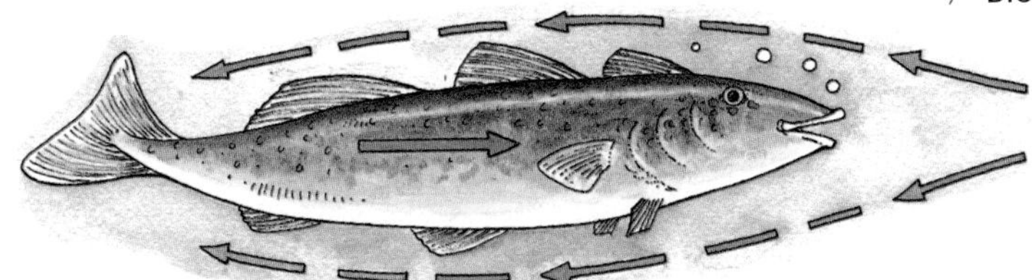

As a fish swims along, the water can flow past it very easily. The fish's streamlined shape reduces friction.

WHAT YOU NEED TO REMEMBER (Copy and complete using the **key words**)

Getting things moving

An object will not start to move unless an __________ force acts on it.

To make an object move, you need a force which is bigger than any __________ force that is also acting.

The friction force when an object moves through air is called __________ __________. When an object moves faster, this air resistance becomes __________.

To reduce the friction force in air or water you need a __________ shape.

More about friction: CORE+ C2.12

Follows on from: 1.4, 1.5

C2.5 Slowing down

REMEMBER from pages 12–13

When something moves, friction forces act in the **opposite** direction.

To keep something moving along at a steady speed you have to keep pushing it. If you don't, it will slow down and then stop.

1 Look at the diagrams. Then copy and complete the sentences.

A car travels at a steady speed when the driving force and the friction forces are ___________.

If the engine stops driving the car, the car ___________ down. This is because the friction forces are then ___________.

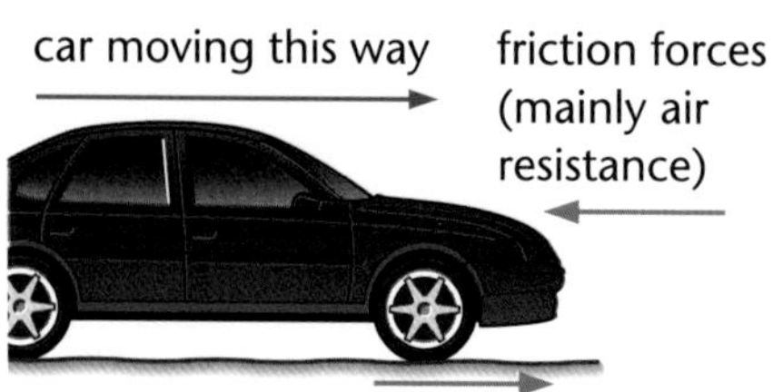

The driving force and friction forces are **balanced**. So the car keeps moving at a steady speed.

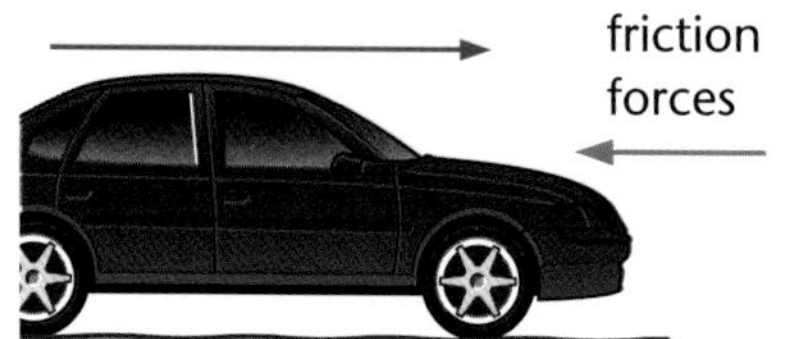

The friction forces are now unbalanced. So they slow the car down.

Using air resistance to slow things down

It isn't safe to jump out of an aeroplane unless you use a parachute. The diagrams show why.

2 Copy and complete the sentences.

Opening a parachute increases air ___________. The parachutist then slows down because the air resistance is ___________ than the force of gravity (weight).

As the speed decreases the air resistance becomes ___________.

Eventually, the forces become ___________ again. This happens when the parachutist is falling at a much ___________ speed.

small air resistance

high speed

weight

Without a parachute a person falls very fast before air **resistance** balances weight.

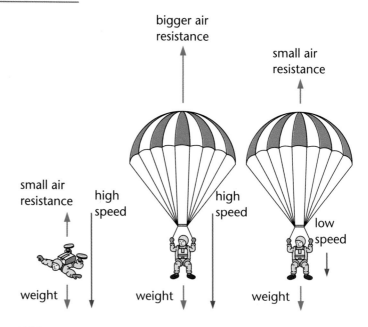

bigger air resistance

high speed

weight

Opening a parachute increases air resistance. The air resistance is bigger than the weight. So the parachutist slows down.

small air resistance

low speed

weight

Eventually the forces balance. The parachutist is falling at a lower speed.

How a skater slows down

There is very little friction on ice. So a skater needs some way of slowing down. The diagram shows how a skater can do this.

movement
The toe of the skate has teeth.
The bottom of the skate is smooth so that there is very little friction with the ice.

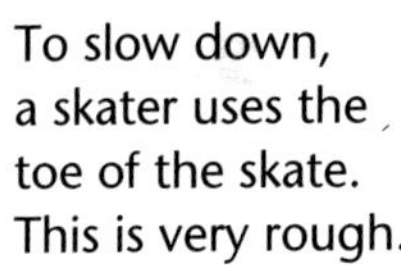
To slow down, a skater uses the toe of the skate. This is very rough.
large force of friction

3 **(a)** What does a skater do to slow down?

(b) How does this work?

Slowing a vehicle down

A driver slows down a car using the brakes. The car's brakes use the friction force between two surfaces which **slide** across each other. The diagram shows what happens.

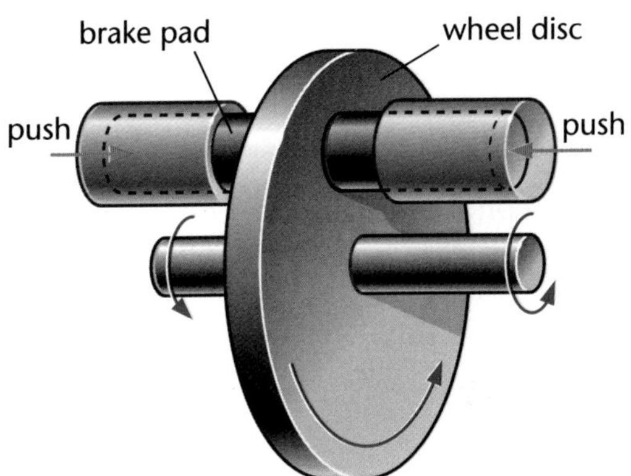
brake pad
wheel disc
push
push

To slow a car down, the brake pads are pressed hard against the wheel disc.

4 Copy and complete the sentence.

A car's brakes slow the car down because of friction between the brake ___________ and the wheel ___________.

5 You must be very careful not to get oil on a brake pad or wheel disc. Explain why.

6 Write down two things that happen to the brake pads and wheel discs when they are used to stop a car.

7 On bicycle brakes rubber blocks rub against the metal rim of the wheels.

(a) Why do the rubber blocks need replacing quite often?

(b) Why do the brakes not work very well in the rain?

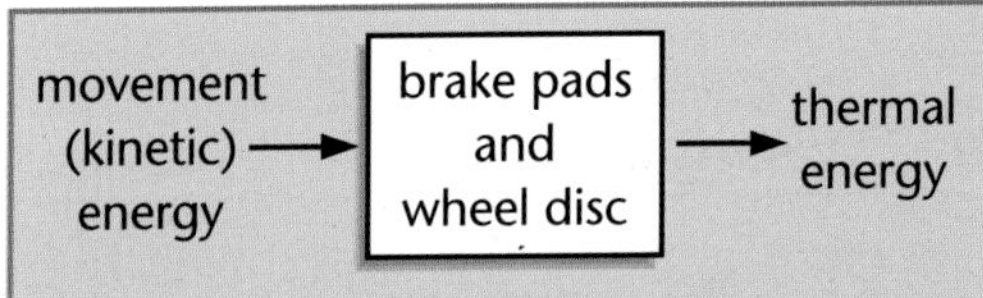
movement (kinetic) energy
brake pads and wheel disc
thermal energy

So the brakes get hot.
Also the pads and the disc wear away and eventually have to be replaced.

WHAT YOU NEED TO REMEMBER (Copy and complete using the key words)

Slowing down

Friction forces always act in the _____________ direction to movement.
So friction forces slow things down unless they are ___________ by a driving force.

We can use friction forces to slow things down:

- a person falls more slowly using a parachute because of greater air ___________;
- brakes use the friction between surfaces which ___________ across each other.

More about falling things: CORE+ C2.13

Follows on from: 1.8

C2.6 Looking at speed

Things sometimes move at a steady speed. For example, police officers often walk at a steady speed when they are on the beat.

You can work out a speed like this:

speed = **distance travelled ÷ time taken**

Example

An athlete runs 400 metres in 50 seconds. His speed is

400 ÷ 50 = 8 metres per second

It takes the police officers 30 seconds to walk along the stretch of pavement shown.

1 Look at the diagrams. Then work out (in metres per second):

(a) the speed of the police officers walking along the pavement;

(b) the speed of the car travelling along the motorway.

2 What is the car's speed in kilometres per hour?

When there aren't too many other cars about, you can travel at a steady speed along a motorway. This car travels 1500 metres every minute.

Average speed

On a journey, you don't usually travel at the same speed all the time. But you can still work out your **average** speed.

3 Look at the information on the diagrams about a car journey. Then copy and complete the following.

Distance travelled = _________ miles

Time taken = _________ hours

Average speed = _________ ÷ _________

= _________ miles per hour

4 The driver stopped to see a friend between 10:30 and 11:30. Work out the average speed of the car during this journey, not counting the time taken for this stop.

depart arrive

car milometer

at start at finish

Showing a journey on a graph

The graph shows the distance travelled during different parts of a cycle ride.

A graph like this is called a distance:time graph.

A steep slope on the graph means a **high** speed.

A flat part on the graph means that the cyclist is stopped.

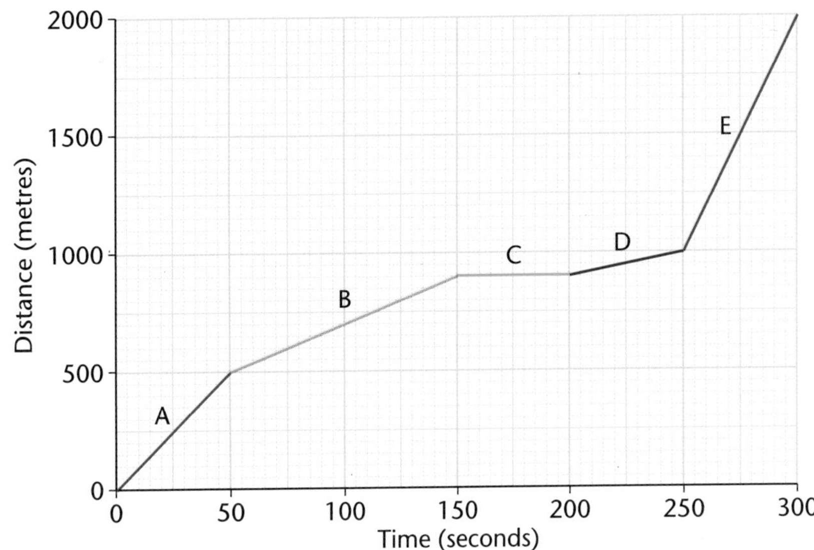

5 Copy and complete the table. Choose from: stopped, very slow, quite slow, quite fast, very fast.

Part of graph	Speed
A	
B	
C	
D	
E	

6 Work out the cyclist's speed during part A of the journey.

7 **(a)** How far does the cyclist travel downhill?

(b) How long does this take?

(c) What is the cyclist's speed downhill?

8 What is the cyclist's average speed for the whole journey?

Find out what the speed limits are on different kinds of roads. Suggest reasons for the differences.

WHAT YOU NEED TO REMEMBER (Copy and complete using the **key words**)

Looking at speed

You can work out speeds like this: speed = ________ ________ ÷ ________ ________

If the speed changes, the answer you get is the ________ speed.

On a distance:time graph, a steep slope means a ________ speed.

More about measuring speed: CORE+ C2.14

Follows on from: 1.6, 1.9

C2.7 Pressure

A gardener is using a new wheelbarrow on some very soft ground. The gardener is pleased that the wheel doesn't sink into the ground as much as the wheel of the old wheelbarrow.

The fat tyre means that the weight is spread over a large **area**. So the tyre doesn't press very hard on the ground. We say that there is only a small **pressure**.

1 Look at the picture of the new wheelbarrow (opposite) and the old one at the bottom of the page. What difference is there between the wheels of the two wheelbarrows?

2 Copy and complete the following.

The new wheelbarrow tyre is fat, so there is a large __________ touching the ground. This means that the pressure on the ground is __________.

Working out pressure

To work out the pressure of the wheelbarrow wheel on the ground you need to know:

- the force of the wheel on the ground;
- the area of tyre touching the ground.

The box shows how you can work out the pressure.

> pressure = **force** ÷ **area**
>
> For the fat tyre:
>
> pressure = 400 ÷ 80
> = 5 N/cm^2 (5 newtons per square centimetre)

The gardener's old wheelbarrow has a narrower wheel. There is only 20 cm^2 of the wheel touching the ground.

3 **(a)** Work out the pressure of the narrower wheel on the ground with the same load in the wheelbarrow. (So there is the same force between the wheel and the ground.)

(b) How does the pressure of the narrow tyre on the ground compare with that of the fat tyre?

Using a spade

The gardener then uses a spade to dig the ground. The diagram shows how the gardener pushes the blade of the spade into the ground.

4 Copy and complete the sentences.

The bottom edge of the blade is quite sharp. It has only a very small __________. This means that it produces a big __________ on the ground.

5 Work out the pressure of the end of the blade on the ground.

6 Why does the top edge of the blade need to be wider than the bottom edge?

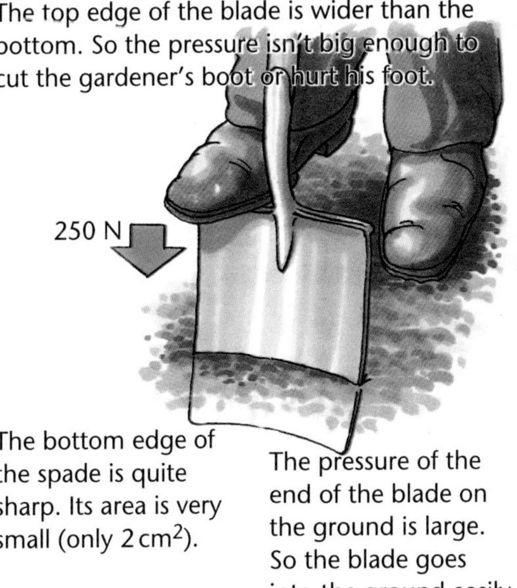
The top edge of the blade is wider than the bottom. So the pressure isn't big enough to cut the gardener's boot or hurt his foot.
250 N
The bottom edge of the spade is quite sharp. Its area is very small (only 2 cm²).
The pressure of the end of the blade on the ground is large. So the blade goes into the ground easily.

Getting the right pressure

Sometimes we want to increase pressure. At other times we want to reduce it.

7 Explain why a fork:

(a) has prongs which are pointed;

(b) has a wide rounded handle.

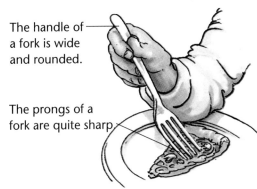

The handle of a fork is wide and rounded.

The prongs of a fork are quite sharp.

8 The diagram shows a builder mending a roof. Why is the builder kneeling on a long wide board?

DANGER
Fragile roof

ATMOSPHERIC PRESSURE

The weight of the air in the atmosphere creates a pressure. This pressure depends on how high up you are and also on the weather.

At sea-level it is about 100 000 N/cm^2.

WHAT YOU NEED TO REMEMBER (Copy and complete using the **key words**)

Pressure

To reduce the pressure a force produces, you can spread it over a large __________.

Making a force act on a small area produces a large __________.

You can work out a pressure like this: pressure = __________ ÷ __________.

More about pressure: CORE+ C2.15

C2.8 Forces that make things turn

To make something move you need an unbalanced force. But an unbalanced force doesn't always make something move <u>along</u>. It sometimes makes it <u>turn</u> around a **pivot**.

This is what happens with a cat flap. The diagrams show how a cat flap works.

Some people have a cat flap fitted to the door. Their cat can then go in and out of the house whenever it wants to.

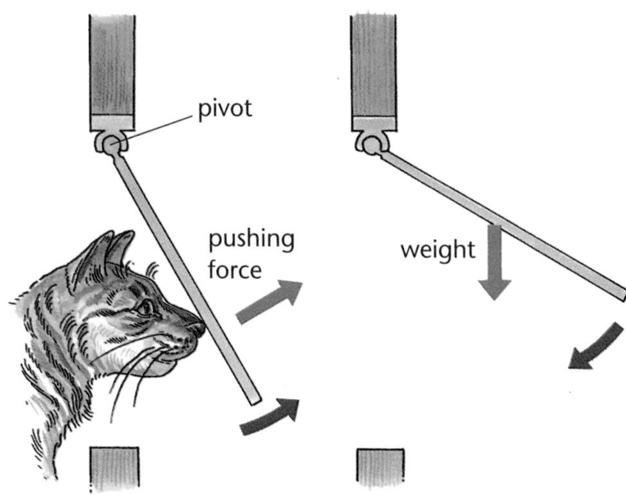

When the cat pushes the flap, it turns about the pivot point. The flap turns anti-clockwise.

After the cat has gone through, the weight of the flap turns it back again, in a clockwise direction.

1 Which way does the cat flap turn when the cat pushes it to come into the house?

2 What force makes the cat flap move back again after the cat has gone through?

There is a special name for the turning effect of a force. It is called the **moment** of the force.

Balanced and unbalanced moments

To make something turn, you need an **unbalanced** turning force or moment.

The diagrams show two see-saws with different turning forces acting on them.

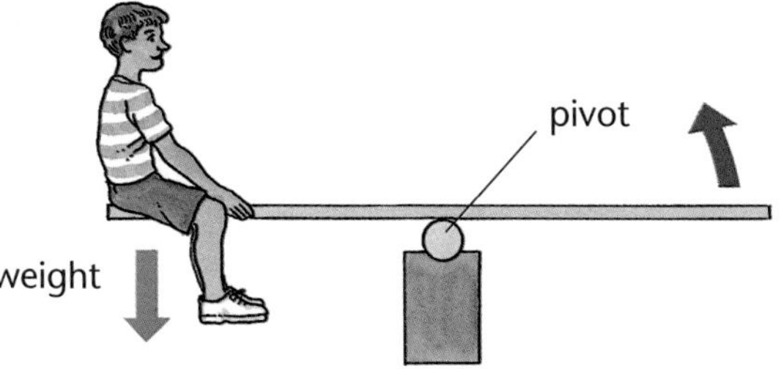

There is an unbalanced anti-clockwise moment. So the see-saw turns anti-clockwise.

Clockwise and anti-clockwise moments balance. So the see-saw does not move.

3 Copy and complete the sentences.

The top see-saw moves because there is an anti-clockwise turning force that is __________.

The bottom see-saw doesn't move because the clockwise moment and the anti-clockwise moment are __________.

What does the moment of a force depend on?

There are two ways of getting a bigger turning effect or moment:

- you can use a **bigger** force;
- you can apply a force **further away** from the pivot.

The diagram shows a small lad and his big sister on a see-saw. The see-saw doesn't move because the clockwise and anti-clockwise moments are **balanced**.

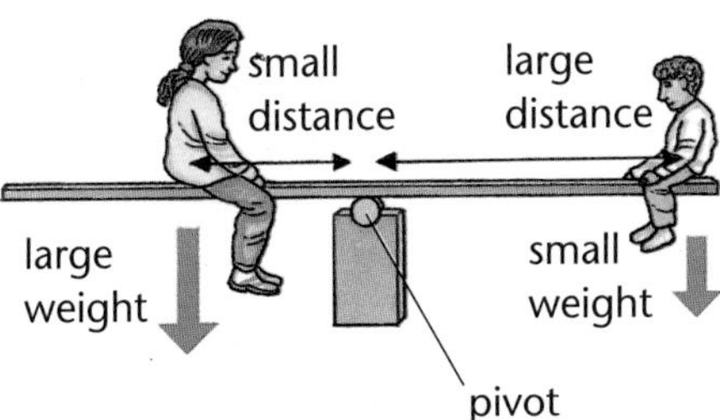

The big sister has a larger weight. But the small lad is further away from the pivot. So they both produce the same moment. The clockwise moment balances the anti-clockwise moment.

4 Explain how the small lad can balance his big sister on a see-saw.

Getting a bigger turning effect

To undo a nut you can use a spanner. The force you apply then has a much bigger moment than just using your fingers.

But the nut could be so tight that you still can't undo it. The diagram shows what you could do.

5 Using the pipe you can get a bigger moment with the same force. Explain why.

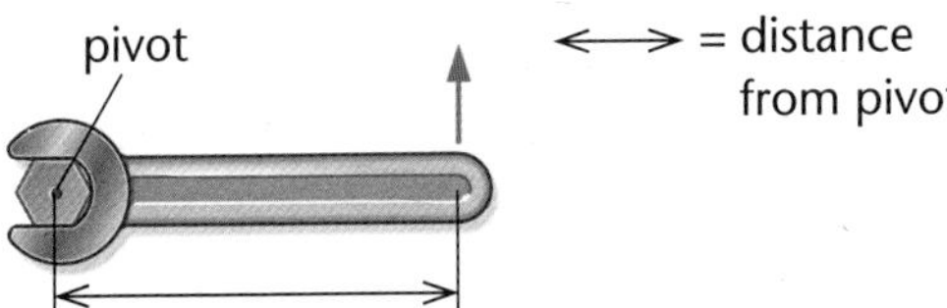

This nut is too tight to slacken with this spanner.

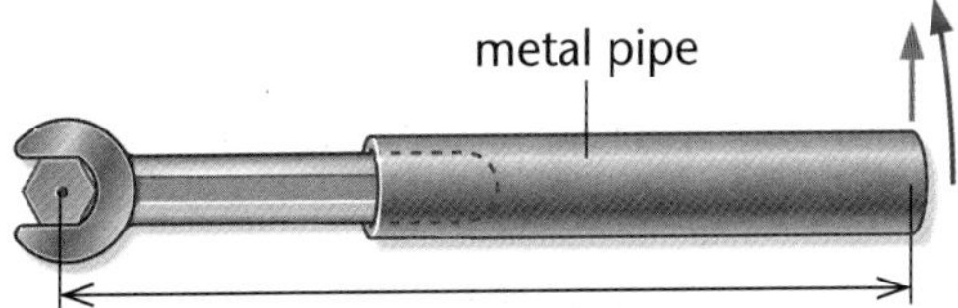

You can add a metal pipe to increase the distance between the force and the pivot.

WHAT YOU NEED TO REMEMBER (Copy and complete using the **key words**)

Forces that make things turn

The point about which something turns is called a ____________.
The turning effect of a force is called its ____________.

To get a bigger moment:
- you can use a ____________ force;
- you can apply a force ____________ ____________ from the pivot.

For an object to turn there must be an ____________ moment acting on it.

An object <u>doesn't</u> turn if the clockwise and anti-clockwise moments are ____________.

More about moments: CORE+ C2.16

CORE +
Follows on from: C2.1

C2.9 Why do magnets point north and south?

REMEMBER from pages 54–55

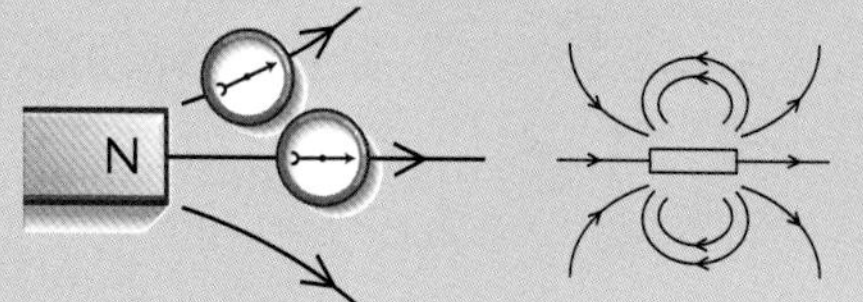

A magnetic compass tells you the direction of the lines of magnetic force in the magnetic field around a magnet.

The needle of a magnetic compass is a small magnet. It is free to turn.

The needle always comes to rest with one end pointing north and the other end pointing south. This happens because the Earth acts like a very big magnet with its own magnetic field.

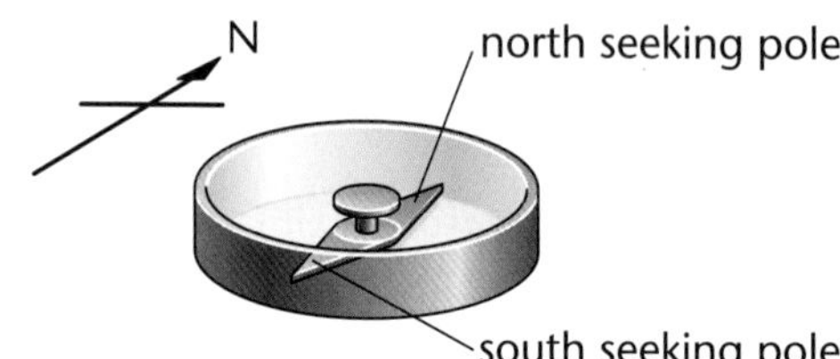

The needle of a magnetic compass points to the north. (So the other end points to the south.)

The lines of force in the Earth's magnetic field run from south to north.

1 What are the ends of a magnetic compass needle called?

2 Copy and complete the sentences.

One end of a compass needle points ___________; the other end points ___________. This means that the Earth must have a magnetic ___________. The lines of magnetic ___________ must run from south to north.

Why the Earth has a magnetic field

The diagram shows why the Earth has a magnetic field with the lines of force running from south to north.

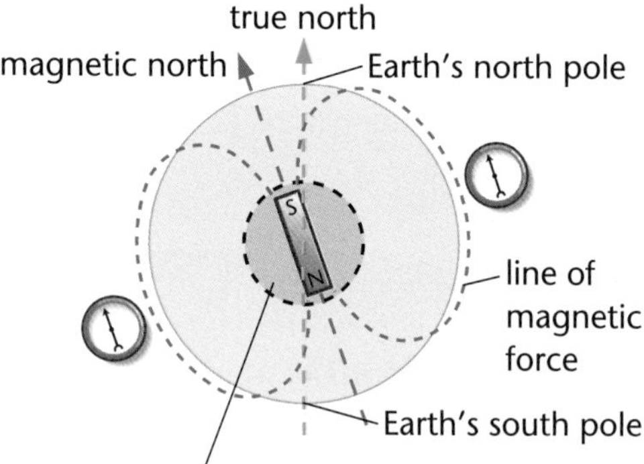

The Earth's core is made of metals called nickel and iron. The core acts just like a bar magnet. This magnet is at an angle to the Earth's axis.

3 Copy and complete the sentences.

The Earth's core is made of ___________ and ___________. These metals produce a magnetic ___________ just like the one from a ___________magnet.

The Earth spins on its own axis. The Earth's north and south poles are at the ends of this axis.

4 Why doesn't a magnetic compass point exactly to the Earth's north and south poles?

WHAT YOU NEED TO REMEMBER

Why do magnets point north and south?

You will need to use Core ideas in different ways like you have on this page.

C2.10 More about gravity and distance

As a spaceship moves further away from the Earth, the pull of the Earth's gravity on it changes. So the weight of the spaceship changes too. The diagram shows how.

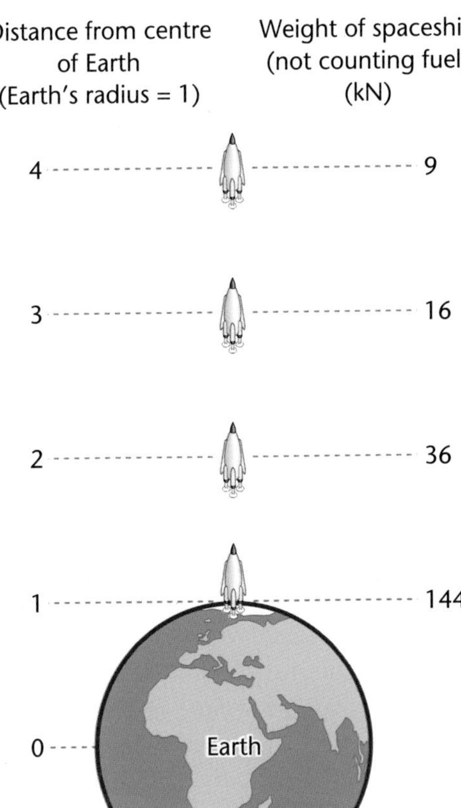

1 What happens to the weight of the spaceship as it gets further away from Earth?

2 (a) Copy and complete the table.

Distance from centre of Earth	(Distance)^2	Weight	(Distance)^2 × weight
1			
2	2 × 2 = 4	36	144
3			
4			

(b) What will the weight of the spaceship be when its distance is six times the radius of the Earth?

A journey to the Moon

A spaceship travels from Earth to the Moon.

The graph shows the force of the Earth's gravity and the force of the Moon's gravity on the spaceship during different parts of the journey.

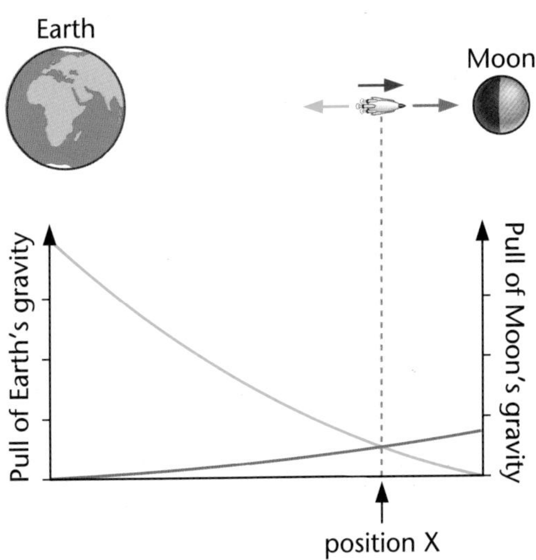

3 Copy and complete the following.

As the spaceship travels from the Earth to the Moon:
- the pull of the Earth's gravity __________;
- the pull of the Moon's gravity __________.

4 What can you say about the forces acting on the spaceship at position X?

WHAT YOU NEED TO REMEMBER

More about gravity and distance

You will need to use Core ideas in different ways like you have on this page.

C2.11 More about orbits

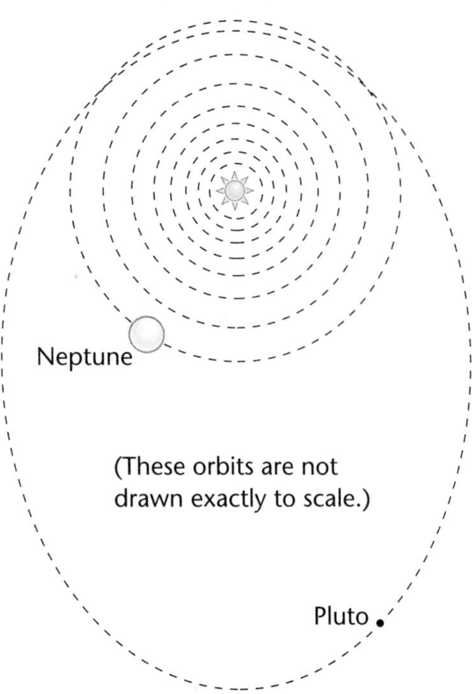
Neptune
(These orbits are not drawn exactly to scale.)
Pluto

The diagram shows the shape of the orbits of the planets.

1 (a) What shape do the orbits of most of the planets seem to be?

(b) Which planet has an orbit that looks a different shape?

2 Which planet is furthest from the Sun? (Look carefully at the diagram. The answer isn't as simple as you might think at first.)

In fact, the orbits of all the other planets are ellipses like Pluto's orbit. But they are only a tiny bit different from circles. Pluto's orbit is a lot more elliptical than the orbits of the other planets.

Find out which scientist, over 400 years ago, suggested that the Earth and the planets move round the Sun, and which scientist realised that the orbits were ellipses rather than circles.

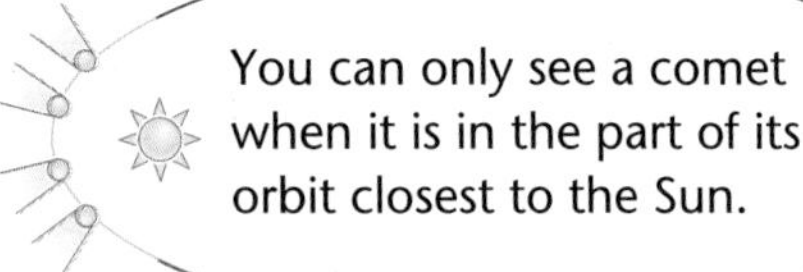
You can only see a comet when it is in the part of its orbit closest to the Sun.
Then you can't see the comet for a long time.

Comets

Comets are large lumps of rock and ice. They move in very elliptical orbits around the Sun. They are a lot smaller than planets so you can't usually see them.

3 During which part of its orbit can you see a comet?

4 You could see comet Hale-Bopp very clearly during the first few months of 1997. When will it be seen again?

Halley's comet was seen when the Normans invaded England in 1066. It has been seen 12 times since then. The last time was in 1986.

5 (a) About how long does it take Halley's comet to go round its orbit?

(b) When will it be seen again?

The orbit time for comet Hale-Bopp is about 4000 years.

WHAT YOU NEED TO REMEMBER

More about orbits

You will need to use Core ideas in different ways like you have on this page.

C2.12 Comparing forces of friction

Friction between sliding surfaces

Suppose you want to compare the friction between different surfaces. The diagram shows how you can do this.

The force of gravity on the block tends to pull it down the slope.

The friction force stops the block from sliding.

angle of slope

You can increase the angle of the slope until the block *just* slides down.

1 Copy and complete the sentence.

The bigger the friction force is, the bigger the ___________ of the slope must be before the block starts to slide.

The table shows the results of some tests.

Type of surface on slope	Type of surface on block	Angle of slope when sliding starts
polished wood	polished wood	40°
	rough wood	50°
	sandpaper	60°
rough wood	polished wood	50°
	rough wood	60°
	sandpaper	70°
sandpaper	polished wood	60°
	rough wood	70°
	sandpaper	80°

2 What do these results tell you about the friction between the different types of surface? Answer as fully as you can.

The friction between sliding surfaces does not increase as the speed increases. In fact, it takes a slightly bigger force to start things sliding than it does to keep them sliding.

Friction in liquids

The diagrams show how you can compare the friction in water and oil.

3 **(a)** In which liquid is the friction greater?

(b) How do you know that it is?

Oil is a 'thicker' liquid than water. Things don't fall so easily through oil as they do through water. Oil also doesn't pour as easily as water. Scientists say that oil is a more viscous liquid than water.

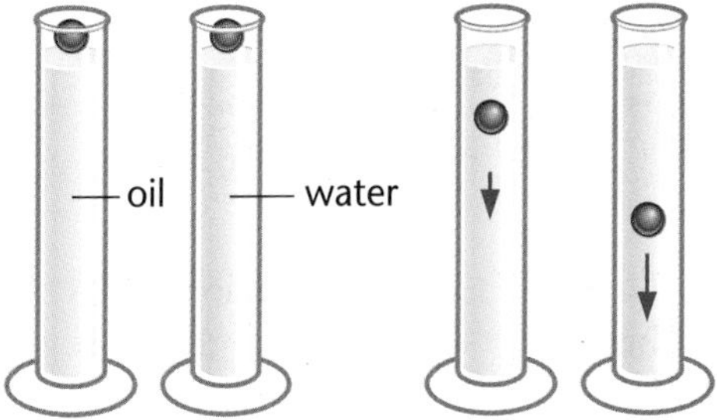

Drop beads into oil and water at the same time.

Then watch how fast the beads fall through the liquids.

WHAT YOU NEED TO REMEMBER

Comparing forces of friction

You will need to use Core ideas in different ways like you have on this page.

C2.13 Raindrops and other falling things

Drops of rain fall down through the air at a steady speed. The diagram shows why.

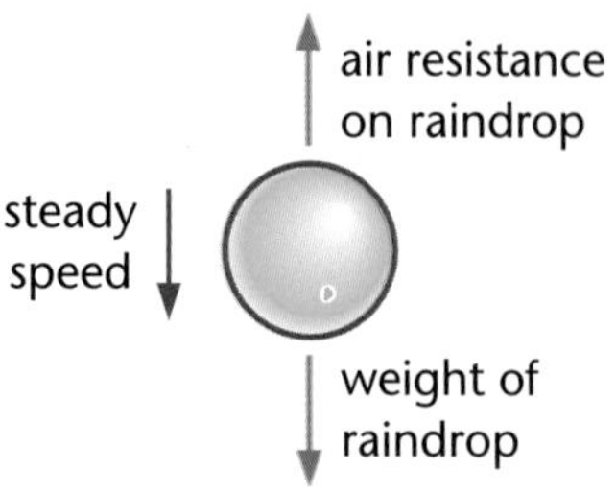

The forces on the raindrop are balanced. So it falls at a steady speed.

1 **(a)** What two forces act on a falling raindrop?

(b) Why does the raindrop fall at a steady speed?

When things fall, they increase in speed at first. Then they reach a steady speed. We call this steady speed the terminal velocity.

REMEMBER from page 129

The air resistance acting on a moving object depends on its speed. The faster it falls, the bigger the air resistance is.

Measuring terminal velocity

There is a lot more resistance when objects fall through a liquid such as water than when they fall through air. So their terminal velocity is smaller.

They also reach their terminal velocity quicker. This makes it easier to measure terminal velocities in water than it is in air.

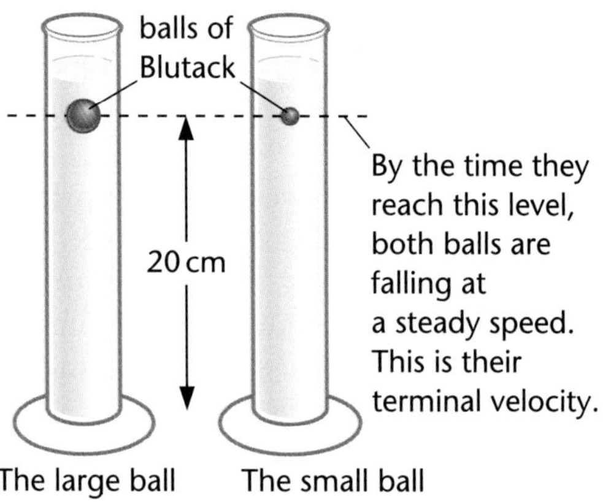

The large ball takes 4 seconds to fall 20 cm.

The small ball takes 10 seconds to fall 20 cm.

2 Look at the diagrams. Copy and complete the table.

	Terminal velocity (cm per second)
larger ball	
smaller ball	

Drops of rain falling through air behave just like balls of Blutack falling through water.

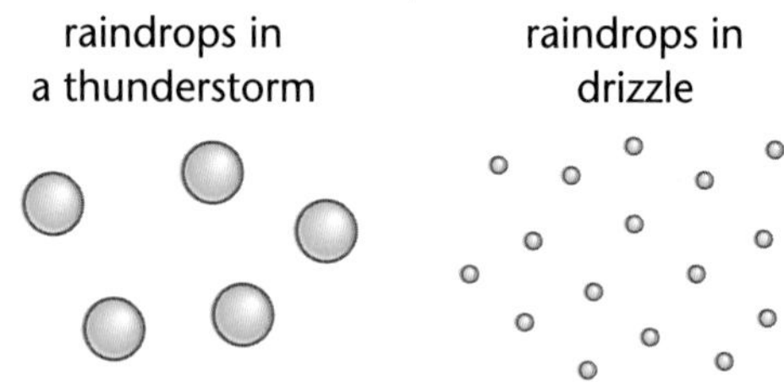

Compared to raindrops in a thunderstorm, raindrops in drizzle have:
- a smaller air resistance;
- a much smaller weight.

3 **(a)** Which falls faster, the large drops of rain in a thunderstorm or the small drops of rain in drizzle?

(b) Explain your answer as fully as you can.

WHAT YOU NEED TO REMEMBER

Raindrops and other falling things

You will need to use Core ideas in different ways like you have on this page.

C2.14 Measuring speed

If you are inside a car, you can easily find out how fast you are travelling.

But when the police want to catch speeding motorists, they must be able to measure a car's speed from outside the car. They need to do this quickly without having to work it out.

A car has a speedometer to tell the driver how fast it is travelling.

The police use a speed sensor to measure a car's speed. It sends out waves which are reflected back from the car.

1 (a) How fast is the car in the picture travelling:

(i) according to the speedometer in the car?

(ii) according to the police speed sensor?

(b) Suggest a reason for the difference.

Measuring speeds in the lab

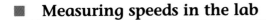

If you make a slope at just the right angle, a trolley will move down the slope at a steady speed. This happens when the force pulling it down the slope exactly balances the forces of friction.

The diagrams show four different ways of measuring the speed of the trolley.

Remember: speed = distance ÷ time

1

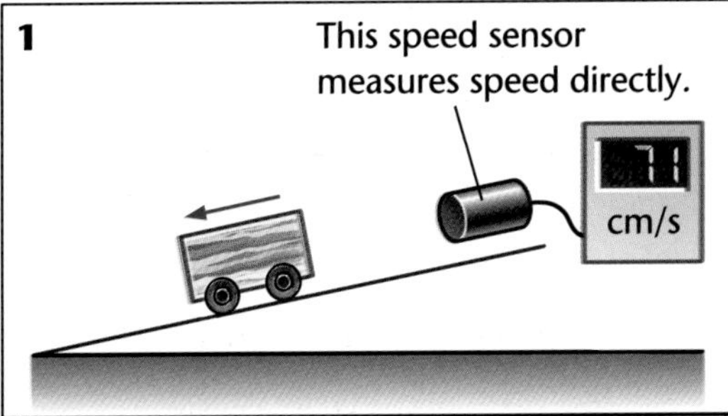

This speed sensor measures speed directly.
71
cm/s

2 Using a timer that you can start and stop with your finger, you find that the trolley takes 0.5 seconds to travel between these points.

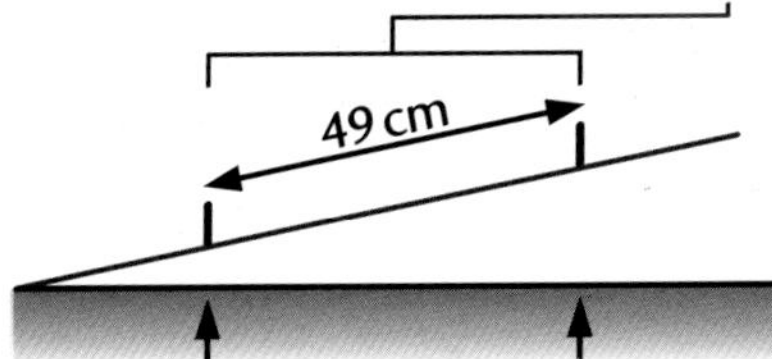

3 You can set up a timer to start and stop automatically when the trolley passes the points. Result: 0.7 seconds.

4

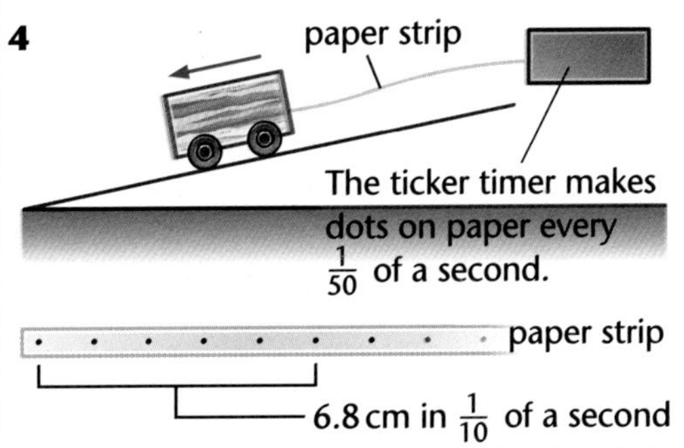

paper strip
The ticker timer makes dots on paper every $\frac{1}{50}$ of a second.
paper strip
6.8 cm in $\frac{1}{10}$ of a second

2 Copy and complete the table.

Method of measuring speed	What the measured speed is (cm per second)
speed sensor	
hand-operated timer	
automatic timer	
ticker tape	

3 (a) Which result is most different from the others?

(b) Suggest why it is different.

WHAT YOU NEED TO REMEMBER

Measuring speed

You will need to use Core ideas in different ways like you have on this page.

C2.15 More about pressure

REMEMBER from page 134

Pressure = force ÷ area

Pressure on your body

Your weight is the force of the Earth's gravity on your body.

If you lie down, your weight is spread over a larger area than when you are standing up. So there is a smaller pressure between your body and what it is resting on.

The diagram shows the same person standing, sitting, lying on a bed and floating in water.

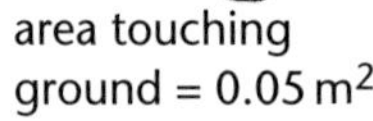

area touching ground = $0.05\,m^2$

area touching chair = $0.1\,m^2$

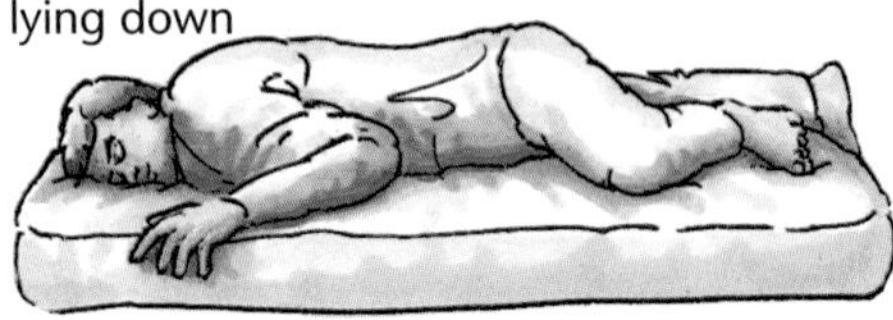

area touching bed = $0.4\,m^2$

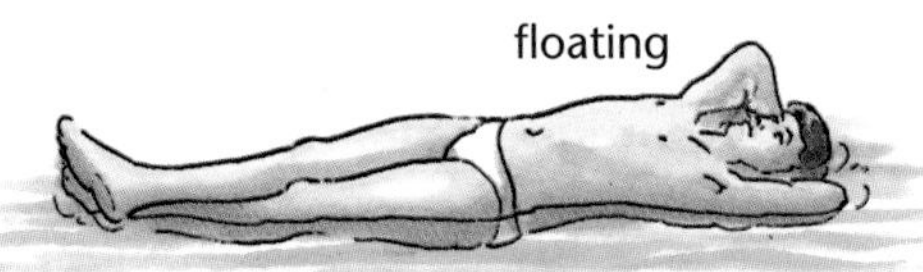

area touching water = $0.5\,m^2$

1 (a) When is the pressure on the person's body:

(i) least? (ii) greatest?

(b) Give reasons for your answers.

2 The person's weight is 600 newtons. Work out the pressure on his body in each case.

Example

Lying down: pressure = 600 ÷ 0.4
= $1500\,N/m^2$

Pressure on a car tyre

The diagrams show a car tyre before and after the driver pumps some more air into it.

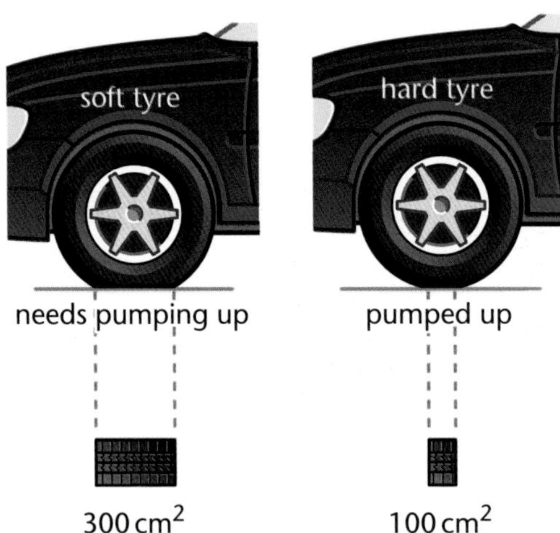

3 What difference does pumping air into the tyre make to its pressure on the ground? Explain your answer.

4 The pressure between the hard tyre and the ground is 30 newtons per square centimetre. What is the force of the tyre on the ground?

force = pressure × area

If the pressure between the soft tyre and the ground is $10\,N/cm^2$,

force = 10 × 300 = 3000 N (newtons)

WHAT YOU NEED TO REMEMBER

More about pressure

You will need to use Core ideas in different ways like you have on this page.

C2.16 More about moments

REMEMBER from pages 136–137 from pages 136–137

The turning effect or moment of a force depends on:

- the size of the force;
- the distance of the force from the pivot.

We sometimes need to work out what happens when two turning forces act on a body. To do this, we need to know exactly how big the moment of each force is.

You can work out the moment of a force like this:

moment of force = **size** of force × **distance** of force from the pivot

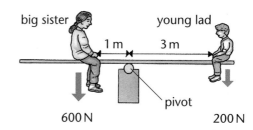

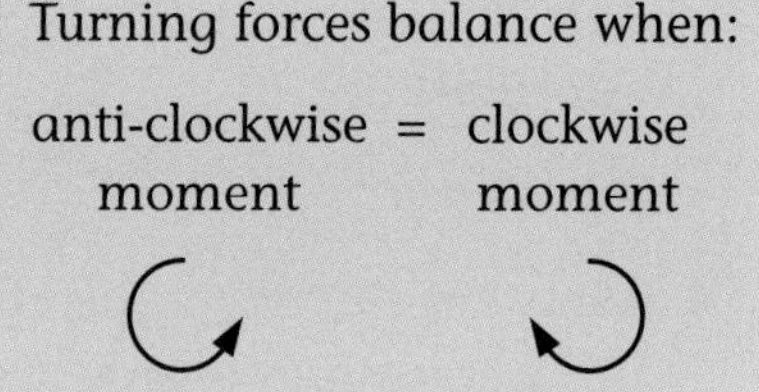

1 Look at the diagram of the see-saw.

(a) Copy and complete the table.

	Weight (N)	Distance from pivot (m)	Moment (N × m)	Clockwise or anti-clockwise?
big sister				
young lad				

(b) Why does the see-saw balance?

Turning forces balance when:

anti-clockwise moment = clockwise moment

Calculating moments

The diagram shows a girl weighing herself using 10 kilograms of potatoes.

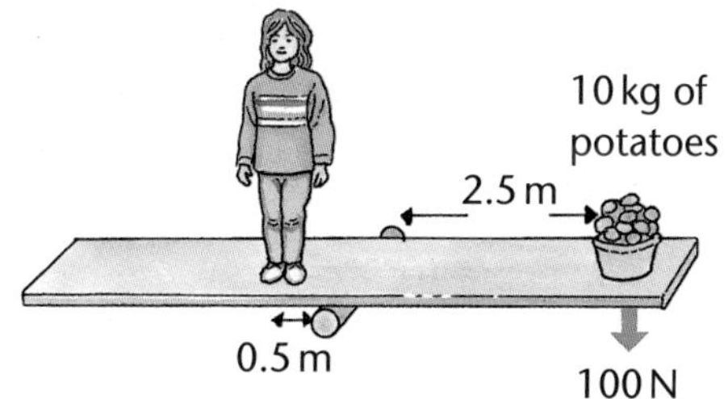

The girl stands quite near to the pivot.

Her friend moves the bucket until the plank balances.

2 (a) What is the clockwise moment caused by the weight of the potatoes?

(b) What must the anti-clockwise moment of the girl's weight be?

(c) What is the weight of the girl (in newtons)?

(d) What is the mass of the girl (in kilograms)?

To undo a nut, you must overcome the moment of the friction force.

3 How big is this moment for the nut shown in the diagram?

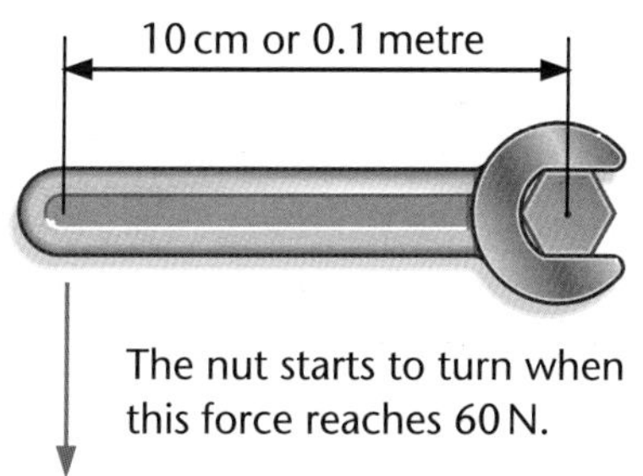

The nut starts to turn when this force reaches 60 N.

WHAT YOU NEED TO REMEMBER (Copy and complete using the **key words**)

More about moments

Moment of a force = ____________ of force × ____________ of force from the pivot

Follows on from: 4.5, 4.6

C3.1 Energy sources

We get energy from energy sources. The diagram tells you about these energy sources.

1 Copy and complete the sentence.

Most of our energy sources depend upon energy which has come from the ___________.

2 We can use energy from the Sun's rays directly to make things warm. Write down two ways of doing this.

3 How does energy from the Sun make:

(a) wind?

(b) waves?

4 Rainwater can be trapped behind dams to make lakes. This water stores energy. Describe how water gets from the sea to the lake behind a dam.

5 Most fuels store energy that has come from the Sun.

(a) Write down the names of four of these fuels.

(b) Which of these fuels are fossil fuels?

(c) Why are they called fossil fuels?

6 Write down the names of three energy sources that do not depend on energy that came from the Sun.

A **renewable** energy source is one that does not get used up. This is because it is being replaced all the time.

7 Copy and complete the table.

Renewable energy sources	Non-renewable energy sources

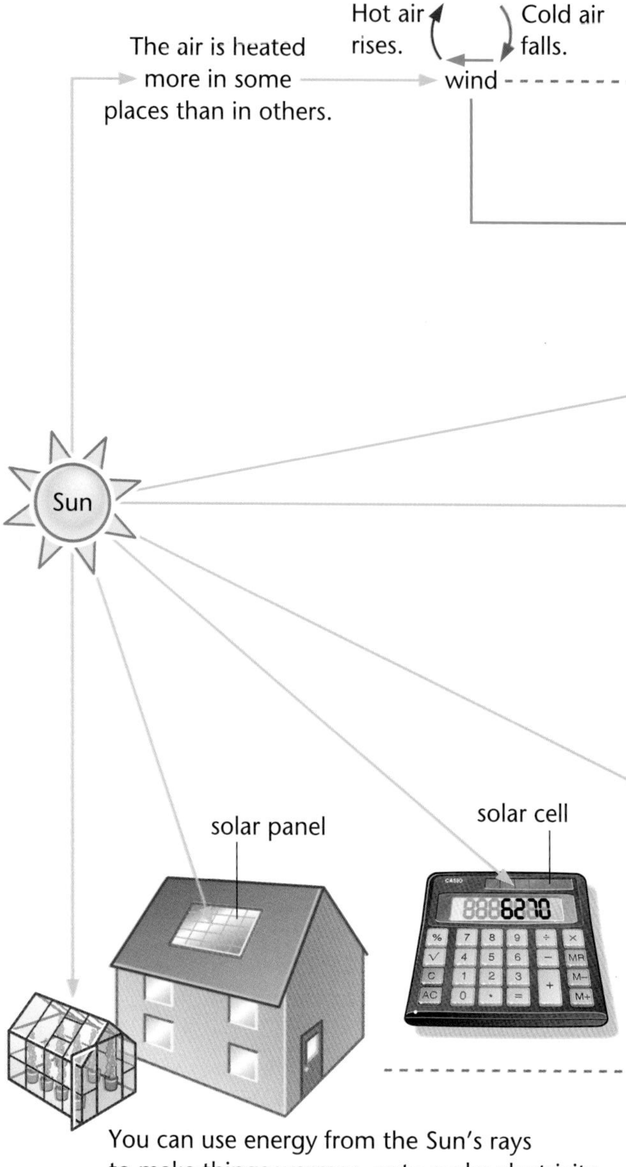

Hot air rises.
Cold air falls.

You can use energy from the Sun's rays to make things warmer, or to make electricity.

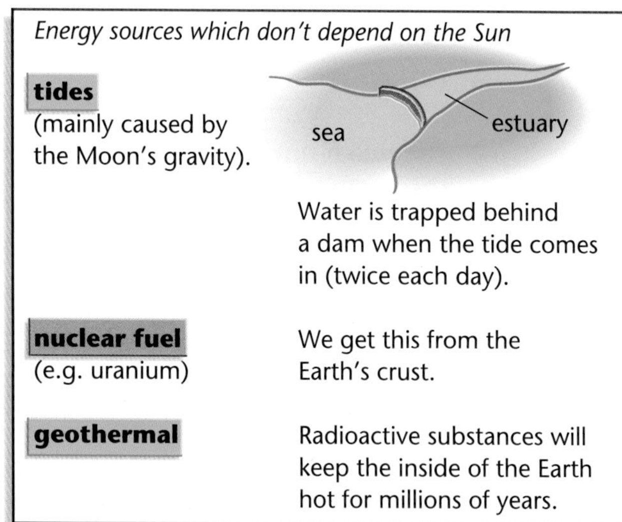

Energy sources which don't depend on the Sun
tides
(mainly caused by the Moon's gravity).
sea
estuary
Water is trapped behind a dam when the tide comes in (twice each day).
nuclear fuel
(e.g. uranium)
We get this from the Earth's crust.
geothermal
Radioactive substances will keep the inside of the Earth hot for millions of years.

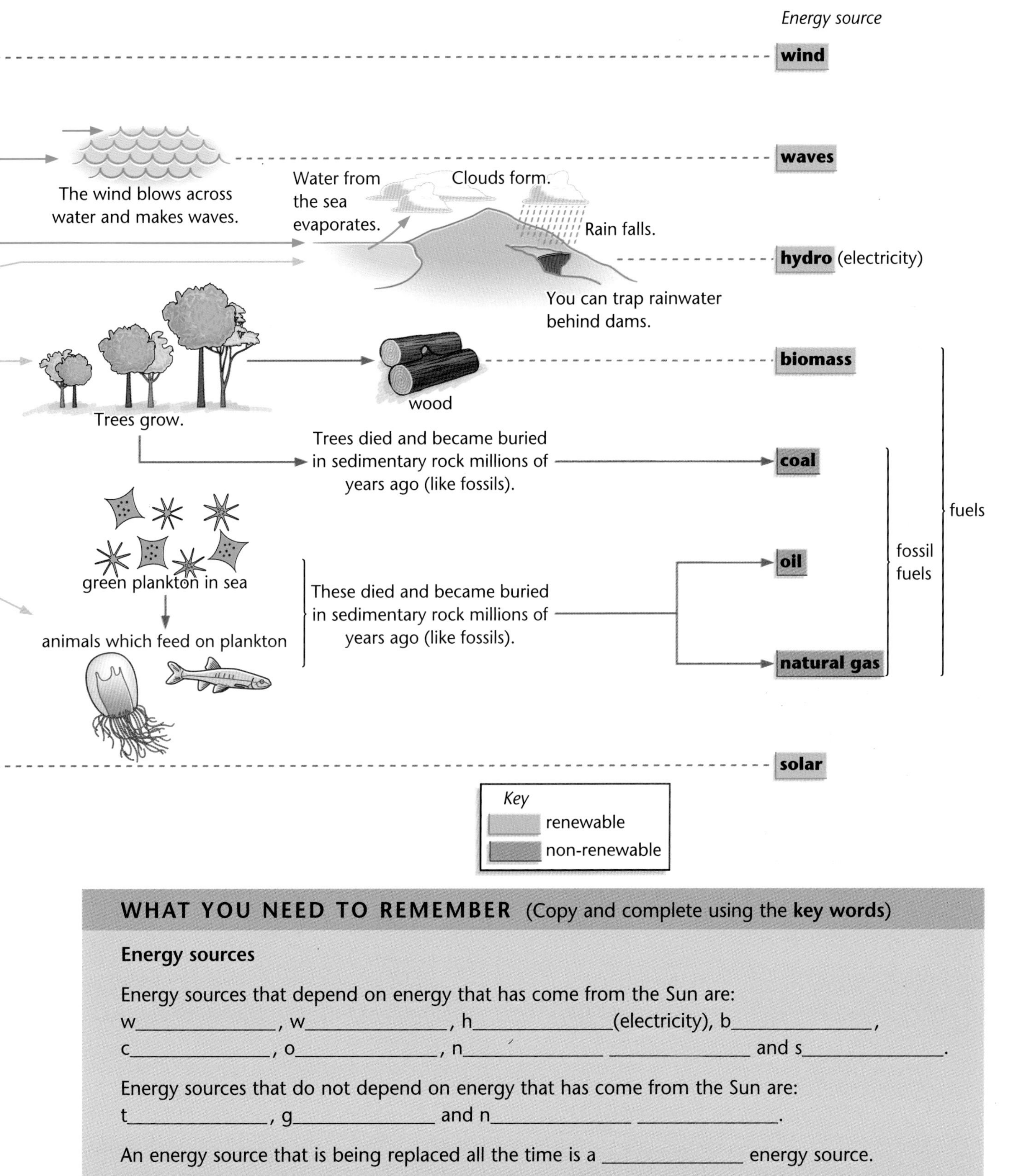
Energy source
wind
waves
The wind blows across water and makes waves.
Water from the sea evaporates.
Clouds form.
Rain falls.
hydro (electricity)
You can trap rainwater behind dams.
biomass
wood
Trees grow.
Trees died and became buried in sedimentary rock millions of years ago (like fossils).
coal
green plankton in sea
animals which feed on plankton
These died and became buried in sedimentary rock millions of years ago (like fossils).
oil
natural gas
fossil fuels
fuels
solar
Key
renewable
non-renewable

WHAT YOU NEED TO REMEMBER (Copy and complete using the **key words**)

Energy sources

Energy sources that depend on energy that has come from the Sun are:
w__________, w__________, h__________(electricity), b__________,
c__________, o__________, n__________ __________ and s__________.

Energy sources that do not depend on energy that has come from the Sun are:
t__________, g__________ and n__________ __________.

An energy source that is being replaced all the time is a __________ energy source.

You should know which energy sources are renewable and which are non-renewable.

More about energy from the Sun: CORE+ C3.9

C3.2 Using energy sources to generate electricity

The diagrams show seven energy sources that we use to generate electricity.

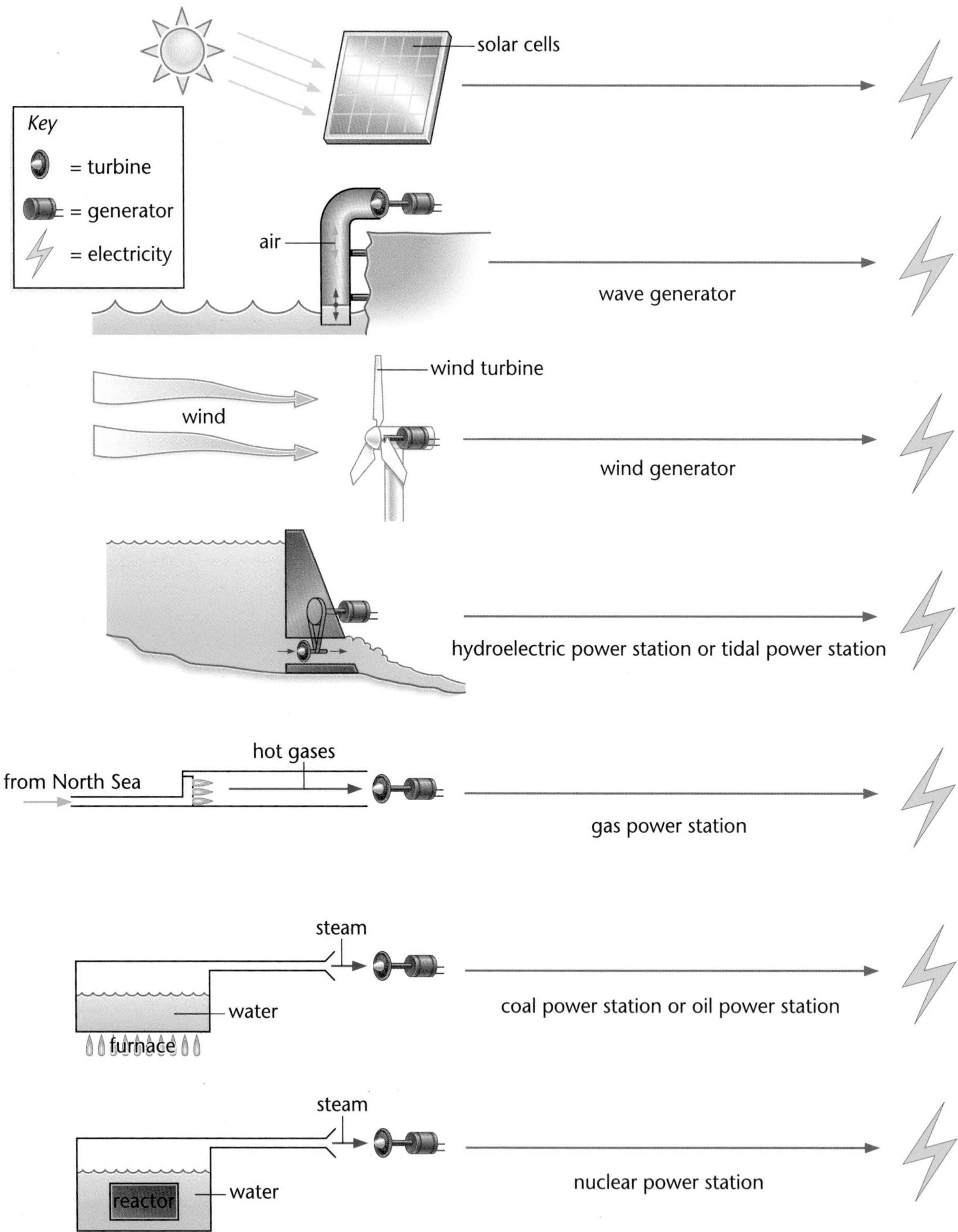

To generate **electricity**, we usually need a **turbine** and a **generator**. We use an energy source to drive the turbine. The diagrams show the type of energy transferred to and from the generator.

REMEMBER from page 69

Things that <u>move</u> have **kinetic** energy.

1 Copy and complete the sentences.

When energy is transferred to a turbine, it makes the turbine ____________. So the turbine has ____________ energy.

The turbine transfers kinetic energy to a ____________. This then transfers energy to homes and factories by ____________.

The turbines rotate. They have kinetic energy. The kinetic energy from the turbines is changed into electricity. This carries energy to houses and factories.

Here is an easy way to write down these energy transfers:

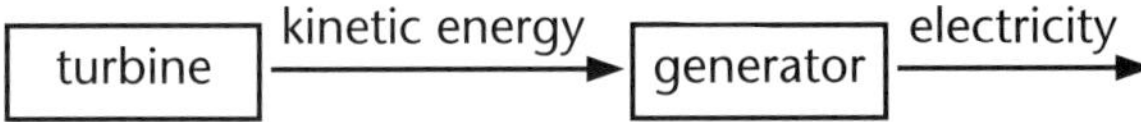

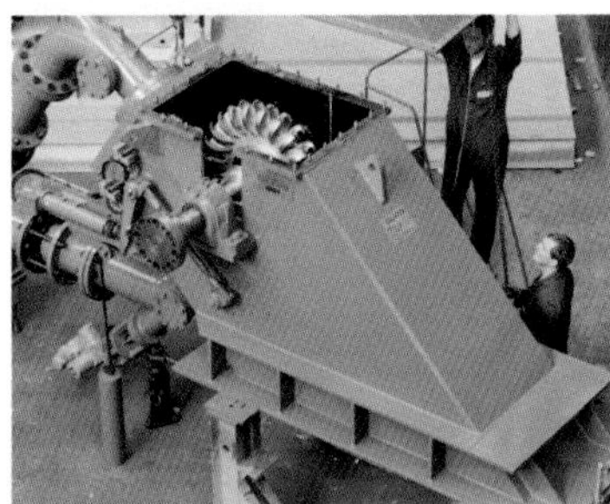

Use the information on the opposite page to answer the following questions.

2 **(a)** Write down <u>three</u> types of power station that use a turbine driven by steam.

(b) Write down <u>three</u> ways of generating electricity that use turbines driven by air or hot gases (not steam).

3 Which <u>two</u> types of power station use a turbine driven by water?

4 How can you produce electricity without using a turbine or a generator at all?

WHAT YOU NEED TO REMEMBER (Copy and complete using the **key words**)

Using energy sources to generate electricity

Most ways of generating electricity use a ____________ to drive a ____________.

turbine → ______ energy → generator → ______

More about energy sources: CORE+ C3.10, C3.11

C3.3 Getting the energy we want from electricity

We transfer energy in lots of ways every day.

When a room is dark, we switch on the light. The light bulb transfers energy to the room.

To boil water, we can switch on a kettle. The kettle transfers energy to the water.

When we want to transfer energy, we often switch on an **electrical** appliance.

The diagrams on the opposite page show what we use some electrical appliances for.

WARNING!

Mains electricity can kill.

NEVER switch things on or off with wet hands.

NEVER use electrical appliances that have broken plugs or loose wires.

1 Copy and complete the following.

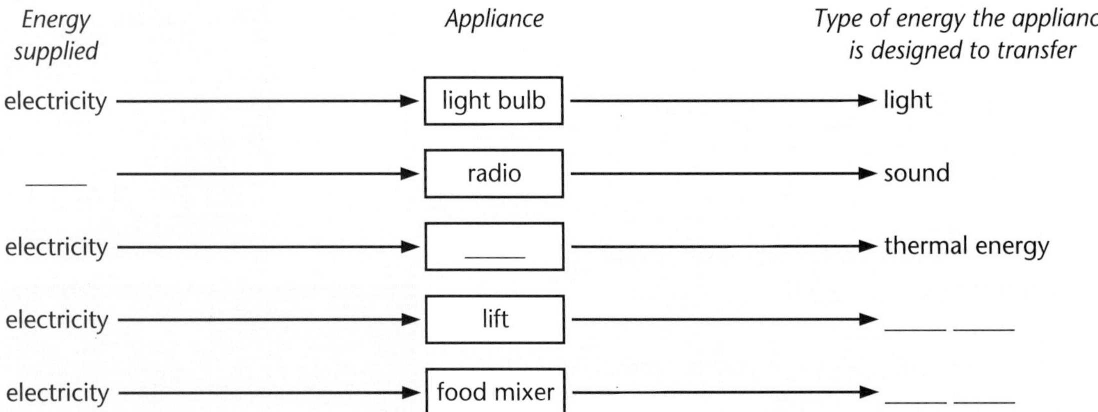

We don't only get what we want

Appliances always transfer **all** the energy we supply to them in some way. The problem is that some of the energy is transferred in ways that we don't really want. This energy is **wasted**.

2 Copy and complete the sentences.

A light bulb is designed to transfer _________ energy to its surroundings.

But it also transfers _________ energy to its surroundings. This is not wanted.

3 Make a list of the unwanted energy that is transferred by each of the appliances on the opposite page.

A light bulb makes its surroundings warmer as well as lighter. It transfers thermal energy ∿∿ *as well as light* — *to its surroundings.*

REMEMBER from pages 70 and 78–79

When we lift things higher up, they have more potential energy.

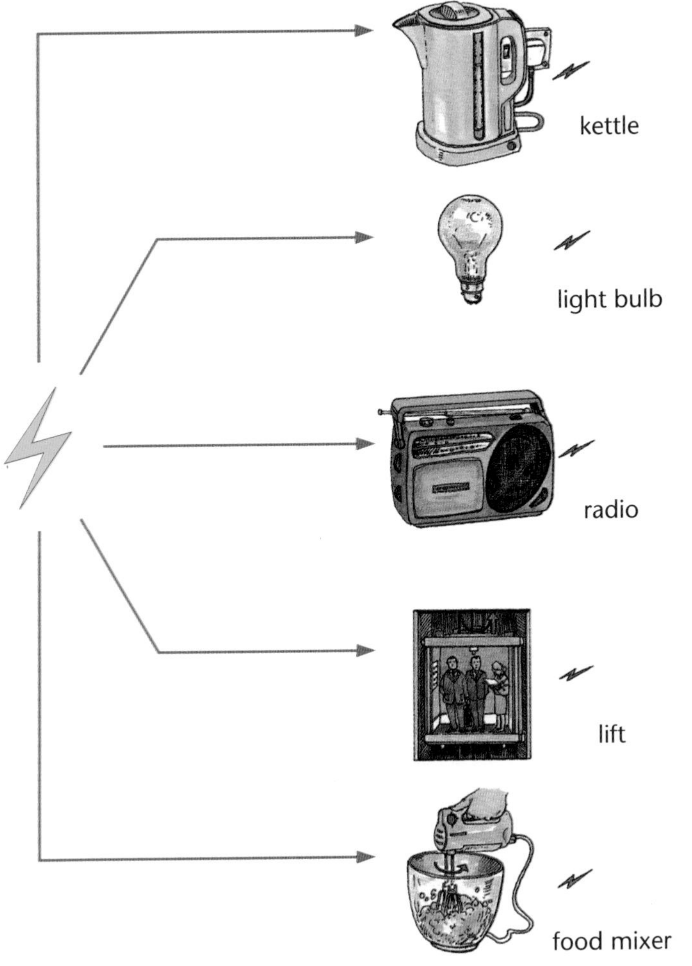

designed to transfer thermal energy (mainly to water) [but also transfers a little sound]

designed to transfer light energy (to surroundings) [but also transfers a lot of thermal energy]

designed to transfer sound energy (to surroundings) [but also transfers thermal energy]

designed to transfer potential energy (to lift) [but also transfers thermal energy and sound]

designed to transfer kinetic (movement) energy (to food) [but also transfers thermal energy and sound]

WHAT YOU NEED TO REMEMBER (Copy and complete using the **key words**)

Getting the energy we want from electricity

To transfer energy to our surroundings, we often use ____________ appliances.

Electrical appliances transfer ____________ the energy we supply to them.

Some of the energy is transferred in ways that we don't want; this energy is ____________ .

You should know the energy transfers that everyday electrical appliances are designed to make and the unwanted energy transfers that they also make.

More about energy transfers: CORE+ C3.12

Follows on from: 3.1, 3.3

C3.4 Static electricity and electric currents

To get an electric current, we need a battery or a generator. Batteries were only invented about 200 years ago and generators about 150 years ago. But people have known about static electricity for more than 2000 years.

REMEMBER from pages 46–49

You can make static electricity by rubbing together two different materials (like plastic and cloth).

Some materials get a positive (+) charge when you rub them. Other materials get a negative (–) charge.

1 How can you produce static electricity?

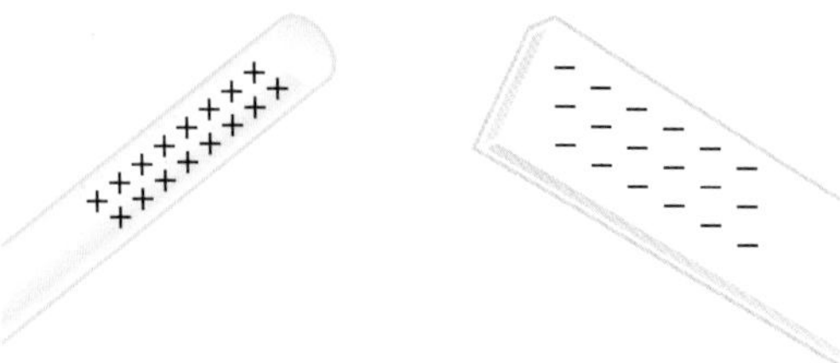

These pieces of plastic are charged with static electricity. The charges stay in **one place**. 'Static' means 'not moving'.

Find out:

- who first discovered static electricity;
- who invented the first battery;
- who invented electric light bulbs.

What's the connection between static electricity and an electric current?

Static electricity and electric currents are both caused by electrical charges.

The diagrams show the differences between static electricity and an electric current.

2 Copy and complete the table.

What happens to the electrical charges	Type of electricity
standing still	__________ electricity
moving	an electric __________

3 Copy and complete the sentence.

Electricity can flow through copper wires because copper is a good __________ of electricity.

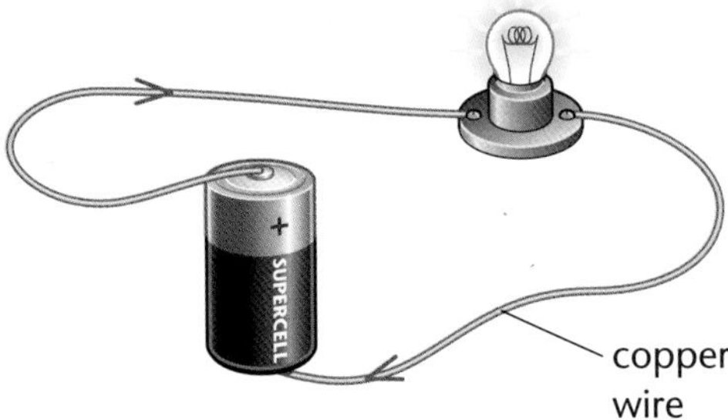

An electric current flows round this circuit. Electrical charges **move** through the wires and the filament of the bulb.

REMEMBER from pages 50–51

A material that lets an electric current pass through it is called a **conductor**. Metals are good electrical conductors.

Getting an electric current from a static charge

You can make an electric current flow from a charged metal object. To do this, you must connect the charged metal object to the **earth** with an electrical conductor. The diagrams show what happens if you do this with a special lamp.

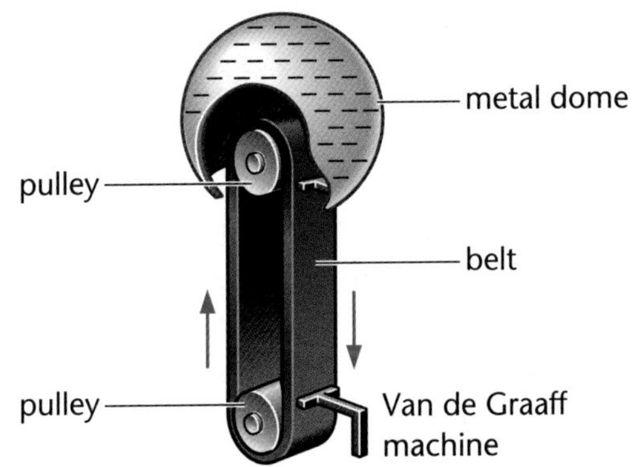

When the belt moves round, it makes a very big static charge on the dome. On many machines the dome gets a positive (+) charge. It all depends on what materials the belt and pulleys are made of.

4 (a) How can you tell that there is an electric current?

(b) How do the electrical charges on the dome make this current?

5 Copy and complete the sentences.

When an object loses its electrical charge, we say that it is ________ .
This happens when the charged object is ________ .

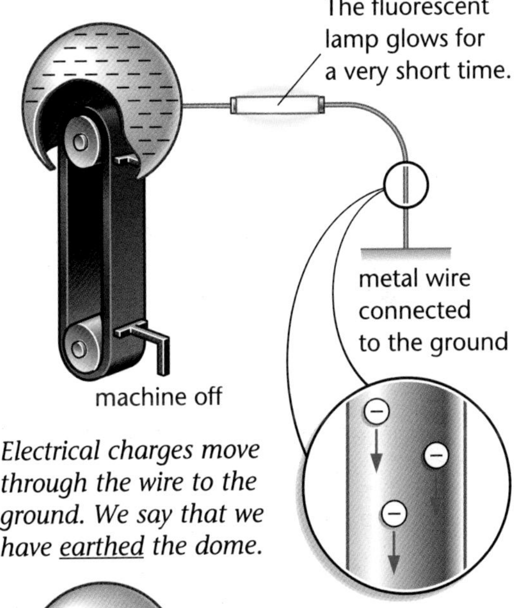

Electrical charges move through the wire to the ground. We say that we have earthed the dome.

The dome has lost its charge. We say that it is discharged.

Why do we need batteries and generators?

When you discharge a charged object, you get only a very small current for a very short time. If you want a larger current for a longer time, you need a battery or a generator.

Some bicycles have lights that do not need batteries. Where does the electricity for these lights come from?

WHAT YOU NEED TO REMEMBER (Copy and complete using the **key words**)

Static electricity and electric currents

On an object charged with static electricity, the electrical charges stay in ________ ________.

In an electric current, electrical charges ________.
The material that an electric current will flow through is called a ________.

You can discharge a charged conductor by connecting it to the ________.

More about batteries: CORE+ C3.13

Follows on from: 3.7, 3.8

C3.5 Measuring currents in circuits

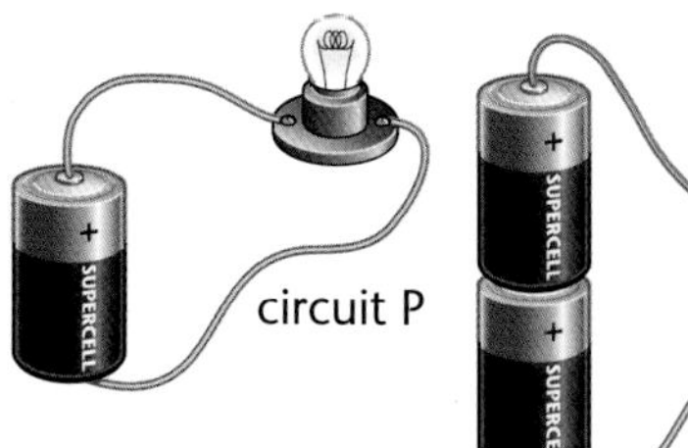

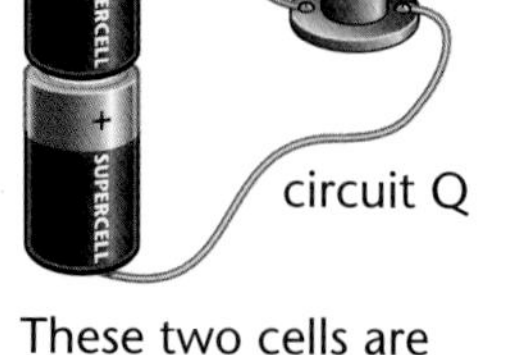

These two cells are connected end to end, facing the same way.

Some circuits have a light bulb in them. A bulb is brighter when a bigger current flows through it. So the brightness of the bulb tells you about the size of the current flowing through the circuit.

1 The diagram shows the same bulb in two different circuits.

(a) Which circuit has the bigger current flowing through it?

(b) How do you know?

(c) Why do you think there is a bigger current in one circuit than in the other?

Using a meter to measure current

If you want to <u>measure</u> the sizes of electric currents, you need to use a meter.

We measure currents in units called <u>amperes</u> (amps or A, for short). The meter we use to measure currents is called an **ammeter**.

The diagrams show the same two circuits as before, but this time with an ammeter.

You can put an ammeter here ...

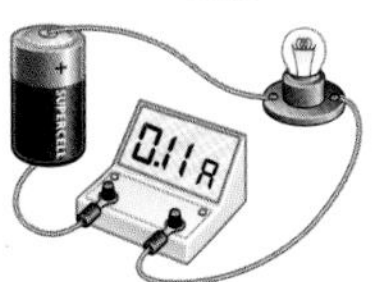

... or here.

The same current flows through the bulb and through the ammeter. We say that the ammeter is in **series** with the bulb.

Measuring the current in circuit P.

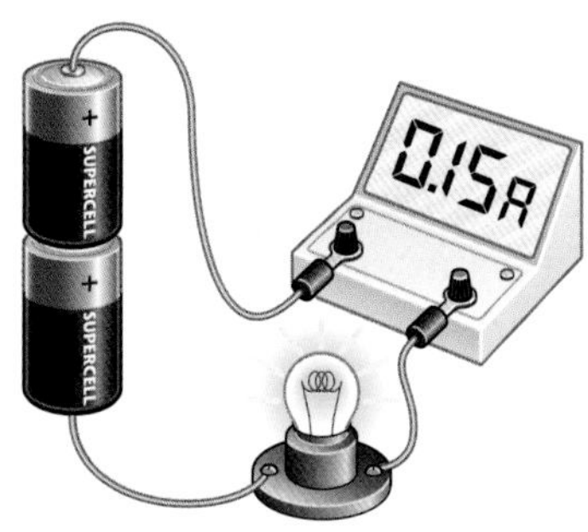

Measuring the current in circuit Q.

2 Copy and complete the sentences.

You measure a current using an _________.

To measure the current through a bulb you must connect the meter in _________ with the bulb.

In circuit P, the current is _________ A (amps).
In circuit Q, the current is _________ A (amps).

3 Draw a circuit diagram for circuit Q with the ammeter in another suitable position.

It doesn't matter which side of the bulb you put the ammeter. Exactly the **same** current flows all the way round the circuit.

REMEMBER from page 59

A simple way to draw circuits is to use symbols. This is how you can draw circuit Q.

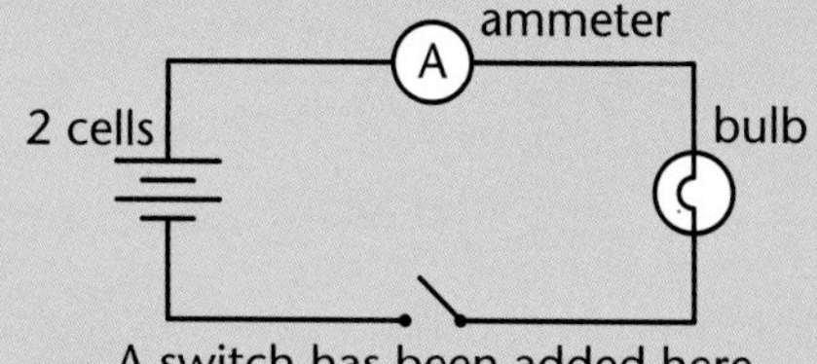

Two bulbs connected in series

The diagram shows one way of connecting two bulbs into the same circuit.

4 Copy and complete the sentences.

When two bulbs are connected in series, there is only __________ circuit for the current to flow round. You can measure the current through the bulbs by putting an __________ in series at any point in this circuit.

5 Draw a circuit diagram for circuit R with an ammeter in position X.

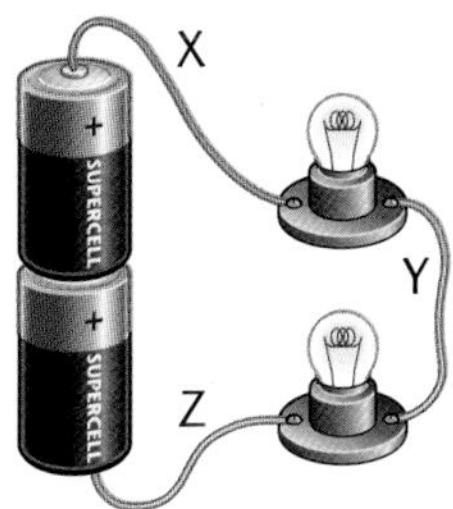

circuit R

These two bulbs are connected so that the current flows through one bulb and then through the other. There is **one** circuit for the current to flow round. The bulbs are connected in <u>series</u>.

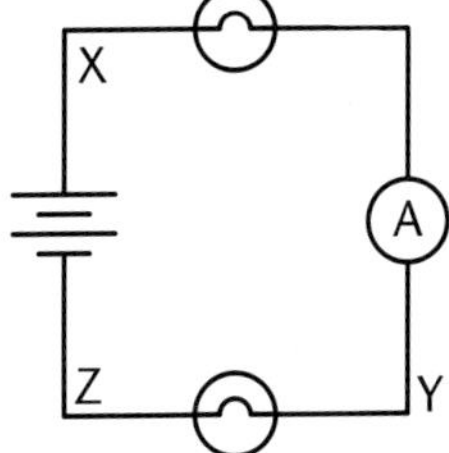

You can measure the current with an ammeter at X (or at Y, or at Z).

Two bulbs connected in parallel

The diagram shows another way of connecting two bulbs into a circuit.

6 Copy and complete the sentences.

When two bulbs are connected in parallel, you have two __________ circuits. To measure the current through one of the bulbs, you must put an ammeter in __________ with that bulb.

7 Draw a circuit diagram for circuit S with an ammeter to measure the current through bulb 2.

These two bulbs are connected to the same two cells in another way. We say that they are connected in **parallel**.

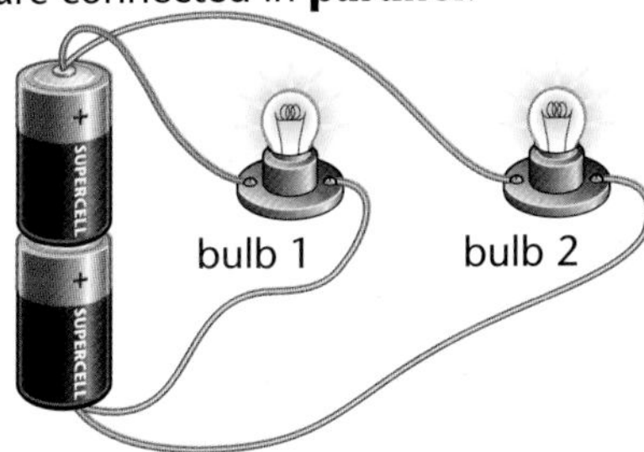

circuit S

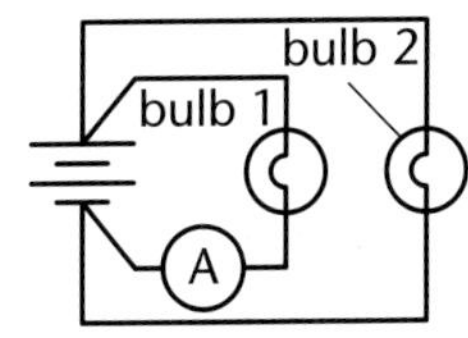

The ammeter has been added in series only with bulb 1. So it only measures the current through bulb 1.

WHAT YOU NEED TO REMEMBER (Copy and complete using the **key words**)

Measuring currents in circuits

To measure electric currents you use an ____________.

To measure the current through a bulb, you connect the ammeter in ____________ with the bulb.

If you connect two or more bulbs in series, there is still only ____________ circuit for the current to flow round. The current through all points in the circuit is exactly the ____________.

Two or more bulbs can be connected to a battery so that they are in separate circuits. We then say that they are connected in ____________.

More about circuits: CORE+ C3.14

Follows on from: 3.5, 3.6

C3.6 Electromagnets

A coil of wire with an electric current flowing through it behaves just like a bar magnet. We call it an **electromagnet**.

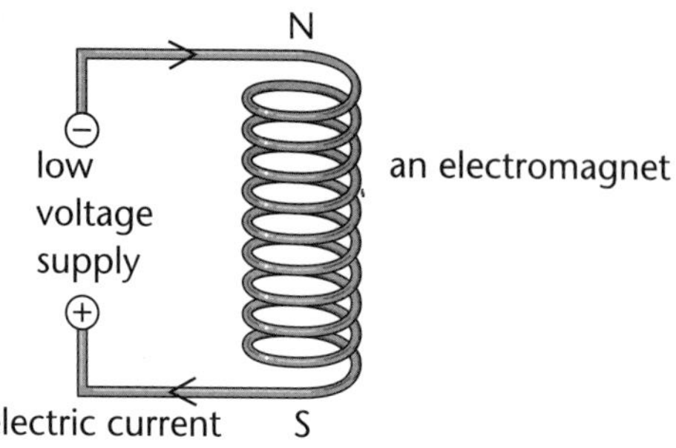

1 **(a)** Copy the diagram of the electromagnet, leaving plenty of space around it.

(b) Now draw the magnetic field around the electromagnet.

REMEMBER from pages 54–55

A magnetic compass shows you the direction of the lines of magnetic force.

S N

N

S

The lines of magnetic force show the magnetic field around the magnet.

A bar magnet has two poles: N = north pole, S = south pole.

Making the electromagnet stronger

The diagram shows how you can test the strength of an electromagnet.

You can make an electromagnet stronger in three different ways. The diagrams below show you how.

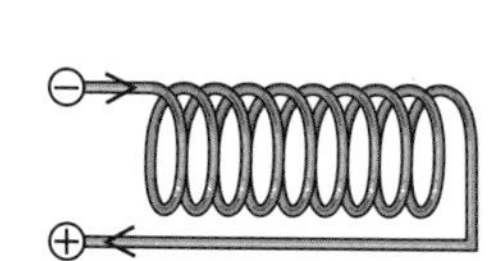

thin thread

steel nut

The stronger the magnet is, the further it pulls the steel nut.

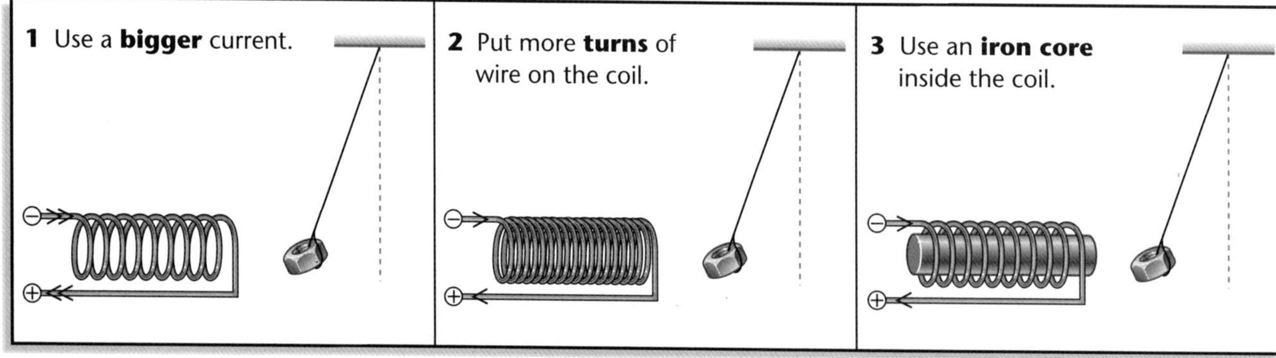

1 Use a **bigger** current.
2 Put more **turns** of wire on the coil.
3 Use an **iron core** inside the coil.

2 What are the three ways of making an electromagnet stronger?

3 You want to make a very strong electromagnet. What should you do?

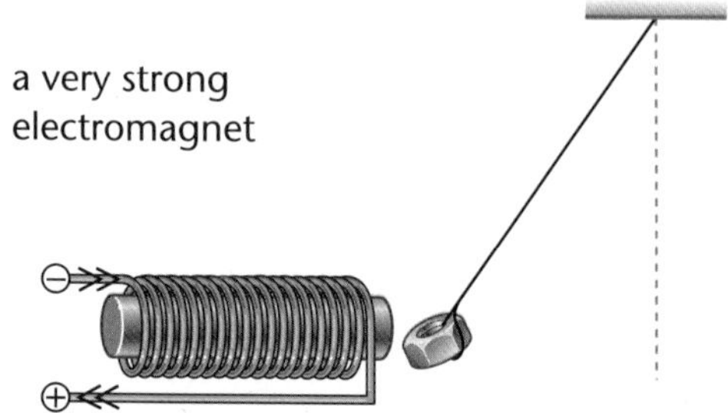

How does a magnet attract iron and steel?

When you put a piece of iron or steel close to a magnet, it is attracted. The diagrams show why this happens.

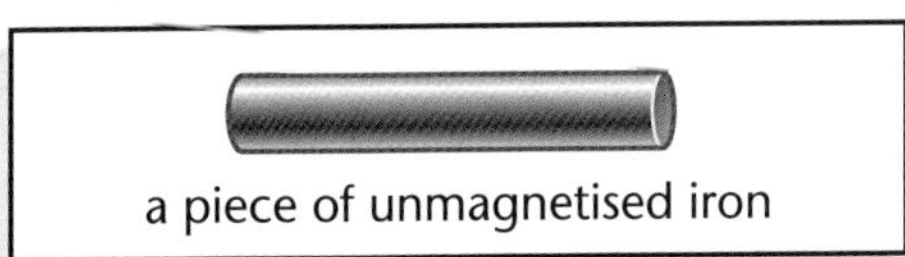

a piece of unmagnetised iron

4 Copy and complete the sentences.

When you put a piece of unmagnetised iron into a magnetic field, it becomes a _________.

The south pole of the magnetised iron is next to the _________ pole of the magnet. So the magnet and the piece of iron _________ each other.

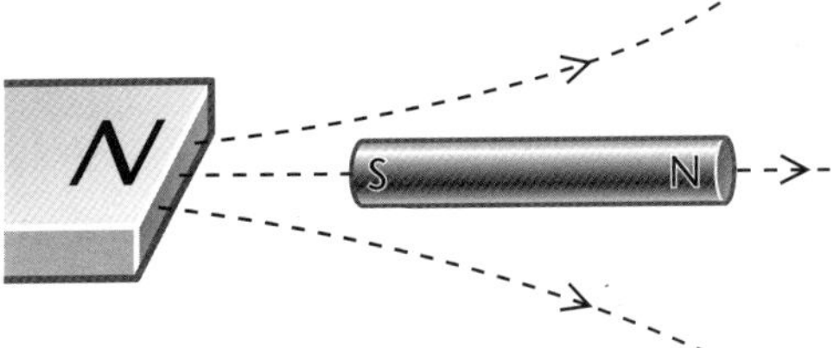

In a magnetic field, the piece of iron becomes a **magnet**.

5 Draw a diagram to show what happens when you put a piece of unmagnetised iron close to the <u>south</u> pole of a magnet.

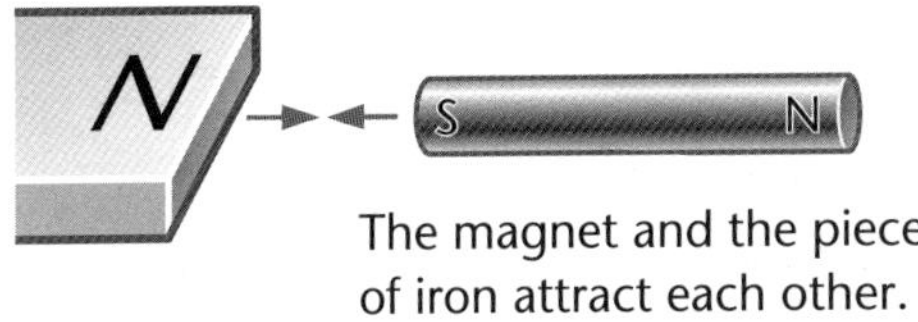

The magnet and the piece of iron attract each other.

Why an iron core makes an electromagnet stronger

A coil with a current flowing through it becomes a **magnet**. The magnetic field of the coil then magnetises the iron core.

6 Copy and complete the sentences.

An iron core makes an electromagnet _________.
This is because the _________ field of the coil makes the core into a magnet. The magnetic field of the coil and the magnetic field of the _________ _________ then add together.

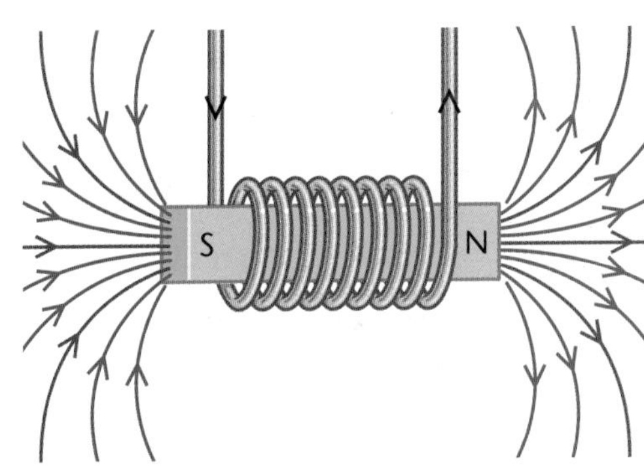

The magnetic field of the iron core adds itself to the magnetic field of the coil.

The magnetic effect of an electric current was accidentally discovered by Hans Christian Oersted in 1820.
Find out how Oersted made this discovery.

WHAT YOU NEED TO REMEMBER (Copy and complete using the **key words**)

Electromagnets

A coil with a current flowing through it becomes an ___________.
You can make this stronger by using a ___________ current, by putting more ___________ of wire on the coil or by using an ___________ ___________ inside the coil.

When you put some unmagnetised iron into a magnetic field, it becomes a ___________.

You should also know what is in the 'Remember' box.

Follows on from: 3.9

C3.7 Using electromagnets

REMEMBER from page 56

You can make an electromagnet by passing an electric current through a coil of wire. The electromagnet is a lot stronger if there is an iron core inside the coil.

A bar magnet stays magnetised all the time. We say that it is a **permanent** magnet.

An electromagnet is only magnetic when electricity flows through the coil. This makes electromagnets a lot more useful. You can **switch** them on and off.

1 Why is a permanent magnet not as useful as an electromagnet on a scrapyard crane?

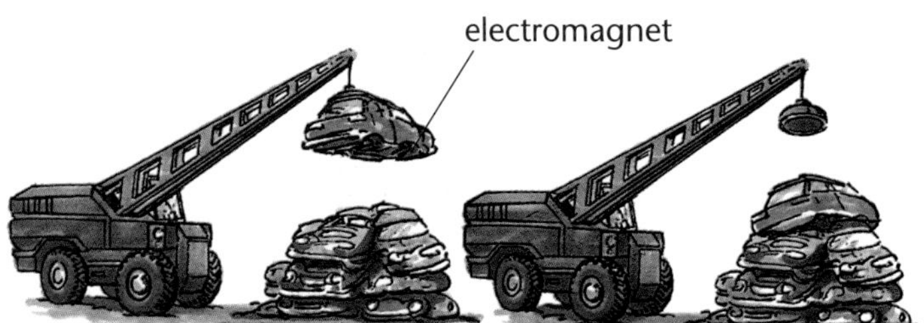

The crane uses an electromagnet to lift scrap cars.

To drop the car, the crane driver switches off the current.

A reed relay

Electromagnets can be used to make relays. A relay is a special kind of switch. It uses one current to switch on another current.

With a relay you can use a small current to switch on a larger current. You can also use a safe low voltage circuit to switch on a dangerous high voltage circuit.

The diagrams show how one sort of relay works.

2 Copy and complete the sentences.

When a small current flows through the coil, the steel strips become __________. So the steel strips __________ each other. When they touch, a __________ can then flow though the relay.

When the current through the coil is switched off, the coil is no longer a __________. So the steel strips __________ apart. The current through the relay is switched __________.

A

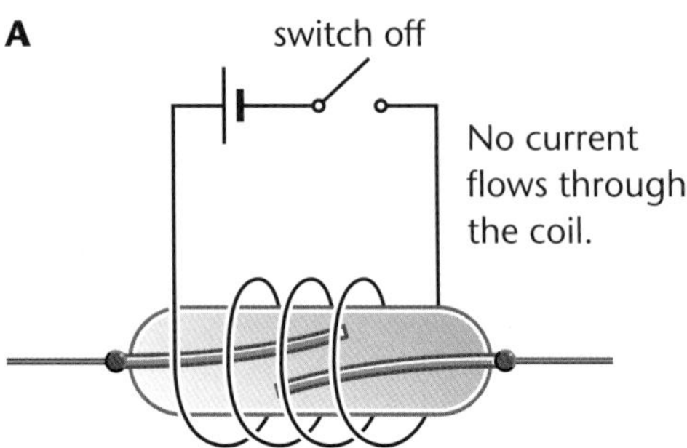

The springy steel strips are apart.

No current flows through the relay.

B

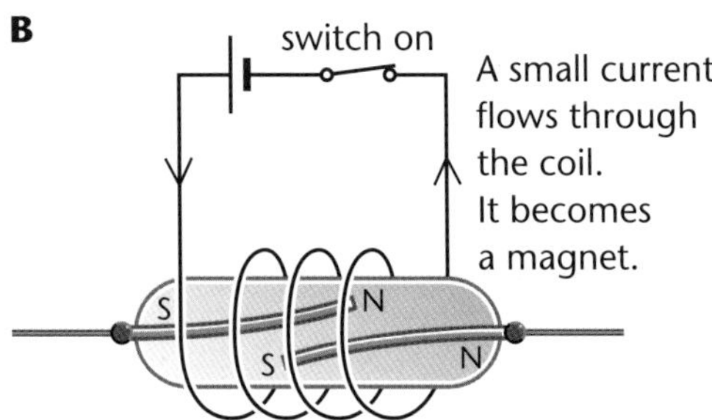

The magnetic field of the coil magnetises both of the steel strips.

C

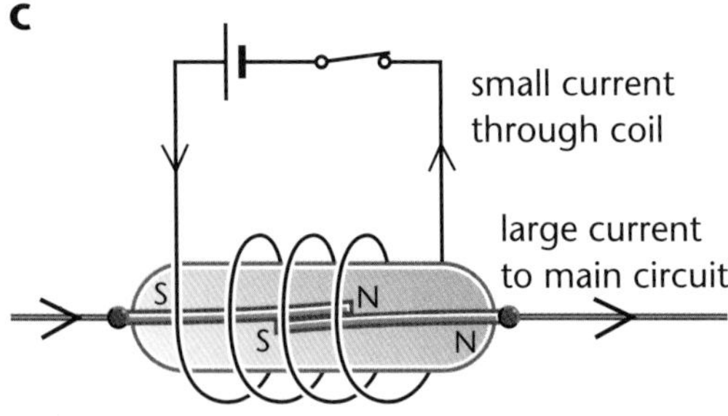

The steel strips attract and touch each other. A large current flows through the relay.

D

When you switch off the current to the coil, it stops being a magnet. So the steel strips spring apart, like they are in diagram A.

An electric bell

An electric bell uses an electromagnet to make it work. The electromagnet keeps switching itself on and off to make the bell ring.

The diagrams show how the bell works.

3 (a) Explain why iron is used in the core of the electromagnet.

(b) Explain why the iron core of the electromagnet is bent into a U-shape.

4 On a copy of the flow-chart, put the following sentences in the correct boxes to explain how the bell works.

The circuit to the electromagnet is broken.

A current flows through the coil of the electromagnet.

The springy steel bends back and touches the contact again.

The iron bar is attracted to the electromagnet.

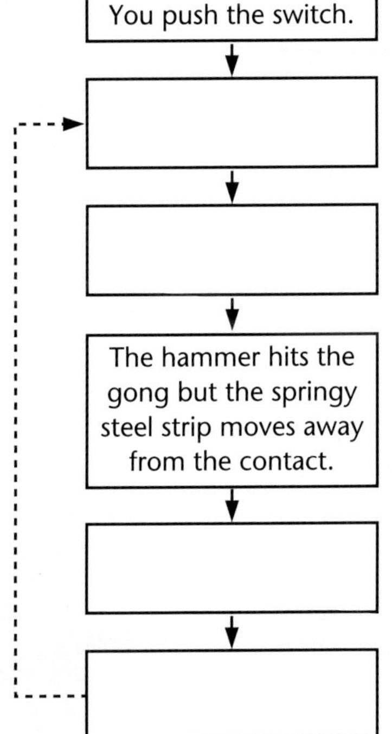

You push the switch.
The hammer hits the gong but the springy steel strip moves away from the contact.

REMEMBER from page 57

The magnetic effect of a magnet is strongest near to its north and south poles (ends).

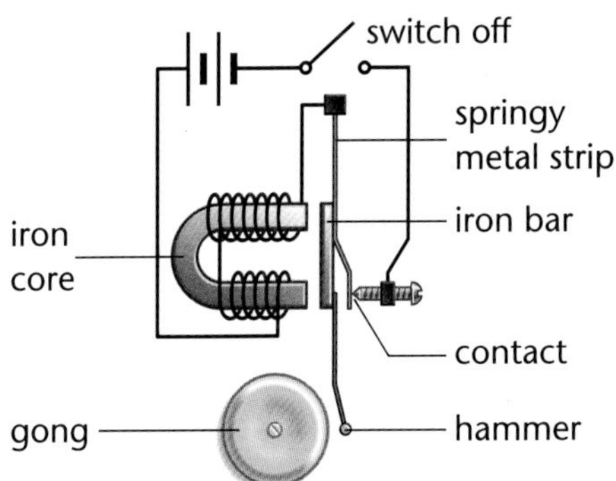

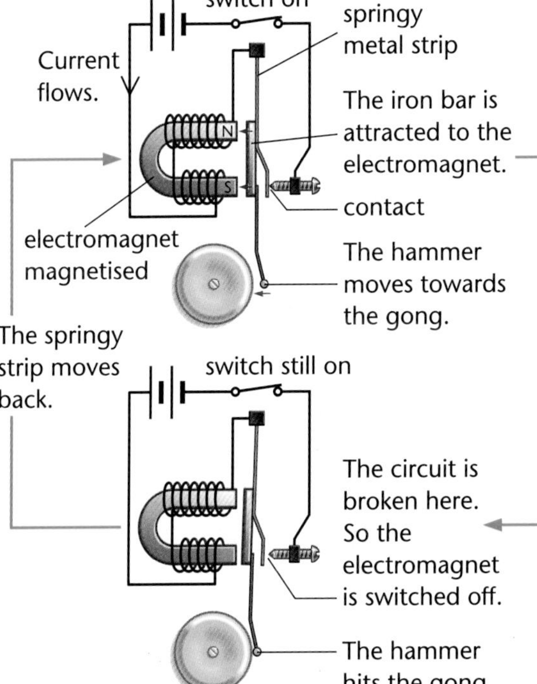

WHAT YOU NEED TO REMEMBER (Copy and complete using the **key words**)

Using electromagnets

A magnet that stays magnetised all the time is called a ____________ magnet.

An electromagnet is more useful than a permanent magnet because you can ____________ it on and off.

You may be given information about things which use electromagnets. You should then be able to explain how they work just like you did on these pages.

More about relays: CORE+ C3.15

C3.8 What happens to all the energy we transfer?

Every day we transfer energy in lots of different ways. For example, we burn petrol in car engines to make cars move.

But most of the energy from the burning petrol isn't transferred to the car as movement energy at all. It just makes the surroundings warmer.

The diagram shows the energy transferred to and from a car engine.

1 Copy and complete the table.

Where energy from burning petrol is transferred	%
to the surroundings as thermal energy	
to the surroundings as sound	
to the car as kinetic (movement) energy	
Total	

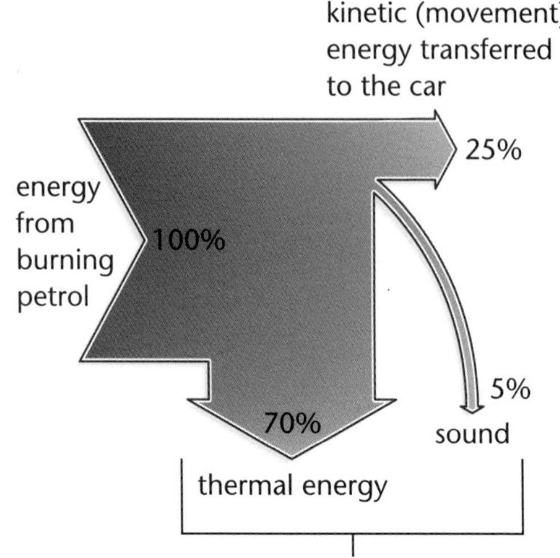

70% + 25% + 5% = 100%
So all the energy is transferred somewhere. Energy is never **lost**. But some is transferred in ways that are not useful to us.

What happens to the energy transferred to the car?

When a car is moving at a steady speed, even the energy usefully transferred to it from the engine doesn't make it move any faster. All it does is stop the car from slowing down.

Energy is transferred from the car to the surroundings by friction forces.

2 (a) What force must be overcome to stop the car from slowing down?

(b) What happens to the energy transferred by the engine to a car when the car travels at a steady speed?

In the end, all the energy from burning petrol in a car engine ends up making the surroundings a little bit **warmer**.

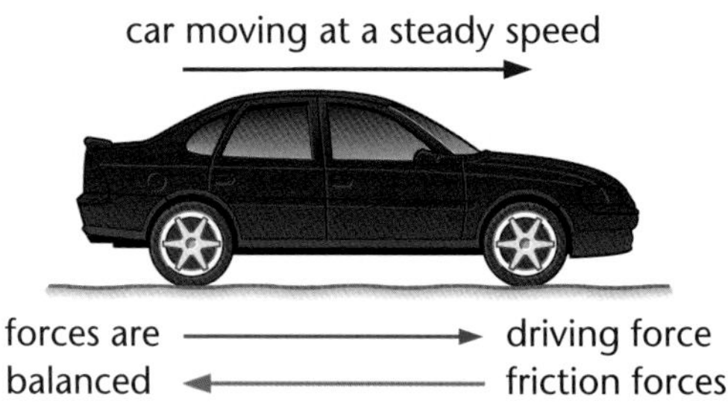

Friction forces transfer kinetic energy from the car to the surroundings as thermal energy and sound. As sounds fade away, this energy too makes the surroundings just a little bit warmer.

Energy transfers in a car engine.

Energy that isn't much use

The energy transferred by a car engine doesn't get used up. It all ends up in the surroundings. But it isn't much use to us any more because it's so spread out.

The diagrams show some <u>very</u> hot things. We can transfer energy from them in useful ways because the thermal energy <u>isn't</u> spread out.

A hot filament produces light. A hot flame can cook things. Hot gases can turn a turbine.

What you can do with very hot things.

3 Write down <u>three</u> useful ways that very hot things can transfer energy.

Each time we transfer energy, it is harder to transfer it again in any useful way.

We can use electricity to transfer energy to the surroundings in many different ways.

Boiling water is useful for making tea. But it is difficult to transfer the energy again to light a room or make a TV set work.

4 Look at the diagrams.

(a) The thermal energy in a kettle of boiling water is less useful for energy transfers than the electricity that was used to make the water hot in the first place. Explain why.

(b) Why is the thermal energy in a kettle of boiling water even less useful if you pour it into a bathful of cold water?

Energy and energy sources

Energy never gets used up, but each time it is transferred it gets more **spread** out. This makes it less useful. We say that the energy has become <u>dissipated</u>.

Energy <u>sources</u> such as fossil fuels <u>can</u> get used up. We say that these energy sources are <u>non-renewable</u>.

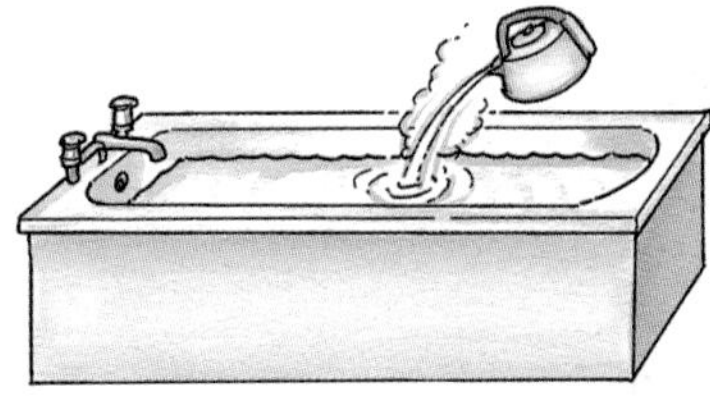

If you pour a kettleful of boiling water into a bathful of cold water, it only warms it up a tiny bit. All the energy is still there, but it is spread out and not much use for anything.

WHAT YOU NEED TO REMEMBER (Copy and complete using the **key words**)

What happens to all the energy we transfer?

When you transfer energy, none is ever ______________ but some is always ______________.

All the energy that we transfer eventually ends up making the surroundings a tiny bit ______________. This energy isn't very useful because it is very ______________ out.

More about storing energy: CORE+ C3.16

C3.9 Energy from the Sun

We measure energy in units called joules.
500 J means 500 joules.

A lot of energy from the Sun reaches the Earth every second of every day.

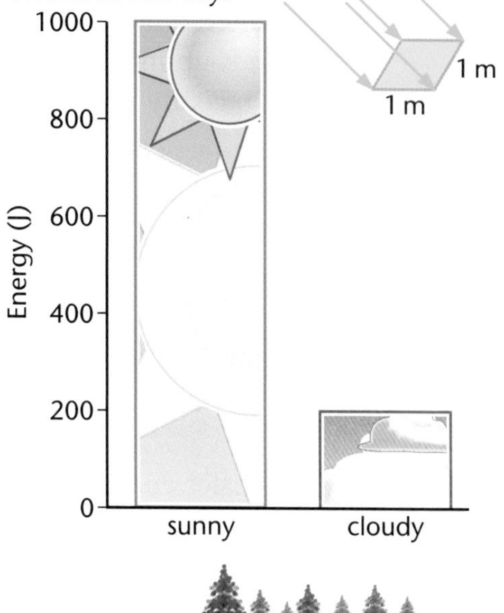

1 Look at the bar-chart. Then copy and complete the table.

	Energy from the Sun in London (per square metre per second)
sunny day	________ J
cloudy day	________ J

Transferring the energy from sunlight

The diagrams show three different ways energy from sunlight can be transferred to do something useful.

Plants transfer about 1% of the energy from sunlight. As plants grow, this energy is stored in the materials the plants are made of. We say that the energy is stored in biomass.

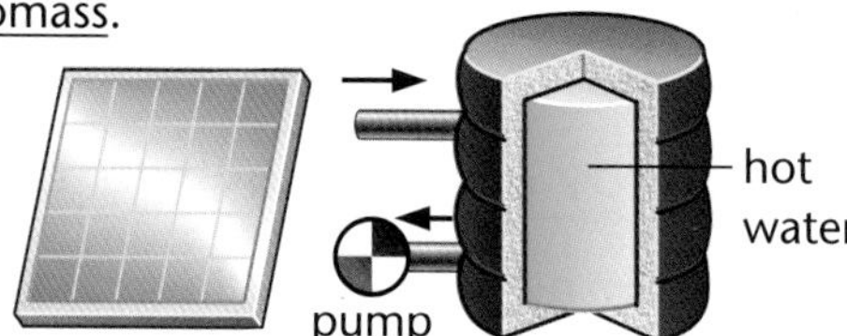

Solar panels transfer about 70% of the energy from sunlight to water by making it hot. The hot water is stored until it is needed.

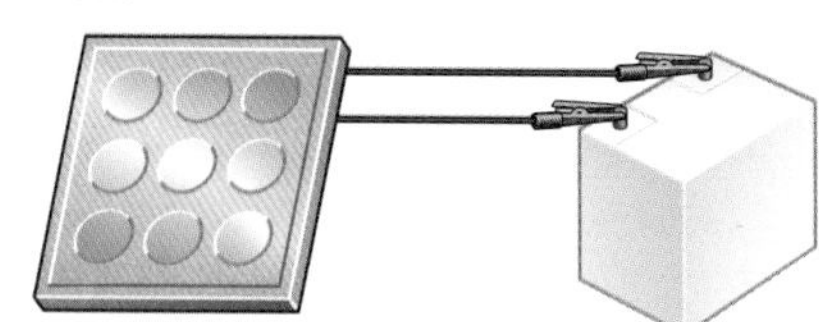

Solar cells transfer about 10% of the energy from sunlight as electricity to the re-chargeable battery. The battery stores chemical energy until it is needed.

2 (a) Which method transfers most of the Sun's energy in a useful way?

(b) Which method transfers least?

In bright sunshine, a 5 m^2 solar panel can supply all the thermal energy a house needs.

3 The solar panel can't supply all the thermal energy the house needs all of the time. Why not?

After the energy from sunlight has been transferred, it is often stored until it is needed.

4 How is the energy stored:

(a) after being transferred to plants?

(b) after being transferred to a solar panel?

(c) after being transferred to solar cells?

WHAT YOU NEED TO REMEMBER

Energy from the Sun

You will need to use Core ideas in different ways like you have on this page.

C3.10 Comparing energy sources

The table compares some energy sources that we use to generate electricity.

Energy source	Building and running costs (except for fuel)	Fuel costs	Pollution problems	Overall cost of each Unit of electricity
nuclear fuel	high	low	Few problems provided there are no accidents. Dangerous wastes need to be stored for a long time.	average
fossil fuel	quite low	high	Burning pollutes the air with carbon dioxide, nitrogen oxides and (for coal and oil) sulphur dioxide.	lower than average
wind	high	zero	On tops of hills so can be seen for miles around. Noisy if near homes.	slightly higher than average
solar	very high	zero	None, but can be used on a large scale only in very sunny areas.	much higher than average
tides	high	zero	Destroys habitats of birds and other things that live in river estuaries.	slightly lower than average

1 Write down the energy sources in order, starting with the cheapest and finishing with the most expensive:

(a) for the building and running costs;

(b) for the fuel costs;

(c) for the overall cost of each Unit of electricity.

2 What problems of pollution are caused by burning fossil fuels?

3 Nuclear power stations do not usually cause much pollution. But some people want to ban them because they believe they are a danger to the environment. What makes people believe this?

4 Renewable energy sources don't pollute air or water. But they can still harm the environment. Describe how two of the renewable energy sources affect the environment.

WHAT YOU NEED TO REMEMBER

Comparing energy sources

You will need to use Core ideas in different ways like you have on this page.

CORE +
Follows on from: C3.2

C3.11 Renewable energy sources in action

This topic was written using a word processor powered by renewable energy sources. The photograph shows how the electricity is generated.

1 Copy and complete the table.

Energy source	Device that produces electricity

This writer's electricity is produced by the wind generator and the arrays of solar cells on the roof.

Electricity when it's wanted

Solar cells don't produce electricity at night or in dull weather. Also it isn't always windy. But there is still electricity in the cottage. The diagram shows why.

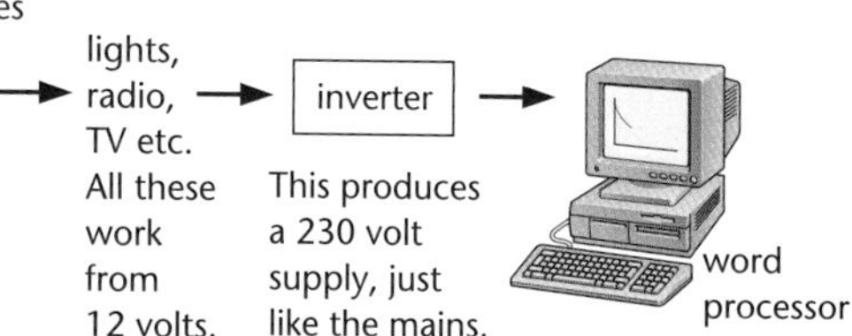
set of large 12 volt batteries
lights, radio, TV etc.
All these work from 12 volts.
inverter
This produces a 230 volt supply, just like the mains.
word processor

2 Why is there still electricity even when none is being generated?

3 Copy and complete the sentences.

Most of the appliances in the cottage work from the 12 volt ___________.

But the word processor works from an ___________.
This provides a 230 volt supply just like the ___________.

REMEMBER from pages 72 and 74

Fossil fuels like coal and oil were formed from living things which died millions of years ago. They are non-renewable. Once they are used up, they cannot be replaced.

Keeping the cottage warm

The wind generator and solar cells don't produce enough electricity to heat the cottage or for cooking. To do this, peat is burned in a stove.

The photograph shows how peat is formed.

Layers of dead moss from previous years.
It takes a few hundred years for the dead moss to turn to peat.

Pieces of peat are cut with a special spade. They are dried and then burned.

4 Peat is both a renewable fuel and a fossil fuel. Explain why.

WHAT YOU NEED TO REMEMBER

Renewable energy sources in action

You will need to use Core ideas in different ways like you have on this page.

CORE +
Follows on from: C3.3

C3.12 More about energy transfers

Some devices transfer energy mainly in the way that we want them to. We say that they are <u>efficient</u>.

An electric kettle, for example, is very efficient. Nearly all of the energy we supply to the kettle is transferred to the water inside it.

The efficiency of an appliance is the percentage of energy it transfers in the way that we want it to.

A light bulb that transferred all the electrical energy to its surroundings as light would be 100% efficient. Real light bulbs are a lot less efficient than this.

The diagrams show how efficient some electrical appliances are.

1 Copy the table below. Then complete the <u>first</u> <u>two</u> columns, putting the appliances in order. Start with the most efficient appliance and end with the least efficient.

Appliance	Efficiency (%)	Wasted energy (%)

Making it all add up

Energy is never lost. <u>All</u> of the energy supplied to an electrical appliance is transferred in one way or another.

For example, the light bulb transfers 5% of the energy supplied to it as light and the other 95% as thermal energy:

5% + 95% = 100%.

We say that energy is <u>conserved</u>.

2 Complete the <u>third</u> column of your table.

kettle

98% to hot water

2% wasted

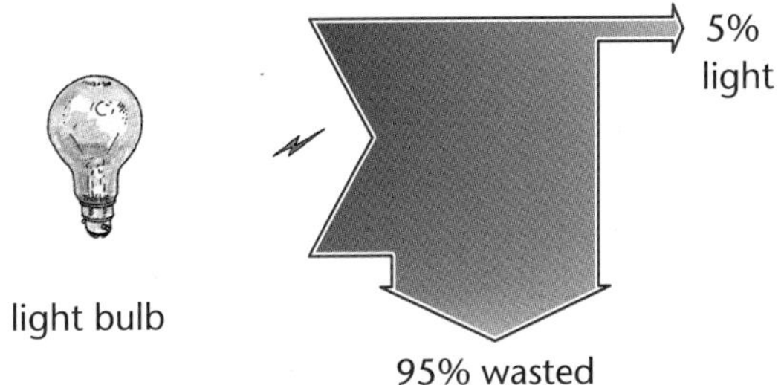

light bulb

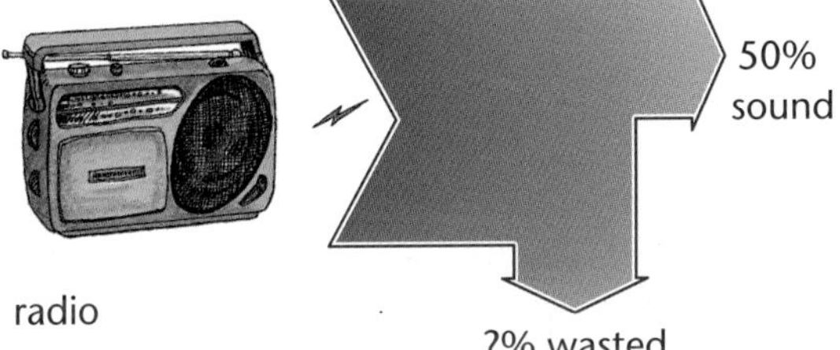

radio

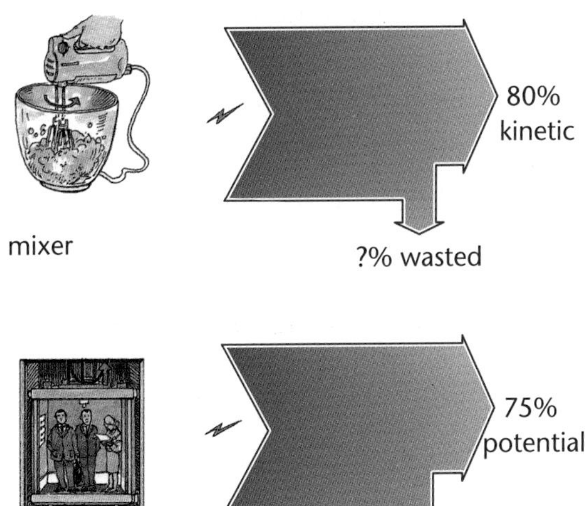

mixer

lift

WHAT YOU NEED TO REMEMBER

More about energy transfers

You will need to use Core ideas in different ways like you have on this page.

C3.13 Cells and batteries

A useful but expensive way to get an electric current is from a battery.

The diagram shows the first kind of battery to be invented.

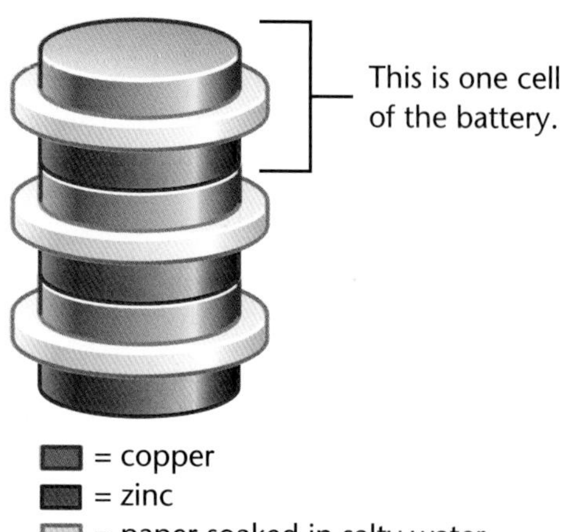

Alessandro Volta (1745–1827) made the first battery in about 1800.

1 **(a)** When was the battery first invented?

(b) What did Volta use to make this battery?

2 How many cells are there in the battery shown in the diagram?

You can make a cell with <u>any</u> two different metals and a solution that will conduct electricity.

A cell works because one of the metals is more reactive than the other.

The diagram shows how reactive some metals are.

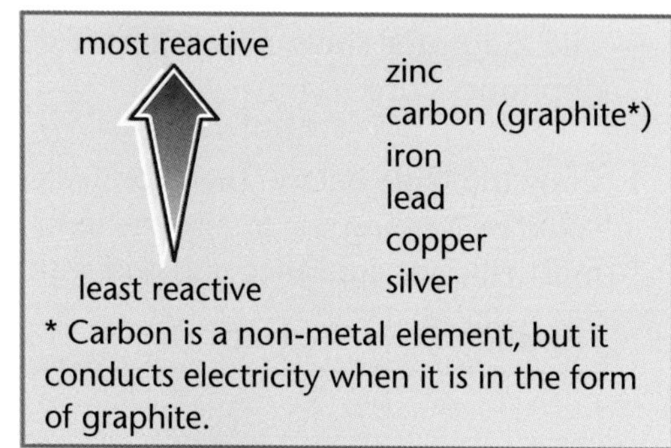

* Carbon is a non-metal element, but it conducts electricity when it is in the form of graphite.

3 Which metal in Volta's cell is the more reactive?

Another type of cell

The diagram shows the cheapest type of cell that you can buy in a shop.

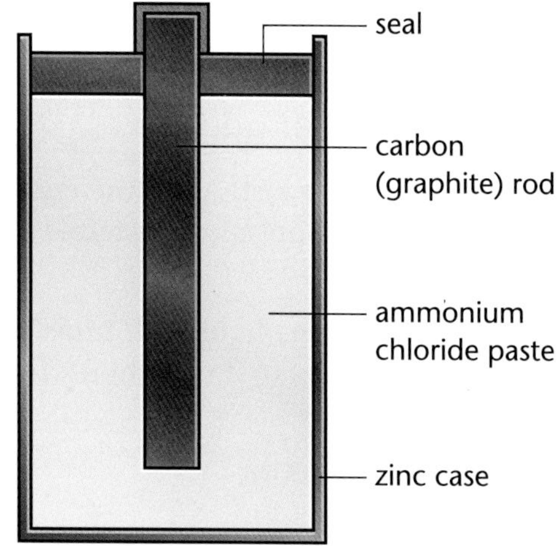

The cell also has manganese dioxide around the carbon rod. This stops bubbles of gas from building up around the rod. The bubbles would stop the cell from working.

4 Copy and complete the following.

The cell is made from:

- a reactive metal called ___________;
- a less reactive element called ___________;
- ammonium chloride made into a ___________.

5 **(a)** What other substance is in the cell?

(b) Why is it there?

WHAT YOU NEED TO REMEMBER

Cells and batteries

You will need to use Core ideas in different ways like you have on this page.

C3.14 More about circuits

A two-way circuit

The diagrams show a circuit that is often used for a light on stairs. You can switch the light on or off from the top of the stairs or from the bottom. It doesn't matter where you last switched the light on or off.

A

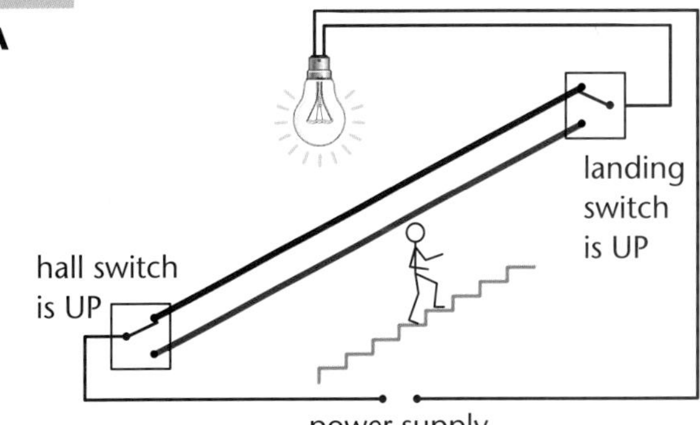

B

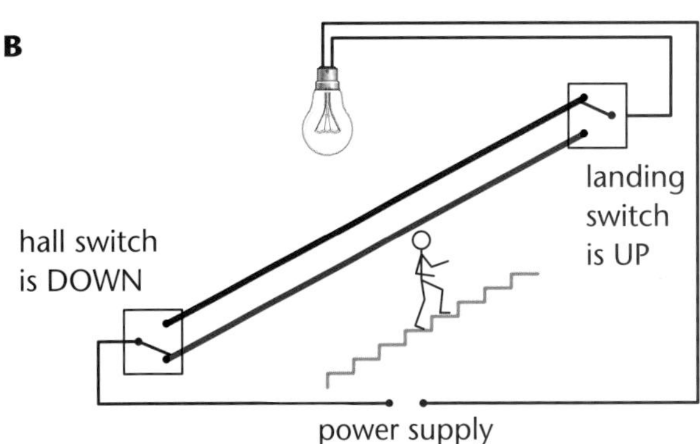

1 Copy and complete the sentences.

On diagram A, both switches are in the __________ position. So a current can flow along the __________ wire. The light is __________.

If one of the switches is put to the DOWN position, the circuit is ___________. This makes the light go ___________.

2 Draw a diagram to show what happens if both switches are DOWN.

Currents in a parallel circuit

The diagram shows two <u>different</u> light bulbs connected in parallel. The ammeters show the currents in different parts of the circuit.

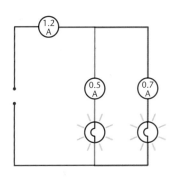

3 Copy and complete the table.

Part of circuit	Current
red	
green	
blue	

4 **(a)** Add together the currents in the green and blue parts of the circuit.

(b) What do you notice about your answer?

In a parallel circuit, the current from the supply is the total of the currents in the separate branches of the circuit.

WHAT YOU NEED TO REMEMBER

More about circuits

You will need to use Core ideas in different ways like you have on this page.

CORE +
Follows on from: C3.7

C3.15 Switching on a car starter motor

To start a car, all the driver has to do is turn the ignition key. Under the bonnet, a large electric motor turns the heavy engine to make it start. The motor needs a very big electric current to turn the engine. This current is too big to go through the ignition switch. So a relay must be used.

The diagrams show what happens when the driver turns the ignition key.

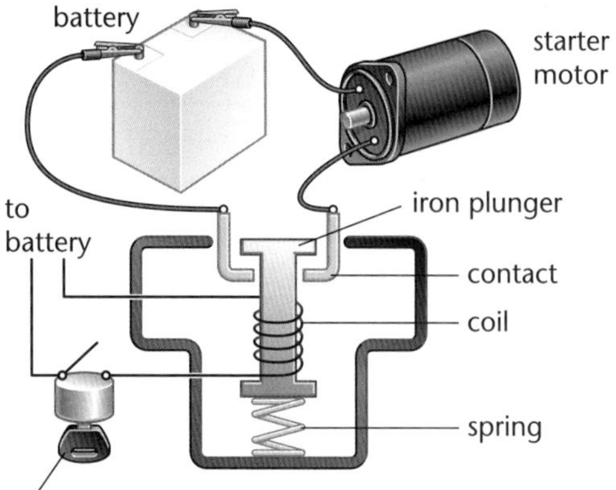
battery
starter motor
to battery
iron plunger
contact
coil
spring

Unless you turn the ignition key, the switch is off.

1 Write down the following sentences in the correct order to describe what happens. The first one is in the right place.

The driver turns the ignition key.

- A large current flows to the starter motor.
- The top of the plunger connects the two contacts.
- A small current flows through the coil.
- The iron plunger is pulled down.

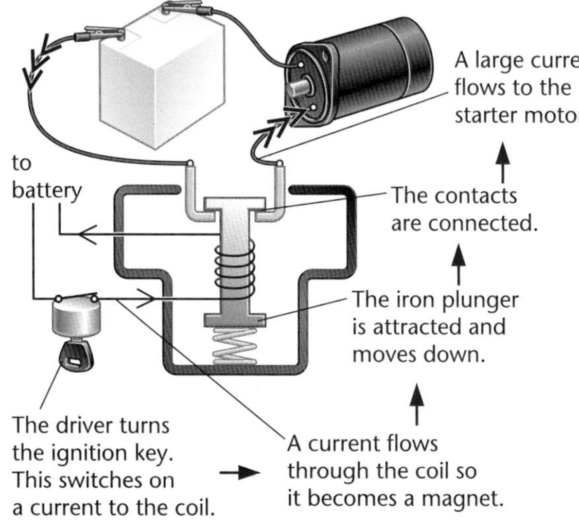
A large current flows to the starter motor.
to battery
The contacts are connected.
The iron plunger is attracted and moves down.
The driver turns the ignition key. This switches on a current to the coil.
A current flows through the coil so it becomes a magnet.

When the driver stops turning the ignition key, the starter motor stops.

2 Copy and complete the sentences.

When the driver stops turning the ignition key, the coil stops being a __________.
The iron plunger is pushed back up by the __________.
So the current to the starter motor is switched __________.

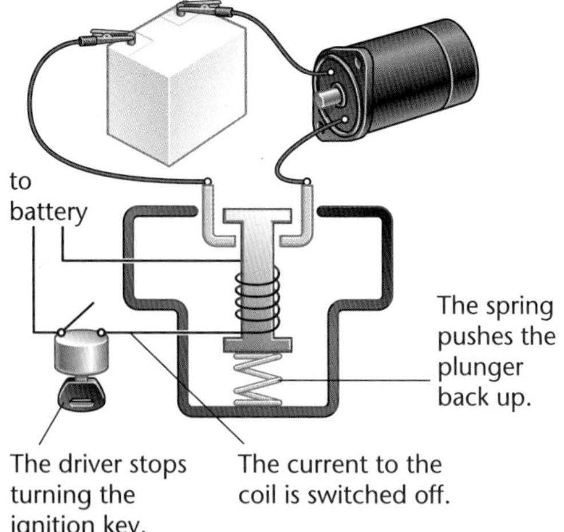
to battery
The spring pushes the plunger back up.
The driver stops turning the ignition key.
The current to the coil is switched off.

WHAT YOU NEED TO REMEMBER

Switching on a car starter motor

You will need to use Core ideas in different ways like you have on this page.

CORE +
Follows on from: 4.8, C3.8

C3.16 Storing energy for when it's needed

Energy for starting a car

A car starter motor needs a very big current. The starter might be used many times every day. This is enough to make even a very big battery go flat very quickly.

The photograph shows why a car battery doesn't go flat.

1 Copy and complete the energy transfer diagrams.

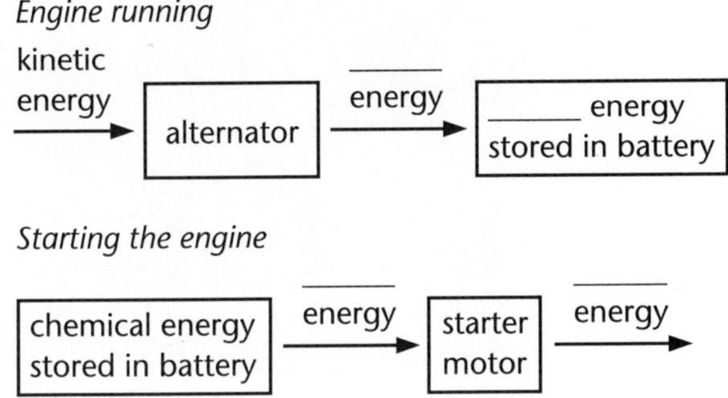

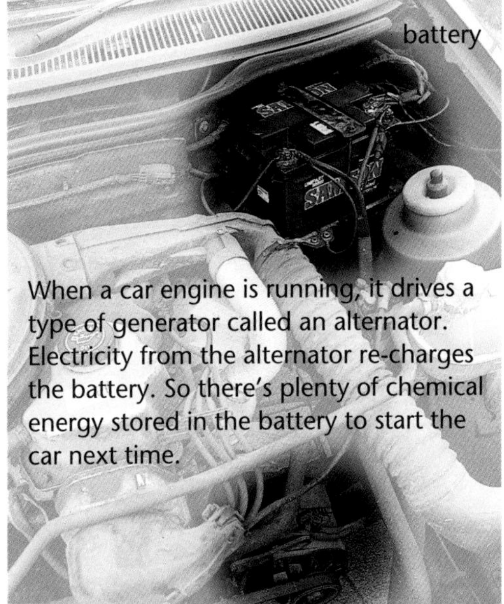

When a car engine is running, it drives a type of generator called an alternator. Electricity from the alternator re-charges the battery. So there's plenty of chemical energy stored in the battery to start the car next time.

Buses with special brakes

Most buses are slowed down using brakes. The brakes get hot and transfer thermal energy to the surroundings. So the kinetic energy the bus had when it was moving is wasted.

The diagrams show how a new type of bus avoids wasting energy when it slows down.

Inside the bus, there is a large heavy wheel called a *flywheel.*

The bus slows down by transferring energy to the flywheel. This makes it spin very fast.

The rotating flywheel stores kinetic energy. Energy from the flywheel can then be transferred back to the bus to start it moving again.

2 Copy and complete the sentences.

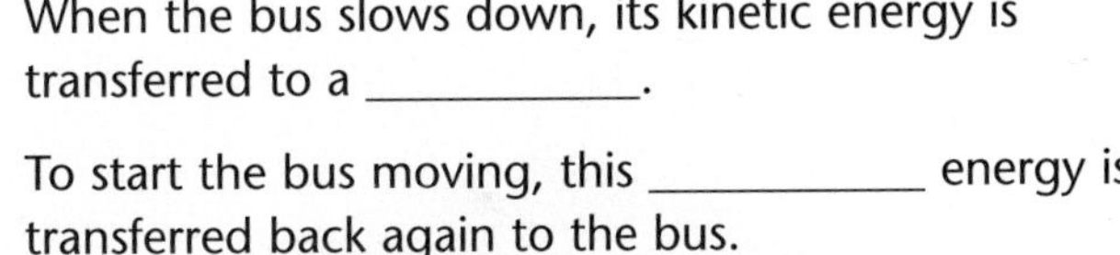

When the bus slows down, its kinetic energy is transferred to a __________.

To start the bus moving, this __________ energy is transferred back again to the bus.

WHAT YOU NEED TO REMEMBER

Storing energy for when it's needed

You will need to use Core ideas in different ways like you have on this page.

Investigating a sliding box

Science isn't just about what other people have found out. It is also about finding things out for yourself. As you read about how John investigates a sliding box you will learn about how to do science.

A wooden box is standing on a rubber mat on a table.
When John tries to pull it along with his finger, the box doesn't move.
To make the box move, John has to pull harder.

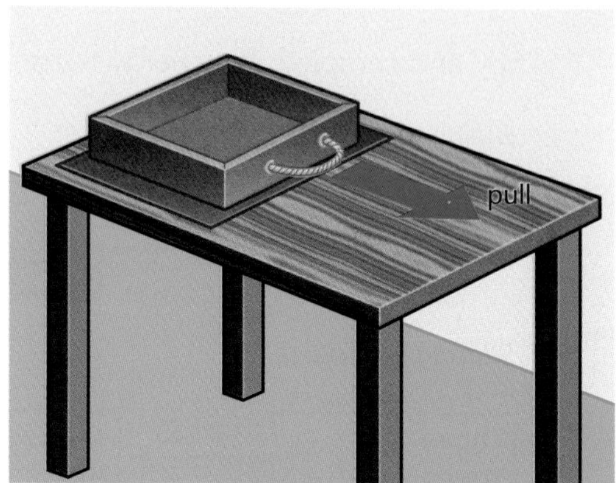

1 Read the 'Information' box.

(a) Why doesn't the box move when John pulls it with his finger?

(b) Why does the box move when John pulls it harder?

INFORMATION

When you try to slide one surface across another, a friction force acts in the opposite direction.

There is a limit to the size of this friction force.

To make the surfaces slide across each other, you must push or pull with a force that is bigger than the maximum friction force.

John pulls the box off the rubber mat and on to the smooth table top. He notices that it is now much easier to pull the box.

2 Why is it much easier to pull the box along the smooth table top?

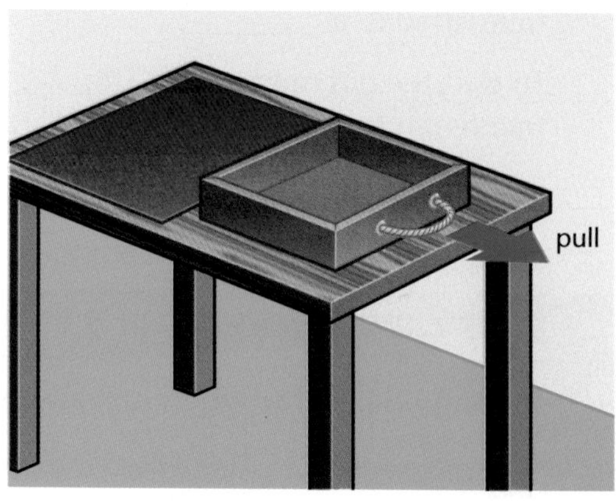

Planning an experiment

John wants to measure how much easier it is to pull the box along the table top than to pull it along the rubber mat.

First, John must decide what measurements he is going to make; he must **plan** his experiment. He begins by trying out a couple of ideas. The diagrams show you what he did.

force meter
pull
It was difficult to pull with a steady force. So the reading on the force meter kept changing.

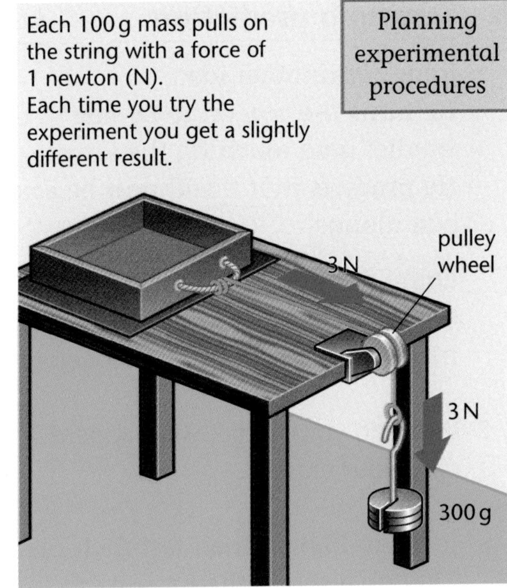
Each 100 g mass pulls on the string with a force of 1 newton (N).
Each time you try the experiment you get a slightly different result.
pulley wheel
3 N
3 N
300 g

Planning experimental procedures

3 Copy the table. Then complete it to show what John should do.

Obtaining evidence

Problem	Plan
How should John pull the box along with a force that is steady and easy to measure?	
What should John do to get an accurate result for the force needed to move the box?*	
How should John record his results?*	

(*Hint: If you don't know the answers to these questions look at the table below.)

John's results

The table shows the results of John's experiment.

Surface that box is standing on	Force needed to keep box just moving along				
	1st try	2nd try	3rd try	4th try	Average
smooth table	4 N	3 N	5 N	4 N	4 N
rubber mat	21 N	20 N	18 N	21 N	20 N

What do John's results tell us?

Look carefully at John's results.

Analysing evidence and drawing conclusions

4 Copy and complete the sentences.

The force needed to make the box slide on the rubber mat is a lot __________ than the force needed to make it slide on the smooth table.

In fact, the force is __________ times bigger.

Testing a prediction

John has another idea.
He turns the box on to its side so that there is a smaller area touching the table.
He **predicts** that it will now be easier to pull the box along.

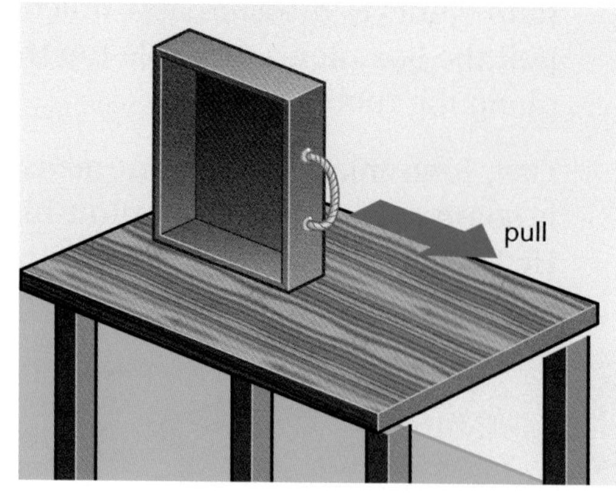

Emily disagrees. She says that there will now be a bigger pressure on the table so she predicts that the friction force will also be bigger.

5 What do you predict will happen?
Give your reasons.

John and Emily then test their predictions.
The table shows their results.

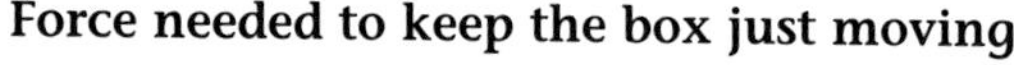

Force needed to keep the box just moving

Box standing on its base	Box standing on its side
4 N	3 N
3 N	5 N
5 N	4 N
4 N	5 N

Considering the strength of evidence

6 **(a)** Work out the average force needed in each case. (See 'How to work out an average' if you need help.)

(b) What difference is there between the averages?

(c) How big is this difference compared to the differences between the results for the same test?

(d) What do you now want to say about John's prediction, Emily's prediction and your own prediction?

How to work out an average

To work out the average of several measurements:
1 add all the measurements together to get the total;
2 divide the total by the number of measurements that there are.

Example
Five measurements: 5 N, 8 N, 6 N, 7 N, 4 N
Total = 30
30 ÷ 5 = 6
Average = 6 N

Testing another prediction

John and Emily both think that putting something inside the box will make it harder for the box to slide.

When they test their prediction, they get the results shown in the table.

Mass of box + contents	Force needed to keep box just moving (average of five tests)
1 kg	3.5 N
2 kg	8.0 N
3 kg	12.5 N
4 kg	15.5 N

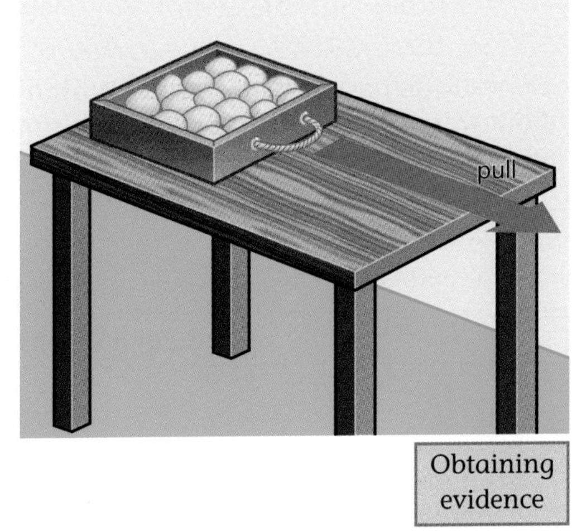

Obtaining evidence

7 Do these results support the prediction made by John and Emily?

Drawing a graph

A graph is often a good way to show the measurements you make in an experiment.

You can then <u>see</u> what the results tell you.

Analysing evidence and drawing conclusions

8 (a) Plot the results from the table above on a graph. (The diagram shows you how to do this.)

(b) Then draw the graph line. (The graph is <u>very nearly</u> a straight line. With very accurate measurements, it probably would be a straight line. So instead of joining the points on the graph dot-to-dot, draw the straight line that is <u>closest</u> to going through <u>all</u> of the points. We call this the **best** straight line.)

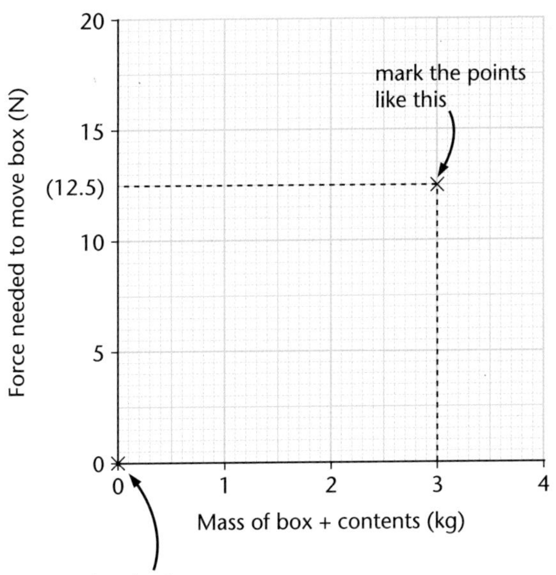

What you need to know about Key Stage 3 Science SATs

Science SATs papers look very long. Don't worry about this. Most pupils have enough time to answer all of the questions.

Easier questions are at the beginning of the paper, but you will be able to answer some, if not all, of most questions. So start with the questions and parts of questions you find easy. Then go back to the more difficult ones.

Read each question carefully to see what you have to do.

- Sometimes you have to choose the right answer from those provided in the question.
  Read *all* the possible answers before you choose.

  This kind of question comes in several different forms.

  - 'Tick the correct box' means tick *one* box. So don't tick more than one box unless the question tells you to.

Which of these fuels is renewable?

Tick the correct box.

coal ☐
wood ☑
oil ☐
nuclear fuel ☐

This gets 1 mark.

Which of these fuels is renewable?

Tick the correct box.

coal ☐
wood ☑
oil ☑
nuclear fuel ☐

This gets 0 mark. →

- Complete a sentence by choosing a word from the list.

  You *must* use a word from the list.

  So Mercury is incorrect because, although it is the planet closest to the Sun, it is not in the list.

Complete the sentence by choosing a word from the list.

Venus **Earth** **Mars** **Jupiter**

Of these planets, the one closest to the Sun is Venus.

- From the information in the chart, choose the best answer to the question.

  The example opposite uses a bar chart. You have to get both planets right to get the mark.

  Other planets such as Jupiter or Saturn are bigger still, but are incorrect because they are not in the chart.

From the information in the chart, choose the **two** biggest planets.

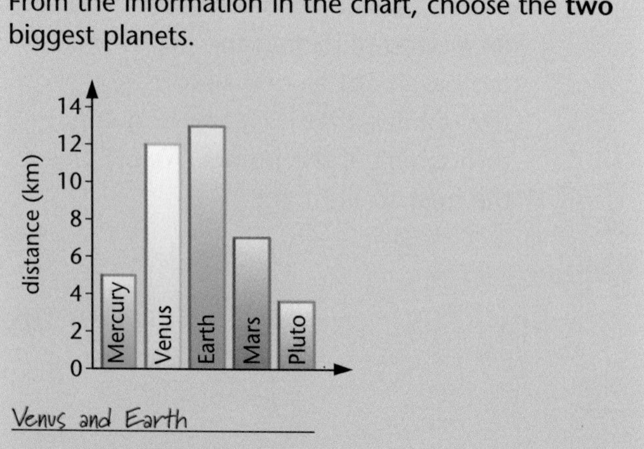

- In some questions you will need to give short answers of one word, a few words or one sentence.

  Clues: there will only be one line for your answer.

  there will only be one mark for a correct answer (shown in the margin).

  There's no need to write any more (e.g. *red, orange, yellow, green, blue and violet* or *different colours are refracted different amounts*). There's only 1 mark, so it's a waste of time.

What happens to a thin beam of white light when you pass it through a glass prism.

It splits up into colours. 1 mark

or

What happens to a thin beam of white light when you pass it through a glass prism.

It produces a spectrum. 1 mark

- In other questions you will need to give longer answers.

  Clues: there will be two or more lines for your answer.

  there will be two or more marks for a correct answer.

  These questions will often ask you to 'describe' or 'explain'. Make sure you know the difference between these two instructions.

A thin beam of white light passes through a glass prism.

Describe what happens to the light.

Explain why this happens.

this describes → *The light splits up into a spectrum of colours.*

this explains → *This happens because the light is refracted as it goes into and out of the prism. Different colours of light are refracted different amounts.*

- Often in a question you will see a word or words in **bold** type. This usually emphasises what you need to give in your answer.

  To give more reasons is time wasted.

Give **one** way of making an electromagnet stronger.

use an iron core 1 mark

The diagram shows a fish.

How does its **shape** help it to move through the water?

It is streamlined.

Your answer must be about the shape of the fish, so '*It is long and thin*' is also correct, but an answer '*It has fins*' is incorrect.

- When asked to 'calculate' an answer, you may be told to show your working. This is important because you may gain some of the marks even if your final answer is wrong.

  (a) Units may be provided.
  If they are provided do *not* change them.

A cyclist travels 50 metres in 10 seconds.
What is her average speed in **metres per second?**
Show your working.

speed $= \frac{\text{distance}}{\text{time}} = \frac{50}{10}$

= 5 metres per second

  (b) You may be asked to write in the units.

  You may not get any marks without the units.

A man weighs 800 newtons.
The total area of his shoes is 400 cm^2.
What is the pressure he exerts on the ground?
Show your working. Give the units.

pressure $= \frac{\text{force}}{\text{area}} = \frac{800}{400} = 2\ N/cm^2$

- When you are asked to complete a diagram, you must do so neatly and accurately and exactly as instructed.

  Use a ruler for lines that should be straight.

  The diagram opposite has been completed but has several errors.
  How many mistakes can you spot?

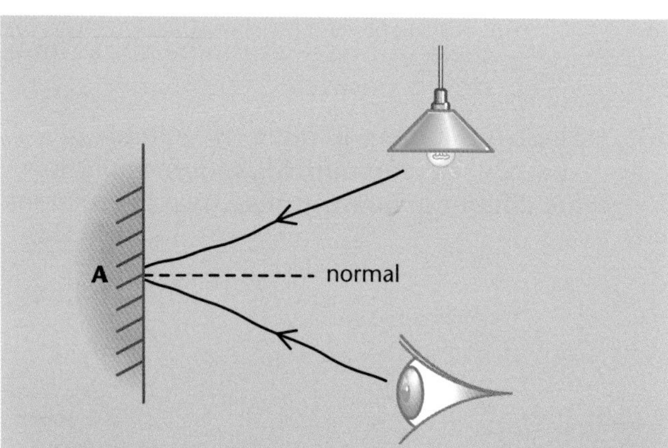

Draw one ray of light on the diagram from the bulb to point A on the mirror. Use a ruler.
Put an arrow on the ray to show the direction of the light.
The ray is reflected from the mirror to the eye of the girl. Draw in this reflected ray.

This is a correct completion.

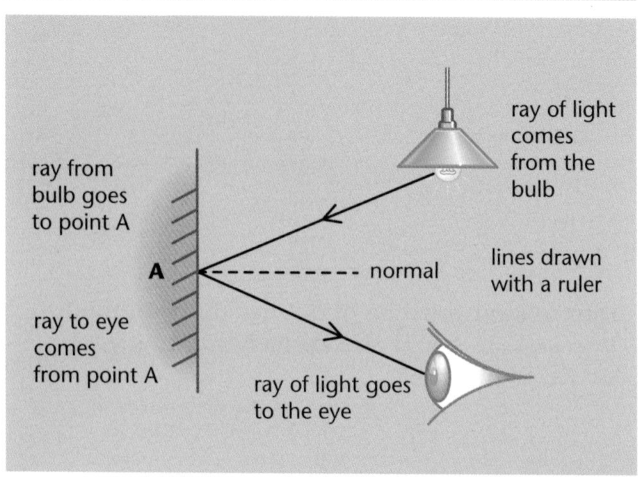

- In some questions you have to draw lines for labels or to join boxes.
  - When you are asked to label a diagram, draw the guide lines accurately and precisely.

    The line to the earth wire is well drawn. The line to the fuse is <u>not</u> well drawn. It could be pointing to the live terminal.

On the diagram of the plug
draw a line from letter E to the earth wire,
draw a line from letter F to the fuse.

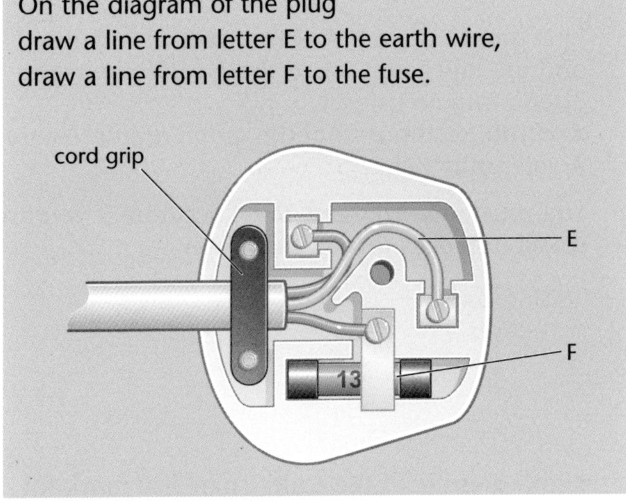

  - Joining boxes: read *all* the information before you begin. Link together pairs of boxes only with clear lines.

Draw **one** line from each symbol to the name of what it stands for.

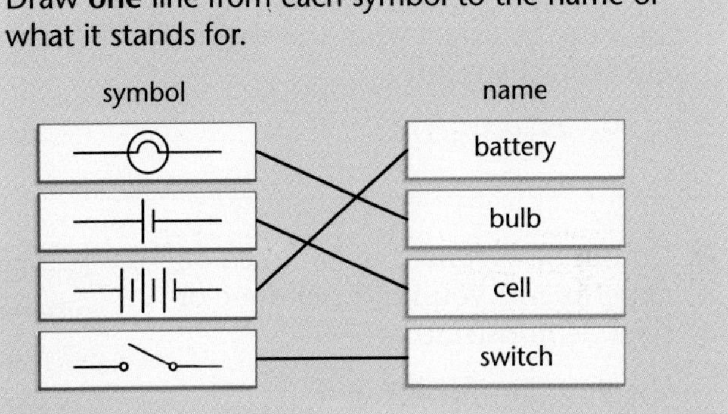

- In all your answers, try to be as precise as possible. You won't get any marks for vague answers.

The Sun seems to move across the sky.
The drawing shows the position of the Sun during a day in summer.

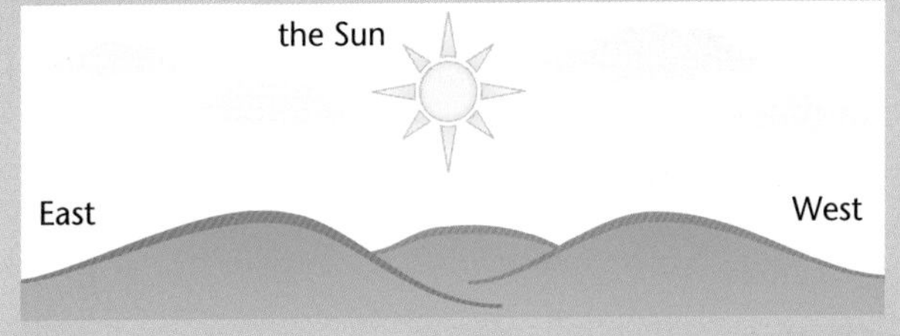

(a) At what time is the Sun highest in the sky?

12 o'clock

(b) Why does the Sun seem to move across the sky?

The Earth turns on its axis ✓ and goes round the Sun. ✗

In part (a) 'midday' or 'noon' are also correct but 'at lunchtime' is too vague.

Don't write down two different answers when you're not sure. That way you are bound to get no marks.

So 0 mark.

Choose the answer you think is most likely to be correct.

- Some questions are about graphs.

Line graphs often have both axes with scales and are labelled. Look at these carefully before attempting an answer.
Accurate readings from the graph are necessary. A ruler may help.

You must also take care to be accurate if you are asked to plot points on the graph.

The graph shows Sam's journey to school.

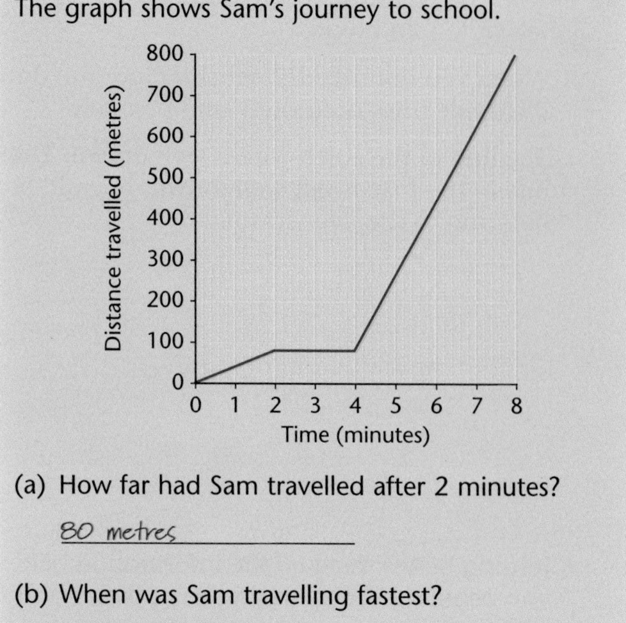

Look carefully at the scale. There is 0 mark for 99 or 90 metres.

(a) How far had Sam travelled after 2 minutes?

80 metres

You may be asked what the shape of the graph tells you (the trend).

(b) When was Sam travelling fastest?

between 4 and 8 minutes

- Do not be surprised to be asked about experiments you have not done or seen demonstrated.

Use your knowledge and understanding of scientific methods and apply these to new or unfamiliar situations.

Amy used a light meter to measure the brightness of two different bulbs.

The diagrams show what she did and what results she got.

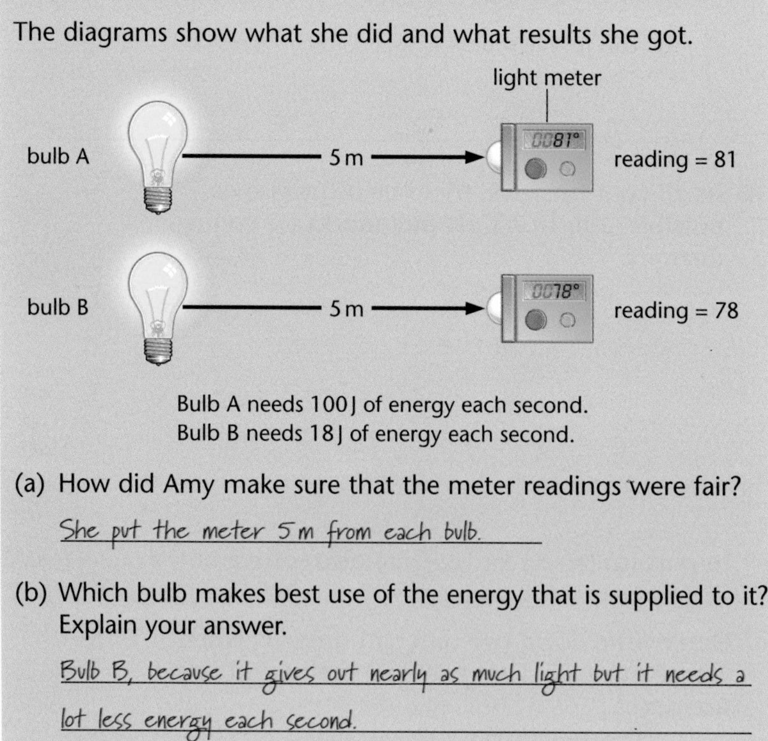

Bulb A needs 100 J of energy each second.
Bulb B needs 18 J of energy each second.

(a) How did Amy make sure that the meter readings were fair?

She put the meter 5 m from each bulb.

(b) Which bulb makes best use of the energy that is supplied to it? Explain your answer.

Bulb B, because it gives out nearly as much light but it needs a lot less energy each second.

Remember that if you have some time left, go back to try any difficult parts of questions that you left and to check your answers for careless mistakes.

'What you need to remember' completed passages

FORCES

1.1 How to make things move

To start something moving, to speed it up or to change its direction, you must make a **force** act on it. This force must be in the same **direction** as you want the thing to move.

If you want to slow something down, the force must be in the **opposite** direction to the way it is moving.

1.2 Why do things slow down?

Moving things slow down because of **friction** forces. Friction forces act in the **opposite** direction to the way an object is moving.

There is friction between things which **slide** over each other.

There is also friction when things move through the air. This is called air resistance or **drag**.

1.3 How to reduce friction

You can reduce sliding friction between hubs and spindles:

- by using **smooth** surfaces;
- by using ball **bearings**;
- by lubricating moving parts with **oil**.

You can reduce air resistance by giving things a **streamlined** shape.

1.4 Making good use of friction

Between tyres and the road there must be a lot of **friction**.
If there isn't, the tyre might **skid**.

You slow down cars and bicycles by using the **brakes**. These use **sliding** friction to slow the wheels down.

A parachute uses **air resistance** to slow the parachutist down.

1.5 Balanced forces

A force doesn't always change the way something moves.
This is because the force may be **balanced** by another force.

To change the way something moves, you need an **unbalanced** force.

1.6 How hard is it pressing?

If you spread out a force over a big area, it will only produce a small **pressure**.

To get a big pressure, you must make a force act on a small **area**.

1.7 Using forces to make things turn

Forces can make things turn around a **pivot** point.

If a force makes something turn clockwise, the opposite force will make it turn **anti-clockwise**.

If a clockwise turning force is the same as an anti-clockwise turning force, the forces **balance**.

1.8 How fast is it moving?

The distance something travels in a certain time is called its **speed**.

You can work out speed like this: speed = **distance** travelled ÷ **time** taken

Many things don't move at the same speed all the time. So the speed we work out is their **average** speed.

1.9 Working out the pressure

The pressure of a force depends on the **area** it acts on.

Forces are measured in **newtons** (N for short).

You can work out pressure like this: pressure = **force** ÷ area

LIGHT AND SOUND

2.1 How you see things

You can only see when there is some **light**.
The things you see either give out light or **reflect** light into your eyes.

Light travels in **straight lines**. So it can't go round **corners**.

When light can't pass through something, it makes a **shadow**.

2.2 Reflecting light

We can see some things because they give out **light**. We can see other things because they **reflect** light into our eyes.

Most things reflect light in all **directions**.

Shiny surfaces, such as mirrors, reflect light at the same **angle** as the light strikes them.

2.3 Using mirrors

When light is reflected from a mirror, angles X and Y are **equal**.

2.4 Colours of the rainbow

Light from the Sun is **white**.

When white light is split up by drops of rain, we get a **rainbow**.

We can split up white light into colours using a **prism** made of clear plastic. We call the colours a **spectrum**.

We can also make coloured light from white light by using **filters**. Filters let some colours pass through but **absorb** other colours.

2.5 Why do things look coloured?

Things look coloured in white light because they **reflect** some colours of light but **absorb** other colours.

White things and grey things don't look coloured because they reflect the same amount of **all** the colours of the spectrum.

Things which reflect hardly any light at all look **black**.

2.6 Comparing light and sound

We see when **light** enters our eyes. We hear when **sound** enters our ears.

Light travels **faster** than sound through the air. The further light and sound travel, the **fainter** they get. Light, but not sound, can travel through **empty space**.

Light can be different **colours**. Sounds can have a **different pitch**.

2.7 Making and hearing sounds

Sounds are made when things **vibrate**. These vibrations then travel through the **air** to your ears.

Sounds can also travel through **solids** and **liquids**.

When sounds enter your ear, they strike your **eardrum** and make it vibrate.

2.8 Different sounds

Sounds can be different in two ways:

- one sound can be **louder** than another;
- the sounds can have a different **pitch**.

Loud sounds are caused by large **vibrations**. We say that these vibrations have a big **amplitude**.

The pitch of a sound depends on **how many** vibrations there are each second. This is called the **frequency** of the sound.

A frequency of 200 **hertz** (Hz for short) means 200 vibrations each second.

2.9 How to bend light

Light bends when it passes across the **boundary** between two different substances. We say that the light is **refracted**.

A line at 90° to a boundary is called a **normal**.

When light passes from glass or water into air, it is refracted **away from** the normal.

When light passes from air into glass or water, it is refracted **towards** the normal.

When light crosses a boundary at **right angles**, it is not refracted.

ELECTRICITY

3.1 Making electricity by rubbing

If you rub an object with a different material, it becomes **charged** with electricity. The electrical charge stays where it is, so we call it **static** electricity.

A charged object will **attract** other things such as bits of dust or paper.

3.2 Two sorts of charges

Electrical charges can be **positive** (+) or **negative** (–).

A positive charge and a negative charge **attract** each other. Two charges that are the same **repel** each other.

3.3 Electric currents

You can get a safe electric current from a **cell**.

Two or more cells joined together is called a **battery**.

A current will only flow if there is a **complete** circuit of **conductors**.

To stop a current flowing you must make a **break** in the circuit. You usually do this using a **switch**.

3.4 Other things that attract and repel

Some rocks attract things made of **iron** or steel. We say that the rocks are **magnetised**.

If a magnetised rock or a magnet is free to move, one end will point **north** and the other end will point south. The ends of a magnet are called the **poles**.

The north pole of one magnet will **attract** the south pole of another magnet.
Two poles that are the same **repel** each other.

3.5 Magnetic fields

The area around a magnet is called a magnetic **field**.

You can explore a magnetic field using iron **filings** or a small magnetic **compass**.

The lines on a magnetic field are called lines of magnetic **force**.

The arrows show the direction that the **north** pole of a compass needle will point.

The magnetic field around a **bar** magnet.

3.6 Using an electric current to make a magnet

You can make a magnet by passing an electric current through a **coil** of wire.
This is called an **electromagnet**.
The magnet works better with an iron **core** inside the coil.

The magnetic field of the electromagnet is the same shape as for a **bar** magnet.

An electromagnet is very useful because you can **switch** it off.

3.7 Building up circuits

If a current flows through one bulb and then through another, we say that the bulbs are connected in **series**.

If two bulbs are connected separately to a cell or a power supply, we say that they are connected in **parallel**.

We can draw circuits using special **symbols** for cells, bulbs, and switches.
Circuits drawn with these symbols are called **circuit diagrams**.

3.8 Using series and parallel circuits

You must put a switch in **series** with the bulb that you want to switch on or off.
If two bulbs are in series, the switch will turn off the current to **both** of them.

A bulb with a broken filament is just like a **switch** which is off.
In a series circuit, if one bulb breaks, the other bulb **doesn't light**.
In a parallel circuit, if one bulb breaks, the other bulb **stays on**.

3.9 Using electromagnets

Electromagnets are very useful because you can easily **switch** them on and off.

ENERGY

4.1 Switch on for energy

We need energy for light, for sound, to make things hot and to make things **move**.

We transfer energy to a light bulb by **electricity**. The bulb then **transfers** energy to its surroundings by light.

When something becomes hotter, it has more **thermal** energy.

4.2 Energy from fuels

We sometimes get the energy we need by burning **fuels**.
The energy stored in fuels is called **chemical** energy.

When we burn fuels, energy is transferred to the surroundings as **thermal** energy.
For fuels to burn, **oxygen** is also needed.

4.3 Using fuels to make electricity

Electricity is **generated** in power stations. The main energy sources used are all **fuels**.

In a power station:

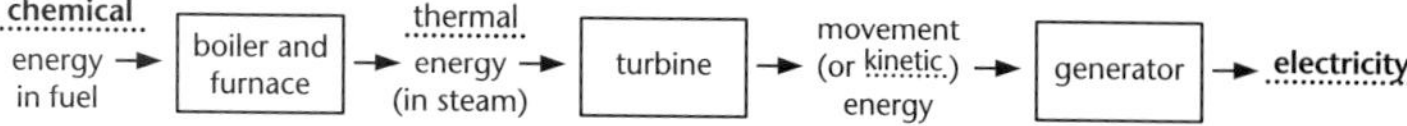

4.4 Some other ways of generating electricity

To generate electricity we need an energy **source**.

Some of the energy sources we can use, besides fuels, are **wind**, **water trapped behind dams**, **waves**, **tides**, **potential** and **geo-thermal** energy.

4.5 Thank you, Sun!

Most of our energy sources depend on energy from the **Sun**.

Energy sources which don't depend on the Sun are **nuclear fuel**, **tides** and **geo-thermal energy**.

4.6 Will our energy sources last for ever?

Some energy sources will last for ever because the energy is constantly being **replaced**. We say that these energy sources are **renewable**.

Some energy sources will eventually run out. We say they are **non-renewable** energy sources.

4.7 Energy for your body

Your body gets the energy it needs from **foods**.

Food stores **chemical** energy. Your body transfers the energy from food mainly as **thermal** energy and **kinetic** energy.

When you lift something up, you give it more **potential** energy.

4.8 Ways of storing energy

You can store energy as **chemical** energy, **gravitational** potential energy or **elastic** potential energy.

Electricity is great for **transferring** energy, but you can't **store** electricity.
Batteries store energy as **chemical** energy.

4.9 You don't only get what you want

When energy is transferred, it is **all** transferred in some way.
But some is transferred in ways we don't really want, so it is **wasted**.

In the end, all transferred energy is wasted because it gets very **spread out**.

THE EARTH AND BEYOND

5.1 The Sun and the stars

Every day the Sun seems to move across the sky from **east** to **west**.
Every night the stars seem to go around the **Pole** star.
This is because the Earth **spins** round once each day.

5.2 Why are the days longer in summer?

The Earth moves around the Sun once each **year**.

When it is summer in the UK, the north of the Earth is **tilted** towards the Sun.
This means that the days are **longer** than the nights.

When the north of the Earth is tilted away from the Sun, it is **winter** in the UK.
This means that the nights are **longer** than the days.

5.3 Stars and planets

All the stars except the **Sun** are a very long way away. Like the Sun, they give out their own **light**.

The planets all go round the **Sun**. They **reflect** light from the Sun. The Earth is a **planet**.

5.4 The solar system

All the planets, including Earth, go round the Sun. We say they **orbit** the Sun.
The Sun and all the planets make up the **solar system**.

We can see some planets more easily than others. This is mainly because they come **nearer** to Earth. The nearer to Earth a planet is, the **brighter** it looks.

5.5 Moons

The Moon is the Earth's **satellite**.
Most of the other **planets** also have satellites.

We can see the Moon because it **reflects** light from the Sun.

An eclipse of the Moon happens when the Moon moves into the Earth's **shadow**.

5.6 Artificial satellites

The natural satellite of the Earth is called the **Moon**.

We can also put **artificial** satellites into orbit around the Earth. These can be used by **astronomers** for observing stars.

Artificial satellites can also be used for **observing** things on Earth.
Observation satellites are usually put into a **polar** orbit.

5.7 What holds the solar system together?

Planets and satellites stay in their orbits because of the force of **gravity**, and because they are **moving**.
The force of gravity between two objects is the **same** on both objects.
But a planet has a lot less **mass** than the Sun, so the planet orbits the Sun.
A satellite has a lot less mass than a planet, so the satellite **orbits** the planet.

5.8 Why we need the Sun

All life on Earth depends on **energy** from the Sun.

The Sun has been shining for about 5 **billion** years.
During that time it has used up about **half** of its nuclear fuel.

MORE LIGHT AND SOUND

C1.1 The Sun and the Earth's satellites

The Sun gives out its own **light**.

Light travels in **straight** lines.

The side of the Earth that faces away from the Sun is in **darkness**. This is because it is in the Earth's **shadow**.

The Moon **orbits** the Earth. We say that it is a **satellite** of the Earth.

We can see the Moon and other satellites because light from the Sun is **reflected** from them.

C1.2 The solar system and the stars

You can see stars because they give out their own light, just like the **Sun**.

You can see planets because they **reflect** the Sun's light.

Planets seem to move through the **constellations** of stars.

The constellations seem to move across the sky because the Earth **spins**.

C1.3 Driving at night

White or pale surfaces **reflect** light better than black or dark surfaces.

A piece of white paper reflects light in all directions; it **scatters** the light.

The diagram shows how a mirror reflects a beam of light.

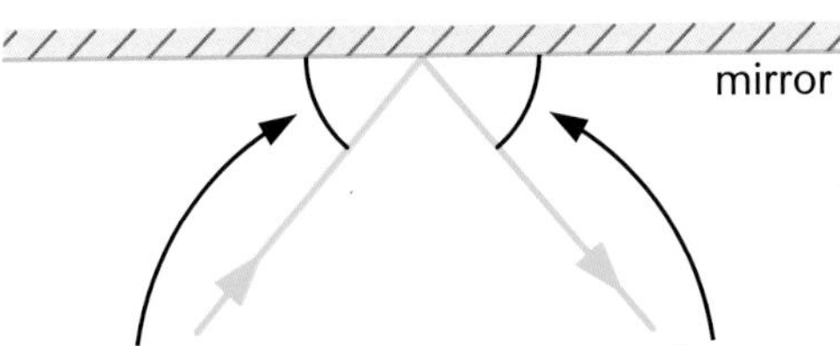
mirror

These two angles are **equal**.

C1.4 Colour

White light is a **mixture** of many different colours.

We can split white light into a **spectrum** using a glass or plastic prism. We say that the prism **disperses** the white light.

An object looks coloured because it **reflects** only some of the colours in white light. The other colours from the white light are **absorbed**.

A coloured filter only lets some colours pass through; it **absorbs** other colours.

C1.5 What prisms do to light

When light passes from one substance into another it is **refracted**.

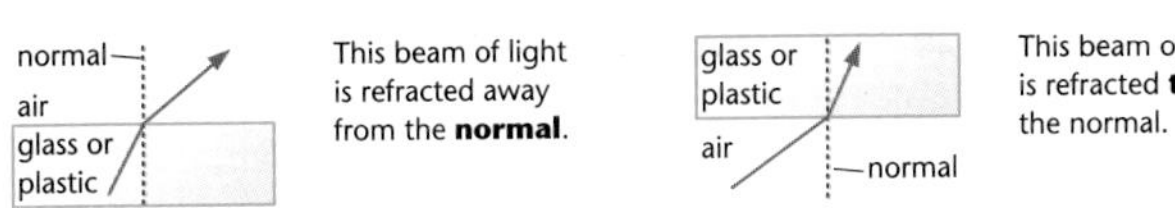
normal
air
glass or plastic
This beam of light is refracted away from the **normal**.
glass or plastic
air
normal
This beam of light is refracted **towards** the normal.

Light at the red end of the spectrum is refracted **less** than light at the violet end of the spectrum.

C1.6 'Bent' rulers and 'shallow' water

Water always looks **shallower** than it really is. A ruler that dips below water looks **bent**. These things happen because light is **refracted** away from the normal when it passes from water into **air**.

C1.7 A rock band on the Moon

All sounds are caused by **vibrations**. These can travel through solids, liquids or gases but not through empty **space**. Another word for empty space is a **vacuum**.

Sound travels a lot **slower** than light does.

Sound can be **reflected**, especially from hard surfaces.

Loud sounds are made by vibrations which have a large **amplitude**. Loud sounds can **damage** your ears.

C1.8 Two different stringed instruments

If a string vibrates faster, we say that it has a higher **frequency**.

Vibrations with a high frequency produce sounds with a high **pitch**.

You also need to know what is in the 'Remember' boxes.

CORE+ C1.9–C1.16

You will need to use Core ideas in different ways like you have on these pages.

MORE FORCES

C2.1 Things that can attract or repel

A magnet has a **north** pole and a **south** pole.
Like poles **repel**.
Unlike poles **attract**.

Electric charges can be **positive** (+) or **negative** (–).
Like charges repel.
Unlike charges attract.

You also need to know what is in the 'Remember' box.

C2.2 Gravity – a force that attracts

Any two objects attract each other with a force called **gravity**. This force is very weak unless one (or both) of the objects has a large **mass**.

The force of gravity that acts on an object is what we call its **weight**.

Gravity keeps a planet or a satellite moving around its **orbit**. The force of gravity keeps changing the **direction** in which planets and satellites move.

C2.3 Looking at orbits

The further away from the Sun a planet is, the longer is its **orbit** time.

Artificial satellites need to be above the atmosphere so they aren't slowed down by **friction** with the air.

Satellites that are used to watch the Earth are put into quite **low** orbits.

You also need to know the order of the planets in the solar system (page 89).

C2.4 Getting things moving

An object will not start to move unless an **unbalanced** force acts on it.

To make an object move, you need a force which is bigger than any **friction** force that is also acting.

The friction force when an object moves through air is called **air resistance**. When an object moves faster this air resistance becomes **larger**.

To reduce the friction force in air or water you need a **streamlined** shape.

C2.5 Slowing down

Friction forces always act in the **opposite** direction to movement. So friction forces slow things down unless they are **balanced** by a driving force.

We can use friction forces to slow things down:
- a person falls more slowly using a parachute because of greater air **resistance**;
- brakes use the friction between surfaces which **slide** across each other.

C2.6 Looking at speed

You can work out speeds like this:
speed = **distance travelled ÷ time taken**

If the speed changes, the answer you get is the **average** speed.

On a distance:time graph, a steep slope means a **high** speed.

C2.7 Pressure

To reduce the pressure a force produces, you can spread it over a large **area**.

Making a force act on a small area produces a large **pressure**.

You can work out a pressure like this:
pressure = **force** ÷ **area**

C2.8 Forces that make things turn

The point about which something turns is called a **pivot**. The turning effect of a force is called its **moment**.

To get a bigger moment:
- you can use a **bigger** force;
- you can apply a force **further away** from the pivot.

For an object to turn there must be an **unbalanced** moment acting on it.

An object doesn't turn if the clockwise and anti-clockwise moments are **balanced**.

CORE+ C2.9–C2.15

You will need to use Core ideas in different ways like you have on these pages.

C2.16 More about moments C+

Moment of a force = **size** of force × **distance** of force from the pivot

ENERGY AND ELECTRICITY

C3.1 Energy sources

Energy sources that depend on energy that has come from the Sun are:
wind, **waves**, **hydro** (electricity), **biomass**, **coal**, **oil**, **natural gas** and **solar**.

Energy sources that do not depend on energy that has come from the Sun are:
tides, **geothermal** and **nuclear fuel**.

An energy source that is being replaced all the time is a **renewable** energy source.

You should know which energy sources are renewable and which are non-renewable.

C3.2 Using energy sources to generate electricity

Most ways of generating electricity use a **turbine** to drive a **generator**.

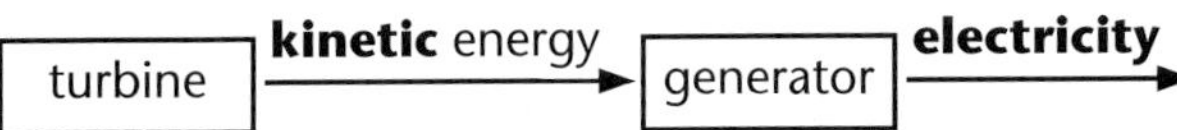

C3.3 Getting the energy we want from electricity

To transfer energy to our surroundings, we often use **electrical** appliances.

Electrical appliances transfer **all** the energy we supply to them.

Some of the energy is transferred in ways that we don't want; this energy is **wasted**.

You should know the energy transfers that everyday electrical appliances are designed to make and the unwanted energy transfers that they also make.

C3.4 Static electricity and electric currents

On an object charged with static electricity, the electrical charges stay in **one place**.

In an electric current, electrical charges **move**. The material that an electric current will flow through is called a **conductor**.

You can discharge a charged conductor by connecting it to the **earth**.

C3.5 Measuring currents in circuits

To measure electric currents you use an **ammeter**.

To measure the current through a bulb, you connect the ammeter in **series** with the bulb.

If you connect two or more bulbs in series, there is still only **one** circuit for the current to flow round. The current through all points in the circuit is exactly the **same**.

Two or more bulbs can be connected to a battery so that they are in separate circuits. We then say that they are connected in **parallel**.

C3.6 Electromagnets

A coil with a current flowing through it becomes an **electromagnet**. You can make this stronger by using a **bigger** current, by putting more **turns** of wire on the coil or by using an **iron core** inside the coil.

When you put some unmagnetised iron into a magnetic field, it becomes a **magnet**.

You should also know what is in the 'Remember' box.

C3.7 Using electromagnets

A magnet that stays magnetised all the time is called a **permanent** magnet.

An electromagnet is more useful than a permanent magnet because you can **switch** it on and off.

You may be given information about things which use electromagnets. You should then be able to explain how they work just like you did on these pages.

C3.8 What happens to all the energy we transfer?

When you transfer energy none is ever **lost** but some is always **wasted**.

All the energy that we transfer eventually ends up making the surroundings a tiny bit **warmer**. This energy isn't very useful because it is very **spread** out.

CORE+ C3.9–C3.16

You will need to use Core ideas in different ways like you have on these pages.

Glossary/index

A few words that occur very often such as force, energy and electricity, are not included. Some of these words are the headings of the topics in the book. Words in *italics* appear elsewhere in the glossary.

A

absorb, absorption: when something 'soaks up' light rather than *reflecting* it or letting it pass through **35–37, 104, 117**

air resistance: the *friction force* on something moving through air; also called *drag* **13, 15–16, 19, 129–130**

ammeter: a meter that is used to measure electric *currents* in *amperes* **154–155**

ampere (amp, A): the unit of electric *current* **154–155**

amplitude: the size of the *vibrations* that produce a sound; a large amplitude produces a *loud* sound **42, 111**

anti-clockwise: opposite of *clockwise*

attract, attraction: things pulling towards each other **48–51, 53, 94–95, 112–115**

B

balanced forces: forces that are the same size but act in opposite directions **48–51, 53, 94–95, 112–115**

battery: made from two or more electrical *cells* joined together **50, 166**

bell: a device that uses an *electromagnet* to make it ring **159**

brakes: these use *friction* to slow down bicycles and motor vehicles **16, 131**

buzzer: this uses an *electromagnet* to make a sound **63**

C

cell: contains chemicals that produce an electric *current* when it is connected to a *complete circuit* **50, 154–155, 166**

charges: these produce an electric *current* when they are moving and *static electricity* when they are standing still **46–50, 123, 152–153**

circuit diagram: an electric *circuit* drawn using circuit *symbols* **59–61, 164**

clockwise: the direction that the hands of a clock move round **22–23, 136–137, 145**

comet: a lump of rock and ice that moves in a very elliptical *orbit* around the *Sun* **140**

compass: see *magnetic compass*

complete circuit: an unbroken chain of things that conduct electricity **50–51, 58–61**

constellation: a group of *stars* that form a pattern **101**

current: electric *charges* flowing around a *complete circuit* **50–51, 58–61, 152–155**

D

disperse: splitting white light into different colours by *refracting* it through a *prism* **104**

distance–time graph: graph which plots the distance something travels against the time it takes to travel; the slope of the graph represents *speed* **133**

drag: see *air resistance*

E

eardrum: the part of your ear that picks up sound *vibrations* from the air **41**

eclipse: when the *Moon* is in the Earth's shadow, or the Earth in the Moon's shadow **114**

efficiency: the fraction, or percentage, of the energy supplied that is transferred in the way that we want **165**

electromagnet: a magnet made by passing an electric *current* through a coil of wire; it usually has an iron core **56–57, 62–63, 156–159, 165, 168**

F

filter: a thin piece of glass or plastic that only some colours of light can pass through **35, 104**

fossil fuels: fuels that were formed from the remains of animals or plants that died millions of years ago; they are burned to release *thermal energy* **72, 76, 147–149, 163**

frequency: the number of *vibrations* in a *second*; this gives a sound its particular *pitch*; units are *hertz* **43, 112–113, 123**

friction: a force that acts in the opposite direction to something that moves or is trying to move; friction can be between solid surfaces or when things move in gases or liquids **12–17, 19, 128–131, 141–142**

fuels: substances that are burned; stored chemical energy is transferred as *thermal energy*; see also *fossil fuels* and *nuclear fuels* **8, 66–69, 74, 78**

G

generator: produces electricity when it is supplied with *kinetic energy* **69–71, 148–149**

geothermal energy: energy stored in hot rocks in the Earth's crust **71, 73, 75, 146**

gravity: force of *attraction* between two objects because of their *mass* **94–95, 124–125, 139**

H

hertz (Hz): the number of *vibrations* each second; the unit of *frequency* **43, 113, 121**

hydroelectricity: electricity produced by transferring the *potential energy* of water trapped behind a dam **70–71, 73, 78, 96**

I

insulator: a substance that will not let an electric *current* pass through it **51**

J

joule (J): the unit of energy **154**

K

kinetic energy: the energy that an object has because it is moving **68–69, 76–77, 149**

L

lines of magnetic force: these tell you which way a *magnetic compass* will point in a *magnetic field* **54–55, 57, 138**

loud: a loud sound is produced by *vibrations* with a large *amplitude* **111**

M

magnetic compass: a magnet that is free to pivot; it comes to rest with one end (*pole*) pointing north and the other pole pointing south **52–55, 122, 138**

magnetic field: area around a magnet where it *attracts* or *repels* **54–55, 57, 138, 156–157**

mass: the amount of stuff in an object; it is measured in grams (g) or kilograms (kg) **124**

mirror: a surface that reflects each narrow beam (*ray*) of light in one direction **103, 116**

moment: the turning effect of a force **136–137, 145**

Moon: the natural *satellite* of the Earth **90–91, 99**

N

negative: one of the two types of electrical *charge*; the other type is called *positive* **48–49, 123, 152–153**

newton (N): the unit of force **27, 124**

non-renewable: energy sources, such as *fossil fuels*, that are not replaced and will eventually be used up **74–75, 146–149, 163**

normal: a line drawn at right angles (90°) to a boundary **44–45, 106**

north pole: the end of a magnet that points north when the magnet is free to move **52–55**

nuclear fuel: a *fuel*, such as uranium, that is used in nuclear power stations **69, 73, 146, 148, 163**

O

orbit: the path of a *satellite* as it moves round a *planet*, or of a planet (or comet) as it moves round the *Sun* **88–95, 99–100, 115, 125–127, 186**

P

parachute: uses *air resistance* to slow down things falling through air **16, 19, 130**

parallel: a way of connecting more than one bulb etc. to a *cell* or a power supply so that a *current* flows through each of them separately **58–61, 155, 167**

periscope: this is used to see over the top of things **33**

pitch: a squeak has a higher pitch than a growl; it is produced by *vibrations* with a higher *frequency* **39, 43, 112–113, 121**

pivot: the point around which something turns, or tries to turn **136–137, 145**

planet: very large objects, including the Earth, that move in *orbits* around the *Sun* **86–89, 91, 94–95, 100–101, 125–126, 140**

poles: the ends of a magnet that *attract*, or *repel*, other magnets; if the magnet is free to move one pole points north and the other pole points south **122**

positive: one of the two types of electrical *charge*; the other type is called *negative* **48–49, 123, 152–153**

potential energy: the energy that is stored in something because it is high up (gravitational) or because it is bent or stretched (elastic) **70–71, 77–79**

pressure: how much force there is on a certain area **20–21, 26–27, 134–135, 144**

prism: a triangular block of clear glass or plastic **34, 104, 106–107, 118**

R

rainbow: a *spectrum* of the colours in sunlight made by raindrops **34**

ray: a narrow beam of light **31**

reflect, reflection: light, or sound, bouncing off whatever it strikes **28–33, 36–37, 99, 101–104, 110, 116, 118**

refract, refraction: light bending when it passes from one transparent substance into another **44–45, 106–110, 119**

relay: a *switch* that works using an *electromagnet* **62, 158**

renewable: an energy source that is constantly being replaced and won't get used up **74–75, 147–149, 162–164**

repel: when things push each other away **48–49, 52–53, 122–123**

S

satellite: an object that *orbits* a *planet*; it may be natural like the *Moon* or artificial like a weather or communications satellite **91–93, 99, 125, 127**

series: a way of connecting two or more bulbs etc. to a *cell* or power supply so that a *current* flows through each of them in turn **58–61, 154–155**

shadow: the dark area formed behind an object when light can't pass through it **29, 98, 114**

sliding friction: the *friction* force between two solid surfaces which slide, or try to slide, across each other **12, 14, 16–17, 170–173**

Acknowledgements

We are grateful to the following for permission to reproduce photographs.

J Allan Cash Photolibrary p. 25t, 25b; **Allsport UK Ltd** pp. 24b (Phil Cole), 25c and 76b (Gray Mortimore); **Aviation Picture Library** pp. 118, 120 (Lockheed Aircraft Corporation); **Trevor Clifford Photography** pp. 112tl, 112tr, 112br, 113t, 113c; **Environmental Images** pp. 24c (© EPL/Martin Bond), 68 (Martin Bond), 70t (Stan Gamester), 75 (© John Novis); **Gilbert Gilkes & Gordon Ltd** p. 149c; **Holt Studios International** p. 70c (Primrose Peacock); **Chris Howes FRPS** p. 169; **Image Bank** pp. 39cr (David Hamilton), 76c; **Nicholas Judd** p. 102; **Andrew Lambert** p. 42c; **Bryan Milner** p. 164(3); **Redferns Music Picture Library** pp. 42t and 112bl (David Redferns), 42br (Mick Hutson); **Science Photo Library** pp. 86 (US Geological Survey), 93l (NRSC Ltd), 93r (NASA), 140 (Frank Zullo), 149b (Bill Longchore); **Still Pictures** p. 149t (David Hoffman); © **John Walmsley Photo Library** pp. 39cl, 42bl.

Picture research: Maureen Cowdroy